9th SIGdial Workshop on Discourse and Dialogue 2008

(SIGdial 08)

Held in conjunction with ACL-HLT 2008

Columbus, Ohio, USA
19-20 June 2008

Editors:

David Schlangen **Beth Ann Hockey**

ISBN: 978-1-61738-548-3

Printed from e-media with permission by:

Curran Associates, Inc.
57 Morehouse Lane
Red Hook, NY 12571

Some format issues inherent in the e-media version may also appear in this print version.

Printed by Curran Associates, Inc. (2010)

For permission requests, please contact the Association for Computational Linguistics
at the address below.

Association for Computational Linguistics
209 N. Eighth Street
Stroudsburg, Pennsylvania 18360

Phone: 1-570-476-8006
Fax: 1-570-476-0860

acl@aclweb.org

Additional copies of this publication are available from:

Curran Associates, Inc.
57 Morehouse Lane
Red Hook, NY 12571 USA
Phone: 845-758-0400
Fax: 845-758-2634
Email: curran@proceedings.com
Web: www.proceedings.com

Introduction

We are pleased to present in this volume, the Proceedings of the 9th SIGdial Workshop on Discourse and Dialogue. These proceedings could not have been produced without the assistance of this year's excellent program committee. The quality of the collection is a result of their efforts and we are indebted to them for donating their time and expertise. 19 of the 46 submissions were accepted as long papers and another 10 were accepted as short papers. This selection of papers follows the SIGdial tradition of providing a venue for work on theory, implemented systems, developed work and new approaches. The topics covered include generation for dialogue systems, dialogue system evaluation, opinions, persuasion, multi-party dialogue, probabilistic methods for dialogue, grounding and the use of dialogue features for improving speech processing. We are optimistic that the breadth and quality of the selected papers will contribute to a lively and interesting workshop event and will prove a valuable resource for the SIGdial readership.

There are many to thank for their assistance with the organization of the 2008 SIGdial event; we mention a few of them here. We would like to thank ACL for providing workshop support, and Priscilla Rasmussen for handling the financial transactions and providing us with valuable information about the mysteries of matters budgetary. The SIGdial Board was very supportive and provided sage advice to us on a number of questions that arose in the course of organizing the event. David Traum gave us extra assistance on several issues and was very responsive to our numerous questions. Additional thanks go to Harry Bunt, Tim Paek and Livia Polyani for helping us secure sponsorship, to Crystal Nakatsu for giving us excellent advice on potential reception locations, and to the SIGdial webmaster, Torben Madsen, for putting up the website.

We also thank Prof. Julia Hirschberg of Columbia University for giving the 2008 SIGdial keynote address on "Lexical, Acoustic/Prosodic, and Discourse Entrainment in Spoken Dialogue Systems".

And finally, thank you, the SIGdial audience, for your continued support in making SIGdial a premier venue for work in Discourse and Dialogue.

Beth Ann Hockey & David Schlangen
SIGdial 2008 Co-Chairs

We thank our sponsors:

Microsoft Research

JOHN BENJAMINS PUBLISHING COMPANY

SemanticEdge
FIRST CHOICE

Powerset
NATURAL LANGUAGE SEARCH

Organizers:

Beth Ann Hockey, UC Santa Cruz (USA)
David Schlangen, University of Potsdam (Germany)

Program Committee:

Jan Alexandersson, DFKI GmbH (Germany)
Masahiro Araki, Kyoto Institute of Technology (Japan)
Srinivas Bangalore, ATT Research, (USA)
Robbert-Jan Beun, Universiteit Utrecht (Netherlands)
Nate Blaylock, IHMC (USA)
Dan Bohus, Microsoft Research (USA)
Johan Bos, La Sapienza (Italy)
Pierrette Bouillon, University of Geneva (Switzerland)
Johan Boye, Telia Research (Sweden)
Harry Bunt, Tilburg University (Netherlands)
Donna Byron, Ohio State University (USA)
Sandra Carberry, University of Delaware (USA)
Rolf Carlson, KTH (Sweden)
Justine Cassell, Northwestern University (USA)
Christine Doran, MITRE (USA)
Laila Dybkjaer, University of Southern Denmark (Denmark)
Myroslava Dzikovska, University of Edinburgh (UK)
Jens Edlund, KTH (Sweden)
Stephanie Elzer, Millersville University (USA)
Raquel Fernández, Stanford (USA)
Mary Ellen Foster, Technical University Munich (Germany)
Reva Freedman, Northern Illinois University (USA)
Kallirroi Georgila, University of Edinburgh (UK)
Jonathan Ginzburg, King's College (UK)
Genevieve Gorrell, Sheffield University (UK)
Nancy Green, University of North Carolina at Greensboro (USA)
Alexander Gruenstein, MIT (USA)
Joakim Gustafson, Teliasonera Sweden (Sweden)
Patrick Healey, Queen Mary University London (UK)
Mattias Heldner, KTH (Sweden)
Kristiina Jokinen, University of Helsinki (Finland)
Arne Jonsson, University of Linkoping (Sweden)
Pamela Jordan, University of Pittsburgh (USA)
Simon Keizer, Cambridge University (UK)
Alistair Knott, Otago University (NewZealand)
Jörn Kreutel, Semantic Edge and University of Potsdam (Germany)
Geert-Jan Kruijff, DFKI (Germany)
Staffan Larsson, Göteborg University (Sweden)
Alex Lascarides, University of Edinburgh (UK)
Lin-Shan Lee, National Taiwan University (Taiwan)
Oliver Lemon, University of Edinburgh (UK)
Piroska Lendvai, Tilburg University (The Netherlands)
Diane Litman, University of Pittsburgh (USA)
Ramón López-Cózar, University of Granada (Spain)
Colin Matheson, University of Edinburgh (UK)
Michael McTear, University of Ulster (UK)

Wolfgang Minker, University of Ulm (Germany)
Sebastian Möller, Deutsche Telekom Labs and Technical University Berlin (Germany)
Mikio Nakano, Honda Research Institute (Japan)
Yukiko Nakano, Tokyo University of Agriculture and Technology (Japan)
Tim Paek, Microsoft Research (USA)
Patrick Paroubek, LIMSI-CNRS (France)
Norbert Pfleger, DFKI GmbH (Germany)
Roberto Pieraccini, Speech Cycle (USA)
Paul Piwek, Open University (UK)
Livia Polanyi, Powerset (USA)
Andrei Popescu-Belis, IDIAP Research Institute (Switzerland)
Matt Purver, Stanford (USA)
Manny Rayner, University of Geneva (Switzerland)
Norbert Reithinger, DFKI GmbH (Germany)
Laurent Romary, LORIA (France)
Antonio Roque, USC ICT (USA)
Alex Rudnicky, CMU (USA)
Yoshinori Sagisaka, Waseda University (Japan)
Stephanie Seneff, MIT (USA)
Gabriel Skantze, KTH (Sweden)
Ronnie Smith, East Carolina University (USA)
Claudia Soria, CNR (Italy)
Manfred Stede, University of Potsdam (Germany)
Amanda Stent, Stony Brook University (USA)
Matthew Stone, Rutgers University (USA)
Thora Tenbrink, University of Bremen (Germany)
Stefanie Tomko, Microsoft Corp (USA)
David Traum, USC/ICT (USA)
Nigel Ward, University of Texas at El Paso (USA)
Art Ward, University of Pittsburgh (USA)
Janyce Wiebe, University of Pittsburgh (USA)
Jason Williams, AT&T Labs (USA)
Steve Young, Cambridge University (UK)
Ingrid Zukerman, Monash University (Australia)

Additional Reviewers:

Paul Crook, University of Edinburgh (UK)
Verena Rieser, University of Edinburgh (UK)
Niels Kasch, East Carolina University (USA)

Invited Speaker:

Julia Hirschberg, Columbia University (USA)

Table of Contents

Conference Program

Thursday, June 19, 2008

9:00–9:15 Opening Remarks

Session 1: Dialogue Features and Speech Processing

9:15–9:40 *Optimizing Endpointing Thresholds using Dialogue Features in a Spoken Dialogue System*
Antoine Raux and Maxine Eskenazi

9:40–10:05 *Response-Based Confidence Annotation for Spoken Dialogue Systems*
Alexander Gruenstein

10:05–10:30 *Learning N-Best Correction Models from Implicit User Feedback in a Multi-Modal Local Search Application*
Dan Bohus, Xiao Li, Patrick Nguyen and Geoffrey Zweig

10:30–11:00 Coffee Break

Session 2: Grounding in Dialogue

11:00–11:25 *Agreement and Disputes in Dialogue*
Alex Lascarides and Nicholas Asher

11:25–11:50 *Reactive Redundancy and Listener Comprehension in Direction-Giving*
Rachel Baker, Alastair Gill and Justine Cassell

11:50–12:15 *Semantic negotiation in dialogue: the mechanisms of alignment*
Gregory Mills and Pat Healey

12:15–12:40 *Degrees of Grounding Based on Evidence of Understanding*
Antonio Roque and David Traum

12:40–2:40 Lunch and Poster Session

Thursday, June 19, 2008 (continued)

Poster Session

Thursday, June 19, 2008 (continued)

Session 3: Probabilistic Methods

Friday, June 20, 2008

Session 4: Opinions, Persuasion, and Multi-Party Dialogue

Friday, June 20, 2008 (continued)

11:50–12:15 *Modeling Vocal Interaction for Text-Independent Participant Characterization in Multi-Party Conversation*
Kornel Laskowski, Mari Ostendorf and Tanja Schultz

12:15–12:45 *Modelling and Detecting Decisions in Multi-party Dialogue*
Raquel Fernández, Matthew Frampton, Patrick Ehlen, Matthew Purver and Stanley Peters

12:45–2:15 Lunch

Session 5: Evaluation

2:15–2:40 *User Simulation as Testing for Spoken Dialog Systems*
Hua Ai and Fuliang Weng

2:40–3:05 *Evaluation Understudy for Dialogue Coherence Models*
Sudeep Gandhe and David Traum

3:05–3:30 *A Framework for Model-based Evaluation of Spoken Dialog Systems*
Sebastian Möller and Nigel Ward

3:30–4:00 Coffee Break

Session 6: Generation

4:00–4:25 *The Effect of Dialogue System Output Style Variation on Users' Evaluation Judgments and Input Style*
Ivana Kruijff-Korbayova and Olga Kukina

4:25–4:50 *Making Grammar-Based Generation Easier to Deploy in Dialogue Systems*
David DeVault, David Traum and Ron Artstein

4:50–5:00 Closing Remarks

5:00 End of SIGdial 2008

Optimizing Endpointing Thresholds using Dialogue Features in a Spoken Dialogue System

Antoine Raux and **Maxine Eskenazi**
{antoine,max}@cs.cmu.edu
Language Technologies Institute
Carnegie Mellon University
Pittsburgh, PA 15213, USA

Abstract

This paper describes a novel algorithm to dynamically set endpointing thresholds based on a rich set of dialogue features to detect the end of user utterances in a dialogue system. By analyzing the relationship between silences in user's speech to a spoken dialogue system and a wide range of automatically extracted features from discourse, semantics, prosody, timing and speaker characteristics, we found that all features correlate with pause duration and with whether a silence indicates the end of the turn, with semantics and timing being the most informative. Based on these features, the proposed method reduces latency by up to 24% over a fixed threshold baseline. Offline evaluation results were confirmed by implementing the proposed algorithm in the Let's Go system.

1 Introduction

1.1 Responsiveness in Dialogue

Although the quality of speech technologies has improved drastically and spoken interaction with machines is becoming a part of the everyday life of many people, dialogues with artificial agents still fall far short of their human counterpart in terms of both comfort and efficiency. Besides lingering problems in speech recognition and understanding, Ward et al (Ward et al., 2005) identified turn-taking issues, specifically responsiveness, as important shortcomings. Dialogues with artificial agents are typically rigid, following a strict one-speaker-at-a-time structure with significant latencies between turns. In a previous paper, we concurred with these findings when analyzing issues with the Let's Go system (Raux et al., 2006). In contrast, empirical studies of conversation have shown that human-human dialogues commonly feature swift exchanges with little or no gap between turns, or even non-disruptive overlap (Jaffe and Feldstein, 1970; Sacks et al., 1974). According to Conversation Analysis and psycholinguistic studies, responsiveness in human conversations is possible because participants in the conversation exchange cues indicating when a turn might end, and are able to anticipate points at which they can take over the floor smoothly. Much research has been devoted to finding these cues, leading to the identification of many aspects of language and dialogue that relate to turn-taking behavior, including syntax (Sacks et al., 1974; Ford and Thompson, 1996; Furo, 2001), prosody (Duncan, 1972; Oreström, 1983; Chafe, 1992; Ford and Thompson, 1996; Koiso et al., 1998; Furo, 2001), and semantics (Oreström, 1983; Furo, 2001). However, regarding this last aspect, Orestrom notes about his corpus that "there is no simple way to formalizing a semantic analysis of this conversational material". This difficulty in formalizing higher levels of conversation might explain the relatively low interest that conversational analysts have had in semantics and discourse. Yet, as conversational analysts focused on micro-levels of dialogue such as turn-taking, computational linguists uncovered and formalized macro-level dialogue structure and devised well-defined representations of semantics for at least some forms of dialogues (Allen and Perrault, 1980; Grosz and Sidner, 1986; Clark, 1996), which have in turn been implemented in spoken dialogue systems (Rich and Sidner, 1998; Allen et al., 2005).

Proceedings of the 9th SIGdial Workshop on Discourse and Dialogue, pages 1–10,

1.2 Current Approaches to Turn-Taking in Spoken Dialogue Systems

Unfortunately, while socio- and psycho-linguists revealed the complexity of conversational turn-taking behavior, designers of practical spoken dialogue systems have stuck to a simplistic approach to end-of-turn detection (hereafter *endpointing*). Typically, silences in user speech are detected using a low-level Voice Activity Detector (VAD) and a turn is considered finished once a silence lasts longer than a fixed threshold. This approach has the advantage of being simple, only relying on easily computable low-level features. However, it leads to suboptimal behavior in many instances. First, False Alarms (FA) happen when a pause lasts longer than the threshold and gets wrongly classified as a gap[1]. Second, latency occurs at every gap, because the system must wait for the duration of the threshold before classifying a silence as gap. When setting the threshold, system designers must consider the trade-off between these two issues: setting a low threshold reduces latency but increases FA rate, while setting a high threshold reduces FA rate but increases latency.

To help overcome the shortcomings of the single-threshold approach, several researchers have proposed to exploit various features. Sato et al (Sato et al., 2002) used decision trees to classify pauses longer than 750 ms as gap or pause. By using features from semantics, syntax, dialogue state, and prosody, they were able to improve the classification accuracy from a baseline of 76.2% to 83.9%. While this important study shows encouraging results on the value of using various sources of information in a dialogue system, the proposed approach (classifying long silences) is not completely realistic (what happens when a gap is misclassified as a pause?) and does not attempt to optimize latency. An extension to this approach was proposed in (Takeuchi et al., 2004), in which a turn-taking decision is made every 100 ms during pauses. However, in this latter work the features are limited to timing, prosody, and syntax (part-of-speech). Also the reported classification results, with F-measures around 50% or below do not seem to be sufficient for practical use.

[1]We use the terminology from (Sacks et al., 1974) where a *pause* is a silence within a turn while a *gap* is a silence between turns. We use the term *silence* to encompass both types.

Similarly, Ferrer and her colleagues (Ferrer et al., 2003) proposed the use of multiple decision trees, each triggered at a specific time in the pause, to decide to either endpoint or defer the decision to the next tree, unless the user resumes speaking. Using features like vowel duration or pitch for the region immediately preceding the silence, combined with a language model that predicts gaps based on the preceding words, Ferrer et al are able shorten latency while keeping the FA rate constant. On a corpus of recorded spoken dialogue-like utterances (ATIS), they report reductions of up to 81% for some FA rates. While very promising, this approach has several disadvantages. First it relies on a small set of possible decision points for each pause, preventing fine optimization between them. Second, the trees are trained on increasingly smaller datasets requiring smoothing of the tree scores to compensate for poor training of the later trees (which are trained on increasingly small subsets of pauses from the training set). Finally, and perhaps most importantly, these authors have investigated prosodic and lexical features, but not other aspects of dialogue, such as discourse structure, timing, and semantics.

In this paper, we propose a new approach to endpointing that directly optimizes thresholds using automatically extracted dialogue features ranging from discourse to timing and prosody. Section 2 outlines the proposed algorithm. Section 3 describes the analysis of the relationship between silences and a wide range of features available to a standard spoken dialogue system (hereafter *dialogue features*). Evaluation results, both offline and in the deployed Let's Go system are given in Section 4.

2 Dynamic Endpointing Threshold Decision Trees

2.1 Overview

One issue with current approaches to endpointing is that they rely on binary gap/pause classifiers and the relationship between optimizing for classification accuracy vs optmizing to minimize latency is unclear. Also, the performance we obtained when applying classification-based approaches to the Let's Go data was disappointing. The accuracy of the classifiers was not sufficient for practical purposes, even with the improvements proposed by (Ferrer et al.,

2003). We hypothesize that the discrepancy between these results and the good performances reported by others is due to the noisiness of the Let's Go data (see Section 3.1.1). To overcome these issues, we propose a method that directly optimizes endpointing thresholds using a two-stage process. First, silences are clustered based on dialogue features so as to create groups of silences with similar properties. Second, a single threshold is set for each cluster, so as to minimize the overall latency at a given false alarm rate. The result of the training process is thus a decision tree on dialogue features that contains thresholds at its leaves. At runtime, every time a silence is detected, the dialogue system runs the decision tree and sets its endpointing threshold accordingly. The following sections describe the two training stages.

2.2 Feature-based Silence Clustering

The goal of the first stage of training is to cluster silences with a similar FA rate/latency tradeoff. The intuition is that we would like to generate low-threshold clusters, which contain mostly gaps and short pauses, and clusters where long pauses would be concentrated with no or very few gaps, allowing to set high thresholds that reduce cut-in rate without hurting overall latency. We used a standard top-down clustering algorithm that exhaustively searches binary splits of the data based on feature values. The split that yields the minimal overall cost is kept, where the cost C_n of cluster K_n is defined by the following function:

$$C_n = G_n \times \sqrt{\frac{1}{|K|} \sum_{p \in K} Duration(p)^2} \quad (1)$$

where G_n the number of gaps in K_n and $Duration(p)$ the duration of a pause p, set to zero for gaps. While other cost functions are possible, the intuition behind this formula is that it captures both the cluster's gap ratio (first factor) and its pause duration distribution (second factor: root mean square of pause duration). The splitting process is repeated recursively until the reduction in cost between the original cost and the sum of the costs of the two split clusters falls below a certain threshold. By minimizing $C(K)$, the clustering algorithm will find questions that yield clusters with either a small G_n, i.e. mostly pauses, or a small root mean square pause duration. Ultimately, at the leaves of the tree are sets of silences that will share the same threshold.

2.3 Cluster Threshold Optimization

Given the clusters generated by the first phase, the goal of the second phase is to find a threshold for each cluster so that the overall latency is minimized at a given FA rate. Under the assumption that pause durations follow an exponential distribution, which is supported by previous work and our own data (see Section 3.2), we show in Figure 3 in appendix that there is a unique set of thresholds that minimizes latency and that the threshold for any cluster n is given by:

$$\theta_n = \frac{\mu_n \times log(\beta_n \times \frac{E \times \mu_n}{\sum \mu_n})}{G_n} \quad (2)$$

where μ_n and β_n can be estimated from the data.

3 Silences and Dialogue Features

3.1 Overview of the Data

3.1.1 The Let's Go Corpus

Let's Go is a telephone-based spoken dialogue system that provides bus schedule information for the Pittsburgh metropolitan area. It is built on the Olympus architecture (Bohus et al., 2007), using the RavenClaw dialogue management framework, and the Apollo interaction manager (Raux et al., 2007) as core components. Outside of business hours callers to the bus company's customer service are offered the option to use Let's Go. All calls are recorded and extensively logged for further analysis. The corpus used for this study was collected between December 26, 2007 and January 25, 2008, with a total of 1326 dialogues, and 18013 user turns. Of the calls that had at least 4 user turns, 73% were complete, meaning that the system provided some schedule information to the user.

While working on real user data has its advantages (large amounts of data, increased validity of the results), it also has its challenges. In the case of Let's Go, users call from phones of varying quality (cell phones and landlines), often with background noises such as cars, infant cries, loud television sets, etc. The wide variability of the acoustic conditions makes any sound processing more prone to error than on carefully recorded corpora. For example, as reported in (Raux et al., 2005), the original speech recognizer had been found to yield a 17% word error rate on a corpus of dialogues collected by recruiting subjects to call the system from an office. On the live Let's Go data, that same recognizer had a 68% WER. After acoustic and language model retraining/adaptation, that number was brought down to about 30% but it is still a testimony to the difficulty of obtaining robust features, particularly from acoustics.

3.1.2 Correcting Runtime Endpointing Errors

Let's Go uses a GMM-based VAD trained on previously transcribed dialogues. Endpointing decisions are based on a fixed 700 ms threshold on the duration of the detected silences. One issue when analyzing pause distributions from the corpus is that observed user behavior was affected by system's behavior at runtime. Most notably, because of the fixed threshold, no recorded pause lasts more than 700 ms. To compensate for that, we used a simple heuristic to rule some online endpointing decisions as erroneous. If a user turn is followed within 1200 ms by another user turn, we consider these two turns to be in fact a single turn, unless the first turn was a user barge-in. This heuristic was established by hand-labeling 200 dialogues from a previous corpus with endpointing errors (i.e. each turn was annotated as correctly or incorrectly endpointed). On this dataset, the heuristic has a precision of 70.6% and a recall of 75.5% for endpointing errors. Unless specified, all subsequent results are based on this modified corpus.

3.2 Turn-Internal Pause Duration Distribution

Overall there were 9563 pauses in the corpus, which amounts to 0.53 pauses per turn. The latency / FA rate trade-off for the corpus is plotted in Figure 1. This curve follows an exponential function (the R^2 on the linear regression of latency on $Log(FA)$ is 0.99). This stems from the fact that pause duration approximately follows an exponential distribution, which has been observed by others in the past (Jaffe and Feldstein, 1970; Lennes and Anttila, 2002).

One consequence of the exponential-like distribution is that short pauses strongly dominate the distribution. We decided to exclude silences shorter than

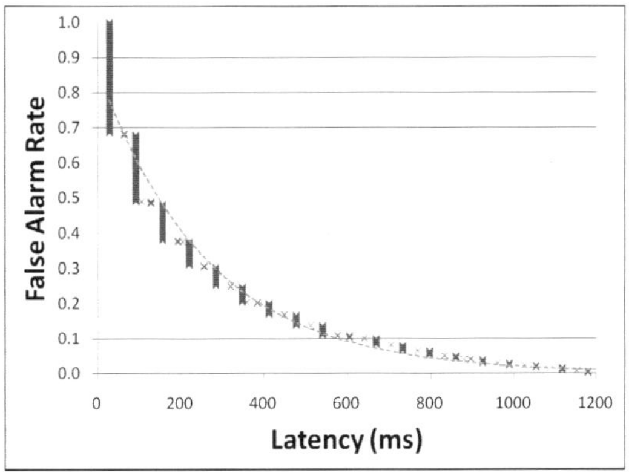

Figure 1: Overall False Alarm / Latency trade-off in the Let's Go corpus. The dashed line represents a fitted curve of the form $FA = e^{\beta+\alpha \cdot Latency}$.

200 ms from most of the following analysis for two reasons: 1) they are more prone to voice activity detection errors or short non-pause silences within speech (e.g. unvoiced stop closure), and 2) in order to apply the results found here to online endpointing by the system, some amount of time is required to detect the silence and compute necessary features, making endpointing decisions on such very short silences impractical. Once short silences have been excluded, there are 3083 pauses in the corpus, 0.17 per turn.

3.3 Relationship Between Dialogue Features and Silence Distributions

3.3.1 Statistical Analysis

In order to get some insight into the interaction of the various aspects of dialogue and silence characteristics, we investigated a number of features automatically extracted from the dialogue recordings and system logs. Each feature is used to split the set of silences into two subsets. For nominal features, all possible splits of one value vs all the others are tested, while for continuous and ordinal features, we tried a number of thresholds and report the one that yielded the strongest results. In order to avoid extreme cases that split the data into one very large and one very small set, we excluded all splits where either of the two sets had fewer than 1000 silences. All the investigated splits are reported in Appendix, in Table 1 and 2. We compare the two subsets generated by each possible split in terms of two metrics:

- Gap Ratio (GR), defined as the proportion of

gaps among all silences of a given set. We report the absolute difference in GR between the two sets, and use chi-square in a 2x2 design (pause vs gap and one subset vs the other) to test for statistical significance at the 0.01 level, using Bonferroni correction to compensate for multiple testings.

- Mean pause duration. The strength of the interaction is shown by the difference in mean pause duration, and we use Mann Whitney's Rank Sum test for statistical significance, again at the 0.01 level, using Bonferroni correction.

We group features into five categories: discourse, semantics, prosody, turn-taking, and speaker characteristics, described in the following sections.

3.3.2 Discourse Structure

Discourse structure is captured by the system's dialogue act immediately preceding the current user turn. In the Let's Go dialogues, 97.9% of system dialogue acts directly preceding user turns are questions[2]. Of these, 13% are open questions (e.g. "What can I do for you?"), 39% are closed questions (e.g. "Where are you leaving from?") and 46% are confirmation requests (e.g. "Leaving from the airport. Is this correct?")[3]. There are many more pauses in user responses to open questions than to the other types (cf Table 1). One explanation is that user answers to open questions tend to be longer (2046 ms on average, to be contrasted with 1268 ms for turns following closed questions and 819 ms for responses to confirmation questions). Conversely, confirmation questions lead to responses with significantly fewer pauses. 78% of such turns contained only one word, single YES and NO answers accounting for 81% of these one-word responses, which obviously do not lend themselves to pauses. Discourse context also has an effect on pause durations, albeit a weak one, with open questions leading to turns with shorter pauses. One possible explanation for this is that pauses after closed and confirmation questions tend to reflect more hesitations and/or confusion on the user's side, whereas responses to open questions also have pauses in the normal flow of speech.

3.3.3 Semantics

Semantic features are based on partial speech recognition results and on their interpretation in the current dialogue context. We use the most recent recognition hypothesis available at the time when the silence starts, parse it using the system's standard parser and grammar, and match the parse against the "expectation agenda" that RavenClaw (Bohus and Rudnicky, 2003) maintains. The expectation level of a partial utterance indicates how well it fits in the current dialogue context. A level of 0 means that the utterance can be interpreted as a direct answer to the last system prompt (e.g. a "PLACE" concept as an answer to "Where are you leaving from?", a "YES" or a "NO" after a confirmation question). Higher levels correspond to utterances that fit in a broader dialogue context (e.g. a place name after the system asks "Leaving from the airport. Is this correct?", or "HELP" in any context). Finally, non-understandings, which do not match any expectation, are given a matching level of $+\infty$.

Expectation level is strongly related to both finality and pause duration. Pauses following partial utterances of expectation level 0 are significantly more likely to be gaps than those matching any higher level. Also, very unexpected partial utterances (and non-understandings) contain shorter pauses than more expected ones. Another indicative feature for finality is the presence of a positive marker (i.e. a word like "YES" or "SURE") in the partial utterance. Utterances that contain such a marker are more likely to be finished than others. In contrast, the effect of negative markers is not significant. This can be explained by the fact that negative responses to confirmation often lead to longer corrective utterances more prone to pauses. Indeed, 91% of complete utterances that contain a positive marker are single-word, against 67% for negative markers.

3.3.4 Prosody

We extracted three types of prosodic features: acoustic energy of the last vowel, pitch of the last voiced region, and duration of the last vowel. Vowel

[2]The remaining 2.1% belong to other cases such as the user barging in right after the system utters a statement.

[3]The high number of confirmations comes from the fact that Let's Go is designed to ask the user to explicitly confirm every concept.

location and duration were estimated by performing phoneme alignment with the speech recognizer. Duration was normalized to account for both vowel and speaker identity. Energy was computed as the log-transformed signal intensity on 10ms frames. Pitch was extracted using the Snack toolkit (Sjolander, 2004), also at 10ms intervals. For both energy and pitch, the slope of the contour was computed by linear regression, and the mean value was normalized by Z-transformation using statistics of the dialogue-so-far. As a consequence, all threshold values for means are expressed in terms of standard deviations from the current speaker's mean value.

Vowel energy, both slope and mean, yielded the highest correlation with silence finality, although it did not rank as high as features from other categories. As expected, vowels immediately preceding gaps tend to have lower and falling intensity, whereas rising intensity makes it more likely that the turn is not finished. On the other hand, extremely high pitch is a strong cue to longer pauses, but only happen in 5.6% of the pauses.

3.3.5 Timing

Timing features, available from the Interaction Manager, provide the strongest cue to finality. The longer the on-going turn has been, the less likely it is that the current silence is a gap. This is true both in terms of time elapsed since the beginning of the utterance and number of pauses observed so far. This latter feature also correlates well with mean pause duration, earlier pauses of a turn tending to be longer than later ones.

3.3.6 Speaker Characteristics

These features correspond to the observed pausal behavior so far in the dialogue. The idea is that different speakers follow different patterns in the way they speak (and pause), and that the system should be able to learn these patterns to anticipate future behavior. Specifically, we look at the mean number of pauses per utterance observed so far, and the mean pause duration observed so far for the current dialogue. Both features correlate reasonably well with silence finality: a higher mean duration indicates that upcoming silences are also less likely to be final, so does a higher mean number of pauses per turn.

3.4 Discussion

What emerges from the analysis above is that features from all aspects of dialogue provide information on silence characteristics. While most previous research has focused on prosody as a cue to detect the end of utterances, timing, discourse, semantic and previously observed silences appear to correlate more strongly with silence finality in our corpus. This can be partly explained by the fact that prosodic features are harder to reliably estimate on noisy data and that prosodic features are in fact correlated to higher levels of dialogue such as discourse and semantics. However, we believe our results make a strong case in favor of a broader approach to turn-taking for conversational agents, making the most of all the features that are readily available to such systems. Indeed, particularly in constrained systems like Let's Go, higher level features like discourse and semantics might be more robust to poor acoustic conditions than prosodic features. Still, our findings on mean pause durations suggest that prosodic features might be best put to use when trying to predict pause duration, or whether a pause will occur or not. The key to more natural and responsive dialogue systems lies in their ability to combine all these features in order to make prompt and robust turn-taking decisions.

4 Evaluation of Threshold Decision Trees

4.1 Offline Evaluation Set-Up

We evaluated the approach introduced in Section 2 on the Let's Go corpus. The set of features was extended to contain a total of 4 discourse features, 6 semantic features, 5 timing/turn-taking features, 43 prosodic features, and 6 speaker characteristic features. All evaluations were performed by 10-fold cross-validation on the corpus. Based on the proposed algorithm, we built a decision tree and computed optimal cluster thresholds for different overall FA rates. We report average latency as a function of the proportion of turns for which any pause was erroneously endpointed, which is closer to real performance than silence FA rate since, once a turn has been endpointed, all subsequent silences are irrelevant.

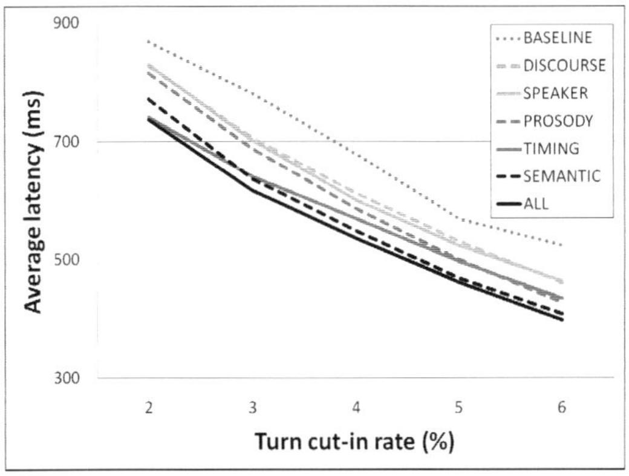

Figure 2: Performance of the proposed approach using different feature sets.

4.2 Performance of Different Feature Sets

First we evaluated each feature set individually. The results are shown in Figure 2. We concentrate on the 2-6% range of turn cut-in rate where any reasonable operational value is likely to lie (the 700 ms threshold of the baseline Let's Go system yields about 4% cut-in rate). All feature sets improve over the baseline. Statistical significance of the result was tested by performing a paired sign test on latencies for the whole dataset, comparing, for each FA rate the proportion of gaps for which the proposed approach gives a shorter threshold than the single-threshold baseline. Latencies produced by the decision tree for all feature sets were all found to be significantly shorter ($p < 0.0001$) than the corresponding baseline threshold.

The best performing feature set is semantics, followed by timing, prosody, speaker, and discourse. The maximum relative latency reductions for each feature set range from 12% to 22%. When using all features, the performance improves by a small but significant amount compared to any single set, up to a maximum latency reduction of 24%. This confirms that the algorithm is able to combine features effectively, and that the features themselves are not completely redundant. However, while removing semantic or timing features from the complete set degrades the performance, this is not the case for discourse, speaker, nor prosodic features. This result, similar to what (Sato et al., 2002) reported in their own experiment, indicates that prosodic features might be redundant with semantic and timing features.

4.3 Live Evaluation

We confirmed the offline evaluation's findings by implementing the proposed approach in Let's Go's Interaction Manager. Since prosodic features were not found to be helpful and since their online extraction is costly and error-prone, we did not include them. At the beginning of each dialogue, the system was randomly set as a baseline version, using a 700 ms fixed threshold, or as an experimental version using the tree learned from the offline corpus. Results show that median latency (which includes both the endpointing threshold and the time to produce the system's response) is significantly shorter in the experimental version (561 ms) than in the baseline (957 ms). Overall, the proposed approach reduced latency by 50% or more in about 48% of the turns. However, global results like these might not reflect the actual improvement in user experience. Indeed, we know from human-human dialogues that relatively long latencies are normal in some circumstances while very short or no latency is expected in others. The proposed algorithm reproduces some of these aspects. For example, after open questions, where more uncertainty and variability is expected, the experimental version is in fact slightly slower (1047 ms vs 993 ms). On the other hand, it is faster after closed question (800 ms vs 965 ms) and particularly after confirmation requests (324 ms vs 965 ms), which are more predictable parts of the dialogue where high responsiveness is both achievable and natural. This latter result indicates that our approach has the potential to improve explicit confirmations, which are often thought to be tedious and irritating to the user.

5 Conclusion

In this paper, we described an algorithm to dynamically set endpointing threshold for each silence. We analyzed the relationship between silence distribution and a wide range of automatically extracted features from discourse, semantics, prosody, timing and speaker characteristics. When all features are used, the proposed method reduced latency by up to 24% for reasonable false alarm rates. Prosodic features did not help threshold optimization once other feature were included. The practicality of the approach and the offline evaluation results were confirmed by implementing the proposed algorithm in the Let's Go system.

Acknowledgments

This work is supported by the US National Science Foundation under grant number 0208835. Any opinions, findings, and conclusions or recommendations expressed in this material are those of the authors and do not necessarily reflect the views of the NSF. We would like to thank Alan Black for his many comments and advice.

References

J. F. Allen and C. R. Perrault. 1980. Analyzing intention in utterances. *Artificial Intelligence*, 15:143–178.

J. F. Allen, G. Ferguson, A. Stent, S. Stoness, M. Swift, L. Galescu, N. Chambers, E. Campana, and G. S. Aist. 2005. Two diverse systems built using generic components for spoken dialogue (recent progress on trips). In *Interactive Demonstration Track, Association of Computational Linguistics Annual Meeting*, Ann Arbor, MI.

D. Bohus and A. Rudnicky. 2003. RavenClaw: Dialog management using hierarchical task decomposition and an expectation agenda. In *Eurospeech03*, Geneva, Switzerland.

D. Bohus, A. Raux, T. Harris, M. Eskenazi, and A. Rudnicky. 2007. Olympus: an open-source framework for conversational spoken language interface research. In *HLT-NAACL 2007 workshop on Bridging the Gap: Academic and Industrial Research in Dialog Technology*, Rochester, NY, USA.

W. L. Chafe, 1992. *Talking Data: Transcription and Coding Methods for Language Research*, chapter Prosodic and Functional Units of Language, pages 33–43. Lawrence Erlbaum.

H.H. Clark. 1996. *Using language*. Cambridge University Press.

S. Duncan. 1972. Some signals and rules for taking speaking turns in conversations. *Journal of Personality and Social Psychology*, 23(2):283–292.

L. Ferrer, E. Shriberg, and A. Stolcke. 2003. A prosody-based approach to end-of-utterance detection that does not require speech recognition. In *ICASSP*, Hong Kong.

C. E. Ford and S. A. Thompson, 1996. *Interaction and Grammar*, chapter Interactional Units in Conversation: Syntactic, Intonational, and Pragmatic Resources for the Management of Turns, pages 134–184. Cambridge University Press.

H. Furo. 2001. *Turn-Taking in English and Japanese. Projectability in Grammar, Intonation, and Semantics.* Routeledge.

B. J. Grosz and C. Sidner. 1986. Attention, intentions, and the structure of discourse. *Computational Linguistics*, 12(3):175–204.

J. Jaffe and S. Feldstein. 1970. *Rhythms of Dialogue*. Academic Press.

H. Koiso, Y. Horiuchi, S. Tutiya, A. Ichikawa, and Y. Den. 1998. An analysis of turn-taking and backchannels based on prosodic and syntactic features in japanese map task dialogs. *Language and Speech*, 41(3-4):295–321.

Mietta Lennes and Hanna Anttila. 2002. Prosodic features associated with the distribution of turns in finnish informal dialogues. In Petri Korhonen, editor, *The Phonetics Symposium 2002*, volume Report 67, pages 149–158. Laboratory of Acoustics and Audio Signal Processing, Helsinki University of Technology.

B. Oreström. 1983. *Turn-Taking in English Conversation*. CWK Gleerup, Lund.

A. Raux, B. Langner, D. Bohus, A. W. Black, and M. Eskenazi. 2005. Let's Go Public! taking a spoken dialog system to the real world. In *Proc. Interspeech 2005*, Lisbon, Portugal.

A. Raux, D. Bohus, B. Langner, A. W. Black, and M. Eskenazi. 2006. Doing research on a deployed spoken dialogue system: One year of Let's Go! experience. In *Proc. Interspeech 2006*, Pittsburgh, PA, USA.

A. Raux, , and M. Eskenazi. 2007. A multi-layer architecture for semi-synchronous event-driven dialogue management. In *Proc. ASRU 2007*, Kyoto, Japan.

C. Rich and C.L. Sidner. 1998. Collagen: A collaboration manager for software interface agents. *An International Journal: User Modeling and User-Adapted Interaction*, 8(3-4):315–350.

H. Sacks, E. A. Schegloff, and G. Jefferson. 1974. A simplest systematics for the organization of turn-taking for conversation. *Language*, 50(4):696–735.

R. Sato, R. Higashinaka, M. Tamoto, M. Nakano, and K. Aikawa. 2002. Learning decision trees to determine turn-taking by spoken dialogue systems. In *ICSLP 2002*, Denver, CO.

Kare Sjolander. 2004. The snack sound toolkit. http://www.speech.kth.se/snack/.

M. Takeuchi, N. Kitaoka, and S. Nakagawa. 2004. Timing detection for realtime dialog systems using prosodic and linguistic information. In *Proc. Speech Prosody 04*, Nara, Japan.

N. Ward, A. Rivera, K. Ward, and D. Novick. 2005. Root causes of lost time and user stress in a simple dialog system. In *Interspeech 2005*, Lisbon, Portugal.

Category	Feature test	Number of Silences	Gap Ratio	Difference
Timing	Pause start time $\geq$ 3000 ms	1836 / 19260	65% / 87%	-23%
Timing	Pause number $\geq$ 2	3379 / 17717	69% / 88%	-19%
Discourse	Previous question is open	3376 / 17720	70% / 88%	-18%
Semantics	Utterance expectation level $\geq$ 1	10025 / 11071	78% / 92%	-14%
Individual	Mean pause duration $\geq$ 500 ms	1336 / 19760	72% / 86%	-14%
Semantics	Utterance contains a positive marker	4690 / 16406	96% / 82%	13%
Prosody	Mean energy of last vowel $\geq$ 5	1528 / 19568	74% / 86%	-12%
Prosody	Slope of energy on last vowel $\geq$ 0	6922 / 14174	78% / 89%	-10%
Individual	Mean number of pauses per utterance $\geq$ 3	1929 / 19267	76% / 86%	-10%
Semantic	Utterance is a non-understanding	6023/15073	79% / 88%	-9%
Discourse	Previous question is a confirmation	8893 / 12203	90% / 82%	8%
Prosody	Duration of last vowel $\geq$ 1	1319 / 19777	78% / 86%	-8%
Prosody	Mean pitch on last voiced region $\geq$ 5	1136 / 19960	92% / 85%	7%
Prosody	Slope of pitch on last voiced region $\geq$ 0	6617 / 14479	82% / 87%	-4%
Semantics	Utterance contains a negative marker	2667 / 18429	87% / 85%	2%*
Discourse	Previous question is closed	8451 / 12645	86% / 85%	1%*

Table 1: Effect of Dialogue Features on Pause Finality. In columns 3 and 4, the first number is for silences for which the condition in column 2 is true, while the second number is for those silences where the condition is false. * indicates that the results are not statistically significant at the 0.01 level.

Category	Feature test	Number of Pauses	Mean pause Duration (ms)	Difference (ms)
Prosody	Mean pitch on last voiced region $\geq$ 4	172 / 2911	608 / 482	126
Semantics	Utterance Expectation Level $\geq$ 4	2202 / 881	475 / 526	-51
Prosody	Slope of energy on last vowel $\geq$ 1	382 / 2701	446 / 495	-39
Timing	Pause number $\geq$ 2	1031 / 2052	459 / 504	-45
Discourse	Previous question is open	1015 / 2068	460 / 504	-43
Individual	Mean pause duration $\geq$ 500 ms	370 / 2713	455 / 494	-39*
Prosody	Mean energy of last vowel $\geq$ 4.5	404 / 2679	456 / 494	-38*
Semantics	Utterance contains a positive marker	211 / 2872	522 / 487	35*
Discourse	Previous question is closed	1178 / 1905	510 / 477	33*
Timing	Pause start time $\geq$ 3000 ms	650 / 2433	465 / 496	-31*
Semantic	Utterance is a non-understanding	1247 / 1836	472 / 502	-30*
Prosody	Duration of last vowel $\geq$ 0.4	1194 / 1889	507 / 478	29*
Individual	Mean number of pauses per utterance $\geq$ 2	461 / 2622	474 / 492	-19*
Semantics	Utterance contains a negative marker	344 / 2739	504 / 488	16*
Prosody	Slope of pitch on last voiced segment $\geq$ 0	1158 / 1925	482 / 494	-12*
Discourse	Previous question is a confirmation	867 / 2216	496 / 487	9*

Table 2: Effect of Dialogue Features on Pause Duration. In columns 3 and 4, the first number is for silences for which the condition in column 2 is true, while the second number is for those silences where the condition is false. * indicates that the results are not statistically significant at the 0.01 level.

Let (K_n) be a set of n silence clusters, the goal is to set the thresholds (θ_n) that minimize overall mean latency, while yielding a fixed, given number of false alarms E. let us define G_n the number of gaps among the silences of K_n. For each cluster, let us define $E_n(\theta_n)$ the number of false alarms yielded by threshold θ_n in cluster n, and the total latency L_n by:

$$L_n(\theta_n) = G_n \times \theta_n \tag{3}$$

Assuming pause durations follow an exponential distribution, as shown in Section 3, the following relation holds between L_n and E_n:

$$e^{\frac{L_n(\theta_n)}{\mu_n}} = \beta_n \times E_n(\theta_n) \tag{4}$$

where μ_K and β_K are cluster-specific coefficients estimated by linear regression in the log domain. If we take the log of both sides, we obtain:

$$L_n(\theta_n) = \mu_n \times log(\beta_n \times E_n(\theta_n)) \tag{5}$$

Theorem 1. *If (θ_n) is a set of thresholds that minimizes $\sum_n L_n$ such that $\sum_n E_n(\theta_n) = E$, then $\exists A s.t. \forall n, \frac{dL_n}{dE_n}(\theta_n) = A$*

Informal proof. The proof can be done by contradiction. Let us assume (θ_n) is a set of thresholds that minimizes $\sum_n L_n$, and $\exists (p,q) s.t. \frac{dL_p}{dE_p}(\theta_p) > \frac{dL_q}{dE_q}(\theta_q)$. Then, there exists small neighborhoods of θ_p and θ_q where $L_p(E_p)$ and $L_q(E_q)$ can be approximated by their tangents. Since their slopes differ, it is possible to find a small ϵ such that the decrease in FA yielded by $\theta_p + \epsilon$ is exactly compensated by the increase yielded by $\theta_q - \epsilon$, but the reduction in latency in K_q is bigger than the increase in K_p, which contradicts the fact that (θ_n) minimizes L. □

From Theorem 1, we get $\exists A s.t. \forall n \frac{dL_n}{dE_n} = A$. Thus, by deriving Equation 5, $\frac{\mu_n}{E_n} = A$ which gives $E_n = \frac{\mu_n}{A}$. Given that $\sum E_n = E$, $\frac{\sum \mu_n}{A} = E$. Hence, $A = \frac{\sum \mu_n}{E}$. From 5, we can infer the values of $L_n(\theta_n)$ and, using 3, the optimal threshold θ_n for each cluster:

$$\theta_n = \frac{\mu_n \times log(\beta_n \times \frac{E \times \mu_n}{\sum \mu_n})}{G_n} \tag{6}$$

where the values of μ_n and β_n can be estimated by linear regression from the data based on 5.

Figure 3: **Derivation of the formula for optimal thresholds**

Response-Based Confidence Annotation for Spoken Dialogue Systems

Alexander Gruenstein
Spoken Language Systems Group
M.I.T. Computer Science and Artificial Intelligence Laboratory
32 Vassar St, Cambridge, MA 02139 USA
alexgru@csail.mit.edu

Abstract

Spoken and multimodal dialogue systems typically make use of confidence scores to choose among (or reject) a speech recognizer's N-best hypotheses for a particular utterance. We argue that it is beneficial to instead choose among a list of candidate system *responses*. We propose a novel method in which a confidence score for each response is derived from a classifier trained on acoustic and lexical features emitted by the recognizer, as well as features culled from the generation of the candidate response itself. Our response-based method yields statistically significant improvements in F-measure over a baseline in which hypotheses are chosen based on recognition confidence scores only.

1 Introduction

The fundamental task for any spoken dialogue system is to determine how to respond at any given time to a user's utterance. The challenge of understanding and correctly responding to a user's natural language utterance is formidable even when the words have been perfectly transcribed. However, dialogue system designers face a greater challenge because the speech recognition hypotheses which serve as input to the natural language understanding components of a system are often quite errorful; indeed, it is not uncommon to find word error rates of 20-30% for many dialogue systems under development in research labs. Such high error rates often arise due to the use of out-of-vocabulary words, noise, and the increasingly large vocabularies of more capable systems which try to allow for greater naturalness and variation in user input.

Traditionally, dialogue systems have relied on confidence scores assigned by the speech recognizer to detect speech recognition errors. In a typical setup, the dialogue system will choose to either accept (that is, attempt to understand and respond to) or reject (that is, respond to the user with an indication of non-understanding) an utterance by thresholding this confidence score.

Stating the problem in terms of choosing whether or not to accept a particular utterance for processing, however, misses the larger picture. From the user's perspective, what is truly important is whether or not the system's response to the utterance is correct. Sometimes, an errorful recognition hypothesis may result in a correct response if, for example, proper names are correctly recognized; conversely, a near-perfect hypothesis may evoke an incorrect response. In light of this, the problem at hand is better formulated as one of assigning a confidence score to a system's candidate response which reflects the probability that the response is an acceptable one. If the system can't formulate a response in which it has high confidence, then it should clarify, indicate non-understanding, and/or provide appropriate help.

In this paper, we present a method for assigning confidence scores to candidate system responses by making use not only of features obtained from the speech recognizer, but also of features culled from the process of generating a candidate system response, and derived from the distribution of candidate responses themselves. We first compile a list of unique candidate system responses by processing

Proceedings of the 9th SIGdial Workshop on Discourse and Dialogue, pages 11–20,
Columbus, June 2008.

each hypothesis on the recognizer's N-best list. We then train a Support Vector Machine (SVM) to identify acceptable responses. When given a novel utterance, candidate responses are ranked with scores output from the SVM. Based on the scores, the system can then either respond with the highest-scoring candidate, or reject all of the candidate responses and respond by indicating non-understanding.

Part of the motivation for focusing our efforts on selecting a system response, rather than a recognition hypothesis, can be demonstrated by counting the number of unique responses which can be derived from an N-best list. Figure 1 plots the mean number of unique system responses, parses, and recognition hypotheses given a particular maximum N-best list length; it was generated using the data described in section 3. Generally, we observe that about half as many unique parses are generated as recognition hypotheses, and then half again as many unique responses. Since many hypotheses evoke the same response, there is no value in discriminating among these hypotheses. Instead, we should aim to gain information about the quality of a response by pooling knowledge gleaned from each hypothesis evoking that response.

We expect a similar trend of multiple hypotheses mapping to a single parse in any dialogue system where parses contain a mixture of key syntactic and semantic structure—as is the case here—or where they contain only semantic information (*e.g.*, slot/value pairs). Parsers which retain more syntactic structure would likely generate more unique parses, however many of these parses would probably map to the same system response since a response doesn't typically hinge on every syntactic detail of an input utterance.

The remainder of our discussion proceeds as follows. In section 2 we place the method presented here in context in relation to other research. In section 3, we describe the City Browser multimodal dialogue system, and the process used to collect data from users' interactions with the system. We then turn to our techniques for annotating the data in section 4 and describe the features which are extracted from the labeled data in section 5. Finally, we demonstrate how to build a classifier to rank candidate system responses in section 6, which we evaluate in section 7.

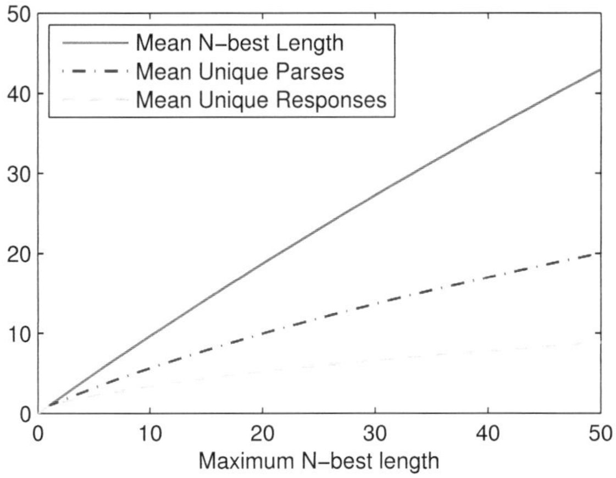

Figure 1: The mean N-best recognition hypothesis list length, mean number of unique parses derived from the N-best list of recognition hypotheses, and mean number of unique system responses derived from those parses, given a maximum recognition N-best list length.

2 Related Work

There has been much research into deriving utterance-level confidence scores based on features derived from the process of speech recognition. The baseline utterance-level confidence module we make use of in this paper was introduced in (Hazen et al., 2002); we use a subset of the recognizer-derived features used by this module. In it, confidence scores are derived by training a linear projection model to differentiate utterances with high word error rates. The utterance-level confidence scores are used to decide whether or not the entire utterance should be accepted or rejected, while the decision as to how to respond is left out of the classification process. Of course, most other recognizers make use of utterance or hypothesis level confidence scores as well; see, for example (San-Segundo et al., 2000; Chase, 1997).

(Litman et al., 2000) demonstrate the additional use of prosodic features in deriving confidence scores, and transition the problem from one of word error rate to one involving concept error rate, which is more appropriate in the context of spoken dialogue systems. However, they consider only the top recognition hypothesis.

Our work has been heavily influenced by (Gabsdil and Lemon, 2004), (Bohus and Rudnicky, 2002), (Walker et al., 2000), and (Chotimongkol and Rudnicky, 2001) all of which demonstrate the utility of training a classifier with features derived from the natural language and dialogue management components of a spoken dialogue system to better predict the quality of speech recognition results. The work described in (Gabsdil and Lemon, 2004) is especially relevant, because, as in our experiments, the dialogue system of interest provides for map-based multimodal dialogue. Indeed, we view the experiments presented here as extending and validating the techniques developed by Gabsdil and Lemon. Our work is novel, however, in that we reframe the problem as choosing among system responses, rather than among recognizer hypotheses. By recasting the problem in these terms, we are able to integrate information from all recognition hypotheses which contribute to a single response, and to extract distributional features from the set of candidate responses. Another key difference is that our method produces confidence scores for the candidate responses themselves, while the cited methods produce a decision as to whether an utterance, or a particular recognition hypothesis, should be accepted, rejected, or (in some cases), ignored by the dialogue system.

In addition, because of the small size of the dataset used in (Gabsdil and Lemon, 2004), the authors were limited to testing their approach with leave-one-out cross validation, which means that, when testing a particular user's utterance, other utterances from the same user also contributed to the training set. Their method also does not provide for optimizing a particular metric—such as F-measure—although, it does solve a more difficult 3-class decision problem. Finally, another key difference is that we make use of an n-gram language model with a large vocabulary of proper names, whereas theirs is a context-free grammar with a smaller vocabulary.

(Niemann et al., 2005) create a dialogue system architecture in which uncertainty is propagated across each layer of processing through the use of probabilities, eventually leading to posterior probabilities being assigned to candidate utterance interpretations. Unlike our system, in which we train a single classifier using arbitrary features derived from each stage of processing, each component (recognizer, parser, *etc*) is trained separately and must be capable of assigning conditional probabilities to its output given its input. The method hinges on probabilistic inference, yet it is often problematic to map a speech recognizer's score to a probability as their approach requires. In addition, the method is evaluated only in a toy domain, using a few sample utterances.

3 Experimental Data

The data used for the experiments which follow were collected from user interactions with City Browser, a web-based, multimodal dialogue system. A thorough description of the architecture and capabilities can be found in (Gruenstein et al., 2006; Gruenstein and Seneff, 2007). Briefly, the version of City Browser used for the experiments in this paper allows users to access information about restaurants, museums, and subway stations by navigating to a web page on their own computers. They can also locate addresses on the map, and obtain driving directions. Users can interact with City Browser's map-based graphical user interface by clicking and drawing; and they can speak with it by talking into their computer microphone and listening to a response from their speakers. Speech recognition is performed via the SUMMIT recognizer, using a trigram language model with dynamically updatable classes for proper nouns such as city, street, and restaurant names—see (Chung et al., 2004) for a description of this capability. Speech recognition results were parsed by the TINA parser (Seneff, 1992) using a hand-crafted grammar. A discourse module (Filisko and Seneff, 2003) then integrates contextual knowledge. The fully formed request is sent to the dialogue manager, which attempts to craft an appropriate system response—both in terms of a verbal and graphical response. The GENESIS system (Seneff, 2002) uses hand-crafted generation rules to produce a natural language string, which is sent to an off-the-shelf text-to-speech synthesizer. Finally, the user hears the response, and the graphical user interface is updated to show, for example, a set of search results on the map.

3.1 Data Collection

The set of data used in this paper was collected as part of a controlled experiment in which users worked through a set of scenarios by accessing the City Browser web page from their own computers, whenever and from wherever they liked. Interested readers may refer to (Gruenstein and Seneff, 2007) for more information on the experimental setup, as well as for an initial analysis of a subset of the data used here. Users completed a warmup scenario in which they were simply told to utter "Hello City Browser" to ensure that their audio setup and web browser were working properly. They then worked through ten scenarios presented sequentially, followed by time for "free play" in which they could use the system however they pleased.

As users interact with City Browser, logs are made recording their interactions. In addition to recording each utterance, every time a user clicks or draws with the mouse, these actions are recorded and time-stamped. The outputs of the various stages of natural language processing are also logged, so that the "dialogue state" of the system is tracked. This means that, associated with each utterance in the dataset is, among other things, the following information:

- a recording of the utterance;
- the current dialogue state, which includes information such as recently referred to entities for anaphora resolution;
- the state of the GUI, including: the current position and bounds of the map, any points of interest (POIs) displayed on the map, *etc.*;
- the contents of any dynamically updatable language model classes; and
- time-stamped clicks, gestures, and other user interface interaction performed by the user before and during speech.

The utterances of 38 users who attempted most or all of the scenarios were transcribed, providing 1,912 utterances used in this study. The utterances were drawn only from the 10 "real" scenarios; utterances from the initial warmup and final free play tasks were discarded. In addition, a small number of utterances were eliminated because logging glitches made it impossible to accurately recover the dialogue system's state at the time of the utterance.

The class n-gram language model used for data collection has a vocabulary of approximately 1,200 words, plus about 25,000 proper nouns.

4 Data Annotation

Given the information associated with each utterance in the dataset, it is possible to "replay" an utterance to the dialogue system and obtain the same response—both the spoken response and any updates made to the GUI—which was originally provided to the user in response to the utterance. In particular, we can replicate the *reply_frame* which is passed to GENESIS in order to produce a natural language response; and we can replicate the *gui_reply_frame* which is sent to the GUI so that it can be properly updated (*e.g.*, to show the results of a search on the map).

The ability to replicate the system's response to each utterance also gives us the flexibility to try out alternative inputs to the dialogue system, given the dialogue state at the time of the utterance. So, in addition to transcribing each utterance, we also passed each transcript through the dialogue system, yielding a system response. In the experiments that follow, we considered the system's response to the transcribed utterance to be the *correct* response for that utterance. It should be noted that in some cases, even given the transcript, the dialogue system may *reject* and respond by signally non-understanding—if, for example, the utterance can't be parsed. In these cases, we take the response *reject* to be the correct response.

We note that labeling the data in this fashion has limitations. Most importantly, the system may respond inappropriately even to a perfectly transcribed utterance. Such responses, given our labeling methodology, would incorrectly be labeled as *correct*. In addition, sometimes it may be the case that there are actually several acceptable responses to a particular utterances.

5 Feature Extraction

For each utterance, our goal is to produce a set of candidate system responses, where each response is also associated with a vector of feature values to be used to classify it as *acceptable* or *unacceptable*. Responses are labeled as *acceptable* if they match the system response produced from the transcription, and as *unacceptable* otherwise.

We start with the N-best list output by the speech recognizer. For each hypothesis, we extract a set

Recognition			Distributional	Response
(a) Best across hyps:	**(b) Drop:**	**(c) Other:**	percent_top_3	response_type
total_score_per_word	total_drop	mean_words	percent_top_5	num_found
acoustic_score_per_bound	acoustic_drop	top_rank	percent_top_10	POI_type
lexical_score_per_word	lexical_drop	n-best_length	percent_nbest	is_subset
			top_response_type	parse_status
			response_rank	geographical_filter
			num_distinct	

Table 1: Features used to train the acceptability classifier. Nine features are derived from the recognizer; seven have to do with the distribution of responses; and six come from the process of generating the candidate response.

of acoustic, lexical, and total scores from the recognizer. These scores are easily obtained, as they comprise a subset of the features used to train the recognizer's existing confidence module; see (Hazen et al., 2002). The features used are shown in Table 1a.

We then map each hypothesis to a candidate system response, by running it through the dialogue system given the original dialogue state. From these outputs, we collect a list of *unique* responses, which is typically shorter than the recognizer's N-best list, as multiple hypotheses typically map to the same response.

We now derive a set of features for each unique response. First, each response inherits the best value for each recognizer score associated with a hypothesis which evoked that response (see Table 1a). In addition, the drop in score between the response's score for each recognition feature and the top value occurring in the N-best list is used as a feature (see Table 1b). Finally, the rank of the highest hypothesis on the N-best list which evoked the response, the mean number of words per hypothesis evoking the responses, and the length of the recognizer's N-best list are used as features (see Table 1c).

Distributional features are also generated based on the distribution of hypotheses on the N-best list which evoked the same response. The percent of times a particular response is evoked by the top 3, top 5, top 10, and by all hypotheses on the N-best list are used as features. Features are generated, as well, based on the distribution of responses on the list of unique responses. These features are: the initial ranking of this response on the list, the number of distinct responses on the list, and the type of response that was evoked by the top hypothesis on the recognizer N-best list.

Finally, features derived from the response itself, and natural language processing performed to derive that response, are also calculated. The high-level type of the response, as well as the type and number of any POIs returned by a database query are used as features if they exist, as is a boolean indicator as to whether or not these results are a subset of the results currently shown on the display. If any sort of "geographical filter", such as an address or circled region, is used to constrain the search, then the type of this filter is also used as a feature. Finally, the "best" parse status of any hypotheses leading to this response is also used, where $full\_parse \succ robust\_parse \succ no\_parse$.

Table 1 lists all of the features used to train the classifier, while Table 3 (in the appendix) lists the possible values for the non-numerical features. Figure 3 (in the appendix) gives an overview of the feature extraction process, as well as the classification method described in the next section.

6 Classifier Training and Scoring

For a given utterance, we now have a candidate list of responses derived from the speech recognizer's N-best list, a feature vector associated with each response, and a label telling us the "correct" response, as derived from the transcript. In order to build a classifier, we first label each response as either *acceptable* or *unacceptable* by comparing it to the system's response to the transcribed utterance. If the two responses are identical, then the response is labeled as *acceptable*; otherwise, it is labeled as *unacceptable*. This yields a binary decision problem for each response, given a set of features. We train a Support Vector Machine (SVM) to make this decision, using the Weka toolkit, version 3.4.12 (Witten and Frank, 2005).

Given a trained SVM model, the procedure for processing a novel utterance is as follows. First, classify each response (and its associated feature vector) on the response list for that utterance using the SVM. By using a logistic regression model fit on the training data, an SVM score between -1 and 1 for each response is yielded, where responses with positive scores are more likely to be *acceptable*, and those with negative scores are more likely to be *unacceptable*.

Next, the SVM scores are used to rank the list of responses. Given a ranked list of such responses, the dialogue system has two options: it can choose the top scoring response, or it can *abstain* from choosing any response. The most straightforward method for making such a decision is via a threshold: if the score of the top response is above a certain threshold, this response is accepted; otherwise, the system abstains from choosing a response, and instead responds by indicating non-understanding. Figure 3 (in the appendix) provides a graphical overview of the response confidence scoring process.

At first blush, a natural threshold to choose is 0, as this marks the boundary between *acceptable* and *unacceptable*. However, it may be desirable to optimize this threshold based on the desired characteristics of the dialogue system—in a mission-critical application, for example, it may be preferable to accept only high-confidence responses, and to clarify otherwise. We can optimize the threshold as we like using either the same training data, or a held-out development set, so long as we have an objective function with which to optimize. In the evaluation that follows, we optimize the threshold using the F-measure on the training data as the objective function. It would also be interesting to optimize the threshold in a more sophisticated manner, such as that developed in (Bohus and Rudnicky, 2005) where task success is used to derive the cost of misunderstandings and false rejections, which in turn are used to set a rejection threshold.

While a thresholding approach makes sense, other approaches are feasible as well. For instance, a second classifier could be used to decide whether or not to accept the top ranking response. The classifier could take into account such features as the spread in scores among the responses, the number classified as *acceptable*, the drop between the top score and the second-ranked score, *etc*.

7 Evaluation

We evaluated the response-based method using the data described in section 3, N-best lists with a maximum length of 10, and an SVM with a linear kernel. We note that, in the live system, two-pass recognition is performed for some utterances, in which a key concept recognized in the first pass (*e.g.*, a city name) causes a dynamic update to the contents of a class in the n-gram language model (*e.g.*, a set of street names) for the second pass—as in the utterance *Show me thirty two Vassar Street in Cambridge* where the city name (*Cambridge*) triggers a second pass in which the streets in that city are given a higher weight. This two-pass approach has been shown previously to decrease word and concept error rates (Gruenstein and Seneff, 2006), even though it can be susceptible to errors in understanding. However, since all street names, for example, are active in the vocabulary at all times, the two-pass approach is not strictly necessary to arrive at the correct hypotheses. Hence, for simplicity, in the experiments reported here, we do not integrate the two-pass approach—as this would require us to potentially do a second recognition pass for every candidate response. In a live system, a good strategy might be to consider a second recognition pass based on the top few candidate responses alone, which would produce a new set of candidates to be scored.

We performed 38-fold cross validation, where in each case the held-out test set was comprised of all the utterances of a single user. This ensured that we obtained an accurate prediction of a novel user's experience, although it meant that the test sets were not of equal size. We calculated F-measure for each test set, using the methodology described in figure 4 (in the appendix).

7.1 Baseline

As a baseline, we made use of the existing confidence module in the SUMMIT recognizer (Hazen et al., 2002). The module uses a linear projection model to produce an utterance level confidence score based on 15 features derived from recognizer scores,

Method	*F*
Recognition Confidence (Baseline)	.62
Recog Features Only	.62
Recog + Distributional	.67
Recog + Response	.71*
Recog + Response + Distributional	.72**

Table 2: Average F-measures obtained via per-user cross-validation of the response-based confidence scoring method using the feature sets described in Section 5, as compared to a baseline system which chooses the top hypothesis if the recognizer confidence score exceeds an optimized rejection threshold. The starred scores are a statistically significant (* indicates $p < .05$, ** indicates $p < .01$) improvement over the baseline, as determined by a paired t-test.

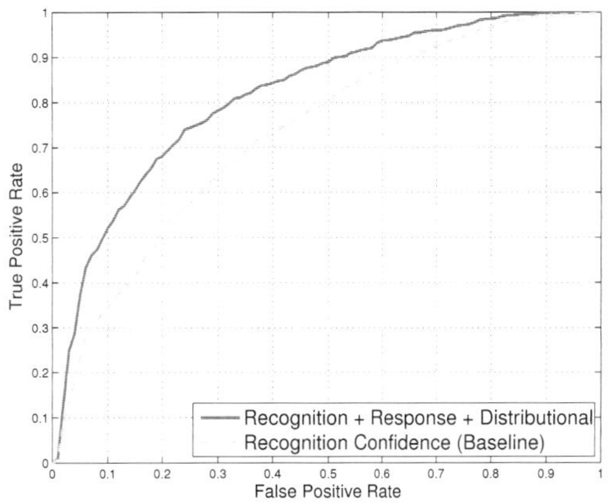

Figure 2: Receiver Operator Characteristic (ROC) curves (averaged across each cross-validation fold) comparing the baseline to the best response-based model.

and from comparing hypotheses on the N-best list. In our evaluation, the module was trained and tested on the same data as the SVM model using cross-validation.

An optimal rejection threshold was determined, as for the SVM method, using the training data with F-measure as the objective function. For each utterance, if the confidence score exceeded the threshold, then the response evoked from the top hypothesis on the N-best list was chosen.

7.2 Results

Table 2 compares the baseline recognizer confidence module to our response-based confidence annotator. The method was evaluated using several subsets of the features listed in Table 1. Using features derived from the recognizer only, we obtain results comparable to the baseline. Adding the response and distributional features yields a 16% improvement over the baseline system, which is statistically significant with $p < .01$ according to a paired t-test. While the distributional features appear to be helpful, the feature values derived from the response itself are the most beneficial, as they allow for a statistically significant improvement over the baseline when paired on their own with the recognizer-derived features.

Figure 2 plots ROC curves comparing the performance of the baseline model to the best response-based model. The curves were obtained by varying the value of the rejection threshold. We observe that the response-based model outperforms the baseline no matter what we set our tolerance for false positives to be.

The above results were obtained by using an SVM with a linear kernel, where feature values were normalized to be on the unit interval. We also tried using a quadratic kernel, retaining the raw feature values, and reducing the number of binary features by manually binning the non-numeric feature values. Each change resulted in a slight decrease in F-measure.

8 Conclusion and Future Work

We recast the problem of choosing among an N-best list of recognition hypotheses as one of choosing the best candidate system response which can be generated from the recognition hypotheses on that list. We then demonstrated a framework for assigning confidence scores to those responses, by using the scores output by an SVM trained to discriminate between acceptable and unacceptable responses. The classifier was trained using a set of features derived from the speech recognizer, culled from the generation of each response, and calculated based on each response's distribution. We tested our methods using data collected by users interacting with the City Browser multimodal dialogue system, and showed that they lead to a significant improvement over a baseline which makes an acceptance decision based on an utterance-level recognizer confidence score.

The technique developed herein could be refined in several ways. First and foremost, it may well be possible to find additional features with discriminatory power. Also, the decision as to whether or not to choose the top-scoring response could potentially be improved by choosing a more appropriate metric than F-measure as the objective function, or perhaps by using a second classifier at this stage.

Finally, our experiments were performed off-line. In order to better test the approach, we plan to deploy the classifier as a component in the running dialogue system. This presents some processing time constraints (as multiple candidate responses must be generated); and it introduces the confounding factor of working with a recognizer that can make multiple recognition passes after language model reconfiguration. These challenges should be tractable for N-best lists of modest length.

Acknowledgments

Thank you to Stephanie Seneff for her guidance and advice. Thanks to Timothy J. Hazen for his assistance with the confidence module. Thanks to Ali Mohammad for discussions about the machine learning aspects of this paper and his comments on drafts. And thanks to four anonymous reviewers for constructive criticism. This research is sponsored by the T-Party Project, a joint research program between MIT and Quanta Computer Inc., Taiwan.

References

Dan Bohus and Alex Rudnicky. 2002. Integrating multiple knowledge sources for utterance-level confidence annotation in the CMU Communicator spoken dialog system. Technical Report CS-190, Carnegie Mellon University.

Dan Bohus and Alexander I. Rudnicky. 2005. A principled approach for rejection threshold optimization in spoken dialog systems. In *Proc. of INTERSPEECH*.

Lin Chase. 1997. Word and acoustic confidence annotation for large vocabulary speech recognition. In *Proc. of 5th European Conference on Speech Communication and Technology*, pages 815–818.

Ananlada Chotimongkol and Alexander I. Rudnicky. 2001. N-best speech hypotheses reordering using linear regression. In *Proc. of 7th European Conference on Speech Communication and Technology*.

Grace Chung, Stephanie Seneff, Chao Wang, and Lee Hetherington. 2004. A dynamic vocabulary spoken dialogue interface. In *Proc. of INTERSPEECH*, pages 327–330.

Ed Filisko and Stephanie Seneff. 2003. A context resolution server for the Galaxy conversational systems. In *Proc. of EUROSPEECH*.

Malte Gabsdil and Oliver Lemon. 2004. Combining acoustic and pragmatic features to predict recognition performance in spoken dialogue systems. In *Proc. of Association for Computational Linguistics*.

Alexander Gruenstein and Stephanie Seneff. 2006. Context-sensitive language modeling for large sets of proper nouns in multimodal dialogue systems. In *Proc. of IEEE/ACL 2006 Workshop on Spoken Language Technology*.

Alexander Gruenstein and Stephanie Seneff. 2007. Releasing a multimodal dialogue system into the wild: User support mechanisms. In *Proc. of the 8th SIGdial Workshop on Discourse and Dialogue*, pages 111–119.

Alexander Gruenstein, Stephanie Seneff, and Chao Wang. 2006. Scalable and portable web-based multimodal dialogue interaction with geographical databases. In *Proc. of INTERSPEECH*.

Timothy J. Hazen, Stephanie Seneff, and Joseph Polifroni. 2002. Recognition confidence scoring and its use in speech understanding systems. *Computer Speech and Language*, 16:49–67.

Diane J. Litman, Julia Hirschberg, and Marc Swerts. 2000. Predicting automatic speech recognition performance using prosodic cues. In *Proc. of NAACL*, pages 218 – 225.

Michael Niemann, Sarah George, and Ingrid Zukerman. 2005. Towards a probabilistic, multi-layered spoken language interpretation system. In *Proc. of 4th IJCAI Workshop on Knowledge and Reasoning in Practical Dialogue Systems*, pages 8–15.

Rubén San-Segundo, Bryan Pellom, Wayne Ward, and José M. Pardo. 2000. Confidence measures for dialogue management in the CU Communicator System. In *Proc. of ICASSP*.

Stephanie Seneff. 1992. TINA: A natural language system for spoken language applications. *Computational Linguistics*, 18(1):61–86.

Stephanie Seneff. 2002. Response planning and generation in the MERCURY flight reservation system. *Computer Speech and Language*, 16:283–312.

Marilyn Walker, Jerry Wright, and Irene Langkilde. 2000. Using natural language processing and discourse features to identify understanding errors in a spoken dialogue system. In *Proc. 17th International Conf. on Machine Learning*, pages 1111–1118.

Ian H. Witten and Eibe Frank. 2005. *Data Mining: Practical machine learning tools and techniques*. Morgan Kaufmann, San Francisco, 2nd edition.

Recognition N-best

Hypothesis	Rank	S_t	S_a	S_l	...	*DS*	Response	Parse	...
thirty two vassal street in cambridge	0	45.3	28.5	26.5		→	R_0	*FULL*	
thirty two vassar street in cambridge	1	45.0	27.1	30.5		→	R_1	*FULL*	
thirty two vassar street in in cambridge	2	44.2	26.0	30.4		→	R_1	*ROBUST*	
at thirty two vassar street <noise>	3	40.1	26.5	29.4		→	R_1	*FULL*	
at thirty two vassal street in cambridge	4	39.5	26.3	29.0		→	R_1	*FULL*	
thirty two vassar street cambridge <noise>	5	38.4	25.8	28.4		→	R_1	*FULL*	
thirty two vassar street in canton	6	38.0	25.8	28.3		→	R_2	*FULL*	
thirty two vassal street in in canton	7	33.5	22.5	27.5		→	R_3	*ROBUST*	
twenty vassar in street in zoom	8	32.4	22.3	26.3		→	R_4	*NONE*	
thirty two vassar street in cambridge <noise>	9	32.0	19.5	26.7		→	R_1	*FULL*	

Response List

Response	Rank	S_t	S_a	S_l	*%Top3*	*%Top5*	*Dist.*	*Parse*	...	*SVM*	Score	
R_0	0	45.3	28.5	26.5	.33	.8	5	*FULL*		→	.42	
R_1	1	45.0	27.1	30.5	.66	.2	5	*FULL*		→	.73	→ **R_1**
R_2	6	38.0	25.8	28.3	0.0	0.0	5	*FULL*		→	-.32	
R_3	7	33.5	22.5	27.5	0.0	0.0	5	*ROBUST*		→	-.55	
R_4	8	32.4	22.3	36.3	0.0	0.0	5	*NONE*		→	-.92	

Figure 3: The feature extraction and classification process. The top half of the digram shows how an N-best list of recognizer hypotheses, with associated scores from the recognizer, are processed by the dialogue system (*DS*) to produce a list of responses. Associated with each response is a set of feature values derived from the response itself, as well as the process of evoking the response (*e.g.* the parse status). The bottom half of the figure shows how the unique responses are collapsed into a list. Each response in the list inherits the best recognition scores available from hypotheses evoking that response; each also has feature values associated with it derived from the distribution of that response on the recognizer N-best list. Each set of feature values is classified by a Support Vector Machine, and the resulting score is used to rank the responses. If the highest scoring response exceeds the rejection threshold, then it is chosen as the system's response.

Feature	Possible Values
response_type top_response_type	geography, give_directions, goodbye, greetings, help_directions_did_not_understand_from_place, help_directions_did_not_understand_to_place, help_directions_no_to_or_from_place, help_directions_subway, hide_subway_map, history_cleared, list_cuisine, list_name, list_street, no_circled_data, no_data, no_match_near, non_unique_near, ok, panning_down, panning_east, panning_south, panning_up, panning_west, presupp_failure, provide_city_for_address, refined_result, reject_or_give_help, show_address, show_subway_map, speak_properties, speak_property, speak_verify_false, speak_verify_true, welcome_gui, zooming, zooming_in, zooming_out
POI_type	none, city, museum, neighborhood, restaurant, subway_station
parse_status	no_parse, robust_parse, full_parse
geographical_filter	none, address, circle, line, list_item, map_bounds, museum, neighborhood, point, polygon, restaurant, subway_station, city

Table 3: The set of possible values for non-numerical features, which are converted to sets of binary features.

Case I

R_0 is *acceptable* and is not *reject*

$S_0 \geq T \rightarrow$ T.P.
$S_0 < T \rightarrow$ F.N.

Response	Score	Type	Label
R_0	S_0	speak_property	acceptable
R_1	S_1	list_cuisine	unacceptable
R_2	S_2	speak_property	unacceptable

Case I: Example Ranked Response List

Case II

No candidate responses *acceptable*, or *acceptable* response is *reject*

(a)
R_0 is not *reject*
$S_0 \geq T \rightarrow$ F.P.
$S_0 < T \rightarrow$ T.N.

(b)
R_0 is *reject*
$S_0 \geq T \rightarrow$ T.N.
$S_0 < T \rightarrow$ T.N.

Response	Score	Type	Label
R_0	S_0	speak_property	unacceptable
R_1	S_1	list_cuisine	unacceptable
R_2	S_2	speak_property	unacceptable
R_3	S_3	reject	unacceptable
R_4	S_4	zooming_out	unacceptable

Case II: Example Ranked Response List

Case III

R_n (with $n > 0$) is *acceptable* and is not *reject*

(a)
R_0 is not *reject*
$S_0 \geq T \rightarrow$ F.P.
$S_0 < T \rightarrow$ F.N.

(b)
R_0 is *reject*
$S_0 \geq T \rightarrow$ F.N.
$S_0 < T \rightarrow$ F.N.

Response	Score	Type	Label
R_0	S_0	speak_property	unacceptable
R_1	S_1	list_cuisine	acceptable
R_2	S_2	speak_property	unacceptable
R_3	S_3	reject	unacceptable
R_4	S_4	zooming_out	unacceptable

Case III: Example Ranked Response List

Figure 4: Algorithm for calculating the F-measure confusion matrix of True Positives (T.P.), False Positives (F.P.), True Negatives (T.N.), and False Negatives (F.N.). The ranking technique described in this paper creates a list of candidate system responses ranked by their scores. The top scoring response is then *accepted* if its score exceeds a threshold T, otherwise all candidate responses are *rejected*. As such, the problem is not a standard binary decision. We show all possible outcomes from the ranking process, and note whether each case is counted as a T.P., F.P., T.N., or F.N. We note that given this algorithm for calculating the confusion matrix, no matter how we set the threshold T, F-measure will always be penalized if Case III occurs.

Learning N-Best Correction Models from Implicit User Feedback in a Multi-Modal Local Search Application

Dan Bohus, Xiao Li, Patrick Nguyen, Geoffrey Zweig
Microsoft Research
One Microsoft Way
Redmond, WA, 98052
{dbohus, xiaol, panguyen, gzweig}@microsoft.com

Abstract

We describe a novel n-best correction model that can leverage implicit user feedback (in the form of clicks) to improve performance in a multi-modal speech-search application. The proposed model works in two stages. First, the n-best list generated by the speech recognizer is expanded with additional candidates, based on confusability information captured via user click statistics. In the second stage, this expanded list is rescored and pruned to produce a more accurate and compact n-best list. Results indicate that the proposed n-best correction model leads to significant improvements over the existing baseline, as well as other traditional n-best rescoring approaches.

1 Introduction

Supported by years of research in speech recognition and related technologies, as well as advances in mobile devices, speech-enabled mobile applications are finally transitioning into day-to-day use. One example is Live Search for Windows Mobile (2008), a speech-enabled application that allows users to get access to local information by speaking a query into their device. Several other systems operating in similar domains have recently become available (TellMeByMobile, 2008; Nuance Mobile Search, 2008; V-Lingo Mobile, 2008; VoiceSignal Search, 2008.)

Traditionally, multi-modal systems leverage the additional input channels such as text or buttons to compensate for the current shortcomings of speech recognition technology. For instance, after the user speaks a query, the Live Search for Windows Mobile application displays a confirmation screen that contains the n-best recognition results. The user selects the correct hypothesis using the buttons on the device, and only then the system displays the corresponding search results (see Figure 1.)

We argue that ideally multi-modal systems could use the additional, more accurate input channels not only for confirmation or immediate correction, but also to learn from the interaction and improve their performance over time, without explicit human supervision. For example, in the interaction paradigm described above, apart from providing the means for selecting the correct recognition result from an n-best list, the user click on a hypothesis can provide valuable information about the errors made by system, which could be exploited to further improve performance.

Consider for instance the following numbers from an analysis of logged click data in the Live Search for Windows Mobile system. Over a certain period of time, the results *Beer* and *Gear* were displayed together in an n-best list 122 times. Out of these cases, *Beer* was clicked 67% of the time, and *Gear* was never clicked. In 25% of the cases when *Beer* was selected, *Gear* was incorrectly presented above (i.e. higher than) *Beer* in the n-best list. More importantly, there are also 82 cases in which *Gear* appears in an n-best list, but *Beer* does not. A manual inspection reveals that, in 22% of these cases, the actual spoken utterance was indeed *Beer*. The clicks therefore indicate that the engine often misrecognizes *Gear* instead of *Beer*.

Proceedings of the 9th SIGdial Workshop on Discourse and Dialogue, pages 21–28,
Columbus, June 2008.

Ideally, the system should be able to take advantage of this information and use the clicks to create an automatic positive feedback loop. We can envision several ways in which this could be accomplished. A possible approach would be to use all the clicked results to adapt the existing language or acoustic models. Another, higher-level approach is to treat the recognition process as a black-box, and use the click feedback (perhaps also in conjunction with other high-level information) to post-process the results recognition results.

While both approaches have their merits, in this work we concentrate on the latter paradigm. We introduce a novel n-best correction model that leverages the click data to improve performance in a speech-enabled multi-modal application. The proposed model works in two stages. First, the n-best list generated by the speech recognizer is expanded with additional candidates, based on results confusability information captured by the click statistics. For instance, in the 82 cases we mentioned above when *Gear* was present in the n-best list but *Beer* was not, *Beer* (as well as potentially other results) would also be added to form an expanded n-best list. The expanded list is then rescored and pruned to construct a corrected, more accurate n-best list.

The proposed approach, described in detail in Section 3, draws inspiration from earlier work in post-recognition error-correction models (Ringger and Allen, 1996; Ringger and Allen, 1997) and n-best rescoring (Chotimongkol and Rudnicky, 2001; Birkenes et al., 2007). The novelty of our approach lies in: (1) the use of user click data in a deployed multi-modal system for creating a positive feedback loop, and (2) the development of an n-best correction model based on implicit feedback that outperforms traditional rescoring-only approaches. Later on, in Section 5, we will discuss in more detail the relationship of the proposed approach to these and other works previously reported in the literature.

Before moving on to describe the n-best correction model in more detail, we give a high-level overview of Live Search for Windows Mobile, the multi-modal, mobile local search application that provided the test-bed for evaluating this work.

2 Live Search for Windows Mobile

Live Search for Windows Mobile is an application that enables local web-search on mobile devices. In its current version, it allows users to find information about local businesses and restaurants, to obtain driving directions, explore maps, view current traffic, get movie show-times, etc. A number of screen-shots are illustrated in Figure 1.

Recently, Live Search for Windows Mobile has been extended with a speech interface (notice the Speak button assigned to the left soft-key in Figure 1.a.) The speech-based interaction with the system proceeds as follows: the user clicks the Speak button and speaks the name of a local business, for instance *A-B-C Hauling,* or a general category such as *Vietnamese Restaurants*. The application endpoints the audio and forwards it over the data channel to a server (Figure 1.b.) Recognition is performed on the server side, and the resulting n-best list is sent back to the client application, where it is displayed to the user (Figure 1.c.) The user can select the correct item from the n-best list, re-speak the request, or abandon the interaction altogether by pressing Cancel. Once the user selects an item in the n-best list, the corresponding search results are displayed (Figure 1.d.)

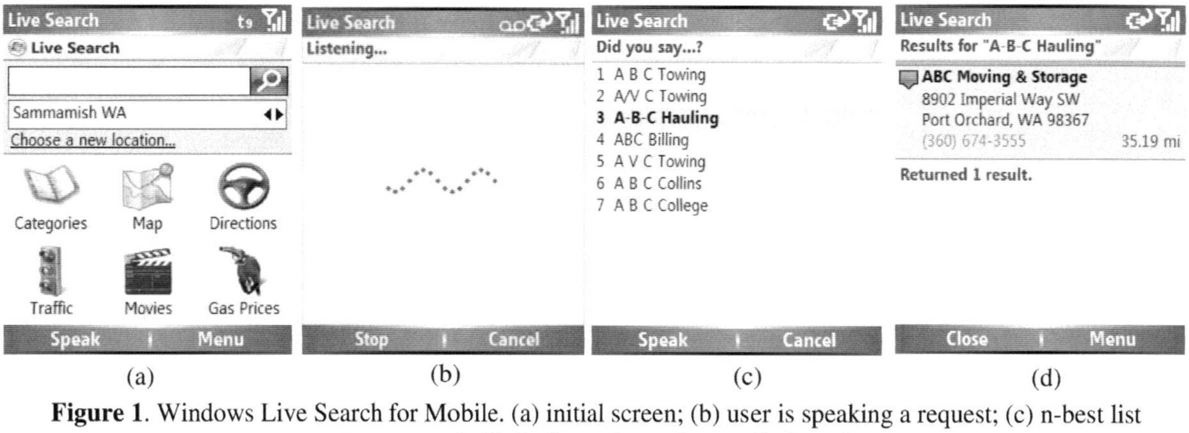

Figure 1. Windows Live Search for Mobile. (a) initial screen; (b) user is speaking a request; (c) n-best list is presented; (d) final search results are displayed

Apart from business names, the system also handles speech input for addresses, as well as compound requests, such as *Shamiana Restaurant in Kirkland, Washington*. For the latter cases, a two-tier recognition and confirmation process is used. In the first stage a location n-best list is generated and sent to the client for confirmation. After the user selects the location, a second recognition stage uses a grammar tailored to that specific location to re-recognize the utterance. The client then displays the final n-best list from which the user can select the correct result.

Several details about the system architecture and the structure of the recognition process have been omitted here due to space considerations. For the interested reader, a more in-depth description of this system is available in (Acero et al., 2008).

3 Approach

We now turn our attention to the proposed n-best correction model

3.1 Overview

The model works in two stages, illustrated in Figure 2. In the first stage the n-best list produced by the speech recognizer is expanded with several alternative hypotheses. In the second stage, the expanded n-best list is rescored to construct the final, corrected n-best list.

The n-best expansion step relies on a result confusion matrix, constructed from click information. The matrix, which we will describe in more detail in the following subsection, contains information about which result was selected (clicked) by the user when a certain result was displayed. For instance, in the example from Figure 2, the matrix indicates that when *Burlington* appeared in the n-best list, *Bar* was clicked once, *Bowling* was clicked 13 times, *Burger King* was clicked twice, and *Burlington* was clicked 15 times (see hashed row in matrix.) The last element in the row indicates that there were 7 cases in which *Burlington* was decoded, but nothing (∅) was clicked. Essentially, the matrix captures information about the confusability of different recognition results.

The expansion step adds to an n-best list generated by the recognizer all the results that were previously clicked in conjunction with any one of the items in the given n-best list. For instance, in the example from Figure 2, the n-best list contains *Sterling, Stirling, Burlington* and *Cooling.* Based on the confusion matrix, this list will be expanded to also include *Bar, Bowling, Burger King, Towing,* and *Turley.* In this particular case, the correct recognition result, *Bowling,* is added in the expanded n-best list.

In the final step, the expanded list is rescored. In the previous example, for simplicity of explanation, a simple heuristic for re-scoring was used: add all the counts on the columns corresponding to each expanded result. As a consequence, the cor-

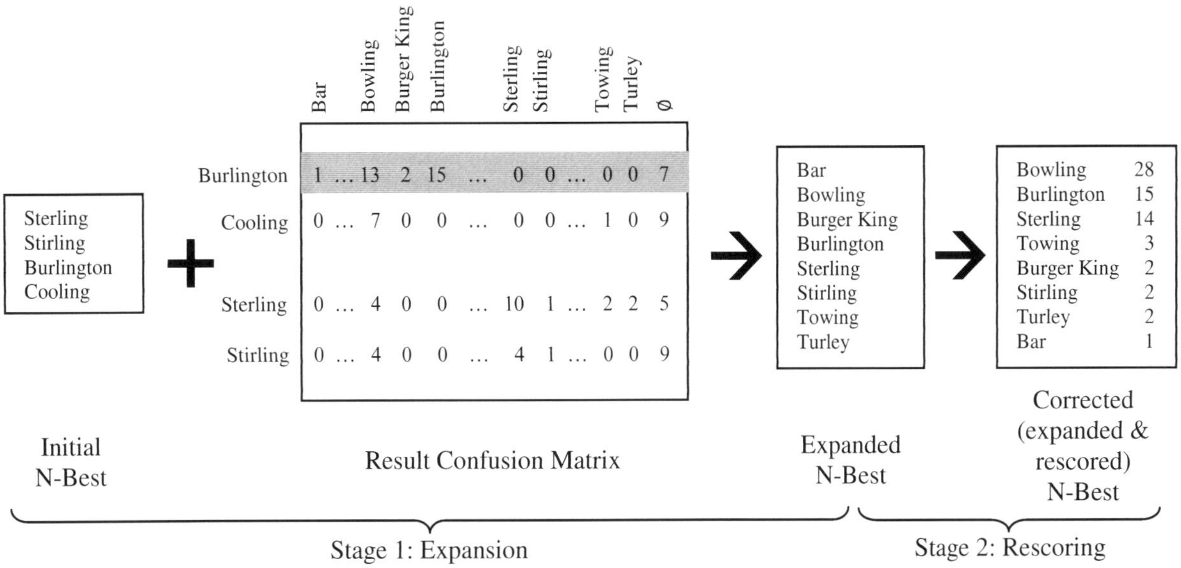

Figure 2. A confusion-based n-best correction model

rect recognition result, *Bowling*, was pushed to the top of the n-best list.

We begin by formally describing the construction of the results confusability matrix and the expansion process in the next two sub-sections. Then, we describe three rescoring approaches. The first one is based on an error-correction model constructed from the confusion matrix. The other two, are more traditional rescoring approaches, based on language model adaptation.

3.2 The Result Confusion Matrix

The result confusion matrix is computed in a simple traversal of the click logs. The rows in the matrix correspond to decoded results, i.e. results that have appeared in an n-best list. The columns in the matrix correspond to clicked (or intended) results, i.e. results that the user has clicked on in the n-best list. The entries at the intersection of row d and column c correspond to the number of times result c was clicked when result d was decoded:

$$m_{d,c} = \#(decoded = d, clicked = c).$$

In addition, the last column in the matrix, denoted $\emptyset$ contains the number of times no result was clicked when result d was displayed:

$$m_{d,\emptyset} = \#(decoded = d, clicked = \emptyset).$$

The rows in the matrix can therefore be used to compute the maximum likelihood estimate for the conditional probability distribution:

$$P_{ML}(c|d) = \frac{m_{d,c}}{\sum_c m_{d,c}}.$$

The full dimensions of the result confusion matrix can grow very large since the matrix is constructed at the result level (the average number of words per displayed result is 2.01). The number of rows equals the number of previously decoded results, and the number of columns equals the number of previously clicked results. However, the matrix is very sparse and can be stored efficiently using a sparse matrix representation.

3.3 N-Best Expansion

The first step in the proposed n-best correction model is to expand the initial n-best list with all results that have been previously clicked in conjunction with the items in the current n-best list.

Let's denote by $N = \{d_r\}_{r=1..n}$ the initial n-best list produced by the speech recognizer. Then, the expanded n-best list EN will contain all d_r, as well as all previously clicked results c such that there exists r with $m_{d_r,c} > 0$.

3.4 Confusion Matrix Based Rescoring

Ideally, we would like to rank the hypotheses in the expanded list EN according to $P(i|a)$, where i represents the intended result and a represents the acoustics of the spoken utterance. This can be rewritten as follows:

$$P(i|a) = \sum_d P(i|d) \cdot P(d|a). \qquad [1]$$

The first component in this model is an error-correction model $P(i|d)$. This model describes the conditional probability that the correct (or intended) result is i given that result d has been decoded. While this conditional model cannot be constructed directly, we can replace it by a proxy - $P(c|d)$, which models the probability that the result c will be clicked, given that result d was decoded. As mentioned earlier in subsection 3.2, this conditional probability distribution can be computed from the result confusion matrix. In replacing $P(i|d)$ with $P(c|d)$, we are making the assumption that the clicks correspond indeed to the correct, intended results, and to nothing else[1].

Notice that the result confusion matrix is generally very sparse. The maximum likelihood estimator $P_{ML}(c|d)$ will therefore often be inappropriate. To address this data sparsity issue, we linearly interpolate the maximum likelihood estimator with an overall model $P_O(c|d)$:

$$P(c|d) = \lambda P_{ML}(c|d) + (1-\lambda)P_O(c|d).$$

The overall model is defined in terms of two constants, α and β, as follows:

$$P_O(c|d) = \begin{cases} \alpha, if\ c = d \\ \beta, if\ c \neq d \end{cases}$$

where α is the overall probability in the whole dataset of clicking on a given decoded result, and β is computed such that $P_O(c|d)$ normalizes to 1.

[1] While this assumption generally holds, we have also observed cases where it is violated: sometimes users (perhaps accidentally) click on an incorrect result; other times the correct result is in the list but nothing is clicked (perhaps the user was simply testing out the recognition capabilities of the system, without having an actual information need)

Finally, the λ interpolation parameter is determined empirically on the development set.

The second component in the confusion based rescoring model from equation [1] is $P(d|a)$. This is the recognition score for hypothesis d. The n-best rescoring model from [1] becomes:

$$P(c|a) = \sum_{d_r \in N} [\lambda P_{ML}(c|d_r) + (1-\lambda)P_O(c|d_r)] \cdot P(d_r|a)$$

3.5 Language Model Based Rescoring

A more traditional alternative for n-best rescoring is to adapt the bigram language model used by the system in light of the user click data, and re-rank the decoded results by:

$$P(i|a) \propto P(d_r|a) \propto P(a|d_r)P(d_r)$$

Here $P(a|d_r)$ is the acoustic score assigned by the recognizer to hypothesis d_r, and $P(d_r)$ is the adapted language model score for this hypothesis.

A simple approach for adapting the system's language model is to add the word sequences of the user-clicked results to the original training sentences and to re-estimate the language model $P(d)$. We will refer to this method as maximum likelihood (ML) estimation. A second approach, referred to as conditional maximum likelihood (CML) estimation, is to adapt the language model such as to directly maximize the conditional likelihood of the correct result given acoustics, *i.e.*,

$$P(i|a) = \frac{P(a|i)P(i)}{\sum_{d_r \in N} P(a|d_r)P(d_r)}$$

Note that this is the same objective function as the one used in Section 3.4, except that here the click data is used to estimate the language model instead of the error correction model. Again, in practice we assume that users click on correct results, i.e. $i = c$.

4 Experiments

We now discuss a number of experiments and the results obtained using the proposed n-best correction approach.

4.1 Data

For the purposes of the experiments described below we extracted just over 800,000 queries from the server logs in which the recognizer had generated a simple n-best list[2]. For each recognition event, we collected from the system logs the n-best list, and the result clicked by the user (if the user clicked on any result).

In addition, for testing purposes, we also make use of 11529 orthographically transcribed user requests. The transcribed set was further divided into a development set containing 5680 utterances and a test set containing 5849 utterances.

4.2 Initial N-Best Rescoring

To tease apart the effects of expansion and rescoring in the proposed n-best correction model, we began by using the rescoring techniques on the initial n-best lists, without first expanding them.

Since the actual recognition confidence scores $P(d_r|a)$ were not available in the system logs, we replaced them with an exponential probability density function based on the rank of the hypothesis:

$$P(d_r|a) = 2^{-r}$$

We then rescored the n-best lists from the test set according to the three rescoring models described earlier: confusion matrix, maximum likelihood (ML), and conditional maximum likelihood (CML). We computed the sentence level accuracy for the rescored n-best list, at different cutoffs. The accuracy was measured by comparing the rescored hypotheses against the available transcripts.

Note that the maximum depth of the n-best lists generated by the recognizer is 10; this is the maximum number of hypotheses that can be displayed on the mobile device. However, the system may generate fewer than 10 hypotheses. The observed average n-best list size in the test set was 4.2.

The rescoring results are illustrated in Figure 3 and reported in Table 1. The X axis in Figure 3 shows the cutoff at which the n-best accuracy was computed. For instance in the baseline system, the correct hypothesis was contained in the top result in 46.2% of cases, in the top-2 results in 50.5% of the cases and in the top-3 results in 51.5% of the cases. The results indicate that all the rescoring models improve performance relative to the base-

[2] We did not consider cases where a false-recognition event was fired (e.g. if no speech was detected in the audio signal) – in these cases no n-best list is generated. We also did not consider cases where a compound n-best was generated (e.g. for compound requests like *Shamiana in Kirkland, Washington*)

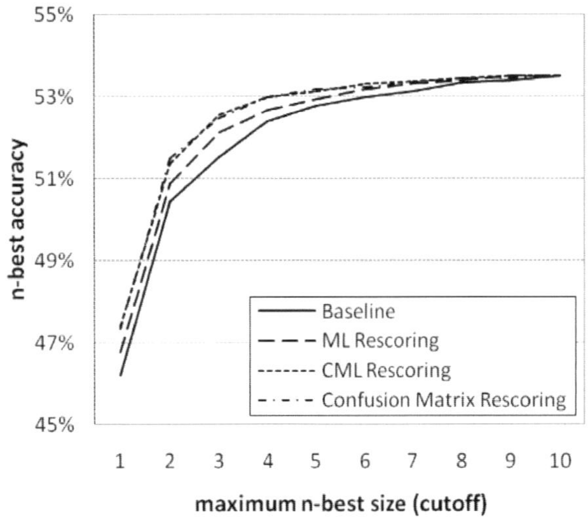

Figure 3. Initial n-best rescoring (test-set)

	Model	1-Best	2-Best	3-Best	10-Best
0	Baseline	46.2	50.5	51.5	53.5
1	ML Rescoring	46.8	50.9	52.1	53.5
2	CML Rescoring	47.4	51.4	52.6	53.5
3	Confusion Matrix Resc.	47.3	51.5	52.5	53.5
4	Expansion + Rescoring (size=7.09)	46.8	52.3	54.5	57.3
5	Expansion + Rescoring (size=4.15)	46.8	52.3	54.4	56.5

Table 1. Test-set sentence-level n-best accuracy; (0) baseline; (1)-(3) initial n-best rescoring; (4)-(5) expansion + rescoring

line. The improvement is smallest for the maximum likelihood (ML) language model rescoring approach, but is still statistically significant ($p = 0.008$ in a Wilcoxon sign-rank test.) The confusion-matrix based rescoring and the CML rescoring models perform similarly well, leading to a 1% absolute improvement in 1-best and 2-best sentence-level accuracy from the baseline ($p < 10^{-5}$). No statistically significant difference can be detected between these two models. At the same time, they both outperform the maximum likelihood rescoring model ($p < 0.03$).

4.3 N-Best Correction

Next, we evaluated the end-to-end n-best correction approach. The n-best lists were first expanded, as described in section 3.3, and the expanded lists were ranked using the confusion matrix based rescoring model described in Section 3.4.

The expansion process enlarges the original n-best lists. Immediately after expansion, the average n-best size grows from 4.2 to 96.9. The oracle performance for the expanded n-best lists increases to 59.8% (versus 53.5% in the initial n-best lists.) After rescoring, we trimmed the expanded n-best lists to a maximum of 10 hypotheses: we still want to obey the mobile device display constraint. The resulting average n-best size was 7.09 (this is lower than 10 since there are cases when the system cannot generate enough expansion hypotheses.)

The sentence-level accuracy of the corrected n-best lists is displayed in line 4 from Table 1. A direct comparison with the rescoring-only models or with the baseline is however unfair, due to the larger average size of the corrected n-best lists. To create a fair comparison and to better understand the performance of the n-best correction process, we pruned the corrected n-best lists by eliminating all hypotheses with a score below a certain threshold. By varying this rejection threshold, we can therefore control the average depth of the resulting corrected n-best lists. At a rejection threshold of 0.004, the average corrected n-best size is 4.15, comparable to the baseline of 4.2 .

The performance for the corresponding corrected (and pruned) n-best lists is shown in line 5 from Table 1 and illustrated in Figure 4. In contrast to a rescoring-only approach, the expansion process allows for improved performance at higher depths in the n-best list. The maximum n-best performance (while keeping the average n-best size at 4.15), is 56.5%, a 3% absolute improvement over the baseline ($p < 10^{-5}$).

Figure 5 provides more insight into the relationship between the sentence-level accuracy of the corrected (and pruned) n-best lists and the average n-best size (the plot was generated by varying the rejection threshold.) The result we discussed above can also be observed here: at the same average n-best size, the n-best correction model significantly outperforms the baseline. Furthermore, we can see that we can attain the same level of accuracy as the baseline system while cutting the average n-best size by more than 50%, from 4.22 to 2. In the opposite direction, if we are less sensitive to the number of items displayed in the n-best list (except for the 10-maximum constraint we already obey), we can further increase the overall performance by another 0.8% absolute to 57.3%; this overall accuracy is attained at an average n-best size of 7.09.

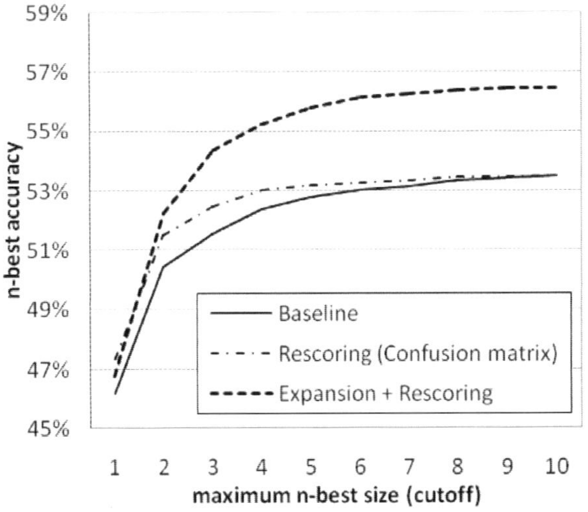

Figure 4. N-Best correction (test-set)

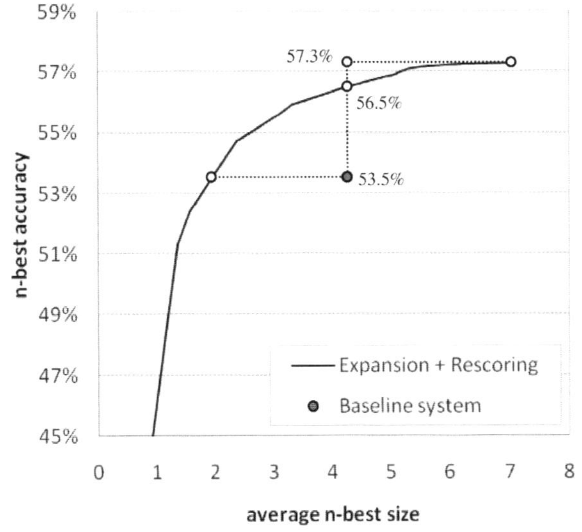

Figure 5. Overall n-best accuracy as a function of the average n-best size

Finally, we also investigated rescoring the expanded n-best lists using the CML approach. To apply CML, an initial ranking of the expanded n-best lists is however needed. If we use the ranking produced by the confusion-matrix based model discussed above, no further performance improvements can be observed.

5 Related work

The n-best correction model we have described in this paper draws inspiration from earlier works on post-recognition error correction models, n-best rescoring and implicitly supervised learning. In this section we discuss some of the similarities and differences between the proposed approach and previous work.

The idea of correcting speech recognition errors in a post-processing step has been proposed earlier by (Ringger and Allen, 1996; Ringger and Allen, 1997). The authors showed that, in the presence of transcribed data, a translation-based post-processor can be trained to correct the results of a speech recognizer, leading to a 15% relative WER improvement in a corpus of TRAINS-95 dialogues.

The n-best correction approach described here is different in two important aspects. First, instead of making use of transcripts, the proposed error-correction model is trained using implicit user feedback obtained in a multi-modal interface (in this case user clicks in the n-best list.) This is a less costly endeavor, as the system automatically obtains the supervision signal directly from the interaction; no transcripts are necessary. Second, the approach operates on the entire n-best list, rather than only on the top hypothesis; as such, it has additional information that can be helpful in making corrections. At Figure 2 illustrates, there is a potential for multiple incorrect hypotheses to point towards and reinforce the same correction hypothesis, leading to improved performance (in this example, *Burlington, Cooling, Sterling* and *Stirling* were all highly confusable with *Bowling*, which was the correct hypothesis).

The n-best correction model we have described includes a rescoring step. N-best rescoring approaches have been investigated extensively in the speech recognition community. In the dialog community, n-best rescoring techniques that use higher-level, dialog features have also been proposed and evaluated (Chotimongkol and Rudnicky, 2001). Apart from using the click feedback, the novelty in our approach lies in the added expansion step and in the use of an error-correction model for rescoring. We have seen that the confusability-based n-best expansion process leads to significantly improved performance, even if we force the model to keep the same average n-best size.

Finally, the work discussed in this paper has commonalities with previous works on lightly supervised learning in the speech community, e.g. (Lamel and Gauvain, 2002) and leveraging implicit feedback for learning from interaction, e.g. (Banerjee and Rudnicky, 2007; Bohus and Rudnicky, 2007). In all these cases, the goal is to minimize the need for manually-labeled data, and learn directly from the interaction. We believe that in the long term this family of learning techniques will play a key role towards building autonomous, self-improving systems.

6 Conclusion and future work

We have proposed and evaluated a novel n-best correction model that leverages implicit user feedback in a multi-modal interface to create a positive feedback loop. While the experiments reported here were conducted in the context of a local search application, the approach is applicable in any multi-modal interface that elicits selection in an n-best list from the user.

The proposed n-best correction model works in two stages. First, the n-best list generated by the speech recognizer is expanded with additional hypotheses based on confusability information captured from previous user clicks. This expanded list is then rescored and pruned to create a more accurate and more compact n-best list. Our experiments show that the proposed n-best correction approach significantly outperforms both the baseline and other traditional n-best rescoring approaches, without increasing the average length of the n-best lists.

Several issues remain to be investigated. The models discussed in this paper focus on post-recognition processing. Other ways of using the click data can also be envisioned. For instance, one approach would be to add all the clicked results to the existing language model training data and create an updated recognition language model. In the future, we plan to investigate the relationship between these two approaches, and to whether they can be used in conjunction. Earlier related work (Ringger and Allen, 1997) suggests that this should indeed be the case.

Second, the click-based error-correction model we have described in section 3.4 operates at the result level. The proposed model is essentially a sentence level, memory-based translation model. In the future, we also plan to investigate word-level error-correction models, using machine translation techniques like the ones discussed in (Ringger and Allen, 1997; Li et al., 2008).

Finally, we plan to investigate how this process of learning from implicit feedback in a multi-modal interface can be streamlined, such that the system continuously learns online, with a minimal amount of human intervention.

Acknowledgments

This work would have not been possible without the help of a number of other people. We would like to especially thank Oliver Scholz, Julian Odell, Christopher Dac, Tim Paek, Y.C. Ju, Paul Bennett, Eric Horvitz and Alex Acero for their help and for useful conversations and feedback.

References

Acero, A., N. Bernstein, et al. (2008). "Live Search for Mobile: Web Services by Voice on the Cellphone". ICASSP'08. Las Vegas, NV.

Banerjee, S. and A. Rudnicky (2007). "Segmenting Meetings into Agenda Items by Extracting Implicit Supervision from Human Note-Taking". IUI'2007. Honolulu, Hawaii.

Birkenes, O., T. Matsui, et al. (2007). "N-Best Rescoring for Speech Recognition using Penalized Logistic Regression Machines with Garbage Class". ICASSP'2007, Honolulu, Hawaii.

Bohus, D. and A. Rudnicky (2007). "Implicitly-supervised learning in spoken language interfaces: an application to the confidence annotation problem". SIGdial 2007, Antwerp, Belgium.

Chotimongkol, A. and A. Rudnicky (2001). "N-best Speech Hypotheses Reordering Using Linear Regression". Eurospeech'2001, Aalborg, Denmark.

Lamel, L. and J.-L. Gauvain (2002). "Lightly Supervised and Unsupervised Acoustic Model Training." Computer Speech and Language 16: 115-129.

Li, X., Y.-C. Ju, et al. (2008). "Language Modeling for Voice Search: a Machine Translation Approach". ICASSP'08, Las Vegas, NV.

Live Search for Windows Mobile (2008): http://mobile.search.live.com

Nuance Mobile Search (2008): http://www.nuance.com/mobilesearch.

Ringger, E. and J. Allen (1996). "Error Correction via Post-Processor for Continuous Speech Recognition". ICASSP'96, Atlanta, GA.

Ringger, E. and J. Allen (1997). "Robust Error Correction of Continuous Speech Recognition". ESCA-NATO Workshop on Robust Speech Recognition for Unknown Communication Channels, Pont-a-Mousson, France.

TellMeByMobile (2008): http://www.tellme.com/products/tellmebymobile.

V-Lingo Mobile. (2008): http://www.vlingomobile.com/downloads.html.

VoiceSignal Search. (2008): http://www.voicesignal.com/solutions/vsearch.php.

Agreement and Disputes in Dialogue

Alex Lascarides
School of Informatics,
University of Edinburgh
alex@inf.ed.ac.uk

Nicholas Asher
IRIT
Université Paul Sabatier, Toulouse
asher@irit.fr

Abstract

In this paper we define agreement in terms of shared public commitments, and implicit agreement is conditioned on the semantics of the relational speech acts (e.g., *Narration*, *Explanation*) that each agent performs. We provide a consistent interpretation of disputes, and updating a logical form with the current utterance always involves extending it and not revising it, even if the current utterance denies earlier content.

1 Introduction

A semantic theory of dialogue should account for what content dialogue agents agree on. This includes *implicit* agreement:

(1) a. A: The room went dark.
    b. A: Max turned out the light.
    c. B: And John drew the blinds.

Intuitively, A and B agree that the room went dark, that Max turned out the light, and that the latter is at least part of the reason why the former occurred. Thus, *implicatures can be agreed upon* (that (1b) is part of the cause of (1a) goes beyond compositional semantics), and *agreement can be implicated* (B does not repeat (1a) and (1b) nor utter *OK* to indicate his agreement with A).

In principle, the *Grounding Acts Model* (GAM, Traum (1994), Traum and Allen (1994)) supports implicit agreement. But it demands an acceptance act for agreement to occur, and its current rules don't predict such an act from (1c). Segmented Discourse Representation Theory (SDRT, Asher and Lascarides (2003)) errs in the opposite direction. It stipulates that lack of disagreement implicates agreement, and so in (1) *too much* is agreed upon; e.g., (1c). Thus, SDRT needs modification to deal with (1), just as GAM needs supplementation.

Agreement can occur even in the context of corrections or disputes. In (2), A asserts (2a) and B its negation, but a consistent interpretation of (2) overall is a pre-requisite to explaining how A and B end up agreeing on (2b).

(2) a. A: It's raining.
    b. B: No it's not.
    c. A: OK.

Since a correction negates content in the discourse context, an obvious strategy for maintaining consistency would be to *revise* the semantic representation of the context when updating it with a correction. But we want to avoid revision, both at the level of model theory and at the level of composing logical form. This is for two reasons. Firstly, revision means that there is in principle no general way of stating what information is preserved from the previous discourse state to the current one. But if we construct logical form in a monotonic way—in our case, this means that the discourse structure for a conversation at turn n is an elementary substructure of the discourse structure at turn $n + 1$—then standard preservation results from model theory apply. Secondly, monotonicity guarantees that interpretation algorithms can proceed incrementally, combining information from various sources in a nondestructive way (Alshawi and Crouch, 1992).

To our knowledge, there is currently no dynamic semantics for dialogue that yields adequate interpretations of corrections and implicit agreement. We will address this gap here. In Section 2, we re-

Proceedings of the 9th SIGdial Workshop on Discourse and Dialogue, pages 29–36,
Columbus, June 2008.

view two existing approaches to motivate our basic strategy, which we then describe in Section 3. We will refine SDRT so that it tracks each dialogue participant's public commitments. Further, while identifying a speech act involves default reasoning, constructing logical form will be monotonic, in the sense that the logical form of an updated discourse always extends that of its discourse context, rather than revising it.

2 Motivation

We will say that a proposition p is *grounded* just in case p is agreed by the dialogue agents to be true. This follows Clark's terminology, in particular the concept of grounding a joint action at level 4 (Clark, 1996, p388). Clark's work focusses almost entirely on grounding at the so-called 'lower' levels; how agents ground an understanding of what was said, for instance. By contrast, in order to focus on grounding at the higher level, we will assume a highly idealised scenario where dialogue agents understand each other perfectly, resolving ambiguities in the same way. One of Clark's main claims is that grounding at all levels occurs only when there is positive evidence for it, and we aim to explore in a logically precise manner exactly what amount of positive evidence suffices for grounding a proposition. In future work, we intend to demonstrate that our definition of grounding can model grounding at the lower levels too; this will involve extending the framework to represent misunderstandings.

GAM links the speech acts performed with its effects, including effects on grounding (Traum, 1994). Each conversational participant builds a *conversational information state* (or CIS). Update effects of particular speech acts (and their preconditions) are specified in terms of changes to (and conditions on) the CIS. For example, Figure 1 is the update rule for the speech act e where B **asserts** K to A. It updates the common ground (G) to include an event e' that B intends A to believe K and a conditional event e'' that should A accept the assertion, then A would be socially committed to B to believe K (shown via the attitude **SCCOE**). The update rules form a hierarchy, so that more specific acts inherit effects from more general ones. The speech act in Figure 1 inherits that B is **SCCOE**-ed to A to K, for instance. Decision trees then predict which speech acts have been performed.

While it is possible in principle for GAM to include rules that accurately predict (1c)'s illocutionary effects, the rules that are actually provided only recognise (1c) as an assertion. Consequently, its effects are under-generated: B is socially committed to (1c), but not to (1a), (1b) or a causal relation between them. GAM needs to be supplemented with rules for inferring that B was also *implicitly accepting* parts of A's contribution.

Such acceptances, we argue, should be conditioned on *relational speech acts*. (1c) continues (1b) as a narrative, and the narrative so formed explains (1a). These are *relational speech acts* (Asher and Lascarides, 2003): they are speech acts because continuing a narrative or explaining something are things that people do with utterances; and they are relational because the successful performance of the speech act *Explanation*, say, is logically dependent on the content of the utterance (or sequence of utterances) that is being explained (in this case, (1a)). Thus even though the compositional semantics of (1c) does not entail (1b) or (1a), its illocutionary contribution does entail them—or, perhaps more accurately, entails that B is publicly committed to them. Similarly, through using (1b) as an *Explanation* of (1a), A is publicly committed to (1a), (1b) and a causal relationship between them. Thus, what is grounded amounts to the shared semantic entailments of the rhetorical relations—or speech acts—that both A and B performed. This explains why positive evidence for grounding is necessary (Clark, 1996): both agents must perform a speech act with appropriate semantic consequences for a proposition to become grounded. An implicit acceptance (or acknowledgement in SDRT terms) is then logically dependent on the formal semantic interpretations of the relational speech acts performed. For instance, B's commitments to (1a) and (1b) stem from *Narration* and *Explanation* acts he performed in uttering (1c).

Since GAM incorporates relational speech acts, the general principles that we propose here could extend it. However, we have chosen to use SDRT because it defines logical form more abstractly, allowing us to exploit its model theory to determine grounded propositions. In contrast to GAM, we will not explicitly represent what's grounded (and what's not) in logical form. Doing so would force us to in-

Name:	**Assert**
Condition on update:	$G :: [e : \mathbf{Assert}(B, A, K)]$
Update	$G {+}{=} [e']e' : \mathbf{Try}(B, \lambda s'.s' : \mathbf{Bel}(A, K)),$ $[e'']e'' : \mathbf{Accept}(A, e) \Rightarrow [s \mid s : \mathbf{SCCOE}(A, B, K)]$

Figure 1: The update rule for assertion

corporate revision should grounded content get disputed, as can happen in a dynamic setting, where facts and beliefs change as the agents engage in dialogue. We will make grounding a property of the interpretation of a logical form, and not part of its form.

SDRT offers a formal semantics of relational speech acts (Asher and Lascarides, 2003). Furthermore, in contrast to theories of discourse interpretation that equate interpreting a discourse with its effects on the agents' beliefs (e.g., Hobbs et al. (1993), Grosz and Sidner (1990)), SDRT separates the glue logic (i.e., the logic for constructing a logical form of what was said) from the logic for *interpreting* the logical form (i.e., reasoning about whether what was said is true, or should be believed). This enables SDRT to maintain a *decidable* procedure for computing logical form, even though identifying the speech acts performed inherently involves commonsense reasoning, and hence consistency tests. Asher and Lascarides (2003, p78) argue that it must be decidable to explain why, as Lewis (1969) claims, people by and large have a common understanding of what was said.

SDRT's current representation of (1) is (1′), where π_1, π_2 and π_3 label the contents of the clauses (1a–c) respectively, and π_0 and π label the content of the dialogue segments that are created by the rhetorical connections:

(1′) $\pi_0 : \mathit{Explanation}(\pi_1, \pi)$
$\pi : \mathit{Narration}(\pi_2, \pi_3)$

In words, (1′) implies that the room went dark, and this was caused by a combination of Max switching off the light followed by John drawing the blinds. In the absence of speech acts of denial such as *Correction*, SDRT stipulates that all content is grounded (Asher and Lascarides, 2003, p363). This leads directly to the wrong predictions for (1).

Unlike GAM, SDRT fails to track the different commitments of individual speakers. Simply labelling each speech act with its speaker doesn't suffice, as dialogue (3) shows.[1]

(3) π_1. A: John went to Harrods.
π_2. B: He bought a suit.
π_3. A: He then entered the food halls.
π_4. B: He looked for foie gras.

Intuitively, A's utterance π_3 publicly commits him not only to $\mathit{Narration}(\pi_2, \pi_3)$, but also to $\mathit{Narration}(\pi_1, \pi_2)$ (for this latter speech act entails, while the former does not, that John bought the suit *at Harrods*). And yet B was the speaker who performed the speech act $\mathit{Narration}(\pi_1, \pi_2)$, for it is B who uttered π_2. Accordingly, we abandon representing dialogue with a single SDRS, and replace it with a *tuple* of SDRSs—one SDRS per discourse participant per turn, representing all his commitments up to and including that turn. We define grounding a proposition p in terms of joint entailments from those commitments, and hence grounding becomes a *semantic* property of the logical form. This solves SDRT's over-generation problems with grounding. For instance in (1), A's public commitments are to $\mathit{Explanation}(\pi_1, \pi_2)$. B, on the other hand, is committed to the content expressed by (1′). The shared public commitments then accurately reflect what A and B agree on. We also avoid the under-generation problems of GAM; grounding need not arise from an acceptance but instead from so-called *veridical rhetorical relations* (e.g., *Explanation* and *Narration*) and the logical relationships among their meanings.

Grounded content is not marked as such in logical form. This makes monotonic construction of logical form feasible, even when grounded propositions get disputed. A further part of our strategy for eschewing revision is to assume that the SDRSs for each turn represent all of A's and B's current commitments,

[1] For simplicity, we use a contructed example here, although Sacks (1992) attests many similar, naturally occurring dialogues where the agents build a narrative together.

from the beginning of the dialogue to the end of that turn. The alternative, where prior but ongoing commitments from turn $i-1$ are not shown in the representation of turn i, and accordingly the input context for interpreting turn i is the output one from interpreting turn $i-1$, would condemn us to incorporating revision into the model theory. This is because A may commit in turn i to something that is inconsistent with his commitments in turn $i-1$ (e.g., A's utterance (2c)), and without revision the output context from turn i would then be $\perp$. We want to avoid revision while maintaining consistency. Representing *all* current commitments in each turn avoids revision in the model theory, because one can compute the current commitments of A and B by dynamically interpreting their SDRSs for just the last turn. One can detect how A's commitments have changed during the dialogue, but only by comparing the SDRSs for the relevant turns.[2]

We will model disputes by adding non-truth preserving operators over relevant segments in the logical form. This avoids the need for downdating and revision in both the construction and the interpretation of logical form.

3 Individuating Commitments

The logical form for a dialogue turn proposed in Section 2 generalises to dialogues with more than two agents in the obvious way: the logical form of a dialogue turn is a set $\{S_a : a \in D\}$, where S_a is an SDRS and D is the set of dialogue agents. The logical form of the dialogue overall will be the logical forms of each of its turns (and all dialogue agents build all the SDRSs in the logical form, not just the SDRSs representing their own commitments). We assume an extremely simple notion of turns, where turn boundaries occur whenever the speaker changes (even if this happens mid-clause), and we ignore for now cases where agents speak simultaneously.

This new logical form for dialogue requires a new dynamic interpretation. The context C_d of evaluation for interpreting a dialogue turn is a set of dynamic contexts for interpreting SDRSs—one for each agent $a \in D$:

$$C_d = \{\langle C_a^i, C_a^o \rangle : a \in D\}$$

Thus C_a^i and C_a^o are world assignment pairs, given the definitions from Asher and Lascarides (2003). For instance, (4) defines the dynamic interpretation of veridical relations (e.g. *Narration*, *Explanation*), where meaning postulates then stipulate the illocutionary effects $\varphi_{R(\alpha,\beta)}$—e.g., for *Narration* they stipulate the spatio-temporal progression of the events (we gloss the content that's labelled π as K_π, and m in $[\![.]\!]_m$ stands for monologue). Equation (5) defines the dynamic interpretation of *Correction*.

(4) $(w,f)[\![R(\alpha,\beta)]\!]_m(w',g)$ iff
$(w,f)[\![K_\alpha \wedge K_\beta \wedge \varphi_{R(\alpha,\beta)}]\!]_m(w',g)$

(5) $(w,f)[\![Correction(\alpha,\beta)]\!]_m(w',g)$ iff
$(w,f)[\![(\neg K_\alpha) \wedge K_\beta \wedge \varphi_{Corr(\alpha,\beta)}]\!]_m(w',g)$

The context change potential (CCP) of a dialogue turn $T = \{S_a : a \in D\}$ is the product of the CCPs of the individual SDRSs:

$$C_d[\![T]\!]_d C'_d \text{ iff } C'_d = \{\langle C_a^i, C_a^o \rangle \circ [\![S_a]\!]_m : \langle C_a^i, C_a^o \rangle \in C_d, a \in D\}$$

Accordingly, dialogue entailments can be defined in terms of the entailment relation $\models_m$ for SDRSs afforded by $[\![.]\!]_m$:

$$T \models_d \phi \text{ iff } \forall a \in D, S_a \models_m \phi$$

This makes $\models_d$ the shared entailment of each agent's public commitments. And we assume that content ϕ is grounded or agreed upon by a dialogue turn T iff $T \models_d \phi$. Finally, given that the SDRSs for a dialogue turn reflect *all* an agent's current commitments, the interpretation of the dialogue overall is the CCP of its last turn.

The logical form of (3) is shown in Table 1 (we have omitted the logical forms of the clauses, labelled π_1 to π_4). The semantics of the SDRSs for the last turn correctly predict the following proposition to be grounded (for it is entailed by them): John went to Harrods, followed by buying a suit (at Harrods), followed by his entering the food halls.

There is a sharing of labels across the SDRSs in Table 1. This general feature reflects the reality that one speaker may perform a relational speech act whose first argument is part of someone else's turn,

[2] Prévot et al. (2006) represent dialogue in terms of commitment slates. Their idea inspired our work, but the details differ considerably, particularly on monotonic construction.

Turn	A's SDRS	B's SDRS
1	π_1	$\emptyset$
2	π_1	π_{2B} : *Narration*(π_1, π_2)
3	π_{3A} : *Narration*$(\pi_1, \pi_2) \wedge$ *Narration*(π_2, π_3)	π_{2B} : *Narration*(π_1, π_2)
4	π_{3A} : *Narration*$(\pi_1, \pi_2) \wedge$ *Narration*(π_2, π_3)	π_{4B} : *Narration*$(\pi_1, \pi_2) \wedge$ *Narration*$(\pi_2, \pi_3) \wedge$ *Narration*(π_3, π_4)

Table 1: The logical form of dialogue (3).

or part of his own previous turns. Sharing labels captures the intuition that an agent's speech acts can reveal his commitments (or lack of them) to contextual content, even if this is linguistically implicit.

Including prior but ongoing commitments in the SDRS for the current turn has consequences for the general architecture of the theory: we must stipulate what commitments persist across turns when constructing the SDRSs. Consider the fourth turn of dialogue (3). Intuitively, uttering π_4 commits B to the illocutionary content of *Narration*(π_3, π_4). But in addition, he is also committed at this point to *Narration*$(\pi_1, \pi_2) \wedge$ *Narration*(π_2, π_3), as shown. Those commitments persist from prior turns; they are even transferred from one speaker to another. However, we will shortly examine other examples, involving corrections and even explicit acknowledgements (or an acceptance in Traum's (1994) terminology), where the commitments do not persist. To handle the data, we must make the 'commitment persistence' principle sensitive to distinct relational speech acts, and it must support a monotonic construction of logical form.

To motivate our persistence principle, consider how A and B get to the commitments shown in Table 1. A's SDRS for the first turn is $\pi_1 : K_{\pi_1}$, where K_{π_1} stands for the representation of *John went to Harrods*. Since B hasn't said anything yet, his SDRS for the first turn is $\emptyset$. SDRT's glue logic uses default axioms to predict the relation that connects π_2 to π_1 (Asher and Lascarides, 2003); here, these defaults should yield that B is committed to π_{2B} : *Narration*(π_1, π_2) (we adopt the convention that the root label of the speaker d's SDRS for turn j is named π_{jd}). A's SDRS for the second turn is the same as the first turn: he hasn't spoken since, and so his commitments are unchanged.

In the third turn, the glue logic should predict that A's utterance π_3 forms a narrative with π_2. But simply adding this to A's prior SDRS isn't sufficient. First, the result is not a well-formed SDRS, because it won't contain a single root label. Secondly, it misses an important interplay between discourse structure and grounding: adding only *Narration*(π_2, π_3) to A's existing commitment to K_{π_1} makes A committed to the compositional semantics of π_2, but *not* to its illocutionary contribution conveyed by B (e.g. that John bought the suit *at Harrods*). And yet intuitively, uttering π_3 implicates that this (linguistically implicit) content is agreed on.

Dialogues (1) and (3) feature discourse relations that occur in monologue as well. Several agents can use these to build up a narrative together, as noted by Sacks (1992). Sacks' observations affirm that such discourse relations can be used to perform 'implicit' acknowledgements, and what's more they suggest that the implicit acknowledgement is not only of the prior contribution's compositional semantics but also its illocutionary effects. These observations lead us to add the following `Persistence` principle to the glue logic, together with axioms that identify undenied commitments ($UC(\alpha)$ stands for the undenied commitments of the utterance or segment α):

- `Persistence:`
  $\lambda : R(\alpha, \beta) \rightarrow \lambda : UC(\alpha)$

Different glue-logic axioms will then identify the undenied commitments for different speech acts. The present case concerns *simple left veridical (slv) relations*—those that do not explicitly endorse or criticise any previous commitments. Note $\phi > \psi$ means "If ϕ then normally ψ", and $T(d, j, \pi)$ means that label π is a part of agent d's SDRS for turn j:

- `Undenied Commitments:`
  $(\lambda : R(\alpha, \beta) \wedge T(d_1, j, \lambda) \wedge slv(R) \wedge$
  $\lambda' : R'(\gamma, \alpha) \wedge T(d_2, j-1, \lambda')) >$
  $(\lambda : UC(\alpha) \rightarrow \lambda : R'(\gamma, \alpha))$

`Undenied Commitments` states that if d_1 commits to $R(\alpha, \beta)$ where R is simple left veridical and d_2 is already committed to $R'(\gamma, \alpha)$, then normally the undenied commitments of α include $R'(\gamma, \alpha)$. Examples of simple left veridical relations include *Narration* and *Explanation* but not *Acknowledgement* (since this *explicitly* endorses prior content) or *Correction* (since this denies prior content).

`Persistence` and `Undenied Commitments` predict that A's SDRS for the third turn of (3) includes π_{3A} : *Narration*(π_1, π_2). This is because default rules yield π_{3A} : *Narration*(π_2, π_3), and *Narration*(π_1, π_2) is in B's SDRS. `Persistence` and `Undenied Commitments` likewise predict that *Narration*(π_1, π_2) and *Narration*(π_2, π_3) are a part of B's SDRS for the fourth turn, as shown in Table 1.

`Undenied Commitments` is defeasible. This is because if the illocutionary contribution of A's (left-veridical) speech act $R(\alpha, \beta)$ conflicts with some proposition p that B conveyed by uttering α, then clearly A's speech act should not be construed as an implicit acknowledgement of p. This affects the analysis of (1), whose logical form is Table 2. B's SDRS after the second turn does *not* include *Explanation*(π_1, π_2), even though his utterance π_3 attaches with the veridical relation *Narration* to π_2, and A's SDRS for turn 1 includes *Explanation*(π_1, π_2). `Persistence` applies to this example (for label π_2) and the antecedent to `Undenied Commitments` is satisfied, but *Explanation*(π_1, π_2) is not an undenied commitment of π_2 because its (nonmonotonic) semantic consequences conflict with those of *Explanation*(π_1, π), a speech act that the glue logic must identify as one that B intended to perform (or, in other words, publicly commit to) as a byproduct of uttering π_3. *Explanation*(π_1, π_2) conflicts with *Explanation*(π_1, π) because the former nonmonotonically entails, via a scalar implicature, that Max turning out the light was the sole cause of the room going dark, while the latter (monotonically) entails it was a strict part of it. This example illustrates how the default logic rendered by $>$ must be specified in terms of the consistency in what follows nonmonotonically, rather than what follows monotonically.

`Undenied Commitments` does not apply for the veridical relation *Acknowledgement*; i.e., utterances of the form *OK*, *I agree*, repeating prior content, and the like. In words, *Acknowledgement*(π_1, π_2) entails K_{π_1}, K_{π_2} and that K_{π_2} implies K_{π_1}; to use the GAM term, it is an act of *explicit acceptance*. Dialogue (6) illustrates why *Acknowledgement* behaves differently from the simple left veridical relations like *Narration*:

(6) π_1. B: John is not a good speaker
π_2. B: because he's hard to understand.
π_3. A: I agree he's hard to understand.

The compositional semantics of π_3 makes A explicit about what in B's turn he acknowledges: A must be committed to (at least) *Acknowledgement*(π_2, π_3). What is outside the scope of the acknowledgement—namely, B's putative explanation for why John is not a good speaker—is not denied in (6). It would be consistent to add *Explanation*(π_1, π_2) to A's commitments, but it's simply not warranted. Dialogue (6) shows that when the explicit endorsement conveys sufficiently specific content, it appears to carry a scalar implicature that this precise content is endorsed, and *no more*.

Another reason for excluding explicit acknowledgements from the set of simple left veridical relations is that such speech acts come with their own grounding requirements. Acknowledgements can have scope over implicatures as well as compositional semantic contents, since the first argument to an *Acknowledgement* relation can be a label of an arbitrarily complex SDRS. So by acknowledging π_j, we do not thereby acknowledge the implicatures of π_j itself; had we wished to do so, we would have included them within the scope of the acknowledgement. That is, we would infer the relation *Acknowledgement*(π'_j, π_i), where π'_j has semantic scope over π_j, making π_j and the rhetorical relations it engages in part of what is (explicitly) endorsed. It is because the discourse function of an acknowledgement is precisely to say what one agent commits to from another agent's turn—i.e., what are the undenied commitments in this case—that `Persistence` applies redundantly.

Explicit acknowledgements have been studied by Traum and Hinkelman (1992), among others. Here, we will ignore interpretations of an utterance π_2 (e.g., *OK*) as an acknowledgement that K_{π_1}

Turn	A's SDRS	B's SDRS
1	π_{1A} : *Explanation*(π_1, π_2)	$\emptyset$
2	π_{1A} : *Explanation*(π_1, π_2)	π_{2B} : *Explanation*(π_1, π) π : *Narration*(π_2, π_3)

Table 2: The logical form of (1).

was said (represented in SDRT with the so-called metatalk relation *Acknowledgement**(π_1, π_2)), instead focussing entirely on an interpretation of π_2 using *Acknowledgement* (i.e., a commitment to K_{π_1}, which in turn entails a commitment that K_{π_1} was said). But even so there is ambiguity, because linguistic form does not always fully determine what the acknowledgement has scope over. Let's assume that A's utterance π_3 in (7) is an acknowledgement of *content* and not just of understanding that content:

(7) π_1. B: John is not a good speaker
π_2. B: because he is hard to understand.
π_3. A: OK.

Acknowledgement(π_2, π_3) entails K_{π_2}. Making π_2 the *only* label that's acknowledged leads to an interpretation where the proposition that π_2 explains π_1 is not acknowledged. This 'narrow scope' attachment permits A to continue by challenging the explanatory link, e.g., by uttering *but that's not why he's not a good speaker.* Another interpretation of (7) is that A commits to *all* of B's commitments, including the implicatures: this is expressed by adding *Acknowledgement*(π_{1B}, π_3) to A's SDRS, where π_{1B} : *Explanation*(π_1, π_2). Indeed, if *OK* is *all* that A says, then one defaults to this wide-scope interpretation. Even if A follows *OK* with *He* IS *hard to understand* with high pitch accents and a falling boundary tone, the preferred interpretation contrasts with (6), to be one where *OK* is an *Acknowledgement* of π_{1B}, and *He's hard to understand* is an explanation of that acknowledgement act (marked with the metatalk relation *Explanation** in SDRT). It is straightforward to add glue-logic axioms for constructing logical form that reflect these principles for identifying the first argument of *Acknowledgement*.

In dialogue (2), A commits to the negation of his prior commitment. As before, constructing B's SDRS for the second turn involves using the glue logic to identify how π_2 connects to π_1. So long as their semantic incompatibility is transferred, in shallow form, to the glue logic, then the general principle that the necessary semantic consequences of a speech act are normally sufficient for inferring that it was performed will apply, yielding π_{2B} : *Correction*(π_1, π_2) (see Table 3). The cue phrase *OK* is then used by the glue logic to infer π_{3A} : *Acknowledgement*(π_2, π_3). This resolves the underspecified content *OK* to K_{π_2}; and thus as before the glue logic also yields π_{3A} : *Correction*(π_1, π_3), as shown. *It's not raining* is entailed by the SDRSs for turn 3. The interpretation of each turn is consistent (i.e., the output state is non-empty), although the SDRSs for turn 2 are mutually inconsistent (A's SDRS entails that it's raining and B's entails it's not). Finally, the content associated with each label does not change from one turn to the next, making the construction of logical form monotonic.

Clark (1996) doesn't make precise exactly what counts as sufficient positive evidence for grounding. Similarly, Traum and Allen (1994) don't provide rules for inferring when a speaker has performed an implicit acceptance. Our framework makes the quantity of positive evidence that's needed for grounding propositions logically precise, in terms of the relational speech acts that both speakers perform, and the logical relationships between the semantics of those speech acts. `Persistence` and `Undenied Commitments` capture a general class of examples involving implicit agreement. Sufficient positive evidence for grounding a proposition through *explicit* endorsements and challenges rests on the formal semantic interpretation of the relevant speech acts—namely *Acknowledgement* and *Correction*—and the rules by which one determines the first argument of these relations.

4 Conclusion

We have presented a novel treatment of agreements and disputes in which the construction of logical form is monotonic in the subsumptive sense

Turn	A's SDRS	B's SDRS
1	$\pi_1 : K_{\pi_1}$	$\emptyset$
2	$\pi_1 : K_{\pi_1}$	π_{2B} : *Correction*(π_1, π_2)
3	π_{3A} : *Correction*$(\pi_1, \pi_3) \wedge$ *Acknowledgement*(π_2, π_3)	π_{2B} : *Correction*(π_1, π_2)

Table 3: The logical form of dialogue (2).

(Shieber, 1986); the semantic representation of the discourse context is an elementary substructure of the representation of the dialogue updated with the current utterance, even if the current utterance denies earlier content. However, the logical form remains a product of complex default reasoning, since identifying the speech acts that were performed involves commonsense reasoning with the linguistic and non-linguistic context.

The relationship between the grounded propositions and the interpretation of the dialogue is entirely transparent and is defined in terms of the model theory of the logical forms. It provides a logical basis for exploring Clark's (1996) notion of *positive evidence* for grounding. A crucial ingredient in our account was the use of relational speech acts, and the logical relationships among their semantics.

We believe our definition of grounding as shared commitment is capable of modelling Clark's more central concern—grounding the *understanding* of what was said. The left-veridical relations that are the hallmark of grounding at level 4 entail grounding at the lower levels thanks to the semantics of DSDRSs. Moreover, SDRT's metatalk relations—such as *Explanation**(α, β) and *Acknowledgement**(α, β)—commit an agent to the fact that K_α was said without committing him K_α. Thus shared commitments that follow from a representation of the dialogue can ground acts at lower levels without grounding (or denying) acts at level 4. A full model of grounding at lower levels, however, requires us to extend the framework to handle misunderstandings.

This paper presents just some first steps towards a dynamic theory of grounding. For instance, we have not yet modelled the impact of questions and imperatives on public commitments and grounding. We have started to explore links between public commitments and other attitudes, such as beliefs, preferences, and intentions (Asher and Lascarides, 2008), but this also remains a matter of ongoing research.

References

H. Alshawi and R. Crouch. Monotonic semantic interpretation. In *Proceedings of ACL*, pages 32–39, 1992.

N. Asher and A. Lascarides. *Logics of Conversation*. CUP, 2003.

N. Asher and A. Lascarides. Commitments, beliefs and intentions in dialogue. In *Proceedings of Londial*, 2008.

H. H. Clark. *Using Language*. CUP, 1996.

B. Grosz and C. Sidner. Plans for discourse. In J. Morgan P. R. Cohen and M. Pollack, editors, *Intentions in Communication*, pages 365–388. MIT Press, 1990.

J. R. Hobbs, M. Stickel, D. Appelt, and P. Martin. Interpretation as abduction. *Artificial Intelligence*, 63(1–2):69–142, 1993.

D. Lewis. *Convention: A Philosophical Study*. Harvard University Press, 1969.

L. Prévot, N. Maudet, and P. Muller. Conversational game-board and discourse structure. In *Proceedings of Constraints in Discourse*, Ireland, 2006.

H. Sacks. *Lectures on Conversation*. Blackwells, 1992.

S. Shieber. *An Introduction to Unification-based Approaches to Grammar*. CSLI Publications, 1986.

D. Traum. *A Computational Theory of Grounding in Natural Language Conversation*. PhD thesis, University of Rochester, 1994.

D. Traum and J. Allen. Discourse obligations in dialogue processing. In *Proceedings of ACL*, pages 1–8, 1994.

D. Traum and E. Hinkelman. Conversation acts in task-oriented spoken dialogue. *Computational Intelligence*, 8(3):575–599, 1992.

Reactive Redundancy and Listener Comprehension in Direction-Giving

Rachel E. Baker
Department of Linguistics
Northwestern University
Evanston, IL 60208
r-baker2@northwestern.edu

Alastair J. Gill, Justine Cassell
Center for Technology and Social Behavior
Northwestern University
Evanston, IL 60208
{alastair,justine}@northwestern.edu

Abstract

We explore the role of redundancy, both in anticipation of and in response to listener confusion, in task-oriented dialogue. We find that direction-givers provide redundant utterances in response to both verbal and non-verbal signals of listener confusion. We also examine the effects of prior acquaintance and visibility upon redundancy. As expected, givers use more redundant utterances overall, and more redundant utterances in response to listener questions, when communicating with strangers. We discuss our findings in relation to theories of redundancy, the balance of speaker and listener effort, and potential applications.

1 Introduction

Our everyday conversations represent a carefully negotiated balance between the perceived needs of the speaker and the listener. These opposing forces affect every aspect of language from phonetics to pragmatics. A careful balance between these two forces allows speakers to produce language that is both efficient and effective at communicating a message (Lindblom, 1990; Horn, 1993). Of course, the same balance is not appropriate for every situation. When accuracy is critical to the message, or when the speaker perceives the listener to have difficulty understanding, the speaker is more likely to prioritize clarity over efficiency, resulting in more explicit communication. In contrast, during casual conversation or when speed is a factor, the speaker may choose a more reduced, efficient, communication style (Lindblom, 1990; Horton and Keysar, 1996). A number of scholars have pointed out that speakers seem to use the information available to themselves rather than that available to the listener to guide certain linguistic decisions, such as clarity of pronunciation and choice of syntactic structure (Bard et al., 2000; Branigan et al., 2003). However, these studies examine utterance form, while our study examines content, which is more influenced by audience design (Branigan et al., 2003). In every utterance, a speaker either reduces the likelihood of listener misunderstanding by being more explicit, or reduces their own effort by providing a minimal amount of information. Regardless of whether speakers pro-actively monitor the information needs of listeners, they do need to respond when listeners say or do something to indicate confusion. Developing a better understanding of the factors that affect how and when speakers respond to signs of listener confusion is important at both theoretical and applied levels: first, it can better explain the variation in discourse strategies used in different communicative situations; second, it can help in the design of dialogue systems (Kopp et al., 2008; Theune et al., 2007).

In this study, we examine what types of listener behavior increase the likelihood that a speaker will produce a redundant utterance. We also examine how communicative context affects the amount redundancy a speaker produces overall (Walker, 1992, 1996) and a speaker's use of redundancy in response to listener confusion. In contrast to previous work, we study *reactive* redundancy, or redundancy produced in response to signs of listener confusion. We investigate two factors that may influence a speaker's tendency to produce redundant utterances and to respond to listener confusion with redundancy: the relationship between the interlocutors and their visual contact.

In the following section, we review relevant literature and present our hypotheses; we then describe the direction-giving experiment which we used to examine redundancy in task-oriented dialogue, and present our results; we discuss our results in light of the literature and conclude by noting potential applications and future work.

Proceedings of the 9th SIGdial Workshop on Discourse and Dialogue, pages 37–45,
Columbus, June 2008.

2 Related Work and Predictions

2.1 Redundancy

Grice's (1975) second Maxim of Quantity: 'Do not make your contribution more informative than is required' has led to the general impression that redundancy (providing discourse-old information) is avoided in language (Stalnaker, 1978), with this mirrored by work in natural language generation (Dalianis, 1999). However, Walker (1992, 1996) points out that such conclusions relating to redundancy are often based on flawed assumptions. For example, they assume that agents have unlimited working memory and the ability to automatically generate all the inferences entailed by every utterance, that utterance production should be minimized, and that assertions by Agent A are accepted by default by Agent B (Walker, 1996: 183).

In fact, redundancy can serve many desirable purposes in communication. Redundancy has been shown to increase text cohesion and readability (Horning, 1991) as well as provide evidence of understanding and grounding, make a proposition salient, and make inferences explicit (Walker, 1996). A computer simulation of a cooperative task dialogue between two agents suggested that the use of certain types of redundant utterances improved the performance of the pair (Walker, 1996).

Fussell and Krauss (1989a) point out that there are two methods that speakers can use to tailor their message for the listener. The first method involves predicting what information it is necessary to communicate, using knowledge of the listener's interests and background. The second method involves modifying the message in response to listener feedback. Walker's model only captures the use of redundancy in the service of the first method. We will refer to this type of redundancy as *proactive* redundancy, whereby a speaker provides redundant information without waiting for the listener to express a need for it. The advantages of providing redundant information proactively include being able to integrate the redundant information with the new information, and avoiding conflict by removing the necessity for the listener to express a lack of understanding (Brown and Levinson, 1987).

We hypothesize that speakers also use redundancy *reactively*, after the listener signals a lack of understanding, either verbally or non-verbally. This is redundancy in service of Fussell and Krauss' second method of message-tailoring. The advantages of providing redundant information reactively include increasing the efficiency of the exchange by only providing redundant information that the listener communicates a need for, and reducing the burden on the speaker of having to decide when to include redundant information.

One important distinction between proactive and reactive redundancy is the grounding status of the redundant information. Reactive redundancy is likely to provide information that has not been accepted by the listener, and is therefore not part of the common ground (Clark and Schaeffer, 1989), even though it is discourse-old. In contrast, proactive redundancy is likely to provide information from the interlocutors' common ground. Indeed, Walker (1996) describes Attitude redundant utterances as providing evidence of grounding. Walker's other types of proactive redundancy (Consequence and Attention) make inferences based on grounded utterances explicit and make elements of the common ground salient again.

Reactive redundancy is one type of repair, like expansions and replacements, which can be used in response to non-understanding or misunderstanding (Hirst et al., 1994). The type of miscommunication may influence a speaker's choice of repair strategy, with reactive redundancy being an appropriate response to mishearing or misremembering.

However, producing redundant information, even when the listener signals a need for it, incurs a cost. Including redundant information increases the length of the dialogue and the speaker's effort, and decreases the amount of new information provided within a certain length of time. In these cases the speaker must decide how much redundant information to provide and when to provide it.

2.2 Signals of Confusion

Listeners can express a need for information to be repeated or restated in a number of ways, both verbally and non-verbally. Brinton et al. (1988) used questions and statements of confusion ("I didn't understand") as signs of communication breakdowns. Morrow et al. (1993) describe inaccurate and partial repetitions of instructions as elements of miscommunication. This prior work leads us to examine questions, utterances signaling non-understanding (e.g. "I don't remember what's next"), incorrect repetitions (e.g. "take the third right" after the direction-giver said "take the second right") and abandoned utterances (e.g. "Then I'll turn...") as possible signs of listener confusion. We predict redundancy after such statements because they all indicate that a piece of information has not been understood.

We also examine eye-gaze as a non-verbal marker of listener comprehension. Goodwin (1981) described gaze towards the speaker as a sign of listener attention. However, Nakano et al. (2003) found that speakers seemed to interpret a listener gazing at them rather than at a map as a sign of listener misunderstanding. Therefore, shifting eye-gaze away from the speaker can signal that a listener is losing attention, perhaps due to confusion, while shifting gaze towards the speaker can signal misunderstanding. In this study there is no map, and listeners who can see the speaker spend most of the conversation gazing at the speaker. Still, due to the opposing findings in the literature, we analyze eye-gaze shifts both towards and away from the speaker as potential signs of listener confusion.

2.3 Relationship and Communication

Speakers are more explicit when communicating with strangers or people with whom they share less common ground. This explicitness can take the form of highly informative self-introductions on the phone (Hornstein, 1985), longer descriptions of abstract figures (Fussell and Krauss, 1989b), and explicit references to utterance topics (Svedsen and Evjemo, 2003). These studies indicate that speakers attempt to make up for the small amount of common ground they share with strangers by including more information in the discourse itself.

Another difference between friends and non-friends is that acquaintances tend to be more formal, more concerned with self presentation, less negative, and less likely to disagree than friends (Schlenker, 1984; Tickle-Degnen and Rosenthal, 1990; Planalp and Benson, 1992). Therefore, we expect that in an initial interaction, a speaker will try to appear competent and avoid conflict.

As noted above, speakers talking to strangers are more explicit, leading us to predict more redundancy overall. They are also more likely to try to impress their interlocutor and avoid conflict, leading to more reactive redundancy in response to confusion when the pair are strangers.

2.4 Visibility and Communication

Visibility also has a number of effects on communication. One of the most basic is that when interlocutors cannot see each other they cannot use non-verbal signals to communicate, so they must rely on verbal communication. For example, the use of eye-gaze as a sign of listener attention (Argyle and Cook, 1976; Goodwin, 1981) is only possible when interlocutors can see each other. When they cannot see each other, they must indicate attention verbally or do without this information.

Visibility affects both the form and the outcomes of a conversation. When interlocutors cannot see each other, conversations are longer and contain more, shorter, utterances than when they can (Nakano et al., 2003). Interlocutors in an investment game who could not see each other also did not establish trust to the same extent as those who met face-to-face (Bos et al., 2002).

Because speakers who cannot see each other have fewer channels of communication available to them, their interaction can be more difficult than a face-to-face interaction. We predict that this will lead them to use more redundancy and more reactive redundancy in an effort to be clear.

2.5 Hypotheses

In order to study how responsive speakers are to signs of listener confusion, we must first determine what signs speakers respond to. In this study we examine a number of verbal and non-verbal signs speakers may use to gauge listener confusion. In particular, we expect that speakers will provide redundancy in response to both verbal signs like questions, statements of non-understanding, incorrect statements, and abandoned utterances, and non-verbal signs like eye-gaze changes. We expect that speakers will strike a different balance between efficiency (minimizing speaker effort) and clarity (minimizing listener effort) depending on the relationship between the speaker and listener, and the physical context of the interaction. We expect speakers to use redundancy strategies focused on minimizing speaker effort when addressing friends and people they can see. Such strategies involve less redundancy (and therefore less speaking), and less reactive redundancy (requiring less listener monitoring). Conversely, we expect to find redundancy strategies maximizing clarity when speakers address strangers and people they cannot see. Such strategies involve more redundancy overall (providing the listener with more information in general) as well as more reactive redundancy (which provides the listener with the specific information they may require).

Hypothesis 1 - Redundancy and Non-Understanding

(a) Verbal cues - Direction-givers will provide redundancy when the receiver verbally expresses a lack of understanding by asking a question, abandoning an utterance, making an incorrect statement or explicitly expressing non-understanding.

(b) Non-verbal cues - Givers will provide redundancy when the receiver non-verbally expresses a lack of understanding by shifting eye-gaze.

Hypothesis 2 - Redundancy and Relationship

Givers will prioritize clarity over efficiency in their redundancy use when speaking to strangers, providing (a) more redundancy and (b) more reactive redundancy than when speaking to friends.

Hypothesis 3 - Redundancy and Visual Contact

Givers will prioritize clarity over efficiency in their redundancy use when they cannot see their partner, providing (a) more redundancy and (b) more reactive redundancy than when they can see them.

3 Methods

3.1 Participants

Twenty-four university students participated, resulting in twelve dyads. All were paid $10 for their participation and received $5 gift certificates if they successfully completed the task. In each dyad the direction-giver was familiar with the building in which the experiment took place, and the direction-receiver was unfamiliar with it. Half the dyads were pairs of friends and half were strangers.

3.2 Procedure

The task consisted of three consecutive direction-giving sessions, as described in Cassell et al. (2007). At the start of each session, the experimenter led the direction-giver to a point in the building, and back to the experiment room. Half of the dyads sat facing each other during the direction-giving (the Vision condition) and half sat back-to-back with a screen between them (the No-vision condition). The direction-giver then explained the route to the direction-receiver. There were no time limits or restrictions on what could be said, but the dyads could not use maps or props. When the dyad decided that direction-giving was complete, they signaled the experimenter, who the receiver led to the goal, following the directions.

The direction-giving sessions were videotaped. Participants' speech was transcribed and coded for possible redundancy triggers and redundant utterances using the coding scheme described below. The time-aligned codings for the giver and receiver were aligned with each other using scripts that calculated which of the receiver's utterances or actions directly preceded which of the giver's utterances. The scripts classify a receiver's utterance or action as 'preceding' a giver's utterance if its start precedes the start of the giver's utterance and its end is not more than two seconds before the start of the giver's utterance. The two-second limit was used to avoid positing connections between a giver's utterance and receiver utterances that came long before it.

3.3 Data Coding

Each dialogue was divided into clauses, defined as units that include a subject and predicate and express a proposition. Each clause was coded using a modified version of DAMSL (Core and Allen, 1997). Direction-givers' and receivers' speech was coded differently because we only studied redundancy produced by the giver. We coded the receiver's speech for signs of confusion. We describe the labels we used in more detail below.

Each direction-giver's clauses were coded for Statements and Info-requests. The Info-request tag marks questions and other requests for information. In a Statement, a speaker makes a claim about the world. The class of Statements was broken down into Non-redundant, in which the speaker is trying to change or add to the hearer's beliefs, and Redundant, which contain only information that has already been stated or entailed.

Each direction-receiver's clauses were coded for Statements, Info-requests, Signal non-understandings (S.N.U.), and Abandoned utterances. The receiver's Statements were classified as either Correct or Incorrect. If an utterance explicitly expressed non-understanding of an earlier utterance it was coded as Signal non-understanding. This label was only used for direct statements of non-understanding, such as "I didn't follow that," and not for signals of non-understanding covered by other labels such as Info-requests and Incorrect Statements. Utterances that were abandoned (the speaker stops the utterance and it provides no content to the dialogue) were coded as Abandoned. Receiver utterances that were not coded as Info-requests, Incorrect Statements, Signal-non-understandings, or Abandoned, were coded as No-trigger. No-trigger utterances included correct statements and statements about task management.

4 Results

We found that a large proportion of giver utterances were redundant, ranging from 17% to 38% with a mean of 25%. Examples of redundancy from our recordings are listed in the Appendix.

We first analyzed the data using a hierarchical loglinear analysis with the variables: visual condition (Vision, No-vision), relationship (Friends, Strangers), receiver-utterance (Info-request, Incorrect statement, Signal non-understanding, Abandoned, No-trigger), and giver-utterance (Redundant, Non-redundant). The overall model is significant ($\chi^2_{(39,5294)}$=13254.157,p<.001), justifying chi-square comparisons of individual factors within the model. We report tests of partial association and chi-square tests to indicate where significant differences lie between groups.

4.1 Redundancy and Non-Understanding

Verbal Signals of Non-Understanding

We tested part (a) of Hypothesis 1 by running a test of partial associations (adjusted for all effects in the model) and an unpartialled chi-square (ignoring variables not included in the effect being tested). These showed a significant association between receiver-utterance and giver-utterance type (Partial $\chi^2_{(4,5294)}$=117.7, p<.001; $\chi^2_{(4,5294)}$=121.2,p<.001).

Chi-square tests comparing giver-utterances following predicted redundancy triggers to giver-utterances after No-trigger receiver utterances, indicate that Info-requests, Incorrect statements and Abandoned utterances all significantly increase the likelihood that the giver will produce a redundant utterance ($\chi^2_{(1,4907)}$=57.3,p<.001; $\chi^2_{(1,4562)}$=28.4, p<.001; $\chi^2_{(1,4651)}$=49.1,p<.001, respectively). Explicit Signal-non-understandings do not have significant effects on the likelihood of a redundant-utterance ($\chi^2_{(1,4539)}$=.3,p=.619). Figure 1 shows the percentages of giver utterances that were redundant following various receiver dialogue acts.

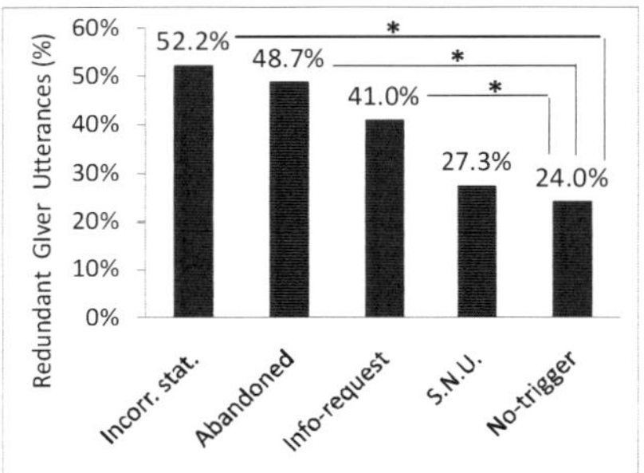

Figure 1. Percent of redundant giver utterances following various receiver dialogue acts.

Non-Verbal Signals of Non-Understanding

We tested part (b) of Hypothesis 1 with a separate hierarchical loglinear analysis examining only the dyads in the Vision condition for the effects of: relationship, receiver-utterance, giver-utterance, and receiver-gaze (Gaze-to, Gaze-away, and No-gaze-change). The first- and second-order effects are significant ($\chi^2_{(59,2815)}$=9582.4, p<.001).

A test of partial associations and a chi-square test indicate a significant association between giver-utterance and receiver-gaze (Partial $\chi^2_{(2,2815)}$= 22.7, p<.001; $\chi^2_{(2,2815)}$=24.7,p<.001). Chi-square tests comparing receiver gaze changes to non-changes show that redundant utterances are significantly more likely after a gaze change toward the giver ($\chi^2_{(1,2433)}$=21.5,p<.001) and after a gaze change away from the giver ($\chi^2_{(1,2475)}$=6.5,p<.05) than after no gaze change. A chi-square test comparing gaze change toward the giver to gaze change away from the giver shows that the difference between them is not significant ($\chi^2_{(1,722)}$=2.7, p=.098). These effects are shown in Figure 2.

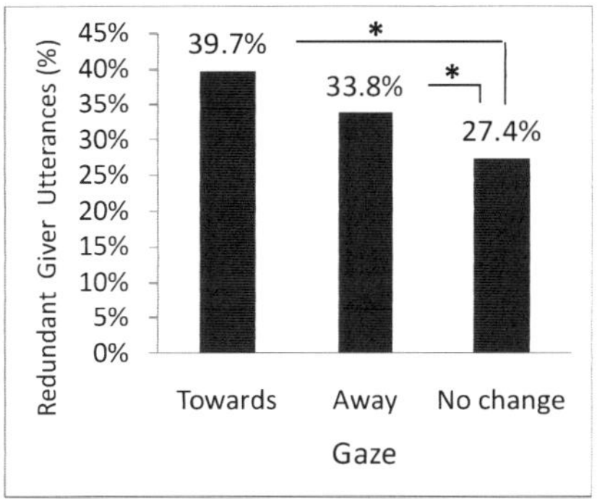

Figure 2. Percent of redundant giver utterances following receiver eye-gaze changes toward and away from the giver, and following no gaze change

4.2 Redundancy and Relationship

Part (a) of Hypothesis 2 was confirmed by the significant association between relationship and giver-utterance (Partial $\chi^2_{(1,5294)}=13.3$, $p<.001$; $\chi^2_{(1,5294)}=6$, $p<.05$) in our original analysis. A larger percentage of giver utterances are redundant in the Strangers condition (27.8%) than in the Friends condition (24.8%).

To examine part (b) of Hypothesis 2 we ran a hierarchical loglinear analysis after collapsing all receiver-utterances into question/non-question categories. This reveals a significant partial association among giver-utterance, receiver-utterance, and relationship (Partial $\chi^2_{(1,5294)}=7.5$, $p<.01$). A chi-square test comparing utterances after questions in the Friends and Strangers conditions shows that redundant utterances are significantly more likely after questions in the Strangers condition than the Friends condition ($\chi^2_{(1,412)}= 14.6$, $p<.0005$), as shown in Figure 3.

Three-way interactions among giver-utterance, receiver-utterance and relationship are not significant in any of the other analyses.

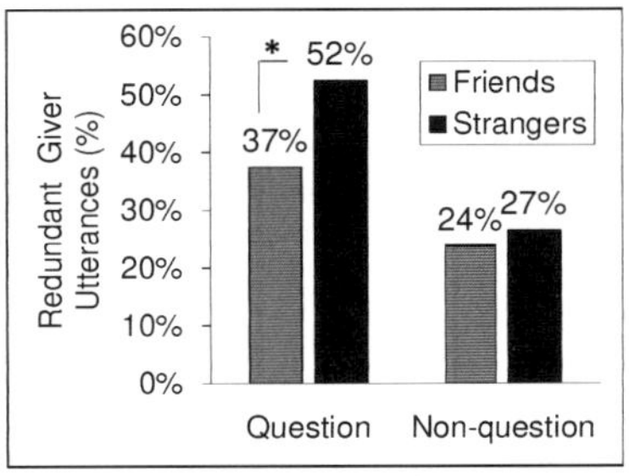

Figure 3. Percent of redundant giver utterances following questions and non-questions, by relationship.

4.3 Redundancy and Visual Contact

There is a trend-level association between visual condition and giver-utterance type (Partial $\chi^2_{(1,5294)}=4.6, p<.05$; $\chi^2_{(1,5294)}=3.3, p=.071$). Contrary to Hypothesis 3, a larger percentage of utterances are redundant in the Vision condition (27.7%) than in the No-vision condition (25.5%). No significant association was found among giver-utterance, receiver-utterance, and visual condition, even when collapsed into question/non-question categories.

5 Discussion

This study set out to discover what verbal and nonverbal behaviors increase the likelihood of redundant utterances in direction-givers' speech. We also examined whether the interlocutors' relationship or visual contact influence whether speakers provide redundant utterances in anticipation of and in response to listener confusion. We found that givers used a large proportion of redundant utterances, (around 25% of utterances). Walker (1996) found that about 12% of utterances were redundant in a corpus of recordings from a call-in financial radio show. The higher proportion of redundant utterances in our study is predicted by Walker's (1996) model, in which a task's tolerance for comprehension errors influences whether redundant utterances are produced. In a radio advice show, a misunderstanding may be more easily recovered from than in direction-giving, in which one wrong turn could make it impossible to reach the goal.

In addition to revealing the impact of task tolerance to error on redundancy, this study sheds light on other circumstances that influence redundancy use. Givers produced reactive redundancy in response to the verbal triggers: Info-requests, Abandoned utterances, and Incorrect statements. However, even these triggers were not always followed by redundancy. In fact, only around 50% of the utterances following these triggers were redundant. Such a low response rate is surprising until we consider the diversity of utterances covered by these labels. For instance, some Info-requests seek new information (e.g. "What's at the top of the stairs?"), and some receiver utterances are abandoned because the giver interrupts with new information. Our study lays the groundwork for future examinations of speaker responses to listener confusion, which can refine these broad categories. We must also consider the variability in responses to listener confusion. We found that givers are more likely to provide redundant utterances in response to questions when speaking to strangers, but this is only one of many factors that could affect levels of responsiveness, including speaker personality, time pressure, and task difficulty.

The non-significant effect of Signals non-understandings on redundancy is surprising. This may be due to the small number of examples of this category in our recordings. We found only 44 instances of Signal non-understandings, in contrast to, for example, 156 Abandoned utterances.

The non-verbal cue gaze change also increased the likelihood of a redundant utterance. Interestingly, gaze changes both to and away from the giver triggered redundancy. This is consistent with both Nakano et al.'s (2003) finding that gazing at the speaker signals listener misunderstanding and Goodwin's (1981) finding that gazing away from the speaker indicates a lack of listener attention.

It is interesting that 24% of giver utterances following No-trigger receiver utterances were redundant. These probably include both redundant utterances triggered by signs of listener confusion that we did not code for, and proactive redundancy. Proactive redundancy can appear within the first description of some directions (see the No-trigger example in the Appendix) and when the whole set of directions is repeated as a memory aid.

The relationship between the interlocutors does affect the amount of redundancy speakers produce overall and in response to listener signs of confusion. Strangers used more redundant utterances than friends and provided more redundant utterances after questions. This supports our hypothesis that direction-givers speaking to strangers will prioritize clarity over efficiency. The more consistent use of reactive redundancy in the Strangers condition may be due to speakers' tendency to avoid confrontation with strangers. When responding to questions from friends, direction-givers may provide some new information because they know that their friend will feel comfortable asking another question if their answer is unclear. However, when answering questions from a stranger, the giver may wish to avoid the embarrassment of further confusion by repeating more discourse-old information.

However, contrary to our predictions, we did not find more redundancy or more reactive redundancy in the No-vision condition than the Vision condition. In fact, we found numerically more redundancy in the Vision condition. Given the low level of significance, we do not discuss this in detail, however we suggest that this could be due to the fact that there are more ways of signaling non-understanding available to the receivers in the Vision condition (both verbal and non-verbal). Therefore, even if givers do not increase their rates of reactive redundancy in the Vision condition, they could provide more reactive redundancy (and more redundancy overall) because they are receiving more cues to react to. Not all situations leading to communication difficulties encourage more redundancy or more reactive redundancy, but the increased explicitness and positivity typical of conversation between strangers do encourage it.

6 Conclusion

This study explored the use of redundancy in task-oriented dialogue, specifically the effects of listener behavior and communicative context on the amount of redundancy produced. We found that direction-givers provided redundant utterances in response to verbal and non-verbal signs of listener confusion. As predicted, givers were more likely to prioritize clarity over efficiency in their redundancy use (using more redundancy overall and more redundancy in response to questions) when speaking to strangers than friends. Contrary to our predictions, givers did not provide more redundant utterances when they could not see their listener.

Direction-giving, due to its high memory load and the need for the receiver to understand the giver almost completely, is a type of discourse that may encourage more redundancy than other types. Indeed, we note that our data have a much greater proportion of redundancies than discussions taken from radio talk shows (Walker, 1996). Future work should examine the nature of proactive and reactive redundancy in more varied discourse contexts, such as negotiation, teaching, and play. It should also explore the effects of memory load on redundancy by varying task complexity, which may be easier with a more controlled task like the Map-task. Researchers could study the relationship between saliency and redundancy by studying correlations between a segment's salience and its likelihood of being used in a redundant utterance.

Our findings can be used to improve the communicative efficacy of natural language generation systems like those used in Embodied Conversational Agents (ECAs; Kopp et al., 2008). For example, like strangers, direction-giving ECAs could use increased overall and reactive redundancy to compensate for the lack of shared common ground with the human user of the system. Analyses of the syntactic structures of different types of redundant utterances will be important for incorporating these results into generation systems.

Acknowledgments

We thank Paul Tepper, Gregory Ward, Darren Gergle, Alex Podbelski, and our anonymous reviewers for their helpful advice and hard work. We are grateful for generous funding from Motorola and NSF HCC 0705901.

References

M. Argyle and M. Cook. 1976. *Gaze and Mutual Gaze*. Cambridge University Press, New York.

E. Bard, A. Anderson, C. Sotillo, M. Aylett, G. Doherty-Sneddon and A. Newlands. 2000. Controlling the intelligibility of referring expressions in dialogue. *J. Memory and Language*, 42(1):1-22.

N. Bos, J. Olson, D. Gergle, G. Olson, and Z. Wright. 2002. Effects of four computer-mediated communication channels on trust development. In *Proceedings of SIGCHI 2002,* pages 135-140, Minneapolis, MN.

H. P. Branigan, J. F. McLean, and H. Reeve. 2003. Something old, something new: Addressee knowledge and the given-new contract. In *Proceedings of the 25th Annual Conference of the Cognitive Science Society,* pages 180-185, Boston, MA.

B. Brighton, M. Fujiki, and E. Sonnenberg. 1988. Responses to requests for clarification by linguistically normal and language-impaired children in conversation. *J. Speech and Hearing Disorders*, 53:383-391.

P. Brown and S. C. Levinson. 1987. *Politeness: Some Universals in Language Usage.* Cambridge University Press, Cambridge, UK.

J. Cassell, A. J. Gill, and P. Tepper. 2007. Coordination in conversation and rapport. In *Proceedings of the Workshop on Embodied Language Processing at ACL,* pages 41-50, Prague.

H. H. Clark and E. F. Schaeffer. 1989. Contributing to discourse. *Cognitive Science,* 13:259-294.

M. G. Core and J. F. Allen. 1997. Coding dialogs with the DAMSL annotation scheme. In *Proceedings of AAAI Fall Symposium on Communicative Action in Humans and Machines*, pages 28-35, Boston, MA.

H. Dalianis. 1999. Aggregation in natural language generation. *J. Computational Intelligence*, 15(4):384-414.

S. R. Fussell and R. M. Krauss. 1989 a. The effects of intended audience on message production and comprehension: Reference in a common ground framework. *European J. Social Psychology,* 25:203-219.

S. R. Fussell and R. M. Kraus. 1989 b. Understanding friends and strangers: The effects of audience design on message comprehension. *European J. Social Psychology*, 19:445-454.

C. Goodwin. 1981. *Conversational Organization: Interaction between Speakers and Hearers.* Academic Press, New York.

H. P. Grice. 1975. Logic and conversation. In P. Cole and J. Morgan, editors, *Syntax and Semantics III – Speech Acts.* Academic Press,New York, pages 41-58.

G. Hirst, S. McRoy, P. Heeman, P. Edmonds, and D. Horton. 1994. Repairing conversational misunderstandings and non-understandings. *Speech Communication*, 15: 213-230.

L. Horn. 1993. Economy and redundancy in a dualistic model of natural language. *SKY 1993: Yearbook of the Linguistic Association of Finland*: 33-72.

A. Horning. 1991. Readable writing: The role of cohesion and redundancy. *J. Advanced Composition, 11*:135-145.

G. Hornstein. 1985. Intimacy in conversational style as a function of the degree of closeness between members of a dyad. *J. Personality and Social Psychology,* 49(3):671-681.

W. Horton and B. Keysar. 1996. When do speakers take into account common ground? *Cognition,* 59:91–117.

S. Kopp, P. Tepper, K. Ferriman, K. Striegnitz and J. Cassell. 2008. Trading spaces: How humans and humanoids use speech and gesture to give directions. In T. Nishida, editor, *Conversational Informatics.* John Wiley & Sons, New York, pages 133-160.

B. Lindlom. 1990. Explaining phonetic variation: A sketch of the H and H theory. In W. Hardcastle & A. Marchal, editors, *Speech Production and Speech Modeling.* Kluwer, Dordrecht, pages 403-439.

D. Morrow, A. Lee, and M. Rodvold. 1993. Analysis of problems in routine controller-pilot communication. *International J. Aviation Psychology*. 3(4): 285-302.

Y. Nakano, G. Reinstein, T. Stocky, and J. Cassell. 2003. Towards a model of face-to-face grounding. In *Proceedings of ACL 2003*, pages 553-561, Sapporo, Japan.

S. Planalp and A. Benson. 1992. Friends' and acquaintances' conversations I: Perceived differences. *J. Social and Personal Relationships,* 9:483-506.

B. Schlenker. 1984. Identities, identifications, and relationships. In V. Derlega, editor, *Communication, Intimacy and Close Relationships.* Academic Press, New York, pages 71-104.

R. Stalnaker. 1978. Assertion. In P. Cole, editor, *Syntax and Semantics, Volume 9: Pragmatics.* Academic Press, New York, pages 315-332.

G. Svendsen and B. Evjemo. 2003. Implicit referring as an indication of familiarity in face-to-face and phone conversations. In *Proceedings of INTERACT '03:* pages 920-923, Zurich.

M. Theune, D. Hofs and M. van Kessel. 2007. The Virtual guide: A direction giving embodied conversational agent. In *Proceedings of Interspeech 2007,* pages 2197-2200, Antwerp, Belgium.

L. Tickle-Degnen and R. Rosenthal. 1990. The nature of rapport and its nonverbal correlates. *Psychological Inquiry*, 1(4):285-293.

M. A. Walker. 1992. Redundancy in collaborative dialogue. In *Proceedings of the 14th International Conference on Computational Linguistics*, pages 345-351, Nantes, France.

M. A. Walker. 1996. The effect of resource limits and task complexity on collaborative planning in dialogue. *Artificial Intelligence Journal*, 85:181-243.

Appendix: Examples from Dialogues

In the following examples, utterances in italics are the triggers produced by the receiver, and underlined utterances are redundant. Commas indicate pauses. Receiver utterances in square brackets overlap with the portion of the preceding giver utterance in brackets.

Question Example

Giver (G): as soon as you come outta the door, uhh on the second floor you'll [see like a window] in front of you
Receiver (R): [mmhm]
G: [and then], you'll wanna take a left
R: [hm]
...
G: if you look to your left you'll see the exit sign, uhh with for the stairwell
R: ok so then I go to this second floor
G: mmhm
R: *and then do I go right?*
G: no
R: *or left?*
G: <u>you go left [once you come outta] the second floor</u>
R: [you go left]

Incorrect Statement Example

G: and you're gonna go towards the computer, and pass the computer, and there will be, copy machines on your right after you pass the computer
R: mhmm
G: so after you, walk, just past the copy machines you're gonna want to take a hard left, almost like a U-turn
...
G: once you turn to the right at after the first stairs you'll you'll see a computer
R: oh a computer right ok *and then I'm gonna take a really hard left like a U-turn*
G: <u>right well you go past the computer and then you'll see copying machines</u>
R: oh ok
G: and then but, the copy machines are like maybe three five feet after the computer
R: ok
G: and then <u>that's when you take the hard left</u>

Abandoned Example

G: and then you're gonna hear some kids and people talking and stuff, you're gonna be heading toward the clinic
R: oh okay
G: okay, the clinic you're is gonna come up on your right, [there's gonna] be, kind of, semi circular blue couches
R: [okay], uhhuh
G: down there, the stapler, is on the floor, right next to a pillar, [um] so basically you're gonna like, you're gonna kind of, turn right to look into the clinic
R: [okay], okay
G: and then, the stapler's kinda just over there to the left, on the floor by one of the pillars
...
G: and you're gonna hear people talking and there's gonna [be kids]
R: *[okay] so and then the, pillar its' like gonna be one of the pillars on the, right by like I guess it's on the*
G: <u>basically, basically um you walk into, the clinic, and there's blue, couches</u>
R: mmhm
G: <u>and then it's just a little bit over to the left</u>
R: oh okay
G: <u>on the floor</u>

No-Trigger Example

G: open the door, and you're gonna see a set of stairs
R: okay
G: go down those stairs, to the second floor
R: mmhm
G so you're gonna be on the third floor, you're gonna <u>then you're gonna take the stairs down to the second floor</u>
R: okay

Semantic negotiation in dialogue: the mechanisms of alignment

Gregory J. Mills
Interaction, Media and Communication Research Group
Department of Computer Science
Queen Mary, University of London
London E1 4NS
gj@dcs.qmul.ac.uk

Patrick G.T. Healey
Interaction, Media and Communication Research Group
Department of Computer Science
Queen Mary, University of London
London E1 4NS
ph@dcs.qmul.ac.uk

Abstract

A key problem for models of dialogue is to explain how semantic co-ordination in dialogue is achieved and sustained. This paper presents findings from a series of Maze Task experiments which are not readily explained by the primary co-ordination mechanisms of existing models. It demonstrates that alignment in dialogue is not simply an outcome of successful interaction, but a communicative resource exploited by interlocutors in converging on a semantic model. We argue this suggests mechanisms of co-ordination in dialogue which are of relevance for a general account of how semantic co-ordination is achieved.

1 Introduction

One of the first things apparent to European travellers on arriving at an American hotel is that the ground floor is also the first floor. Any confusion can be quickly corrected by an observant concierge, whether by explicitly stating the convention, or by implicitly bypassing the problem with a different description, such as "go up 5 flights of stairs". Assuming this description is sufficient to guide the hapless traveller to the correct room, when the same traveller asks for assistance to find another part of the hotel, the concierge is faced with a choice of whether to give a description involving floor numbers or in terms of flights of stairs.

The immediate question that emerges is what motivates this choice between different semantic models of a domain, how they are deployed when interlocutors are faced with problematic understanding, and which semantic model is subsequently used once the problem is resolved. Although existing approaches to dialogue agree that answering this question necessarily involves focusing on the interactional devices available to interlocutors, their primary emphasis is on the information-exchange aspects of language use. Larsson (2007) provides a useful distinction between the co-ordination of information, i.e. establishing common ground (Clark, 1996) and the co-ordination of linguistic resources which are adapted to suit particular communicative situations in order to make such information-exchange possible. Part of this framework involves interlocutors negotiating which particular semantic model to use, and adapting their own interpretations on the basis of successful/unsuccesful use. However, although this framework sketches out a formal account of the mechanisms involved in this process, it is not concerned with predicting which particular semantic model will be adopted by interlocutors.

A model of dialogue which attempts to address this issue is the interactive alignment model of Pickering and Garrod (2004). In this model convergence on a semantic model is arrived at via tacit priming occurring at all levels of representation (phonetic, phonological, lexical, syntactic, semantic and situational): interlocutors are more likely to re-use the representations used by their partner, giving rise to a "winner-takes-all" dynamic (cf. Steels & Belpaeme, 2005) which leads to align-

Proceedings of the 9th SIGdial Workshop on Discourse and Dialogue, pages 46–53,
Columbus, June 2008.

ment of interlocutors' representations. This is further re-inforced by "percolation" occurring between levels, thus lexemes associated with particular semantic models will reinforce the use of these models.

The claims associated with the interactive alignment model (henceforth IM) are drawn from a series of maze task experiments (Garrod & Doherty 1994; Garrod and Anderson, 1987; Anderson and Garrod, 1987). This paper discusses some of the original findings of these experiments and a further set of maze task experiments conducted by Healey and Mills (2006), Mills and Healey (2006). These papers argued that the primary mechanisms provided by the IM are insufficient for explaining observed patterns in maze task dialogue; in particular how semantic co-ordination is achieved. The present paper argues that interlocutors in the Maze task exploit variation in usage in the service of semantic co-ordination. Furthermore we argue this suggests mechanisms which are relevant for a general account of how semantic co-ordination is achieved in dialogue. As the claims developed here are based on the maze task, we first explain the task in more detail. We then discuss a series of examples drawn from this task that raise basic issues for models of semantic co-ordination.

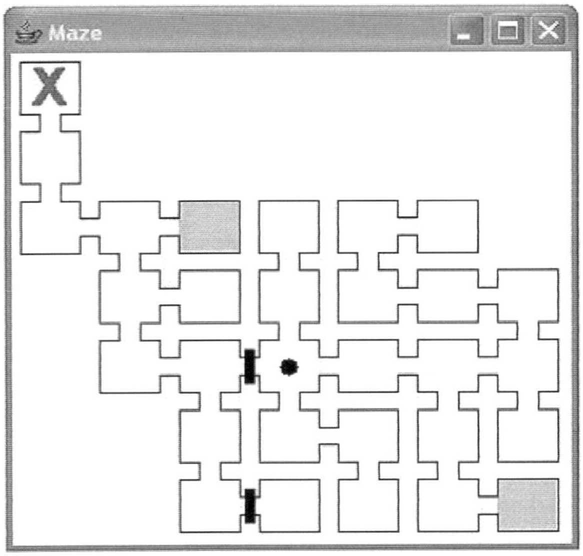

Figure 1: Example maze configuration. The solid black circle shows the player's current position, the cross represents the goal point that the player must reach, solid bars the gates and shaded areas the switch points.

2 The maze task

The maze task developed by Garrod et al involves pairs of participants seated in separate rooms in front of a computer which displays a simple maze consisting of interconnected nodes (see Fig 1). Participants must move their respective position markers through the maze in order to reach a "goal" node. Some of the paths are blocked by gates, which are opened by participants guiding each other onto "switch" nodes (shaded areas). This provides participants with the recurrent co-ordination problem of collaboratively individuating and referring to maze locations in order to solve the maze. The descriptions used by participants to refer to maze locations are classified by Garrod et al. into four distinct types:

Figural: Picks out salient features of the maze:
"The l-shape sticking out at the top"
"The uppermost box"

Path: Traces a route along the connections between nodes:
"Go 2 up, 1 down, 3 along, 5 up"
"up, right, down, up "

Line: Treats the maze as consisting of horizontal or vertical vectors:
"3rd row, 5th box"
"4th column, second square"

Matrix: Cartesian co-ordinate system:
"4,2"
"A1"

It is assumed that these different description types correspond to different semantic models of the maze.

3 Conservatism

The first question, also raised by Healey and Mills (2006), concerns the tension between the interactive alignment model's inherently conservative primary co-ordination mechanism and the migration in description types commonly observed in the Maze task. To the extent that it relies on priming as its basic mechanism the IM cannot provide an account of how once a convention is established and used successfully, it might be supplanted by another.. However, it is consistently observed that the description types used most frequently initially fall into disuse and are not converged on in later games. Across trials there is a general shift from more "concrete" (Figural and Path) descriptions towards more "abstract" (Line and Matrix) descriptions, which runs counter to precedence. A typical pattern of the shift is given in table 1, below:

0 mins:	The piece of the maze sticking out
2 mins:	The left hand corner of the maze
5 mins:	The northenmost box
10 mins:	Leftmost square of the row on top
15 mins:	3rd column middle square
20 mins:	3rd column 1st square
25 mins:	6th row longest column
30 mins:	6th row 1st column
40 mins:	6 r, 1 c
45 mins:	6,1

Table 1: Semantic shift from "Figural" and "Path" descriptions to "Line" and "Matrix" observed in maze task dialogues.

Garrod (1999) discusses this process as an "exploration" process. However, this, in itself, doesn't explain the systematic patterns of change observed in the experiments.

4 Variation

The early explanations of co-ordination in the Maze Task also emphasized the importance of variation in the description types participants are exposed to. Garrod and Doherty (1994) assigned participants to one of three different groups: (1) isolated pairs who always interacted with the same partner in subsequent games, (2) a sub-community group whose members changed partners in each game, only interacting with members from the same sub-community, and (3) a non-community group whose members always interacted with a new partner who was not drawn from the same community. Although initially pairs in the sub-community group were less co-ordinated than the isolated pairs, using a wider variety of referring expressions, by the later trials, this pattern was reversed: participants in the sub-community group had converged on a single Matrix scheme and consistently matched each other's descriptions.

These findings present a problem for accounts of co-ordination which rely on priming, as they make the emphasis of the priority of alignment of representations at all levels problematic. The metaphor of two tightly-coupled production and comprehension systems is the paradigm case of successful co-ordination, as it allows rapid priming between interlocutors' representations. However, these experiments show weaker semantic co-ordination in the isolated dyads than within the group. As Garrod and Doherty (1994) concur, this implies that variation, i.e. differences in interlocutors' representations is important for establishing and sustaining semantic co-ordination.

5 Granularity of analysis

If variation of description types is intrinsic to the development of semantic co-ordination, this strongly suggests the importance of mechanisms involved in dealing with problematic understanding (Healey, forthcoming). All things being equal, variation increases the likelihood that interlocutors will encounter others whose use of language will differ more from their own. Further, any account of misunderstandings must also be able to address semantic differences between descriptions: participants in the maze task do not treat these four description types equally, and consequently are not appropriately modelled as co-ordination equilibria of the kind described by Lewis (1968) (Healey, 2004; forthcoming). Existing experimental data shows that participants systematically favour Figural and Path descriptions when encountering problematic dialogue (Mills and Healey, 2006; Healey, 1997) not the prior most frequently used semantic model as predicted by the IM.

Looking more closely at the dialogues, it is not clear that the co-ordination mechanisms actually operate directly at the level of the four basic semantic models. Consider the following excerpt in which a participant encounters difficulties with a Line description type and its associated counting conventions. The dialogue continues with more Figural descriptions, before resuming at turn (35) with a Line description:

(1) A: go to the 1st row 2nd on the right

(2) B: 2nd?

(3) A: on the right

(4) B: OK, I can only get to the left of the maze

(5) A: go to the highest square on the left

(6) B: yes. And then?

......

(35) B: I'm on the top row 2nd square

Excerpt 1: Deletion of elements from problematic turn.

While superficially, A's turn at (3) appears simply as a repeat of (1), with "on the right" being omitted, the subsequent turns continue with Figural descriptions. On this basis, it is unclear whether (1) and (3) invoke the same Line model or whether (3) invokes a Figural description. There is a large class of similar clarification sub-dialogues which involve deletion of a problematic element and result in the continuation of the dialogue with more Figural descriptions.

This issue is of importance for any theory of semantic co-ordination as it raises the question of the granularity of the mechanisms involved in how interlocutors collaboratively change semantic model. Further, it strongly suggests that alignment is not simply an outcome of successful communication, but can provide the background against which other co-ordination mechanisms operate. Turns (1)-(6) demonstrate high levels of between-speaker alignment, while at the same time involving a shift in semantic model. Before returning to this below, we demonstrate further differences between the informational view of language and an account which focuses on semantic co-ordination.

6 Information vs. semantic co-ordination

From an informational perspective, if an utterance fails to secure reference, there is the general assumption that more information will be provided to allow resolution of the problem. However, in (3), no new information is provided by A. This is a counter-example to Clark and Marshall's (1981) model of definite reference repair, which states that to be effective "repair must add or alter descriptors, but not delete them". Importantly, these CR responses that simply delete elements from the target turn are not treated by participants as repeats and queried again, but appear to promote resolution of the problematic understanding by engendering the use of more Figural descriptions. The words which are omitted do not appear, as with the level of description types, to be dictated by prior frequency of use (Mills, 2007). Instead, the data suggest that this pattern is motivated by a relaxation of the constraints of successful interpretation (Healey and Mills, 2006).

The example above raises a further question concerning the relationship between semantic co-ordination and the exchange of information. In existing "ladder models" of communication such as the collaborative model of Clark (1996) and Allwood (1995), there is the general expectation that on encountering and signalling problematic understanding, interlocutors enter a sub-dialogue to resolve the problem, which on completion proceeds at the same "level". From this perspective, B's turn-initial acknowledgment at (4) should demarcate the end of the sub-dialogue dealing with the problematic understanding. Focusing on the description types, however, shows that it is only at turn (35) that the interlocutors return to using the original problematic line description; the semantic effects persist beyond the immediate sub-dialogue. This highlights the inadequacy of a strict informational view of language as the response provides no additional information, yet still has the effect of resolving the misunderstanding.

7 Exploitation of alignment: patterns of deletion, modification and addition

In addition to deletion of elements contained in referring expressions, the maze task dialogues exhibit a multiplicity of ways in which interlocutors modify descriptions when dealing with problematic understanding, through the addition, substitution and (as described above) deletion of elements of semantic models. We argue that alignment is key to these patterns of modification, as it provides a backdrop against which changes can be made. The canonical example of this is embedded correction (Jefferson, 1983; Saxton, 2007) which exploits the structure provided by alignment to make a figure / ground distinction that allows the corrected element to be identified:

(1) A: You need to go to the top of the 5th row

(2) B: I can't get to the top of the 5th line

Excerpt 2: Substitution of problematic elements .

Embedded corrections in the maze task exhibit very high levels of between-speaker alignment, yet occur at points in the dialogue where there is problematic understanding. This indicates that alignment can not simply be reduced to an index of successful communication. While this particular conversational device which spans 2 turns (and possibly a third) has received much attention, closer inspection of the maze task dialogues reveal a far larger space of possible means of exploiting alignment. Excerpt 1 above showed deletions, Excerpt 2 substitutions, however a similar pattern also appears with the addition of Figural elements.

(1) A: I'm in the 4th row 5th square

(2) B: where's that ?

(3) A: The end bit

(4) B: cheers, I'm on the end bit right at the top

(5) A: can you get to my switch?

....

(23) B: am on the top row 3rd square

Excerpt 3: Addition of "Figural" elements.

At a first glance, this excerpt looks like a straightforward clarification request followed by the provision of more details, specifying that the "5th square" is also "the end bit". B's use of "cheers" in (4) and subsequent provision of her own maze location would appear to demarcate the end of the clarification sequence, as they provide an acknowledgment and a "next relevant contribution" (Clark, 1996). However, focusing on the ensuing turns yields a pattern that parallels the first example. The semantic effects stretch beyond the immediate clarification sub-dialogue: both interlocutors continue with more Figural descriptions until turn (23) where the original, problematic Line description is attempted again.

A further issue emerges when interlocutors finally re-use the original description, as in turn (23) of Excerpt 1, and (35) above: although the surface form of the descriptions are similar, this does not necessarily entail that they individuate the same locations. For example, the counting conventions associated with squares may change, such as counting from the left instead of the right or counting from 0 as opposed to 1, similar to the concierge example above. The axes may also change, with "rows" referring to vertical vectors (i.e. columns).

This raises important questions of the relationship between the problematic utterance, the signalling of the problem, the response, the ensuing figural sub-dialogue and the subsequent return to the superficially similar but potentially altered description type. It appears that alignment is not simply an outcome but an interactional resource that is exploited to facilitate the continuation with more Figural descriptions (cf. Saxton, 2007).

In the first excerpt, turns (1) and (3) only differ minimally from each other, while in the second example, turn (3) can be seen to be operating elliptically on turn (1). However, both engender similar semantic shifts towards Figural descriptions and result in a return to the originally problematic Line description.

This leads to the immediate question of what motivates interlocutors' patterns of alignment and modification, and how they reflect differences of understanding and diagnosis of the problem. The tacit and fine-grained nature of these modifications exacerbates the problem of arriving at a preliminary taxonomy, as these dialogue sequences are not readily categorizable as either "elaborations" or "reformulations" (cf. Purver et al., 2004, Schlangen 2004).

8 Boundary of (mis)communication

During the course of maze task dialogues, participants shift seamlessly and tacitly from one description type to another. This occurs both within problematic and unproblematic dialogue. From an informational perspective, miscommunication is readily describable as a form of mismatch, yet from a semantic perspective, participants match each other more when encountering difficulties.

Thus alignment cannot be taken as a straightforward index of successful interaction.

This also raises a methodological point. Measures of matching of representations, whether at the level of description type or its constituent elements are only an approximate index of semantic co-ordination. The excerpts above demonstrate the importance of the interplay between what is retained and what is modified. What is required is a measure that is sensitive to the kind of model being used and the kind of repair being performed.

In addition, more frequent repair does not necessarily entail that a dialogue is unsuccessful. It is not the case that interlocutors introduce their utterances carefully, and once they are sufficiently coordinated, move on. The general pattern is that when participants introduce abstract (Line and Matrix) descriptions, they do so opportunistically. At the start of the games they frequently attempt both Line and Matrix descriptions, which are associated with higher co-ordination. However, there is evidence that it is only where they can go through the process of detecting and responding to differences in usage, i.e. repair, that co-ordination develops (Healey and Mills, 2006).

If the boundary between description types and also the boundary between successful and unsuccessful use can be as porous as demonstrated in the excerpts above, this also suggests a more complex picture of referential contraction (Krauss and Weinheimer, 1966) than provided by current models of dialogue. In current models this is primarily associated with successful use: in the collaborative model, interlocutors follow the principle of "least collaborative effort" (Clark and Wilkes-Gibbs, 1986), whereby successful use sets a precedent for an expression; co-ordination on precedence allows interlocutors to delete elements of the description on successive mention. It is assumed that the information associated with these deleted elements that are no longer on the conversational surface can be re-accessed in the common ground and mentioned explicitly, e.g. to assist disambiguation.

By contrast, the phenomena from the maze task show how similar processes are operative during problematic dialogue, raising further questions concerning the difference between elements that are removed in successful, as opposed to problematic dialogue and where this boundary lies.

Larsson's model of semantic co-ordination places a strong emphasis on the role of feedback in negotiating this boundary in terms of appropriateness gleamed from feedback (e.g. repair, acknowledgements etc..), and provides a schema which analyzes the effects of novel uses of a word and the subsequent update of interlocutors' representations.

Findings from the maze task experiments augment this approach as they suggest that evidence of appropriateness is also derived in the absence of overt repair from semantic change alone. The excerpts indicate that interlocutors are sensitive to which particular tacit shift in model leads to a relaxation of the constraints on successful communication, and consequently can be exploited to indicate problematic understanding (Mills, 2007). For example, consider the following two excerpts:

(1) A: It's on the 5th row 4th square
(2) B: Huh?
(3) A: The last square

(1) A: It's on the 5th row 4th square
(2) A: The last square

Excerpts 4, 5: Provision of feedback

If the dialogue continues successfully in both these instances, it is unclear how to adequately capture the differences between them, in particular, how both patterns affect subsequent use of the description types,

One of the main challenges facing an account of semantic co-ordination is teasing apart how interlocutors' models are affected by both semantic change exploited as a resource using the mechanisms of alignment outlined above, and feedback concerning that change, as both aspects inhabit the boundary between successful and unsuccessful use.

Evidence from the maze task suggests this boundary is one of the important locii in the development of semantic co-ordination.

9 Semantic plasticity

To describe how interlocutors dynamically adapt the meanings of the words they use to the communicative situation and how they are shaped throughout the course of the dialogue, Larsson (2006) introduces the notion of "semantic plasticity". This model is sensitive to the fact that descriptions can involve a plethora of different "ad-hoc registers", which resonates strongly with the empirical phenomena described here. However, the data from all the maze task experiments presents a further problem for attempts to model these phenomena, as successful co-ordination on the more specific abstract levels appears to be predicated upon prior successful use of less specific Figural descriptions: the Figural descriptions are highly specific to individual mazes and allow participants to co-ordinate on their salient features, whereas the Line and Matrix descriptions abstract away from each individual instance to form dyad-specific conceptualizations of vectors and their associated counting conventions.

While Larsson's account highlights the sheer flexibility of ways in which linguistic resources are mobilized and adapted to particular interaction settings, the data from the maze task suggest an additional level of complexity. Namely that the semantic resources can not be treated as separate, essentially equal encyclopaedias that interlocutors draw on. One way in which the cumulative shift toward Matrix descriptions is achieved is by the combination of different "registers" (Larsson 2007) to form a super-ordinate one. Here the question concerns which specific features of each semantic model are included in the final one, in particular when there are problems of commensurability. For example, as table 1 shows, a common pattern in maze task dialogues is that approximately half-way through the dialogues participants use "Line" descriptions. It can occur that they alternate between describing the maze as consisting of vertical and horizontal vectors, say with one participant favouring horizontal and the other favouring vertical vectors (space considerations preclude a throrough examination of this process, described in Mills, 2007). It frequently occurs that Matrix descriptions emerge when these two different Line models are combined to form a Matrix description. This process, however, is not as a rule simply a matter of combining the two. Frequently, the two types of Line description employ different counting conventions, as in the example of the concierge above, giving rise to the problem of whether to retain different counting conventions for the different axes, or employ the same one. The question then emerges as to how this super-ordinate, more abstract semantic model affects the original models.

Results from the maze task suggest this is achieved tacitly by interlocutors, employing similar patterns of modification to those described in the excerpts above (Mills, 2007).

10 Conclusion

The phenomena described here demonstrate the need for an account of semantic co-ordination that explains how interlocutors converge on a semantic representation. Dialogues from the maze task provide compelling evidence that such an account must necessarily be able to account for how variation, and hence differences in semantic models are resolved. This approach necessarily involves shifting the focus from an informational view of language towards a focus on how interlocutors actually address these differences.

In a sense, this presents a reversal of the priorities of existing models. For the interactive alignment model, as well as the collaborative model, misunderstanding is seen as a secondary problem that emerges as a complication of communication which is ordinarily successful (Healey, 2004; forthcoming). The collaborative model explicitly states that in order for communication to be successful, positive evidence of understanding must be demonstrated.

By contrast, the view presented here brings problematic understanding into the foreground, as it is in such instances, when conventions don't work as expected, that interlocutors gain a sense of their applicability. The phenomena presented here suggest that the processes operating in instances of misunderstanding are as much progenitors of semantic co-ordination, as their traditional counterpart of displays of positive understanding. Interlocutors' separate interaction histories inescapably give rise to problems concerning the development and sustenance of mutual-intelligibility, intrinsically requiring interlocutors to resolve differences of semantic model in interaction. The data from the maze task experiments demonstrate how this can be achieved through tacitly modifying the constituents of semantic models. This modification involves the exploitation of alignment, and has the effect of relaxing the constraints on successful understanding.

Any theory of dialogue must, in the first instance be concerned with what interlocutors actually do. The phenomena presented here demonstrate mechanisms of semantic co-ordination that have previously fallen under the category of information-exchange, and the questions raised present rich opportunities for further experimental investigation.

References

Allwood, J. (1995). An activity based approach to pragmatics. *Technical Report (GPTL) 75*, Gothenburg Papers in Theoretical Linguistics, University of Göteborg.

Clark, H. H. *Using Language*. Cambridge University Press, Cambridge.

Garrod, S. and Doherty, G. 1994. Conversation, co-ordination and convention: an empirical investigation of how groups establish linguistic conventions. *Cognition*, 53:181-215.

Healey, P.G.T. 1997. "Expertise or expert-ese: The emergence of task-oriented sub-languages." *Proceedings of the Ninteenth Annual Conference of The Cognitive Science Society.* M.G. Shafto and Langley, P. (Ed.s) August 7th-10th, Stanford University, CA. pp. 301-306.

Healey, P.G.T. 2004. "Dialogue in the degenerate case?" Peer Commentary on Pickering and Garrod: 'The Interactive Alignment Model'. *Behavioral and Brain Sciences* 27(2) p. 201.

Healey P.G.T. (forthcoming) "Interactive Misalignment: The Role of Repair in the Development of Group Sub-languages" in Cooper R. and and Kempson R. (eds) Language Change.

Healey, P.G.T. and Mills, G.J. 2006. "Participation, Precedence and Co-ordination in Dialogue" in Sun R. and Miyake, N. (eds.) *Proceedings of Cogsci06: The 28th Annual Conference of the Cognitive Science Society*. Vancouver, BC, Canada. 26-29th July. pp. 1470-1475.

Jefferson, G. (1983). On exposed and embedded correction in conversation. *Studium Linguistik*, 14, 58–68.

Krauss, R. M. and Weinheimer, S. 1966. Concurrent feedback, confirmation and the encoding of referents in verbal communication. *Journal of Personality and Social Psychology*, 4:343-346.

Larsson, S. 2007. A general framework for semantic plasticity and negotiation. In Bunt, H. C., and Thijsse, E. C. G. (eds): *Prceedings of the 7th International Workshop on Computational Semantics* (IWCS-7).

Larsson, S. 2006. Semantic plasticity. Paper presented at LCM 2006. (Language, Culture and Mind), July 2006, Paris, France.

Lewis, D. 1969. *Convention: A philosophical study*. Harvard University Press.

Mills, G.J. and Healey, P.G.T. (2006) Clarifying Spatial Descriptions: Local and Global Effects on Semantic Co-ordination. In Schlangen, D. and Fernandez, R. (eds.) *Proceedings of Brandial06 The 10th Workshop on the Semantics and Pragmatics of Dialogue*. University of Potsdam, Germany; September 11th-13th. pp.122-129.

Mills, G. J. 2007. The development of semantic co-ordination in dialogue: the role of direct interaction. Unpublished PhD. Thesis.

Purver, M., Healey, P. G. T., King, J., and Mills, G. 2003. Answering clarification questions. In *Proceedings of the 5th Workshop of the ACL SIG on Discourse and Sialogue (SIGdial03)*, Sapporo, Japan.

Saxton, M. 1997. The contrast theory of negative input. *Journal of Child Language, 24,* 139-161.

Schlangen, D. 2004. Causes and strategies for requesting clarification in dialogue. In *Proceedings of the 5th SIGdial Workshop on Discourse and Dialogue.*

Steels, L. and Belpaeme T. 2005. Coordinating perceptually grounded categories through language: A case study for colour. *Behavioral and Brain Sciences,* 28(4):469-89

Degrees of Grounding Based on Evidence of Understanding

Antonio Roque
USC Institute for Creative Technologies
Marina del Rey, CA, USA
roque@ict.usc.edu

David Traum
USC Institute for Creative Technologies
Marina del Rey, CA, USA
traum@ict.usc.edu

Abstract

We introduce the Degrees of Grounding model, which defines the extent to which material being discussed in a dialogue has been grounded. This model has been developed and evaluated by a corpus analysis, and includes a set of types of evidence of understanding, a set of degrees of groundedness, a set of grounding criteria, and methods for identifying each of these. We describe how this model can be used for dialogue management.

1 Introduction

Dialogue system researchers are active in investigating ways of detecting and recovering from error, including determining when to provide confirmations or rejections, or how to handle cases of complete non-understanding (Bohus and Rudnicky, 2005a; Bohus and Rudnicky, 2005b; Skantze, 2005).

Studying the strategies that humans use when speaking amongst themselves can be helpful (Swerts et al., 2000; Paek, 2003; Litman et al., 2006). One approach to studying how humans manage errors of understanding is to view conversation as a joint activity, in which **grounding**, or the process of adding material to the common ground between speakers, plays a central role (Clark and Schaefer, 1989). From this perspective, conversations are highly coordinated efforts in which participants work together to ensure that knowledge is properly understood by all participants. There is a wide variety of grounding behavior that is determined by the communication medium, among other things (Clark and Brennan, 1991).

This approach is developed computationally by Traum, who presents a model of grounding which adapts Clark and Schaefer's contributions model to make it usable in an online dialogue system (Traum, 1994). Other computational approaches to grounding use decision theory (Paek and Horvitz, 2000a) or focus on modeling belief (Bunt et al., 2007).

Grounding models generally consider material to be in one of three states: ungrounded, in the process of becoming sufficiently grounded, or sufficiently grounded. (An exception is (Paek and Horvitz, 2000b), who use a continuous model of groundedness.) We are developing a model of grounding that is attentive to a larger set of types of evidence of understanding than is typical, and use this to define a model of **Degrees of Grounding**, which tracks the extent to which material has become a part of the common ground.

This model includes a set of types of **Evidence of Understanding** that describes the kinds of cues that the dialogue gives about the state of grounding. A set of **Degrees of Groundedness** describes the extent to which material has achieved mutual belief while being discussed. A set of **Grounding Criteria** describes the degree to which material needs to be grounded. Finally, the model provides algorithms to assist dialogue management.

The next section describes the radio domain which we used to begin developing this model. The dialogues in this domain contain a large amount of confirmation behavior, which make it a good testbed for the initial development of the model. However, because these radio dialogues are highly structured we are not yet able to make strong claims about the

Proceedings of the 9th SIGdial Workshop on Discourse and Dialogue, pages 54–63,
Columbus, June 2008.

generality of this model.

In following sections we describe the components of the model, annotation evaluations, and ongoing development of the model.

2 Domain

The domain for this corpus analysis involves a radio-based military training application. This corpus was developed while building the Radiobot-CFF system (Roque et al., 2006) in which soldiers are trained to perform artillery strike requests over a simulated radio in an immersive virtual environment.

Calls for Fire (CFFs) are coordinated artillery attacks on an enemy. Several teams work together to execute a CFF. A **Forward Observer** (FO) team locates an enemy target and initiates the call. The FO team is made up of two or more soldiers, usually with one soldier dedicated to spotting the enemy and another soldier dedicated to operating the radio. The FO radio operator communicates with the **Fire Direction Center** (FDC) team, which decides whether to execute the attack, and if so, which of the available fire assets to use. An example CFF is given in the Appendix.

3 Evidence of Understanding

An influential description of evidence of understanding was presented in (Clark and Schaefer, 1989), as shown in Table 1. This set of types of evidence was described as being "graded roughly from weakest to strongest" and was part of the acceptance phase of a two-phase grounding process. (Clark and Brennan, 1991) further develop Clark's notion of evidence, describing "the three most common forms of positive evidence" as being acknowledgments, initiation of the relevant next turn, and continued attention.

The Degrees of Grounding model exchanges Clark and Schaefer's two-phase model for an approach that tracks grounding acts in a way similar to (Traum, 1994). Also, rather than concerning itself with the strength of a given type of evidence, the current model tracks the strength of material based on its degree of groundedness, which is derived from sequences of evidence as described in Section 4.

Evidence in the Degrees of Grounding model is tracked per **Common Ground Unit** (CGU) in an information state, as in (Traum and Rickel, 2002). An example of such a CGU is given in Figure 1. Material under discussion is disambiguated by several identifying components of the CGU: in this domain this is the dialogue move, the parameter, the mission number, and the adjust number. Note that parameter value is not used as an identifying component; this allows for reference to the material by participants who may not yet agree on its value.

Evidence	Description
Continued Attention	B shows he is continuing to attend and therefore remains satisfied with As presentation.
Initiation of Relevant Next Contribution	B starts in on the next contribution that would be relevant at a level as high as the current one.
Acknowledgement	B nods or says "uh huh," "yeah," or the like.
Demonstration	B demonstrates all or part of what he has understood A to mean.
Display	B displays verbatim all or part of As presentation.

Table 1: (Clark and Schaefer, 1989)'s Evidence of Understanding between speakers A and B

```
information:
  dialogue move: target location
  parameter: direction
  value: 5940
  mission number: to be determined
  adjust number: 0
evidence history:
  submit-G91, repeat_back-S19
degree of groundedness: agreed-content
grounding criteria met: true
```

Figure 1: Example Common Ground Unit

The remainder of this section describes the kinds of evidence of understanding found in the corpus. Section 6 describes inter-annotator agreement studies that determine that humans can reliably identify these types of evidence.

3.1 Submit

A **Submit** type of evidence is provided when material is introduced into the common ground for the first time. The Submit type of evidence is derived from the Presentation phase of (Clark and Schaefer, 1989).

An example of a Submit is given in line 1 of Table 2: "direction 6120" is information that had not yet been mentioned and has no assumed values.

Line	ID	Utterance	Evidence
1	G91	direction 6120 over	Submit
2	S19	direction 6120 out	Repeat Back
3	G91	correction direction 6210 over	Resubmit

Table 2: Example Dialogue

Dialogue systems that do not specifically model grounding generally assume that material is grounded when it is first Submitted unless there is evidence to the contrary.

3.2 Repeat Back

A **Repeat Back** type of evidence is provided when material that was Submitted by another dialogue participant is presented back to them, often as part of an explicit confirmation.

The Repeat Back evidence is related to the "Display" evidence of (Clark and Schaefer, 1989) and described in Table 1, however here it is renamed to indicate that it pertains to verbal repetitions, rather than general displays which may be in other modalities, such as visual. In fact, there is evidence that grounding behavior related to visual feedback is different from that related to auditory feedback (Clark and Brennan, 1991; Thompson and Gergle, 2008).

An example is given in line 2 of Table 2: the "direction 6120" information given in line 1 is Repeated Back as part of a confirmation.

3.3 Resubmit

A **Resubmit** type of evidence is provided when material that has already been Submitted by a dialogue participant is presented again as part of a self- or other-correction. This is an example of what (Clark and Brennan, 1991) call negative evidence, which indicate a lack of mutual belief.

An example is shown in Table 2; the direction information which was Submitted in turn 1 and Repeated Back in turn 2 is Resubmitted in turn 3.

In this domain, follow-up presentations of material were almost always corrections, usually of information that has been repeated back by the other participant, or based on new occurences in the virtual world (for example, the lifting of smoke that was previously obscuring a target.) Due to the nature of the task, this corpus had few instances of non-correction follow-up behavior, where material was presented a second time for the purposes of further discussion. Such follow-ups are an evidence of understanding whose behavior is probably different from that of the Resubmit type of evidence as described here, and will be examined in future work as described in Section 7.

3.4 Acknowledge

An **Acknowledge** type of evidence is a general statement of agreement that does not specifically address the content of the material. Acknowledges are identified by semantic interpretation. Acknowledges are a part of (Clark and Schaefer, 1989)'s set of types of evidence of understanding.

Table 3 contains an example: in line 1 the speaker G91 Submits information about the target's status, which is then Acknowledged by speaker S19 in turn line 2.

Line	ID	Utterance	Evidence
1	G91	end of mission target destroyed over	Submit
2	S19	roger	Acknowledge

Table 3: Example of an Acknowledgment

3.5 Request Repair

A **Request Repair** type of evidence is a statement that indicates that the speaker needs to have the material Resubmitted by the other participant. Request Repairs are identified by semantic interpretation. Request Repairs are another example of negative evidence (Clark and Brennan, 1991).

Table 4 gives an example: in line 1 G91 submits a map grid coordinate, and in line 2 S19 asks that the other speaker "say again" that grid coordinate, which is a Request for Repair.

Line	ID	Utterance	Evidence
1	G91	grid 5843948	Submit
2	S19	say again grid over	Request Repair

Table 4: Example of a Request Repair

3.6 Move On

A **Move On** type of evidence is provided when a participant decides to proceed to the next step of the task at hand. This requires that the given task have a set of well-defined steps, and that the step being Moved On from needs to be grounded before the next step can be discussed. Move Ons are identified based on a model of the task at hand. Move Ons are related to (Clark and Schaefer, 1989)'s "Initiation of the relevant next contribution," although Clark and Schaefer do not specify that "next contributions" should be dependent on sufficiently grounding the previous step.

A Move On provides evidence because a cooperative dialogue participant would typically not move on to the next step of the task under such conditions unless they felt that the previous step was sufficiently grounded.

Table 5 shows an example of a Move On. In line 1, G91 indicates that the kind of artillery fire they want is a "fire for effect"; this is Repeated Back in line 2. G91 then Submits grid information related to the target location. The task specification of Calls for Fire indicates that fire requests should proceed in several steps: after a Warning Order is established, a Target Location should be given, followed by a Target Description. By moving on to the step in which a Target Location is provided, G91 tacitly indicates that the step in which a Warning Order is established has been dealt with to their satisfaction.

Line	ID	Utterance	Evidence
1	G91	fire for effect over	Submit
2	S19	fire for effect out	Repeat Back
3	G91	grid 45183658	Submit, Move On

Table 5: Example of a Move On

Line	ID	Utterance	Evidence
1	S19	message to observer kilo 2 rounds AB0001 over	Submit
2	G91	mike tango oscar kilo 2 rounds target number AB0001 out	Repeat Back
3	S19	shot over	Submit

Table 6: Example of a non-Move On

Not all typical sequences provide Move On evidence. In the example in Table 6, in line 1 S91 submits a "message to observer" indicating the kind of fire that is being delivered, which is followed in line 2 by a confirmation by G91. S19 then proceeds to the next step of the task by indicating in line 3 that the artillery has been fired. Line 3, however, is not a Move On because although it is typically the next step in the task, providing that information is not dependent on fully grounding the material being discussed in line 2 - in fact, line 3 will be provided when the artillery has been fired, and not based on any other decision by S19.

3.7 Use

A **Use** type of evidence is provided when a participant presents an utterance that indicates, through its semantics, that a previous utterance was understood. Uses are related to (Clark and Schaefer, 1989)'s "Demonstration".

In the Radiobot-CFF corpus, most Uses are replies to a request for information, such as in Table 7, where S19's request for a target description in line 1 is answered with a target description, in line 2.

Line	ID	Utterance	Evidence
1	S19	s2 wants to know whats the target description over	Submit
2	G91	zsu over	Submit, Use

Table 7: Example of a Use

Another example of Use is shown in Table 8, in which S19 is providing an intelligence report in line 1 regarding an enemy target, and line 2 replies with a statement asking whether the target is a vehicle. The utterance in line 2 uses information provided in line 1.

3.8 Lack of Response

A **Lack of Response** type of evidence is provided when neither participant speaks for a given length of time. Identifying a Lack of Response type of evidence involves determining how much silence will be significant for signalling understanding or lack of understanding.

Line	ID	Utterance	Evidence
1	S19	again it should have rather large antennas affixed to it uh they are still sending out signals at the time	Submit
2	G91	this is some kind of vehicle over	Submit, Use

Table 8: Example of a Use

In the example shown in Table 9, G91 submits an identifying utterance to see if S19 is available. After 12 seconds, G91 has heard nothing back; this is negative evidence of grounding, so in line 3 G91 resubmits the utterance.

Line	ID	Utterance	Evidence
1	G91	S 1 9 this is G 9 1	Submit
2		(12 seconds of silence)	Lack of Response
3	G91	S 1 9 this is G 9 1	Resubmit

Table 9: Example of a Lack of Response

A Lack of Response can also be an indication of positive grounding, as in Table 10. In line 1, G91 submits information about a target, which in line 2 is repeated back. Line 3 indicates a period of silence, in which neither speaker took the opportunity to request a repair or otherwise indicate their disapproval with the state of the groundedness of the material. In that sense, the silence of line 3 is positive evidence of understanding.

Line	ID	Utterance	Evidence
1	G91	b m p in the open over	Submit
2	S19	b m p in the open out	Repeat Back
3		(10 seconds of silence)	Lack of Response

Table 10: Example of a Lack of Response

4 Degrees of Groundedness

Degrees of groundedness are defined such that material has a given degree before and after any sequence of evidence given. For example, in Table 10 the target description given in line 1 has a certain degree of groundedness before it is Submitted, another degree after it is Submitted, another degree after it is Repeated Back, and another degree after the Lack of Response.

Degreee	Pattern/Identifier
Unknown	not yet introduced
Misunderstood	(anything,Request Repair)
Unacknowledged	(Submit, Lack of Response)
Accessible	(Submit) or (anything,Resubmit)
Agreed-Signal	(Submit, Acknowledgment)
Agreed-Signal+	(Submit, Acknowledgment, other)
Agreed-Content	(Submit, Repeat Back)
Agreed-Content+	(Submit, Repeat Back, other)
Assumed	grounded by other means

Table 11: Degrees of Groundedness

A key part of defining these degrees is to determine which of these degrees is worth modeling. For example, Table 3 shows a CGU further grounded by a single Acknowledgment. In this domain, for the purposes of determining grounding criteria and dialogue management algorithms, it is not worth distinguishing between the case in which it had been followed by one more Acknowledgment and the case in which it had been followed by two or more Acknowledgments.

Table 11 shows the significant degrees identified during the corpus study, as well as the definition or identifying pattern of evidence. These degrees are shown from Unknown, which is least grounded, to Assumed, which is grounded by other means, such as written information given during a scenario briefing. Most degrees are identified by patterns of evidence. For example, a CGU is misunderstood if the latest item of evidence provided is a Request Repair, and CGU is Unacknowledged if it is Submitted followed by a Lack of Response.

The degree of groundedness is used to compute how much (if any) additional evidence is needed to reach the grounding criterion, or "criterion sufficient for current purposes" as defined by (Clark and Schaefer, 1989). This computation can be used in dialogue management to help select a next utterance.

In this domain, information such as target numbers have high grounding criteria, such as Agreed-Content+; they would need to be Repeated Back, and followed at least by a Lack of Response, giving the other participant an opportunity to correct.

Other information might have a grounding criterion of Agreed-Signal, needing only an Acknowledgment to be grounded, as in Table 3. Future work will address the fact that grounding criteria are variable: for example, in noisy conditions where errors are more probable, the grounding criteria may increase.

5 Dialogue Management

Exploiting this model of grounding for dialogue management involves several steps. Evidence of understanding must be identified given a semantic interpretation and the history of evidence provided so far. Given an utterance's new evidence and a CGU's current degree of groundedness, the CGU's new degree of groundedness must be determined.

Once a CGU's current degree is determined, it can be compared to its grounding criterion to determine whether or not it has been sufficiently grounded, and if not, a new item of evidence may be suggested to help further ground the material.

All of these can be put together in one algorithm, as shown in Figure 2.

```
for each dialogue act parameter,
 identify the relevant CGU
 identify evidence of understanding
 compute the CGU's degree of groundedness

for each CGU not sufficiently grounded
 determine evidence to be given
 compute the CGU's degree of groundedness

if Lack of Response detected
 compute the CGU's degree of groundedness
```

Figure 2: Dialogue Management Algorithm

The specifics of how this algorithm is integrated into a system and how it influences task decisions will vary based on the system being used. To explore the domain-independence of this model, we are currently integrating it into a dialogue manager in a domain unrelated to the CFF task.

6 Evaluation

The validity of this model has been evaluated in several corpus tests to measure inter-annotator agreement in identifying evidence, to ensure that identifying evidence can reliably be done by an algorithm, to measure inter-annotator agreement in identifying the increase or decrease of the degree of groundedness, and to ensure that identifying the increase or decrease of a degree of groundedness can reliably be done by an algorithm.

Human transcribers produced transcriptions of several sessions between two sets of humans acting as Forward Observer and Fire Direction Center radio operators in the training simulation. A subset of the corpus was used for close analysis: this subset was made up of 4 training sessions, composed of 17 fire missions, totaling 456 utterances; this provided a total of 1222 possible indicators of evidence of understanding made up of 886 dialogue move parameters and 336 period of silence.

We automatically performed a dialogue act interpretation on the dialogue move parameters, which were then manually corrected. We then manually annotated the evidence of understanding identified in each dialogue move parameter and period of silence. An example of the data produced from this process is given in the Appendix.

6.1 Inter-Annotator Agreement - Identifying Evidence

An inter-annotator agreement study was performed in which two annotators tagged a subset of the corpus (318 dialogue move parameters and 74 silences) to identify the evidence of understanding, given an utterance and dialogue act interpretation. One annotator was the first author of this paper, and the other was a computer professional who had no previous experience with the domain or with tagging data.

Table 12 shows the results, broken down by the Standalone types of evidence, which could occur by themselves (Submit, Repeat Back, Resubmit, Acknowledge, and Request Repair), the Additional types of evidence, which only occurred with other types of evidence (Move On and Use), and the Silence-Related Lack of Understanding type of evidence. Each of these showed acceptable levels of agreement, with the exception of the Kappa for the additional evidence. The low score on the additional evidence is probably due to the fact that Move On judgments depend on a strong understanding of the domain-specific task structure, as described in section 3.6; to a lesser extent Use judgments tend to rely on an understanding of the scenario as well.

Evidence Type	P(A)	Kappa
Standalone	0.95	0.91
Additional	0.87	0.53
Silence-Related	0.92	0.84

Table 12: Inter-Annotator Agreement - Evidence

Evidence Type	P(A)	Kappa
Standalone	0.88	0.81
Additional	0.98	0.92
Silence-Related	1.0	1.0

Table 13: Algorithm Agreement - Evidence

This highlights the fact that for most of the evidence of understanding (all except for Move On and Use), agreement can be reached with a non-expert annotator.

6.2 Algorithm Agreement - Identifying Evidence

The results of the inter-annotator agreement test were merged into the larger 1222-markable corpus, to create a consensus human-annotated corpus. This was used in the next test, to identify whether an algorithm can automatically identify evidence.

We authored a set of rules to identify evidence of understanding based on the order in which CGUs were introduced into the common ground, the identity of the speaker who introduced them, and the semantic interpretations. The rules were then applied to the 1222-markable corpus, and the resulting identifications were then compared to the identifications made by the human annotators. The results are shown in Table 13. The respectable agreement and kappa values indicate that it is possible for an algorithm to reliably identify evidence.

6.3 Degree Increase/Decrease Agreements

Finally, we explored whether humans could reliably agree on whether a given material's groundedness had increased or decreased after a given turn.

We studied this because we are not here claiming that humans explicitly model degrees of groundedness or perform a computation to compare a given material with something they had grounded previously. It is more likely that humans track evidence, determine whether material is more or less grounded than it was before, and check whether it has reached a grounding criterion. A dialogue system need not be tied to human behavior to be effective, so given these human behaviors, we are interested in whether computer algorithms can be built to produce useful results in terms of task completion and human-realistic behavior. For this reason we evaluate the model of degrees of grounding based on how human-realistic its ability to identify whether a CGU's degree of groundedness has increased or decreased, and in future work study whether a system implementation performs acceptably in terms of task completion and managing human-realistic grounding behavior.

Agreement Type	P(A)	Kappa
Human-Human	0.97	0.94
Human-Algorithm	0.87	0.73

Table 14: Degree Increase/Decrease Agreements

To perform the test of whether degree increase or decrease could be reliable detected, we annotated a subset of the corpus with a non-domain expert. For a set of CGUs, we tracked the sequence of evidence that was provided to ground that CGU. Before and after each item of evidence, we asked the annotators to determine whether the CGU was more or less grounded than it was the turn before.

We also developed a set of rules based on the definition of the degrees of groundedness defined in section 4 to determine after each utterance whether a CGU's degree of groundedness had increased or decreased from the utterance before. We then compared the results of that set of rules with human-consensus judgments about degree increase and decrease.

The results are shown in Table 14, indicating that humans could reliably agree among themselves, and a rule-based algorithm could reliably agree with the human consensus judgments.

7 Discussion and Future Work

In this paper we describe the initial development of the Degrees of Grounding model, which tracks the extent to which material has been grounded in a dialogue. The Degrees of Grounding model contains a richer variety of evidence of understanding than most models of grounding, which allows us to define a full set of degrees of groundedness.

We recognize that the initial domain, although rich in grounding behavior, is not typical of most human conversation. Besides the structured dialogues and the domain-specific word use, the types of evidence of understanding presented in Section 3 does not cover all possible types of evidence. For example, (Clark and Schaefer, 1989) describe "continued attention" as another possibility, which was not available with the radio modality used in this study. Furthermore, it is a feature of this domain that Resubmit evidence generally indicates lack of understanding; in general conversation, it is not true that the repeated mention of material indicates that it is not understood, so a "Follow-Up" evidence is likely, as are variations of "Use."

To explore these questions, we are extending work to other domains, and are currently focusing on one in which virtual humans are used for a questioning task. Also, we plan to run evaluations in implemented systems, exploring performance in terms of task completion and believable human behavior.

Acknowledgments

This work has been sponsored by the U.S. Army Research, Development, and Engineering Command (RDECOM). Statements and opinions expressed do not necessarily reflect the position or the policy of the United States Government, and no official endorsement should be inferred.

The authors would like to thank Kevin Knight and the anonymous reviewers for feedback about the evaluation.

References

Dan Bohus and Alexander Rudnicky. 2005a. Error handling in the RavenClaw dialog management architecture. In *Proceedings of HLT-EMNLP-2005*.

Dan Bohus and Alexander Rudnicky. 2005b. Sorry, I didn't catch that! - an investigation of non-understanding errors and recovery strategies. In *Proceedings of SIGdial-2005*. Lisbon, Portugal.

Harry Bunt, Roser Morante, and Simon Keizer. 2007. An empirically based computational model of grounding in dialogue. In *Proceedings of the 8th SIGdial Workshop on Discourse and Dialogue*.

Herbert H. Clark and Susan E. Brennan. 1991. Grounding in communication. In *Perspectives on Socially Shared Cognition*, pages 127–149. APA Books.

Herbert H Clark and Edward F Schaefer. 1989. Contributing to discourse. *Cognitive Science*, 13:259–294.

Diane Litman, Julia Hirschberg, and Marc Swerts. 2006. Characterizing and predicting corrections in spoken dialogue systems. *Computational linguistics*, pages 417–438.

Tim Paek and Eric Horvitz. 2000a. Conversation as action under uncertainty. In *Proceedings of the 16th Conference on Uncertainty in Artificial Intelligence (UAI)*, pages 455–464.

Tim Paek and Eric Horvitz. 2000b. Grounding criterion: Toward a formal theory of grounding. Technical report, Microsoft Research, April. Microsoft Technical Report, MSR-TR-2000-40.

Tim Paek. 2003. Toward a taxonomy of communication errors. In *Proceedings of the ISCA Tutorial and Research Workshop on Error Handling in Spoken Dialogue Systems*, pages 53–58, August 28-31. Chateau d'Oex, Vaud, Switzerland.

Antonio Roque, Anton Leuski, Vivek Rangarajan, Susan Robinson, Ashish Vaswani, Shri Narayanan, and David Traum. 2006. Radiobot-CFF: A spoken dialogue system for military training. In *9th International Conference on Spoken Language Processing (Interspeech 2006 - ICSLP)*, September.

Gabriel Skantze. 2005. Galatea: a discourse modeller supporting concept-level error handling in spoken dialogue systems. In *Proceedings of SigDial*, pages 178–189). Lisbon, Portugal.

Marc Swerts, Diane Litman, and Julia Hirschberg. 2000. Corrections in spoken dialogue systems. In *Proceedings of the 6th International Conference of Spoken Language Processing (ICSLP-2000)*, October.

Will Thompson and Darren Gergle. 2008. Modeling situated conversational agents as partially observable markov decision processes. In *Proceedings of Intelligent User Interfaces (IUI)*.

David Traum and Jeff Rickel. 2002. Embodied agents for multi-party dialogue in immersive virtual world. In *Proceedings of the First International Joint Conference on Autonomous Agents and Multi-agent Systems (AAMAS 2002)*, pages 766–773, July.

David R. Traum. 1994. *A Computational Theory of Grounding in Natural Language Conversation*. Ph.D. thesis, University of Rochester.

Appendix

Line	ID	Utterance	Semantic Interpretation	Evidence: Standalone	Evidence: Additional
1	G91	fire for effect over	WO-MOF: fire for effect	Submit	
2	S19	fire for effect out	WO-MOF: fire for effect	Repeat Back	
3		Silence: 0.7 seconds			
4	G91	ah roger	ROGER	Acknowledge	
		grid four five four two ah three six three eight	TL-GR: 45423638	Submit	Move On
5		Silence: 2.3 seconds			
6	S19	grid four five four two three six three eight out	TL-GR: 45423638	Repeat Back	
7		Silence: 0.7 seconds			
8	G91	ah roger	ROGER	Acknowledge	
		b r d m	TD-TYPE: b r d m	Submit	Move On
		in the open over	TD-DESC: in the open	Submit	
9		Silence: 1.3 seconds			
10	S19	b r d m	TD-TYPE: b r d m	Repeat Back	
		in the open out	TD-DESC: in the open	Repeat Back	
11		Silence: 9.9 seconds		Lack of Response	

Comments:

This dialogue is between G91 as a Forward Observer identifying a target, and S19 as a Fire Direction Center who will send the artillery fire when given the appropriate information.

In line 1, G19's utterance is interpreted as a Warning Order - Method of Fire (WO-MOF), describing the kind of artillery fire requested, whose value is "fire for effect." This is the first mention of a WO-MOF for this particular CFF, so it is identified as a Submit type of evidence related to a new CGU, which now has an Accessible degree of groundedness.

In line 2, a WO-MOF is again given. The WO-MOF is identified as referring to the CGU introduced in line 1, and a Repeat Back type of evidence is added to that CGU's evidence history, which gives it an Agreed-Content degree of groundedness.

In line 3 there follows a silence that is not long enough to be a Lack of Response.

In line 4, G91 provides an Acknowledge type of evidence, and Moves On to the next task item: identifying the Target Location - Grid (TL-GR) of the CFF. The Acknowledge and Move On, referring to the CGU created in line 1, raise that CGU's degree of groundedness to its grounding criterion of Agreed-Content+, at which point it becomes grounded. At the same time, the introduction of the TL-GR information creates a new CGU, whose degree is Accessible.

In line 6 the TL-GR CGU is Repeated Back, thereby raising its degree of groundedness to Agreed-Content.

In line 8 an Acknowledge is provided and a set of information related to the Target Description (TD-) is given, providing a Move On, thereby grounding the TL-GR CGU. So by line 8, two CGUs (WO-MOF and TL-GR) have been added to the common ground, and two more CGUs (TD-TYPE and TD-DESC) have Accessible degrees and are in the process of being grounded.

In line 10 the TD CGUs are Repeated Back, raising their degree of groundedness to Agreed-Content.

In line 11 the Lack of Response raises the TD CGUs to Agreed-Content+ thereby grounding them. At this point there is enough information in the common ground for S19 to send the artillery fire.

Line	ID	Utterance	Semantic Interpretation	Evidence: Standalone	Evidence: Additional
12	S19	message to observer kilo	MTO-BAT: kilo	Submit	Move On
		two rounds	MTO-NUM: two	Submit	
		target number alpha bravo zero zero one over	TN: AB001	Submit	
13		Silence: 3.1 seconds			
14	G91	a roger mike tango alpha ah alpha	ROGER	Acknowledge	
		target number alpha bravo zero zero zero one	TN: AB0001	Repeat Back	
		a kilo	MTO-BAT: kilo	Repeat Back	
		two rounds out	MTO-NUM: two	Repeat Back	
11		Silence: 11.4 seconds		Lack of Response	
16	S19	shot	SHOT	Submit	
		rounds complete over	RC	Submit	
17		Silence: 0.8 seconds			
18	G91	shot	SHOT	Repeat Back	
		rounds complete out	RC	Repeat Back	
19	S19	splash over	SPLASH	Submit	
20		Silence: 1.5 seconds			
21	G91	splash out	SPLASH	Repeat Back	
22		Silence: 30.4 seconds		Lack of Response	
...					
23	G91	ah end of mission a target number alpha bravo zero zero one	TN: AB001	Submit	
		one	EOM-NUM: one	Submit	
		b r d m	EOM-TYPE: b r d m	Submit	
		destroyed over	EOM-BDA: destroyed	Submit	
24	S19	end of mission b r d des m d correction b r d m	EOM-TYPE: b r d m	Repeat Back	
		destroyed out	EOM-BDA: destroyed	Repeat Back	

Comments:

In line 12, S19 provides information about the artillery fire that is going to be sent. This includes the battery that will be firing (MTO-BAT), the number of rounds to be fired (MTO-NUM) and the target number that will be used to refer to this particular fire mission from that point on (TN).

In line 14, G91 Repeats Back the information presented in line 12 along with an Acknowledge.

In line 16, S19 notifies that the mission has been fired; in line 18 this is confirmed. Likewese, in line 19 S19 notifies that the mission is about the land; in line 21 this is confirmed.

Between lines 22 and 23 several turns have been removed for space reasons. These turns were related to an adjustment of the artillery fire: after the initial bombardment, the Forward Observer requested that the same artillery be fired 100 meters to the left of the original bombardment. This was confirmed and delivered.

In line 23, G91 sends a description of the amount of damage suffered by the target: the number of enemy affected (EOM-NUM), the type of enemy (EOM-TYPE) and the extent of the damage (EOM-BDA). These are Repeated Back by S19, thereby ending the CFF. Note that S19 does not Repeat Back the EOM-NUM. In this particular instance the number of enemies is implied by the EOM-TYPE being singular, but throughout the corpus EOMs are seen to have a low grounding criteria.

Rapidly Deploying Grammar-Based Speech Applications with Active Learning and Back-off Grammars

Tim Paek[1], Sudeep Gandhe[2], David Maxwel Chickering[1]
[1] Microsoft Research, One Microsoft Way, Redmond, WA 98052
[2] USC Institute for Creative Technologies, 13274 Fiji Way, Marina del Rey, CA 90292
{timpaek|dmax}@microsoft.com, gandhe@usc.edu

Abstract

Grammar-based approaches to spoken language understanding are utilized to a great extent in industry, particularly when developers are confronted with data sparsity. In order to ensure wide grammar coverage, developers typically modify their grammars in an iterative process of deploying the application, collecting and transcribing user utterances, and adjusting the grammar. In this paper, we explore enhancing this iterative process by leveraging active learning with back-off grammars. Because the back-off grammars expand coverage of user utterances, developers have a safety net for deploying applications earlier. Furthermore, the statistics related to the back-off can be used for active learning, thus reducing the effort and cost of data transcription. In experiments conducted on a commercially deployed application, the approach achieved levels of semantic accuracy comparable to transcribing all failed utterances with 87% less transcriptions.

1 Introduction

Although research in spoken language understanding is typically pursued from a statistical perspective, grammar-based approaches are utilized to a great extent in industry (Knight et al., 2001). Speech recognition grammars are often manually authored and iteratively modified as follows: Typically, context-free grammars (CFG) are written in a format such as Speech Recognition Grammar Specification (SRGS) (W3C, 2004) and deployed. Once user utterances are collected and transcribed, the grammars are then adjusted to improve their coverage. This process continues until minimal OOG utterances are observed. In this paper, we explore enhancing this iterative process of grammar modification by combining back-off grammars, which expand coverage of user utterances, with active learning, which reduces "the number of training examples to be labeled by automatically processing unlabeled examples, and then selecting the most informative ones with respect to a specified cost function for a human to label" (Hakkani-Tur et al., 2002). This paper comprises three sections. In Section 2, we describe our overall approach to rapid application development (RAD). In Section 3, we explain how data transcription can be reduced by leveraging active learning based on statistics related to the usage of back-off grammars. Finally, in Section 4, we evaluate the active learning approach with simulation experiments conducted on data collected from a commercial grammar-based speech application.

2 RAD Approach & Related Work

Working under the assumption that developers in industry will continue to use CFGs for rapid application development, our approach to grammar modification is as follows:

1. Create a CFG (either manually or automatically).
   1.1 Generate a back-off grammar from the CFG.
2. Deploy the application.
   2.1 Use the back-off grammar for OOG utterances.
3. Gather data from users.
4. Selectively transcribe data by using statistics related to the back-off for active learning; i.e., transcribe only those utterances that satisfy the active learning criterion.
5. Modify CFG either manually or automatically and go to step 1.1.

To begin with, developers start with a CFG in Step 1. If they had access to a grammatical platform

[2] Second author was partly sponsored by the U.S. Army Research, Development, and Engineering Command (RDECOM). Statements and opinions expressed do not necessarily reflect the position or the policy of the U.S. Government, and no official endorsement should be inferred.

Proceedings of the 9th SIGdial Workshop on Discourse and Dialogue, pages 64–67,
Columbus, June 2008.

such as Regulus (Rayner et al., 2006), they could in principle construct a CFG automatically for any new domain, though most developers will probably manually author the grammar. Two steps are added to the typical iterative process. In Step 1.1, we generate a back-off grammar from the CFG. One way to accomplish this is by constructing a back-off CFG using filler models (Paek et al., 2007), which when applied to the same command-and-control task in Section 4 can result in a 35% relative reduction in semantic error rate for OOG utterances. However, the back-off grammar could also be a SLM trained on artificial data created from the CFG (Galescu et al., 1998). Whatever back-off mechanism is employed, its coverage should be wider than the original CFG so that utterances that fail to be recognized by the CFG, or fall below an acceptable confidence threshold, can be handled by the back-off in a second or simultaneous pass. That is the gist of Step 2.1, the second additional step. It is not only important to generate a back-off grammar, but it must be utilized for handling possible OOG utterances.

Our approach attempts to reduce the usual cost associated with grammar modification after the application has been deployed and data collected in Step 4. The idea is simple: Exploit the fast and accurate CFG recognition of in-grammar (ING) utterances by making OOG utterances handled by the back-off grammar ING. In other words, expand CFG coverage to include whatever gets handled by the back-off grammar. This idea is very complementary with a two-pass recognition approach where the goal is to get utterances correctly recognized by a CFG on the first pass so as to minimize computational expenses (Paek et al., 2007).

All of this can be accomplished with reduced transcription effort by keeping track of and leveraging back-off statistics for active learning. If the back-off is a CFG, we keep track of statistics related to which CFG rules were utilized the most, whether they allowed the task to be successfully completed, etc. If the back-off is a SLM, we keep track of similar statistics related to the semantic alignment and mapping in spoken language understanding. Given an active learning criterion, these statistics can be used to selectively transcribe utterances which can then be used to modify the CFG in Step 5 so that OOG utterances become ING. Section 3 covers this in more detail.

Finally, in Step 5, the CFG grammar is modified using the selectively transcribed utterances. Although developers will probably want to do this manually, it is possible to automate much of this step by making grammar changes with minimal edit distance or Levenshtein distance.

Leveraging a wider coverage back-off grammar is of course not new. For grammar-based applications, several researchers have investigated using a CFG along with a back-off grammar either simultaneously via a domain-trained SLM (Gorrell et a1., 2002), or in two-pass recognition using either an SLM trained on CFG data (Gorrell, 2003) or a dictation n-gram (Dusan & Flanagan, 2002). To our knowledge however, no prior research has considered leveraging statistics related to the back-off grammar for active learning, especially as part of a RAD approach.

3 Active Learning

Our overall approach utilizes back-off grammars to provide developers with a safety net for deploying applications earlier, and active learning to reduce transcription effort and cost. We now elaborate on active learning, demonstrate the concept with respect to a CFG back-off.

Active learning aims at reducing transcription of training examples by selecting utterances that are most likely to be informative according to a specified cost function (Hakkani-Tur et al., 2002). In the speech community, active learning has been successfully applied to reducing the transcription effort for ASR (Hakkani-Tur et al., 2002), SLU (Tur et al., 2003b), as well as finding labeling errors (Tur et al., 2003). In our case, the examples are user utterances that need to be transcribed, and the learning involves modifying a CFG to achieve wider coverage of user expressions. Instead of passively transcribing everything and modifying the CFG as such, the grammar can "actively" participate in which utterances are transcribed.

The usual procedure for selecting utterances for grammar modification is to transcribe at least all failed utterances, such as those that fall below a rejection threshold. By leveraging a back-off grammar, developers have more information with which to select utterances for transcription. For a CFG back-off, how frequently a back-off rule fired can serve as an active learning criterion because that is where OOG utterances are handled. Given this active learning criterion, the algorithm would proceed as follows (where i denotes iteration, S_t denotes the set of transcribed utterances, and S_u denotes the set of all utterances):

[1] Modify CFG_i using S_t and generate corresponding back-off_i from the CFG_i.
[2] Recognize utterances in set S_u using CFG_i + back-off_i.
[3] Compute statistics on what back-off rules fired when and how frequently.
[4] Select the k utterances that were handled by the most frequently occurring back-off rule and transcribe them. Call the new transcribed set as S_i.
[5] $S_t = S_t \cup S_i; S_u = S_u - S_i$
[6] Stop when CFG_i achieves a desired level of semantic accuracy, or alternatively when back-off rules only handle a desired percentage of S_u, otherwise go to Step 1.

Note that the set S_u grows with each iteration and follows as a result of deploying an application with a CFG_i + back-off_i. Step [1] corresponds to Step 5, 1.1, and 2.1 of our approach. Steps [2-4] above constitute the active learning criterion and can be adjusted depending on what developers want to optimize. This algorithm currently assumes that runtime efficiency is the main objective (e.g., on a mobile device); hence, it is critical to move utterances recognized in the second pass to the first pass. If developers are more interested in learning new semantics, in Step [4] above they could transcribe utterances that failed in the back-off. With an active learning criterion in place, Step [6] provides a stopping criterion. This too can be adjusted, and may even target budgetary objectives.

4 Evaluation

For evaluation, we used utterances collected from 204 users of Microsoft *Voice Command*, a grammar-based command-and-control (C&C) application for high-end mobile devices (see Paek et al., 2007 for details). We partitioned 5061 transcribed utterances into five sets, one of which was used exclusively for testing. The remaining four were used for iterative CFG modification. For the first iteration, we started with a CFG which was a degraded version of the grammar currently shipped with the *Voice Command* product. It was obtained by using the mode, or the most frequent user utterance, for each CFG rule. We compared two approaches: *CFG_Full*, where each iterative CFG was modified using the full set of transcribed utterances that resulted in a *failure state* (i.e., when a false recognition event occurred or the phrase confidence score fell below 45%, which was set by a proprietary tuning procedure for optimizing word-error rate), and *CFG_Active*, where each iterative CFG was modified using only those transcribed utterances corresponding to the most frequently occurring CFG back-off rules. For both *CFG_Full* and *CFG_Active*, CFG_i was modified using the same set of heuristics akin to minimal edit distance. In order to assess the value of using the back-off grammar as a safety net, we also compared *CFG_Full+Back-off*, where a derived CFG back-off was utilized whenever a failure state occurred with *CFG_Full*, and *CFG_Active+Back-off*, where again a CFG back-off was utilized, this time with the back-off derived from the CFG trained on selective utterances.

As our metric, we evaluated semantic accuracy since that is what matters most in C&C settings. Furthermore, because recognition of part of an utterance can increase the odds of ultimately achieving task completion (Paek et al., 2007), we carried out separate evaluations for the functional constituents of a C&C utterance (i.e., keyword and slot) as well as the complete phrase (keyword + slot). We computed accuracy as follows: For any single utterance, the recognizer can either accept or reject it. If it is accepted, then the semantics of the utterance can either be correct (i.e., it matches what the user intended) or incorrect, hence:

$$accuracy = CA / (CA + IA + R) \quad (1)$$

where CA denotes accepted commands that are correct, IA denotes accepted commands that are incorrect, and R denotes the number of rejections.

Table 2 displays semantic accuracies for both *CFG_Full* and *CFG_Active*. Standard errors about the mean were computed using the jacknife procedure with 10 re-samples. Notice that both *CFG_Full* and *CFG_Active* initially have the same accuracy levels because they start off with the same degraded CFG. The highest accuracies obtained almost always occurred in the second iteration after modifying the CFG with the first batch of transcriptions. Thereafter, all accuracies seem to decrease. In order to understand why this would be case, we computed the coverage of the ith CFG on the holdout set. This is reported in the 'OOG%' column. Comparing *CFG_Full* to *CFG_Active* on

Approach	*i*	Utterances Transcribed	Keyword Accuracy	Slot Accuracy	Keyword + Slot Accuracy	Processing Time (ms)	OOG%
CFG_Full	1	0	50.25% (0.13%)	46.84% (0.22%)	46.84% (0.22%)	387 (3.9005)	61.10%
	2	590	**66.20% (0.12%)**	**71.02% (0.23%)**	**70.59% (0.23%)**	401 (4.0586)	31.92%
	3	1000	65.80% (0.15%)	69.72% (0.19%)	69.06% (0.19%)	422 (4.5804)	31.30%
	4	1393	66.10% (0.13%)	67.54% (0.22%)	66.88% (0.21%)	433 (4.7061)	30.95%
CFG_Full + Back-off	1	0	66.70% (0.10%)	66.23% (0.22%)	66.01% (0.22%)	631 (11.1320)	61.10%
	2	590	**73.32% (0.11%)**	**72.11% (0.22%)**	**71.68% (0.23%)**	562 (10.4696)	31.92%
	3	1000	72.52% (0.12%)	72.11% (0.21%)	71.46% (0.22%)	584 (10.4985)	31.30%
	4	1393	73.02% (0.10%)	71.02% (0.23%)	70.37% (0.23%)	592 (10.6805)	30.95%
CFG_Active	1	0	50.25% (0.13%)	46.84% (0.22%)	46.84% (0.22%)	387 (3.9005)	61.10%
	2	87	64.09% (0.13%)	**74.29% (0.21%)**	**74.07% (0.22%)**	395 (4.1469)	42.09%
	3	138	**64.29% (0.15%)**	70.15% (0.22%)	69.50% (0.24%)	409 (4.3375)	38.02%
	4	193	64.09% (0.15%)	69.72% (0.23%)	69.06% (0.24%)	413 (4.4015)	37.93%
CFG_Active + Back-off	1	0	66.70% (0.10%)	66.23% (0.22%)	66.01% (0.22%)	631 (11.1320)	61.10%
	2	87	**72.52% (0.10%)**	**76.91% (0.19%)**	**76.47% (0.21%)**	568 (10.3494)	42.09%
	3	138	71.72% (0.14%)	71.90% (0.24%)	71.24% (0.27%)	581 (10.6330)	38.02%
	4	193	71.21% (0.15%)	71.90% (0.25%)	71.24% (0.26%)	580 (10.5266)	37.93%

Table 2. Semantic accuracies for partial (keyword or slot) and full phrase recognitions (keyword + slot) using a CFG trained on either "Full" or "Active" transcriptions (i.e., selective transcriptions based on active learning). Parentheses indicate standard error about the mean. The 'i' column represents iteration. The 'Utterances Transcribed' column is cumulative. The 'OOG%' column represents coverage of the *ith* CFG on the hold-out set. Rows containing "Back-off" evaluate 2-pass recognition using both the CFG and a derived CFG back-off.

keyword + slot accuracy, *CFG_Full* decreases in accuracy after the second iteration as does *CFG_Active*. However, the OOG% of *CFG_Full* is much lower than *CFG_Active*. In fact, it seems to level off after the second iteration, suggesting that perhaps the decrease in accuracies reflects the increase in grammar perplexity; that is, as the grammar covers more of the utterances, it has more hypotheses to consider, and as a result, performs slightly worse. Interestingly, after the last iteration, *CFG_Active* for keyword + slot and slot accuracies was slightly higher (69.06%) than *CFG_Full* (66.88%) (p = .05). Furthermore, this was done with 193 utterances as opposed to 1393, or 87% less transcriptions. For keyword accuracy, *CFG_Active* (64.09%) was slightly worse than *CFG_Full* (66.10%) ($p < .05$).

With respect to the value of having a back-off grammar as a safety net, we found that both *CFG_Full* and *CFG_Active* achieved much higher accuracies with the back-off for keyword, slot, and keyword + slot accuracies. Notice also that the differences between *CFG_Full* and *CFG_Active* after the last iteration were much closer to each other than without the back-off, suggesting applications should always be deployed with a back-off.

5 Conclusion

In this paper, we explored enhancing the usual iterative process of grammar modification by leveraging active learning with back-off grammars. Because the back-off grammars expand coverage of user utterances to handle OOG occurrences, developers have a safety net for deploying applications earlier. Furthermore, because statistics related to the back-off can be used for active learning, developers can reduce the effort and cost of data transcription. In our simulation experiments, leveraging active learning achieved levels of semantic accuracy comparable to transcribing all failed utterances with 87% less transcriptions.

References

S. Dusan & J. Flanagan. 2002. Adaptive dialog based upon multimodal language acquisition. In *Proc. of ICMI.*

L. Galescu, E. Ringger, & J. Allen. 1998. Rapid language model development for new task domains. In *Proc. of LREC.*

G. Gorrell, I. Lewin, & M. Rayner. 2002. Adding intelligent help to mixed initiative spoken dialogue systems. In *Proc. of ICSLP.*

G.. Gorrell. 2003. Using statistical language modeling to identify new vocabulary in a grammar-based speech recognition system. In *Proc. of Eurospeech.*

D. Hakkani-Tur, G. Riccardi & A. Gorin. 2002. Active learning for automatic speech recognition. In *Proc. of ICASSP.*

S. Knight, G. Gorrell, M. Rayner, D. Milward, R. Koel-ing, & I. Lewin. 2001. Comparing grammar-based and robust approaches to speech understanding: A case study. In *Proc. of Eurospeech.*

T. Paek, S. Gandhe, D. Chickering & Y. Ju. 2007. Handling out-of-grammar commands in mobile speech interaction using back-off filler models. In *Proc. of ACL Workshop on Grammar-Based Approaches to Spoken Language Processing (SPEECHGRAM).*

M. Rayner, B.A. Hockey, & P. Bouillon. 2006. *Putting Linguistics into Speech Recognition: The Regulus Grammar Compiler*. CSLI.

G. Tur, M. Rahim & D. Hakkani-Tur. 2003. Active labeling for spoken language understanding. In *Proc. of Eurospeech.*

G. Tur, R. Schapire, & D. Hakkani-Tur. 2003b. Active learning for spoken language understanding. In *Proc. of ICASSP.*

W3C. 2004. Speech Recognition Grammar Specification Version 1.0. http://www.w3.org/TR/speech-grammar

Persistent Information State in a Data-Centric Architecture*

Sebastian Varges, Giuseppe Riccardi, Silvia Quarteroni
Department of Information Engineering and Computer Science
University of Trento
38050 Povo di Trento, Italy
{varges|riccardi|silviaq}@disi.unitn.it

Abstract

We present the ADAMACH data centric dialog system, that allows to perform on- and off-line mining of dialog context, speech recognition results and other system-generated representations, both within and across dialogs. The architecture implements a "fat pipeline" for speech and language processing. We detail how the approach integrates domain knowledge and evolving empirical data, based on a user study in the University Helpdesk domain.

1 Introduction

In this paper, we argue that the ability to *store and query* large amounts of data is a key requirement for data-driven dialog systems, in which the data is generated by the spoken dialog system (SDS) components (spoken language understanding (SLU), dialog management (DM), natural language generation (NLG) etc.) and the world it is interacting with (news streams, ambient sensors etc.). We describe an SDS that is built around a database management system (DBMS), uses the web service paradigm (in contrast to the architecture described in (Varges and Riccardi, 2007)), and employs a Voice XML (VXML) server for interfacing with Automatic Speech Recognition (ASR) and Text-to-Speech (TTS) components. We would like to emphasize upfront that this does *not* mean that we follow a VXML dialog model.

*This work was partially supported by the European Commission Marie Curie Excellence Grant for the ADAMACH project (contract No. 022593) and by LUNA STREP project (contract no33549).

The data centric architecture we adopt has several advantages: first, the database concentrates heterogeneous types of information allowing to uniformly query the evolving data at any time, e.g. by performing queries across various types of information. Second, the architecture facilitates dialog evaluation, data mining and online learning because data is available for querying as soon as it has been stored. Third, multiple systems/applications can be made available on the same infrastructure due to a clean separation of its processing modules (SLU, DM, NLG etc.) from data storage and persistency (DBMS), and monitoring/analysis/visualization and annotation tools. Fourth, there is no need for separate 'logging' mechanisms: the state of the SDS is contained in the database, and is therefore persistently available for analysis after the dialog ends.

As opposed to the presented architecture, the Open Agent Architecture (OAA) (Martin et al., 1999) and DARPA Communicator (Seneff et al., 1998) treat data as peripheral: they were not specifically designed to handle large volumes of data, and data is not automatically persistent. In contrast to the CSLI-DM (Mirkovic and Cavedon, 2005), and TrindiKit (Larsson and Traum, 2000), but similar to Communicator, the ADAMACH architecture is server-based, thus enabling continuous operation.

To prove our concept, we test it on a University helpdesk application (section 4).

2 Dialog System Architecture

Figure 1 shows our vision for the architecture of the ADAMACH system. We implemented and evaluated the speech modality based core of this system

Proceedings of the 9th SIGdial Workshop on Discourse and Dialogue, pages 68–71,
Columbus, June 2008.

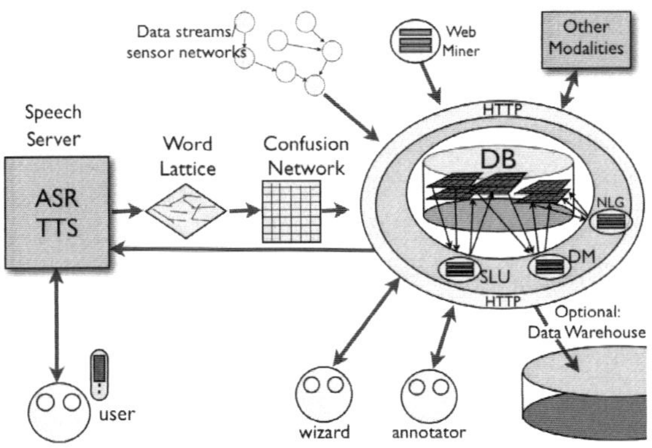

Figure 1: Architecture vision

(figure 2). A typical interaction is initiated by a phone call that arrives at an telephony server which routes it to a VXML platform. A VXML page is continuously rewritten by the dialog manager, containing the system utterance and other TTS parameters, and the ASR recognition parameters for the next user utterance. Thus, VXML is used as a low-level interface to the ASR and TTS engines, but *not* for representing dialog strategies. Once a user utterance is recognized, a web service request is issued to a dialog management server.

All communication between the above-mentioned components is stored in the DBMS: ASR recognition results, TTS parameters and ASR recognition parameters reside in separate tables. The dialog manager uses the basic tables as its communication protocol with ASR and TTS engines, and additionally stores its Information State (IS) in the database. This means that the IS is automatically *persistent*, and that dialog management becomes a function that maps ASR results and old IS to the TTS and ASR parameters and a new IS. The tables of the database are organized into turns, several of which belong to a call (dialog), thus resulting in a tree structure that is enforced by foreign key constraints in the relational database.

The VXML standard is based on the web infrastructure. In particular, a VXML platform can issue HTTP requests that can be served by a web server just like any (HTML) page. The VXML server only sees the generated VXML page, the 'return value' of the HTTP request. This allows us to organize the processing modules of the dialog system (SLU, DM, VXML generator) as web services that are invoked by the HTTP request. As a consequence, each system turn of a dialog is a separate, *stateless* request. The state of the dialog is stored in the database. Furthermore, by threading the VXML session ID through the processing loop (including the VXML pages generated on-the-fly) and distinguishing entries in the DB by sessions, the SDS is inherently parallelizable, just as a conventional web server can serve many users in parallel. Figure 2 shows how information is processed for each turn. The HTTP requests that invoke the processing modules pass on various IDs and parameters, but the actual data is stored in the DB and retrieved only if a processing module requires it. This effectively implements a 'fat pipeline': each speech, language and DM module has access to the database for rescoring and modeling (i.e. data within and across dialogs). At the implementation level, this balances a lightweight communication protocol downstream with data flowing laterally towards the database.

3 Dialog Management

Dialog management works in two stages: retrieving and preprocessing facts (tuples) taken from the database, and inferencing over those facts to generate a system response. We distinguish between the 'context model' of the first phase and the 'dialog move engine' (DME) of the second phase (Larsson and Traum, 2000).

The first stage entails retrieving from the persistent Information State the following information: all open questions for the current dialog from the database, any application information already provided by the user (including their grounding status), the ASR recognition results of last user turn, and confidence and other thresholds. The context model that is applied when retrieving the relevant dialog history from the database can be characterized as a 'linear default model': application parameters provided by the user, such as student ID, are overridden if the user provides a new value, for example to correct a previous misunderstanding. Task boundaries are detected and prevent an application parameter from carrying over directly to the new task.

The second stage employs an inference engine to determine the system action and response: SLU rules match the user utterance to open questions.

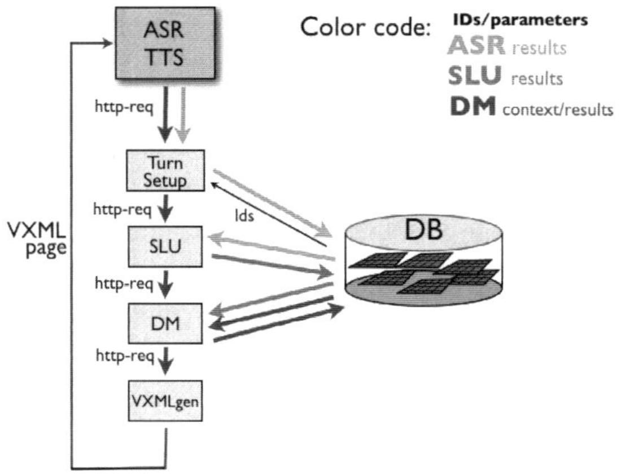

Figure 2: Turn-level information flow

This may result in the decision to verify the application parameter in question, and the action is verbalized by language generation rules. If the parameter is accepted, application dependent task rules determine the next parameter to be acquired, resulting in the generation of an appropriate request. For reasons of space, we cannot provide more details here.

4 Experiments

Our current application is a University helpdesk in Italian which students call to perform 5 tasks: receive information about exams (times, rooms ...), subscribe/cancel subscriptions to exams, obtain exam mark, or request to talk to an operator. Following experimentations, we annotated the dialogs and conducted performance statistics using the system's built-in annotation tool.

Two Italian mothertongues were in charge of manually annotating a total of 423 interactions. Each annotator independently annotated each dialog turn according to whether one of the five available tasks was being requested or completed in it. To compute inter-annotator agreement, 24 dialogs were processed by both annotators; the remaining ones were partitioned equally among them.

We computed agreement at both turn and dialog level. Turn level agreement is concerned with which tasks are requested and completed at a given dialog turn according to each annotator. An agreement matrix is compiled where rows and columns correspond to the five task types in our application. Cohen's κ (Cohen, 1960), computed over the turn matrix, gave a turn agreement of 0.72 resp. 0.77 for requests resp. completions, exceeding the recommended 0.7 threshold. While turn-level agreement refers to *which* tasks occurred and at what turn, dialog level agreement refers to *how many* task requests/completions occurred. Also at the dialog level, the κ statistic gave good results (0.71 for requests and 0.9 for completions).

General dialog statistics The average duration of the 423 annotated dialogs is 63.1 seconds, with an average of 7.43 turn (i.e. adjacency) pairs. 356 of the dialogs contained at least one task; the majority (338) contained exactly one, 17 dialogs contained 2 tasks, and one dialog contained 3. In the remaining 67 dialogs, no tasks were detected: from the audio files, it seems that these generally happened by accident or in noisy environments, hence noinput/hangup events occurred shortly after the initial system prompt.

Furthermore, relative frequencies of task requests and task completions are reported in Table 1. In total, according to the two annotators, there were 375 task requests and 234 task completions. Among the requested tasks, the vast majority was composed by "Get exam mark" –a striking 96%– while "Exam withdrawal" never occurred and the three others were barely performed. Indeed, it seems that students preferred to use the system to carry on "informative" tasks such as obtaining exam marks and general information rather than "active" tasks such as exam subscription and withdrawal.

Table 1: Task request and completion frequencies (%)

Task	**Request**	**Completion**
Get exam mark	96 (360)	96.6 (226)
Info on exam	1.9 (7)	1.7 (4)
Exam subscription	1.1 (4)	0.4 (1)
Exam withdrawal	0.0 (0)	0.0 (0)
Talk to operator	1.1 (4)	1.3 (3)
Total	100 (375)	100 (234)

Task and dialog success Based on the annotation of task requests and completions, we defined task success as a binary measure of whether the request of a given task type is eventually followed by a task completion of the same type. Table 2 reports the average success of each task type according to the annotators[1]. Our results show that the most frequently requested type, "Get exam mark", has a 64.64% success rate (it seems that failure was mostly due to the system's inability to recognize student IDs).

Table 2: Top: annotator (sr_M) and automatic (sr_A) task success rates. Mean $\pm$ binomial proportion confidence interval on the average task success (α= 95%) is reported. Bottom: mean annotator (dsr_M) and automatic (dsr_A) dialog success rates $\pm$ normal law c.i. (α= 95%).

Task	$sr_M(\%)$	$sr_A(\%)$
Get exam mark	64.64	77.97
Info on exam	57.14	71.43
Exam subscription	25	100
Exam withdrawal	-	-
Talk to operator	75	75
Average	64.17±4.96	78.06±4.28
Dialog	$dsr_M(\%)$	$dsr_A(\%)$
Average	64.47±4.95	88.31±9.2

In fact, while it is straightforward to obtain task success information using the manual annotation of dialogs, when the dialog system cannot rely on human judgments, unsupervised approaches must be defined for a rapid (on-line or off-line) evaluation. For this purpose, an automatic approximation of the "manual" task success estimation has been defined using a set of database queries associated to each task type. For instance, the task success query associated to "Info on exam" checks that two conditions are met in the current dialog: 1) it includes a turn where an action is requested the interpretation of which contains "information"; 2) it contains a turn where the concept `Exam_Name` is in focus.

Automatic task success rates have been computed on the same dialogs for which manual task success rates were available and are reported in Table 2, col. 2. The comparison shows that the automatic metric sr_A is more "optimistic" than the manual one sr_M. Indeed, automatic estimators rely on "punctual" indicators (such as the occurrence of confirmations of a given value) in the whole dialog, regardless of the task they appear in (this information is only available from human annotation) and also of the order with which such indicators appear in the dialog.

[1] As several task types occur seldom, we only report the confidence intervals on the means relating to the overall ("Average") task success, computed according to the normal law.

As a by-product of task success evaluation, we defined dialog success rate (dsr) as the average success rate of the tasks in a dialog: $dsr = \frac{\sum_{t_i \in T} sr(t_i)}{|T|}$, T being the set of requested tasks. Depending on whether sr_M or sr_A is used, we obtain two metrics, dsr_M resp. dsr_A.

Our dialog success results (last row of Table 2) are comparable to the task success ones; also, the difference between the automatic and manual estimators of dialog success is similar to their difference at the the task level. This is not surprising when considering that most of the dialogs contained only one task.

5 Conclusions

We have presented a data-centric Spoken Dialog System whose novel aspect is the storage and retrieval of dialog management state, ASR results and other information in a database. As a consequence, dialog management can be lightweight and operate on a turn-by-turn basis, and dialog system evaluation and logging are facilitated.

Acknowledgments

We would like to thank Pierluigi Roberti for helping with the speech platform and annotation tools, and LOQUENDO for providing the VXML platform.

References

J. Cohen. 1960. A coefficient of agreement for nominal scales. *Educational and Psychological Measurement*, 20:37–46.

S. Larsson and D. Traum. 2000. Information State and dialogue management in the TRINDI Dialogue Move Engine Toolkit. *Natural Language Engineering*, 6(3–4):323–340.

D. L. Martin, A. J. Cheyer, and D. B. Moran. 1999. The Open Agent Architecture: A framework for building distributed software systems. *Applied Artificial Intelligence: An International Journal*, 13(1-2):91–128.

D. Mirkovic and L. Cavedon. 2005. Practical Plug-and-Play Dialogue Management. In *Proceedings of PACLING*, Tokyo, Japan.

S. Seneff, E. Hurley, R. Lau, C. Pao, P. Schmid, and V. Zue. 1998. GALAXY-II: A reference architecture for conversational system development. In *Proc. of ICSLP 1998*, Sydney, Australia.

S. Varges and G. Riccardi. 2007. A data-centric architecture for data-driven spoken dialogue systems. In *Proceedings of ASRU*, Kyoto, Japan.

Speaking without knowing what to say… or when to end

Anna Hjalmarsson
Centre for Speech Technology
KTH
SE-10044, Stockholm, Sweden
annah@speech.kth.se

Abstract

Humans produce speech incrementally and on-line as the dialogue progresses using information from several different sources in parallel. A dialogue system that generates output in a stepwise manner and not in preplanned syntactically correct sentences needs to signal how new dialogue contributions relate to previous discourse. This paper describes a data collection which is the foundation for an effort towards more human-like language generation in DEAL, a spoken dialogue system developed at KTH. Two annotators labelled cue phrases in the corpus with high inter-annotator agreement (kappa coefficient 0.82).

1 Introduction

This paper describes a data collection with the goal of modelling more human-like language generation in DEAL, a spoken dialogue system developed at KTH. The DEAL objectives are to build a system which is fun, human-like, and engaging to talk to, and which gives second language learners of Swedish conversation training (as described in Hjalmarsson et al., 2007). The scene of DEAL is set at a flea market where a talking animated agent is the owner of a shop selling used objects. The student is given a mission: to buy items from the shop-keeper at the best possible price by bargaining. From a language learning perspective and to keep the students motivated, the agent's language is crucial. The agent needs to behave human-like in a way which allows the users to suspend some of their disbeliefs and talk to DEAL as if talking to another human being. In an experimental study (Hjalmarsson & Edlund, in press), where a spoken dialogue system with human behaviour was simulated, two different systems were compared: a replica of human behaviour and a constrained version with less variability. The version based on human behaviour was rated as more human-like, polite and intelligent.

1.1 Human language production

Humans produce speech incrementally and on-line as the dialogue progresses using information from several different sources in parallel (Brennan, 2000; Aist et al., 2006). We anticipate what the other person is about to say in advance and start planning our next move while this person is still speaking. When starting to speak, we typically do not have a complete plan of how to say something or even what to say. Yet, we manage to rapidly integrate information from different sources in parallel and simultaneously plan and realize new dialogue contributions. Pauses, corrections and repetitions are used to stepwise refine, alter and revise our plans as we speak (Clark & Wasow, 1998). These human behaviours bring valuable information that contains more than the literal meanings of the words (Arnold et al., 2003).

In order to generate output incrementally in DEAL we need extended knowledge on how to signal relations between different segments of speech. In this paper we report on a data collection of human-human dialogue aiming at extending the knowledge of human interaction and in particular to distinguish different types of cue phrases used in the DEAL domain.

Proceedings of the 9th SIGdial Workshop on Discourse and Dialogue, pages 72–75,
Columbus, June 2008.

2 The DEAL corpus collection

The dialogue data recorded was informal, human-human, face-to-face conversation. The task and the recording environment were set up to mimic the DEAL domain and role play.

2.1 Data collection

The data collection was made with 6 subjects (4 male and 2 female), 2 posing as shop keepers and 4 as potential buyers. Each customer interacted with the same shop-keeper twice, in two different scenarios. The shop-keepers and customers were instructed separately. The customers were given a mission: to buy items at a flea market at the best possible price from the shop-keeper. The task was to buy 3 objects for a specific purpose (e.g. to buy tools to repair a house). The customers were given a certain amount of toy money, however not enough to buy what they were instructed to buy without bargaining. The shop-keeper sat behind a desk with images of different objects pinned to the wall behind him. Some of the object had obvious flaws, for example a puzzle with a missing piece, to open up for interesting negotiation. None of the shop-keepers had any professional experience of bargaining, which was appropriate since we were more interested in capturing naïve conceptual metaphors of bargaining rather than real life price negotiation. Each dialogue was about 15 minutes long, so about 2 hours of speech were collected altogether. The shop-keepers used an average of 13.4 words per speaker turn while the buyers' turns were generally shorter, 8.5 words per turn (in this paper *turn* always refers to speaker turns). In total 16357 words were collected.

3 Annotation

All dialogues were first transcribed orthographically including non-lexical entities such as laughter and hawks. Filled pauses, repetitions, corrections and restarts were also labelled manually.

3.1 Cue phrases

Linguistic devices used to signal relations between different segments of speech are often referred to as *cue phrases*. Other frequently used terms are discourse markers, pragmatic markers or discourse particles. Typical cue phrases in English are: *oh, well, now, then, however, you know, I mean, because, and, but* and *or*. Much research within discourse analysis, communicative analysis and psycholinguistics has been concerned with these connectives and what kind of relations they hold (for an overview see Schourup, 1999). Our definition of cue phrases is broad and all types of linguistic entities that the speakers use to hold the dialogue together at different communicative levels are included. A rule of thumb is that cue phrases are words or chunks of words that have little lexical impact at the local speech segment level but serve significant pragmatic function. To give an exact definition of what cue phrases are is difficult, as these entities often are ambiguous. According to the definition used here, cue phrases can be a single word or larger units, occupy various positions, belong to different syntactic classes, and be realized with different prosodic contours.

The first dialogue was analyzed and used to decide which classes to use in the annotation scheme. Nine of the classes were a subset of the functional classification scheme of discourse markers presented in Lindström (2008). A tenth class, *referring*, was added. There were 3 different classes for *connectives*, 3 classes for *responsives* and 4 remaining classes. The classes are presented in Table 1; the first row contains an example in its context from data, the word(s) in bold are the labelled cue phrase, and the second row presents frequently used instances of that class.

Additive Connectives (CAD)
och grönt är ju fint [**and** green is nice]
och, alltså, så [and, therefore, so]
Contrastive Connectives (CC)
men den är ganska antik [**but** it is pretty antique]
men, fast, alltså [but, although, thus]
Alternative Connectives (CAL)
som jag kan titta på **istället** [which I can look at **instead**]
eller, istället [or, instead]
Responsive (R)
ja jag tycker ju det [yeah I actually think so]
ja, mm, jaha, ok [yes, mm, yeah, ok]
Responsive New Information (RNI)
jaha har du några sådana [**right** do you have any of those]
jaha, ok, ja, mm [right, ok, yes, mm]

Responsive Disprefrence (RD)
ja men det är klart dom funkar [**yeah** but of course they work]
ja, mm, jo [yes, mm, sure]
Response Eliciting (RE)
vad ska du ha för den **då** [how much do you want for that one **then**]
då, eller hur [then, right]
Repair Correction (RC)
nej nu sa jag fel [**no** now I said wrong]
nej, jag menade [no, I meant]
Modifying (MOD)
ja jag tycker **ju** det [yeah I **actually** think so]
ju, liksom, jag tycker ju det [of course, so to speak, I like]
Referring (REF)
fyra hundra kronor **sa vi** [four hundred crowns **we said**]
sa vi, sa vi inte det [we said, wasn't that what we said]

Table 1: The DEAL annotation scheme

The labelling of cue phrases included a two-fold task, both to decide if a word was a cue phrase or not – a binary task – but also to classify which functional class it belongs to according to the annotation scheme. The annotators could both see the transcriptions and listen to the recordings while labelling. 81% of the speaker turns contained at least one cue phrase and 21% of all words were labelled as cue phrases. Table 2 presents the distribution of cue phrases over the different classes.

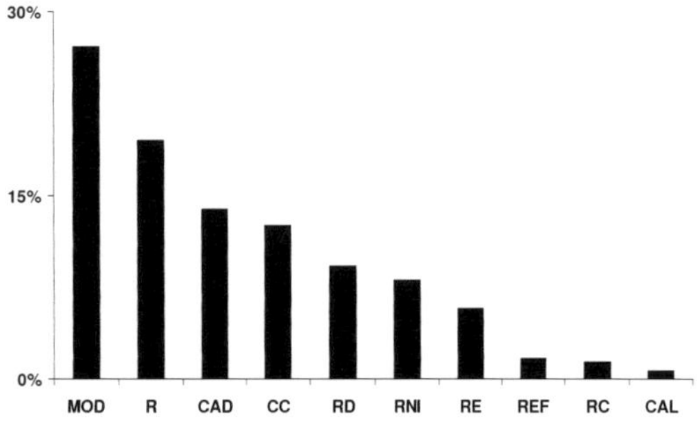

Table 2: Cue phrase distribution over the different classes

Two of the eight dialogues were annotated by two different annotators. A kappa coefficient was calculated on word level. The kappa coefficient for the binary task, to classify if a word was a cue phrase or not, was 0.87 (p=0.05). The kappa coefficient for the classification task was 0.82 (p=0.05). Three of the classes, referring, connective alternative and repair correction, had very few instances. The agreement in percentage distributed over the different classes is presented in Table 3.

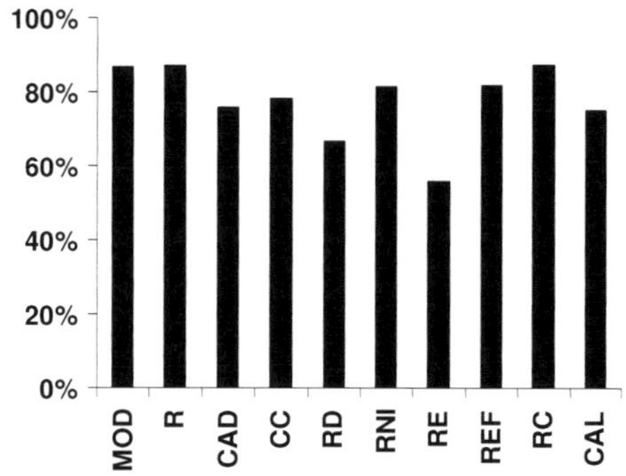

Table 3: % agreement for the different classes

4 Data analysis

To separate cue phrases from other lexical entities and determine what they signal is a complex task. The DEAL corpus is rich in disfluencies and cue phrases; 86% of the speaker turns contained at least one cue phrase or disfluency. The annotators had access to the context and were allowed to listen to the recordings while labelling. The *responsives* were generally single words or non lexical units (e.g. "mm") and appeared in similar dialogue contexts (i.e. as responses to assertions). The classification is likely based on their prosodic realization. Acoustic analysis is needed in order to see if and how they differ in prosodic contour. In Hirschberg & Litman (1993) prosodic analysis is used to distinguish between discourse and sentential use of cue phrases. Table 4 presents how the different cue phrases were distributed over speaker turns, at initial, middle or end position.

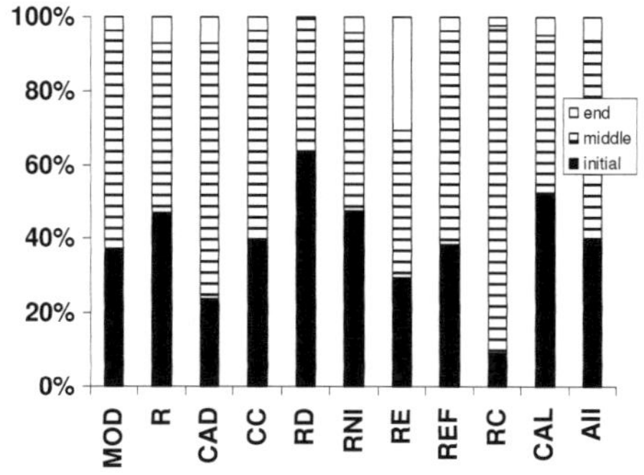

Table 4: Turn position distribution

5 Generation in DEAL

The collected and labelled data is a valuable resource of information for what cue phrases signal in the DEAL domain as well as how they are lexically and prosodically realized. To keep the response times constant and without unnaturally long delays, DEAL needs to be capable of grabbing the turn, hold it while the system is producing the rest of the message, and release it after completion. DEAL is implemented using components from the Higgins project (Skantze et al., 2006) an off-the-shelf ASR system and a GUI with an embodied conversational agent (ECA) (Beskow, 2003). A current research challenge is to redesign the modules and architecture for incremental processing, to allow generation of conversational speech. Deep generation in DEAL – the decision of what to say on an abstract semantic level – is distributed over three different modules; (1) the action manger, (2) the agent manager and the (3) communicative manager. The action manger is responsible for actions related to user input and previous discourse[1]. The agent manager represents the agents' personal motivations and personality. DEAL uses mixed initiative and the agent manager takes initiatives. It may for example try to promote certain objects or suggest prices of objects in focus. It also generates emotional facial gestures related to events in the dialogue. The communicative manager generates responses on a communicative level based on shallow analysis of input. For example, it initiates requests for confirmations if speech recognition confidence scores are low. This module initiates utterances when the user yields the floor, regardless of whether the system has a complete plan of what to say or not. Using similar strategies as the subjects recorded here, the dialogue system can grab the turn and start to say something before having completed processing input. Many cue phrases were used in combination, signalling function on different discourse levels; first a simple responsive, saying that the previous message was perceived, and then some type of connective to signal how the new contribution relates.

6 Final remarks

Since DEAL focuses on generation in role play, we are less interested in the ambiguous cue phrases and more concerned with the instances where the annotators agreed. The DEAL users are second language learners with poor knowledge in Swedish, and it may even be advisable that the agent's behaviour is exaggerated.

[1] For more details on the discourse modeller see Skantze et al, 2006.

Acknowledgments

This research was carried out at Centre for Speech Technology, KTH. The research is also supported by the Swedish research council project #2007-6431, GENDIAL and the Graduate School for Language Technology (GSLT). Many thanks to Jenny Klarenfjord for help on data collection and annotation and thanks to Rolf Carlson, Preben Wik and Jens Edlund for valuable comments.

References

G. Aist, J. Allen, E. Campana, L. Galescu, C. A. Gómez Gallo, S. Stoness, M. Swift, and M. Tanenhaus. 2006. Software Architectures for Incremental Understanding of Human Speech. In *Proc. of Interspeech.*

J. Arnold, M. Fagano, and M. Tanenhaus. 2003. Disfluencies signal theee, um, new information. *Journal of Psycholinguistic Research*, 32, 25-36.

J. Beskow. 2003. Talking heads - Models and applications for multimodal speech synthesis. *Doctoral dissertation, KTH.*

S. Brennan. 2000. Processes that shape conversation and their implications for computational. In *Proc. of the 38th Annual Meeting of the ACL.*

H. Clark, and T. Wasow. 1998. Repeating words in spontaneous speech. *Cognitive Psychology*, 37(3), 201-242.

J. Hirschberg, and D. Litman. 1993. Empirical studies on the disambiguation of cue phrases. *Computational Linguistics*, 19(3), 501-530.

A. Hjalmarsson, and J. Edlund. In press. Human-likeness in utterance generation: effects of variability. To be published in *Proc. of the 4th IEEE Workshop on Perception and Interactive Technologies for Speech-Based Systems.* Kloster Irsee, Germany.

A. Hjalmarsson, P. Wik, and J. Brusk. 2007. Dealing with DEAL: a dialogue system for conversation training. In *Proc. of SigDial.* Antwerp, Belgium.

J. Lindström. 2008. Diskursmarkörer. In *Tur och ordning; introduktion till svensk samtalsgrammatik* (pp. 56-104). Norstedts Akademiska Förlag. Stockholm, Sweden.

L. Schourup. 1999. Discourse markers. *Lingua*, 107(3-4), 227-265.

G. Skantze, J. Edlund, and R. Carlson. 2006. Talking with Higgins: Research challenges in a spoken dialogue system. In *Perception and Interactive Technologies* (pp. 193-196). Berlin/Heidelberg: Springer.

Learning Contrastive Connectives in Sentence Realization Ranking

Crystal Nakatsu
Department of Linguistics
The Ohio State Univeristy
Columbus, OH, USA
cnakatsu@ling.osu.edu

Abstract

We look at the average frequency of contrastive connectives in the SPaRKy Restaurant Corpus with respect to realization ratings by human judges. We implement a discriminative n-gram ranker to model these ratings and analyze the resulting n-gram weights to determine if our ranker learns this distribution. Surprisingly, our ranker learns to avoid contrastive connectives. We look at possible explanations for this distribution, and recommend improvements to both the generator and ranker of the sentence plans/realizations.

1 Introduction

Contrastive discourse connectives are words or phrases such as *however* and *on the other hand*. They indicate a contrastive discourse relation between two units of discourse. While corpus-based studies on discourse connectives usually look at naturally occurring human-authored examples, in this study, we investigate the set of connectives used in the automatically generated SPaRKy Restaurant Corpus[1]. Specifically, we consider the relationship between connective usage and judges ratings, and investigate whether our n-gram ranker learns the preferred connective usage. Based on these findings and previous work on contrastive connectives, we present suggestions for modifying both the generator and the ranker in order to improve the generation of realizations containing contrastive connectives.

[1]We thank Marilyn Walker and her research team for making all of the MATCH system data available for our study, especially including the SPaRKy Restaurant Corpus.

2 Corpus Study

2.1 SPaRKy Restaurant Corpus

The SPaRKy Restaurant Corpus was generated by the MATCH Spoken Language Generator (Walker et al., 2007) which consists of a dialog manager, SPUR text planner (Walker et al., 2004), SPaRKy sentence planner (Walker et al., 2007), and RealPro surface realizer (Lavoie and Rambow, 1997).

The corpus contains realizations for 3 dialogue strategies:

- RECOMMEND (REC): recommend an entity from a set of entities
- COMPARE-2 (C2): compare 2 entities
- COMPARE-3 (C3): compare 3 or more entities

Each strategy contains 30 content plans from which either 16 or 20 sentence plans were generated by the SPaRKy sentence plan generator. 4 sentence plans were discarded due to duplication upon realization, totaling 1756 realizations in the corpus.[2]

A content plan consists of several assertions and the relations which hold between them. Content plans from the RECOMMEND strategy exclusively employ the Rhetorical Structure Theory (RST) (Mann and Thompson, 1987) relation JUSTIFY while those from COMPARE-2 use CONTRAST and ELABORATION. COMPARE-3 content plans consists mostly of CONTRAST and ELABORATION relations, though some use only JUSTIFY. In addi-

[2]The total number of realizations reported here is inconsistent with the information reported in (Walker et al., 2007). In corresponding with the authors of that paper, it is unclear why this is the case; however, the difference in reported amounts is quite small, and so should not affect the outcome of this study.

Proceedings of the 9th SIGdial Workshop on Discourse and Dialogue, pages 76–79,
Columbus, June 2008.

Strategy	Alt #	Rating	Rank	Realization
C2	3	3	7	Sonia Rose has very good decor but Bienvenue has decent decor.
	7	1	16	Sonia Rose has very good decor. On the other hand, Bienvenue has decent decor.
	8	4.5	13	Bienvenue has decent decor. Sonia Rose, on the other hand, has very good decor.
	10	4.5	5	Bienvenue has decent decor but Sonia Rose has very good decor.
	11	1	12	Sonia Rose has very good decor. However, Bienvenue has decent decor.
	13	5	14	Bienvenue has decent decor. However, Sonia Rose has very good decor.
	14	5	3	Sonia Rose has very good decor while Bienvenue has decent decor.
	15	4	4	Bienvenue has decent decor while Sonia Rose has very good decor.
	17	1	15	Bienvenue's price is 35 dollars. Sonia Rose's price, however, is 51 dollars. Bienvenue has decent decor. However, Sonia Rose has very good decor.

Figure 1: Some alternative [Alt] realizations of SPaRKy sentence plans from a COMPARE-2 [C2] plan, with averaged human ratings [Rating] (5 = highest rating) and ranks assigned by the n-gram ranker [Rank] (1 = top ranked).

tion, the SPaRKy sentence plan generator adds the INFER relation to assertions whose relations were not specified by the content planner.

During the sentence planning phase, SPaRKy orders the clauses and combines them using randomly selected clause-combining operations. During this process, a clause-combining operation may insert 1 of 7 connectives according to the RST relation that holds between two discourse units (i.e. inserting *since* or *because* for a JUSTIFY relation; *and*, *however*, *on the other hand*, *while*, or *but* for a CONTRAST relation; or *and* for an INFER relation).

After each sentence plan is generated, it is realized by the RealPro surface realizer and the resulting realization is rated by two judges on a scale of 1-5, where 5 is highly preferred. These ratings are then averaged, producing a range of 9 possible ratings from $\{1, 1.5, ..., 5\}$.

2.2 Ratings/Connectives Correlation

From the ratings of the examples in Figure 1, we can see that some of the SPaRKy sentence plan realizations seem more natural than others. Upon further analysis, we noticed that utterances containing many contrastive connectives seemed less preferred than those with fewer or no contrastive connectives.

To quantify this observation, we calculated the average number of connectives (ave_{c_i}) used per realization with rating i, using $ave_{c_i} = Total_{c_i}/N_{r_i}$, where $Total_{c_i}$ is the total number of connectives in realizations with rating i, and N_{r_i} is the number of realizations with rating i.

We use Pearson's r to calculate each correlation (in each case, $df = 7$). For both COMPARE strategies (represented in Figure 2(a) and 2(b)), we find a significant negative correlation for the average number of connectives used in realizations with a given rating (C2: $r = -0.97, p < 0.01$; and C3: $r = -0.93$, $p < 0.01$). These correlations indicate that judges' ratings decreased as the average frequency of the connectives increased.

Further analysis of the individual correlations used in the comparative strategies show that there is a significant negative correlation for *however* (C2: $r = -0.91$, $p < 0.01$; and C3: $r = -0.86$, $p < 0.01$) and *on the other hand* (C2: $r = -0.89$, $p < 0.01$; and C3: $r = -0.84$, $p < 0.01$) in both COMPARE strategies. In addition, in COMPARE-3, the frequencies of *while* and *but* are also significantly and strongly negatively correlated with the judges' ratings ($r = -0.86$, $p < 0.01$ and $r = -0.90$, $p < 0.01$, respectively), though there is no such correlation between the use of these connectives and their ratings in COMPARE-2.

Added together, all the contrastive connectives show strong, significant negative correlations between their average frequencies and judges' ratings for both comparative strategies (C2: $r = -0.93$, $p < 0.01$; C3:$r = -0.88, p < 0.01$).

Interestingly, unlike in the COMPARE strategies, there is a positive correlation ($r = 0.73, p > 0.05$) between the judges' ratings and the average frequency of all connectives used in the RECOMMEND strategy (see Figure 2(c)). Since this strategy only uses *and*, *since*, and *because* and does not utilize any contrastive connectives, this gives further evidence that only contrastive connectives are dispreferred.

2.3 N-gram Ranker and Features

To acertain whether these contrastive connectives are being learned by the ranker, we re-implemented the n-gram ranker using SVM-light (Joachims,

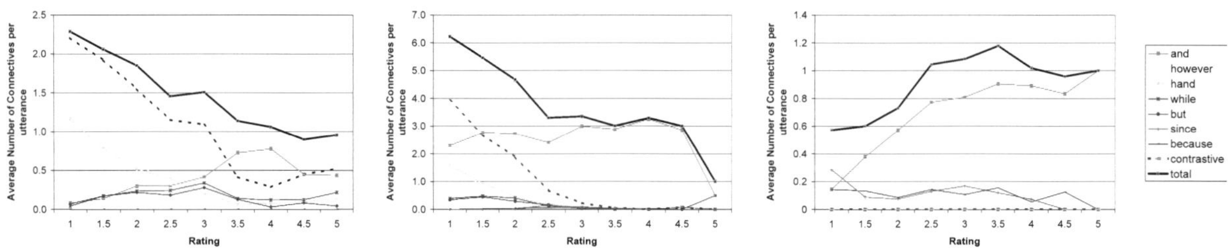

(a) Compare 2 (b) Compare 3 (c) Recommend

Figure 2: Correlation Graphs: The thick solid line indicate the correlation of all the connectives summed together, while the thick dashed line indicates the correlation of the 4 contrastive connectives summed together.

Strategy	however	o.t.o.h	while	but	all contrastives
C2	25.0%	25.0%	0.9%	2.7%	53.6%
C3	9.9%	10.9%	0.0%	3.1%	24.0%

Table 1: The proportion of the 20% most negatively weighted features for all contrastive connectives.

2002). As in Walker et. al (2007), we first prepared the SPaRKy Restaurant Corpus by replacing named entity tokens (e.g numbers, restaurant names, etc.) with their corresponding type (e.g. NUM for *61*), and added BEGIN and END tokens to mark the boundaries of each realization. We then trained our ranker to learn which unigrams, bigrams, and trigrams are associated with the ratings given to the realizations in the training set.

Although we implemented our ranker in order to carry out an error analysis on the individual features (i.e. n-grams) used by the ranker, we also found that our n-gram ranker performed comparably (REC: 3.5; C2: 4.1; C3: 3.8)[3] to the full-featured SPaRKy ranker (REC: 3.6; C2: 4.0; C3: 3.6) out of a possible best (human-performance) score of (REC: 4.2; C2: 4.5; C3: 4.2).

Using a perl script[4], we extracted feature weights learned by the ranker from the models built during the training phase. After averaging the feature weights across 10 training partitions, we examined the top 20% (C2:112/563 features; C3: 192/960 features) most negatively weighted features in each strategy to see whether our ranker was learning to avoid contrastive connectives. Table 1 shows that features containing contrastive connectives make up 53.6% of the 20% most negatively weighted features in COMPARE-2 and 24.0% of the 20% of the most negatively weighted features used in COMPARE-3. Interestingly, COMPARE-2 features that contained either *however* or *on the other hand* (*o.t.o.h*) make up the bulk of the contrastive connectives found in the negatively weighted features, mirroring the results of the correlations for COMPARE-2. This indicates that the discriminative n-gram ranker learns to avoid using contrastive connectives.

3 Contrastive Connectives Usage

3.1 Usage Restrictions

Previous work on contrastive connectives have found that these connectives often have different restrictions on their location in the discourse structure, with respect to maintaining discourse coherance (Quirk et al., 1972; Grote et al., 1995).

Quirk et. al. (1972) classifies *however* and *on the other hand* as subordinating conjuncts, a class of connectives that do not allow their clauses to be reordered without changing the perlocutionary force of the sentence (e.g. contrast C2: Alts # 11 & 13 in Figure 1). In addition, *on the other hand* prompts readers to regard the 2nd clause as more important (Grote et al., 1995). Given that both *however* and *on the other hand* contain the same restrictions on clause ordering, it seems reasonable that they would pattern the same with respect to assigning clausal prominence. This predicts that if the human judges rated the SPaRKy realizations based on the expectation of a particular perlocutionary act (e.g., that the comparison highlights the restaurant with the best decor), they would prefer realizations where *however* or *on the other hand* were attached to the more

[3]These scores were calculated using using the TopRank evaluation metric (Walker et al., 2007).

[4]written by Thorsten Joachims

desirable of the contrasted qualities. When we examine the SPaRKy realizations and ratings, this indeed seems to be the case – when the better property is ordered last, the realization was rated very highly (e.g. Alt 8 & 13 in Figure 1), but when the lesser property was ordered last, the realization was rated poorly (e.g. Alt 7 & 11 in Figure 1).

In contrast, *while* and *but* are not subordinating conjuncts and so are not subject to the clause ordering restriction. Thus, realizations with their contrasted clauses in either order should be rated similarly, and indeed, this is what we find in the corpus (e.g. Alts 3&10, and 14&15 in Figure 1).

3.2 Other Factors

In addition to clause order, another factor that may contribute to the awkwardness of *however* and *on the other hand* in some usages is that both of these connectives seem to be rather "grand" for these simple contrasts. Intuitively, these connectives seem to indicate a larger contrast than *while* and *but*, so when they are used to indicate small contrasts (e.g. contrasting only one quality), or contrasts close together on the scale (e.g. good vs. decent) instead of diametric opposites, they sound awkward. In addition, *however* and *on the other hand* may also be seeking "heavy" arguments that contain more syllables, words, or complex syntax. Lastly, human-authored comparisons, such as in this example from CNET.com:

> ...[it] has two convenient USB ports at the bottom of the front panel. Its beige predecessor, **on the other hand**, supplied these **only** on the back of the box.

seem to indicate that when our expectations of argument order are violated, the 2nd clause is often qualified by words such as "just" or "only", as if to acknowledge the flaunted preference.

4 Discussion and Future Work

Due to the poverty of highly rated instances of contrastive connective usage (particularly for *however* and *on the other hand*), our ranker learns to avoid these connectives in most situations. However, the ratings suggest that people do not dislike these contrastives unilaterally, but rather prefer them in specific usage patterns only. One way to combat this problem is to modify the sentence planner to take into account these semantic preferences for argument ordering when selecting a contrastive connective. This should produce a wider variety of candidates that observe this ordering preference, and thus provide the ranker with more highly rated candiates that use contrastive connectives. This is not to say that only candidates observing this preference should be generated, but merely that a wider variety of candiates should be generated so that the ranker has more opportunities to learn the restrictions surrounding the use of contrastive connectives.

As for the ranker, we can also identify features that are sensitive to these linguistic properties. Currently, n-gram features don't capture the semantic nuances such as argument order or the scalar distance between property values, so identifying features that capture this type of information should improve the ranker. Together, these improvements to both the quality of the generated candidate space and the ranking model should improve the accuracy of the top-rated/selected candidate.

References

B. Grote, N. Lenke, and M. Stede. 1995. Ma(r)king concessions in english and german. In *Proceedings of the Fifth European Workshop on Natural Language Generation.*, May.

Thorsten Joachims. 2002. Optimizing search engines using clickthrough data. In *Proc. KDD*.

B. Lavoie and O. Rambow. 1997. A fast and portable realizer for text generation systems. In *Proceedings of the 5th. Conference on Applied Natural Language Processing*, pages 265–268, San Francisco, CA, USA. Morgan Kaufmann Publishers Inc.

William C. Mann and Sandra A. Thompson. 1987. Rhetorical structure theory: A theory of text organization. Technical Report ISI/RS-87-190, University of Southern California Information Sciences Instuture.

R. Quirk, S. Greenbaum, G. Leech, and J. Svartvik. 1972. *A Comprehensive Grammar of the English Language*. Longman.

M. A. Walker, S. J. Whittaker, A. Stent, P. Maloor, J. D. Moore, M. Johnston, and G Vasireddy. 2004. Generation and evaluation of user tailored responses in multimodal dialogue. *Cognitive Science*, 28(5):811–840.

M. Walker, A. Stent, F. Mairesse, and Rashmi Prasad. 2007. Individual and domain adaptation in sentence planning for dialogue. *Journal of Artificial Intelligence Research (JAIR)*, 30:413–456.

What Are Meeting Summaries? An Analysis of Human Extractive Summaries in Meeting Corpus

Fei Liu, Yang Liu
Erik Jonsson School of Engineering and Computer Science
The University of Texas at Dallas
Richardson, TX, USA
{feiliu,yangl}@hlt.utdallas.edu

Abstract

Significant research efforts have been devoted to speech summarization, including automatic approaches and evaluation metrics. However, a fundamental problem about what summaries are for the speech data and whether humans agree with each other remains unclear. This paper performs an analysis of human annotated extractive summaries using the ICSI meeting corpus with an aim to examine their consistency and the factors impacting human agreement. In addition to using Kappa statistics and ROUGE scores, we also proposed a sentence distance score and divergence distance as a quantitative measure. This study is expected to help better define the speech summarization problem.

1 Introduction

With the fast development of recording and storage techniques in recent years, speech summarization has received more attention. A variety of approaches have been investigated for speech summarization, for example, maximum entropy, conditional random fields, latent semantic analysis, support vector machines, maximum marginal relevance (Maskey and Hirschberg, 2003; Hori et al., 2003; Buist et al., 2005; Galley, 2006; Murray et al., 2005; Zhang et al., 2007; Xie and Liu, 2008). These studies used different domains, such as broadcast news, lectures, and meetings. In these approaches, different information sources have been examined from both text and speech related features (e.g., prosody, speaker activity, turn-taking, discourse).

How to evaluate speech summaries has also been studied recently, but so far there is no consensus on evaluation yet. Often the goal in evaluation is to develop an automatic metric to have a high correlation with human evaluation scores. Different methods have been used in the above summarization research to compare system generated summaries with human annotation, such as F-measure, ROUGE, Pyramid, sumACCY (Lin and Hovy, 2003; Nenkova and Passonneau, 2004; Hori et al., 2003). Typically multiple reference human summaries are used in evaluation in order to account for the inconsistency among human annotations.

While there have been efforts on speech summarization approaches and evaluation, some fundamental problems are still unclear. For example, what are speech summaries? Do humans agree with each other on summary extraction? In this paper, we focus on the meeting domain, one of the most challenging speech genre, to analyze human summary annotation. Meetings often have several participants. Its speech is spontaneous, contains disfluencies, and lacks structure. These all post new challenges to the consensus of human extracted summaries.

Our goal in this study is to investigate the variation of human extractive summaries, and help to better understand the gold standard reference summaries for meeting summarization. This paper aims to answer two key questions: (1) How much variation is there in human extractive meeting summaries? (2) What are the factors that may impact interannotator agreement? We use three different metrics to evaluate the variation among human summaries, including Kappa statistic, ROUGE score, and a new proposed divergence distance score to reflect the coherence and quality of an annotation.

2 Corpus Description

We use the ICSI meeting corpus (Janin et al., 2003) which contains 75 naturally-occurred meetings, each about an hour long. All of them have been transcribed and annotated with dialog acts (DA) (Shriberg et al., 2004), topics, and abstractive and extractive summaries in the AMI project (Murray et al., 2005).

We selected 27 meetings from this corpus. Three annotators (undergraduate students) were recruited to extract summary sentences on a topic basis using the topic segments from the AMI annotation. Each sentence corresponds to one DA annotated in the corpus. The annotators were told to use their own judgment to pick summary sentences that are informative and can preserve discussion flow. The recommended percentages for the selected summary sentences and words were set to 8.0% and 16.0% respectively. Human subjects were provided with both the meeting audio files and an annotation Graphi-

Proceedings of the 9th SIGdial Workshop on Discourse and Dialogue, pages 80–83,
Columbus, June 2008. ©2008 Association for Computational Linguistics

cal User Interface, from which they can browse the manual transcripts and see the percentage of the currently selected summary sentences and words.

We refer to the above 27 meetings **Data set I** in this paper. In addition, some of our studies are performed based on the 6 meeting used in (Murray et al., 2005), for which we have human annotated summaries using 3 different guidelines:

- **Data set II**: summary annotated on a topic basis. This is a subset of the 27 annotated meetings above.
- **Data set III**: annotation is done for the entire meeting without topic segments.
- **Data set IV**: the extractive summaries are from the AMI annotation (Murray et al., 2005).

3 Analysis Results

3.1 Kappa Statistic

Kappa coefficient (Carletta, 1996) is commonly used as a standard to reflect inter-annotator agreement. Table 1 shows the average Kappa results, calculated for each meeting using the data sets described in Section 2. Compared to Kappa score on text summarization, which is reported to be 0.38 by (Mani et al., 2002) on a set of TREC documents, the inter-annotator agreement on meeting corpus is lower. This is likely due to the difference between the meeting style and written text.

Data Set	I	II	III	IV
Avg-Kappa	0.261	0.245	0.335	0.290

Table 1: Average Kappa scores on different data sets.

There are several other observations from Table 1. First, comparing the results for Data Set (II) and (III), both containing six meetings, the agreement is higher for Data Set (III). Originally, we expected that by dividing the transcript into several topics, human subjects can focus better on each topic discussed during the meeting. However, the result does not support this hypothesis. Moreover, the Kappa result of Data Set (III) also outperforms that of Data Set (IV). The latter data set is from the AMI annotation, where they utilized a different annotation scheme: the annotators were asked to extract dialog acts that are highly relevant to the given abstractive meeting summary. Contrary to our expectation, the Kappa score in this data set is still lower than that of Data Set (III), which used a direct sentence extraction scheme on the whole transcript. This suggests that even using the abstracts as a guidance, people still have a high variation in extracting summary sentences. We also calculated the pairwise Kappa score between annotations in different data sets. The inter-group Kappa score is much lower than those of the intragroup agreement, most likely due to the different annotation specifications used in the two different data sets.

3.2 Impacting Factors

We further analyze inter-annotator agreement with respect to two factors: **topic length** and **meeting participants**. All of the following experiments are based on Data Set (I) with 27 meetings.

We computed Kappa statistic for each topic instead of the entire meeting. The distribution of Kappa score with respect to the topic length (measured using the number of DAs) is shown in Figure 1. When the topic length is less than 100, Kappa scores vary greatly, from -0.065 to 1. Among the entire range of different topic lengths, there seems no obvious relationship between the Kappa score and the topic length (a regression from the data points does not suggest a fit with an interpretable trend).

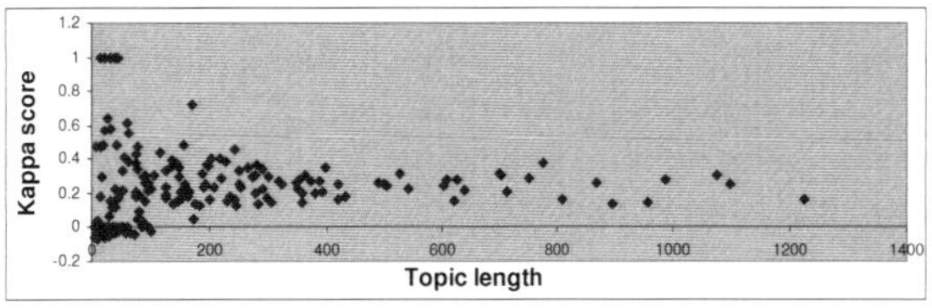

Figure 1: Relationship between Kappa score and topic length.

Using the same Kappa score for each topic, we also investigated its relationship with the number of speakers in that topic. Here we focused on the topic segments longer than a threshold (with more than 60 DAs) as there seems to be a wide range of Kappa results when the topic is short (in Figure 1). Table 2 shows the average Kappa score for these long topics, using the number of speakers in the topic as the variable. We notice that when the speaker number varies from 4 to 7, kappa scores gradually decrease with the increasing of speaker numbers. This phenomenon is consistent with our intuition. Generally the more participants are involved in a conversation, the more discussions can take place. Human annotators feel more ambiguity in selecting summary sentences for the discussion part. The pattern does not hold for other speaker numbers, namely, 2, 3, and 8. This might be due to a lack of enough data points, and we will further analyze this in the future research.

# of speakers	# of topics	Avg Kappa score
2	2	0.204
3	6	0.182
4	26	0.29
5	26	0.249
6	33	0.226
7	19	0.221
8	7	0.3

Table 2: Average Kappa score with respect to the number of speakers after removing short topics.

3.3 ROUGE Score

ROUGE (Lin and Hovy, 2003) has been adopted as a standard evaluation metric in various summarization tasks. It is computed based on the n-gram overlap between a summary and a set of reference summaries. Though the Kappa statistics can measure human agreement on sentence selection, it does not account for the fact that different annotators choose different sentences that are similar in content. ROUGE measures the word match and thus can compensate this problem of Kappa.

Table 3 shows the ROUGE-2 and ROUGE-SU4 F-measure results. For each annotator, we computed ROUGE scores using other annotators' summaries as references. For Data Set (I), we present results for each annotator, since one of our goals is to evaluate the quality of different annotator's summary annotation. The low ROUGE scores suggest the large variation among human annotations. We can see from the table that annotator 1 has the lowest ROUGE score and thus lowest agreement with the other two annotators in Data Set (I). The ROUGE score for Data Set (III) is higher than the others. This is consistent with the result using Kappa statistic: the more sentences two summaries have in common, the more overlapped n-grams they tend to share.

		ROUGE-2	ROUGE-SU4
data (I)	Annotator 1	0.407	0.457
	Annotator 2	0.421	0.471
	Annotator 3	0.433	0.483
data (III)	2 annotators	0.532	0.564
data (IV)	3 annotators	0.447	0.484

Table 3: ROUGE F-measure scores for different data sets.

3.4 Sentence Distance and Divergence Scores

From the annotation, we notice that the summary sentences are not uniformly distributed in the transcript, but rather with a clustering or coherence property. However, neither Kappa coefficient nor ROUGE score can represent such clustering tendency of meeting summaries. This paper attempts to develop an evaluation metric to measure this property among different human annotators.

For a sentence i selected by one annotator, we define a distance score d_i to measure its minimal distance to summary sentences selected by other annotators (distance between two sentences is represented using the difference of their sentence indexes). d_i is 0 if more than one annotator have extracted the same sentence as summary sentence. Using the annotated summaries for the 27 meetings in Data Set (I), we computed the sentence distance scores for each annotator. Figure 2 shows the distribution of the distance score for the 3 annotators. We can see that the distance score distributions for the three annotators differ. Intuitively, small distance scores mean better coherence and more consistency with other annotators' results. We thus propose a mechanism to quantify each annotator's summary annotation by using a random variable (RV) to represent an annotator's sentence distance scores.

When all the annotators agree with each other, the RV d will take a value of 0 with probability 1. In general, when the annotators select sentences close to each other, the RV d will have small values with high probabilities. Therefore we create a probability distribution Q for the ideal situation where the annotators have high agreement, and use this to quantify the quality of each annotation. Q is defined as:

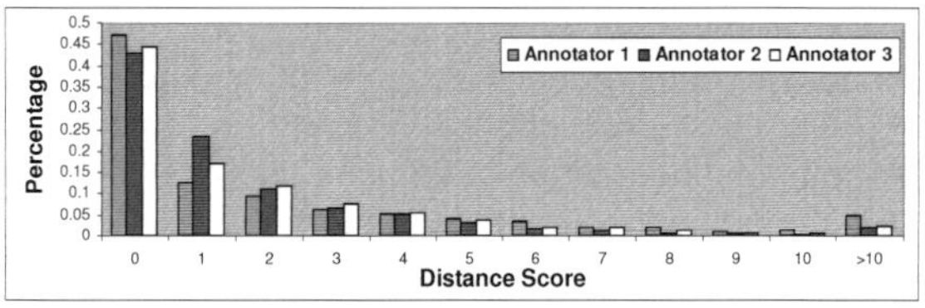

Figure 2: Percentage distribution of the summary sentence distance scores for the 3 annotators in Data Set (I).

$$Q(i) = \begin{cases} (d_{max} - i + 1) \times q & i \neq 0 \\ 1 - \sum_{i=1}^{d_{max}} Q(i) & \\ = 1 - \frac{d_{max} \times (d_{max}+1)}{2} \times q & i = 0 \end{cases}$$

where d_{max} denotes the maximum distance score based on the selected summary sentences from all the annotators. We assign linearly decreasing probabilities $Q(i)$ for different distance values i ($i > 0$) in order to give more credit to sentences with small distance scores. The rest of the probability mass is given to $Q(0)$. The parameter q is small, such that the probability distribution Q can approximate the ideal situation.

For each annotator, the probability distribution P is defined as:

$$P(i) = \begin{cases} \frac{w_i \times f_i}{\sum_i w_i \times f_i} & i \in D_p \\ 0 & \text{otherwise} \end{cases}$$

where D_p is the set of the possible distance values for this annotator, f_i is the frequency for a distance score i, and w_i is the weight assigned to that distance (w_i is i when $i \neq 0$; w_0 is p). We use parameter p to vary the weighting scale for the distance scores in order to penalize more for the large distance values.

Using the distribution P for each annotator and the ideal distribution Q, we compute their KL-divergence, called the Divergence Distance score (DD-score):

$$DD = \sum_i P(i) \log \frac{P(i)}{Q(i)}$$

We expect that the smaller the score is, the better the summary is. In the extreme case, if an annotator's DD-score is equal to 0, it means that all of this annotator's extracted sentences are selected by other annotators.

Figure 3 shows the DD-score for each annotator calculated using Data Set (I), with varying q parameters. Our experiments showed that the scale parameter p in the annotator's probability distribution only affects the absolute value of the DD-score for the annotators, but does not change the ranking of each annotator. Therefore we simply set $p = 10$ when reporting DD-scores. Figure 3 shows that different weight scale q does not impact the ranking of the annotators either. We observe in Figure 3, annotator 1 has the highest DD score to the desirable distribution. We found this is consistent with the cumulative distance score obtained from the distance score distribution, where annotator 1 has the least cumulative frequencies for all the distance values greater than 0. This is also consistent with the ROUGE scores, where annotator 1 has the lowest ROUGE score. These suggest that the DD-score can be used to quantify the consistency of an annotator with others.

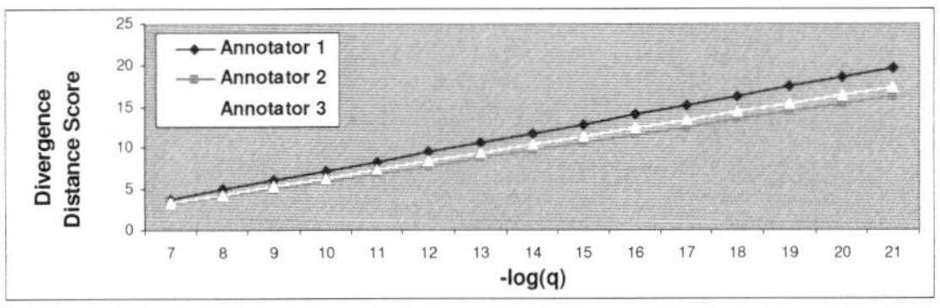

Figure 3: Divergence distance score when varying parameter q in the ideal distribution Q.

We also investigated using the sentence distance scores to improve the human annotation quality. Our hypothesis is that those selected summary sentences with high distance scores do not contain crucial information of the meeting content and thus can be removed from the reference summary. To verify this, for each annotator, we removed the summary sentences with distance scores greater than some threshold, and then computed the ROUGE score for the newly generated summary by comparing to other two summary annotations that are kept unchanged. The ROUGE-2 scores when varying the threshold is shown in Figure 4. No threshold in the X-axis means that no sentence is taken out from the human summary. We can see from the figure that the removal of sentences with high distance scores can result in even better F-measure scores. This suggests that we can delete the incoherent human selected sentences while maintaining the content information in the summary.

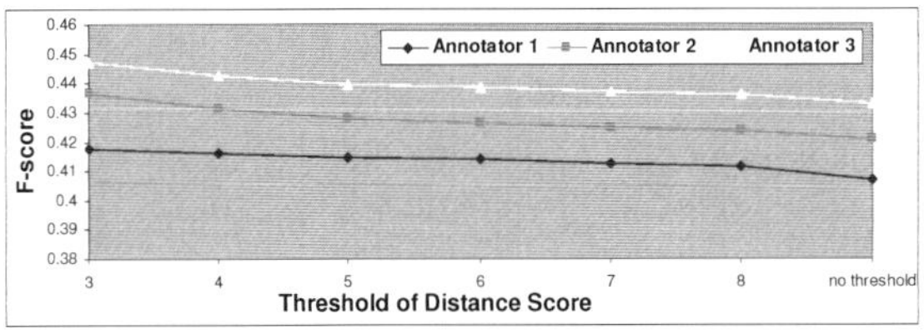

Figure 4: ROUGE-2 score after removing summary sentences with a distance score greater than a threshold.

4 Conclusion

In this paper we conducted an analysis about human annotated extractive summaries using a subset of the ICSI meeting corpus. Different measurements have been used to examine interannotator agreement, including Kappa coefficient, which requires exact same sentence selection; ROUGE, which measures the content similarity using n-gram match; and our proposed sentence distance scores and divergence, which evaluate the annotation consistency based on the sentence position. We find that the topic length does not have an impact on the human agreement using Kappa, but the number of speakers seems to be correlated with the agreement. The ROUGE score and the divergence distance scores show some consistency in terms of evaluating human annotation agreement. In addition, using the sentence distance score, we demonstrated that we can remove some poorly chosen sentences from the summary to improve human annotation agreement and preserve the information in the summary. In our future work, we will explore other factors, such as summary length, and the speaker information for the select summaries. We will also use a bigger data set for a more reliable conclusion.

Acknowledgments

The authors thank University of Edinburgh for sharing the annotation on the ICSI meeting corpus. This research is supported by NSF award IIS-0714132. The views in this paper are those of the authors and do not represent the funding agencies.

References

A. H. Buist, W. Kraaij, and S. Raaijmakers. 2005. Automatic summarization of meeting data: A feasibility study. In *Proc. of the 15th CLIN conference*.

J. Carletta. 1996. Assessing agreement on classification tasks: the kappa statistic. *Computational Linguistics*, 22(2):249–254.

M. Galley. 2006. A skip-chain conditional random field for ranking meeting utterances by importance. In *Proc. of EMNLP*, pages 364–372.

C. Hori, T. Hori, and S. Furui. 2003. Evaluation methods for automatic speech summarization. In *Proc. of Eurospeech*, pages 2825–2828.

A. Janin, D. Baron, J. Edwards, D. Ellis, D. Gelbart, N. Morgan, B. Peskin, T. Pfau, E. Shriberg, A. Stolcke, and C. Wooters. 2003. The ICSI meeting corpus. In *Proc. of ICASSP*.

C. Y. Lin and E. Hovy. 2003. Automatic evaluation of summaries using n-gram co-occurrence statistics. In *Proc. of HLT–NAACL*.

I. Mani, G. Klein, D. House, L. Hirschman, T. Firmin, and B. Sundheim. 2002. Summac: a text summarization evaluation. *Natural Language Engineering*, 8:43–68.

S. Maskey and J. Hirschberg. 2003. Automatic summarization of broadcast news using structural features. In *Proc. of EUROSPEECH*, pages 1173–1176.

G. Murray, S. Renals, J. Carletta, and J. Moore. 2005. Evaluating automatic summaries of meeting recordings. In *Proc. of the ACL Workshop on Intrinsic and Extrinsic Evaluation Measures for Machine Translation*.

A. Nenkova and R. Passonneau. 2004. Evaluating content selection in summarization: The pyramid method. In *Proc. of HLT-NAACL*.

E. Shriberg, R. Dhillon, S. Bhagat, J. Ang, and H. Carvey. 2004. The ICSI meeting recorder dialog act (MRDA) corpus. In *Proc. of 5th SIGDial Workshop*, pages 97–100.

S. Xie and Y. Liu. 2008. Using corpus and knowledge-based similarity measure in maximum marginal relevance for meeting summarization. In *Proc. of ICASSP*.

J. Zhang, H. Chan, P. Fung, and L. Cao. 2007. A comparative study on speech summarization of broadcast news and lecture speech. In *Proc. of Interspeech*.

A Simple Method for Resolution of Definite Reference in a Shared Visual Context

Alexander Siebert
Berlin-Brandenburgische
Akademie der Wissenschaften
siebert@bbaw.de

David Schlangen
Department of Linguistics
University of Potsdam, Germany
das@ling.uni-potsdam.de

Abstract

We present a method for resolving definite exophoric reference to visually shared objects that is based on a) an automatically learned, simple mapping of words to visual features ("visual word semantics"), b) an automatically learned, semantically-motivated utterance segmentation ("visual grammar"), and c) a procedure that, given an utterance, uses b) to combine a) to yield a resolution. We evaluated the method both on a pre-recorded corpus and in an online setting, where it performed with 81% (chance: 14%) and 66% accuracy, respectively. This is comparable to results reported in related work on simpler settings.

1 The Task

The method described in this paper is a module of a dialogue system that acts as a collaborator of a human player in the task of manipulating visually present puzzle objects. An example scene is shown in Figure 1 (the indices *a* and *b* are added here for illustrative purposes). Given utterances like those in (1), the task of the module is to identify the likely referents (here, *a* and *b*, respectively).[1]

(1) a.Take the piece in the middle on the left side.
b.Take the piece in the middle.

More formally, the task can be characterised as follows: possibly starting with an *a priori* assumption about likely referents (e.g., from knowledge of

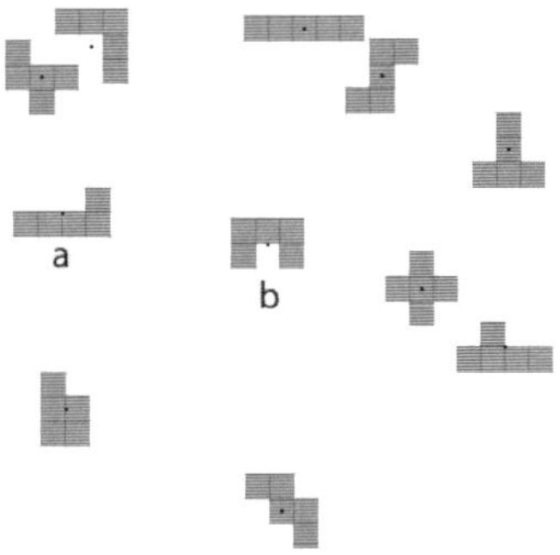

Figure 1: Example Scene

discourse salience), the module uses the evidence present in the utterance (words, syntax) and in the visual scene (visual features) to derive at a new assumption about likely referents. If we call such an assumption a *confidence function* c that assigns to each object in the domain $\mathcal{O}$, a number between 0 and 1; i.e., $c : \mathcal{O} \rightarrow \mathbb{R}$, then *reference resolution* is a function r that takes a triple of an initial confidence function c, an utterance u, and a visual scene representation v to yield an updated confidence function c'. Formally: $r : \mathcal{C} \times \mathcal{U} \times \mathcal{V} \rightarrow \mathcal{C}$.

In the following, we describe the resources needed to set up the module, its subcomponents, and the evaluation we performed. We close by relating the proposed method to prior work and discussing future extensions.

2 Resources

2.1 Corpus

As our method is based on automatically learned models, a corpus is required. Our intended use case is similar to the setting described in (Schlangen and Fernández, 2007), but with the addition of a shared visual context. We collected 300 scene descriptions

[1] Our system is implemented for German input; for ease of description we use examples from our corpus translated into English here.

Proceedings of the 9th SIGdial Workshop on Discourse and Dialogue, pages 84–87,
Columbus, June 2008.

(of scenes containing between 1 and 12 distinct, monochrome shapes, randomly placed and rotated on a rectangular area) using the two-part methodology of (Siebert et al., 2007) that yields recordings and quality assessments (here: attempts to follow other subjects' instructions). We also later recorded an additional 300 scene descriptions by a single speaker, to further increase our data base.

After transcription of the recordings (239 minutes of audio material), we discarded roughly 6% of the instructions because they could not be followed by the evaluators, and a further 4% because the complexity of the descriptions was outside the scope of what we wanted to model. The remaining instructions were then automatically cleaned from dysfluencies, morphologically lemmatised and POS tagged, and annotated as described below.

2.2 Computer Vision

The other required resource is a visual perception algorithm. We use it to compute a feature representation of every visual scene as presented in the data collection:[2] First, each object is represented by a number of *object features* such as size / length / height of the bounding box, center of gravity, number of edges. Second, *topological features* note for each object the distance to certain points on the board (edges, center, etc.) and to other objects. (For details on the computation of such features see for example (Regier and Carlson, 2001).) Lastly, we also compute groupings of objects by clustering along columns and rows or both (see Figure 2 for an illustration). For each group, we compute two sets of *topological features*, one for the objects within the group (e.g., distance to the center of the group), and one for the configuration of groups (distance of group to other objects). This set of features was selected to be representative of typical basic visual features.

3 Components

3.1 Visual Grammar

The 'visual grammar' segments utterances according to functional aspects on two levels. The first

[2]At the moment, the input to the algorithm is a symbolic representation of the scene (which object is where); the features are designed to also be derivable from digital images instead, using standard computer vision techniques (Shapiro and Stockman, 2001); this is future work, however.

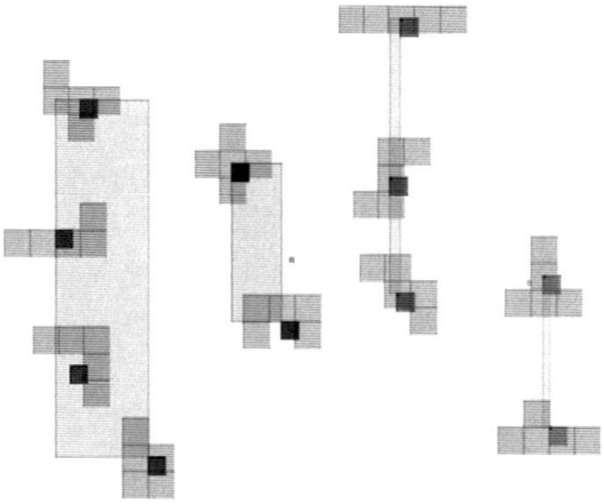

Figure 2: Scene with Horizontal Group Detection

describes the macro-structure of a spatial expression, i.e., the division into *target* (the denoted object; T) and optional *landmarks* (other objects; LM) and their *relation* to the target (R; see example in Table 2). The second level annotates the spatial-lexical function of each word, e.g., whether the word denotes a piece or a configuration of pieces (Table 1). A fully 'parsed' example is shown in Table 2.

Name	Description	Examples
l	lexical reference	***T,piece,cross***
d_r	topological direction	***top left*** *Corner*
d_s	topological distance	***outer*** *left*
d_n	numeric	***second*** *column*
p_g	group (perceptually active)	*from the left* ***column***
g_s	synthetic group	*the three* ***pieces*** *on the left*
f	landmark field N	in the *Middle*
r	prepositional relation	***in*** *the middle*
grad	grading function	***exactly*** *right*

Table 1: Visual Lexical Functions of Words

the	cross	from	the	second	column	from	left	at the top
	l	r		d_n	p_g	r	d_r	d_r

(a) - Annotation of spatial lexical functions

	T	R		LM	LM	LM	LM	T

(b) - Segmentation of visual spatial parts

Table 2: Example Annotation / 'Parse'

Given the requirement for robustness, we decided against a hand-written grammar for deriving such annotations; the moderate size of our corpus on the other hand made for example Markov model-based approaches difficult to apply. We hence chose transformation-based learning to create this (shallow) segmentation grammar, converting the segmentation task into a tagging task (as is done in

(Ramshaw and Marcus, 1995), *inter alia*). In our approach, each token that is to be tagged is itself represented in three different forms or layers: lemmatised word, as POS-tag, and by its spatial-functional tag (as in Table 1; added by simple look-up). All these layers can be accessed in the learned rules. Apart from this, the module is a straightforward implementation of (Ramshaw and Marcus, 1995), which in turn adapts (Brill, 1993) for syntactic chunking.

3.2 Visual Word Semantics

To learn the visual semantics of words we implemented a simple technique for grounding words in perceptions. Roughly, the idea is to extract from all instances in which a word was used in the training corpus and all associated scenes a prototypical visual meaning representation by identifying those features whose values best predict the appropriateness of the word given a scene. (This is similar in spirit to the approach used in (Roy, 2002).)

As material for learning, we only used the simple expressions (target only, no landmark) in the corpus, to ensure that all words used were in some way 'about' the target. The algorithm iterates over all pairs of utterance and scene and saves for each lemma all visual information. This creates for each lemma a matrix of feature values with as many rows as there were occurrences of the lemma. The values in each column (that is, for each feature) are then normalised to the interval [-1, 1] and the standard deviation is recorded.

The next tasks then are a) to compute one single representative value for each feature, but only b) for those features that carry semantic weight for the given word (i.e., to compute a dimensionality reduction). E.g., for the lemma 'left', we want the feature *x_distance_to_center* to be part of the semantic model, but not *y_distance_to_center*.

One option for a) is to simply take the average value as representative for a feature (for a given word). While this works for some words, it causes problems for others which imply a maximisation and not a prototypisation. E.g., the lemma *left* is best represented by *maximal* values of the feature *x_distance_to_center*, not by the average of all values for all occurrences of *left* (this will yield something like *leftish*). Perhaps surprisingly, representation through the majority value, i.e., choosing the most frequent value as representative for a feature (for a given word), performed better, and is hence the method we chose.

For b), dimensionality reduction, we again chose a very simple approach (much simpler than for example (Roy, 2002)): features are filtered out as irrelevant for a given lemma features if their variance is above a certain threshold. To give an example, for the lemma *left* the distribution of values of the feature *x_distance_to_center* varies with a σ of 0.05, that of *y_distance_to_center* with a σ of 0.41. We empirically determined the setting of the threshold such that it excluded the latter.[3]

3.3 Combination

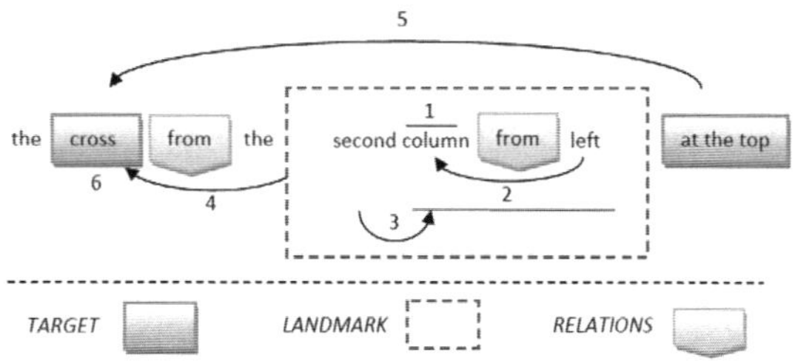

Figure 3: Steps of the Algorithm for Example Utterance

The combination algorithm works through the segmented utterance and combines visual word semantics to yield a reference hypothesis. Figure 3 illustrates this process for the example from Table 2. On detecting a landmark segment (Step 1), the resolution algorithm 'activates' the appropriate group; which one this is is determined by the *p_g* item in the landmark segment. (Here: *column*). The group is then treated as a single object, and (Step 2) the semantics of topological terms (d_r or d_s) in the landmark segment is applied to it (more on this in a second). For our example, this yields a ranking of all columns with respect to their 'left-ness'. The ordinal 'second' finally simply picks out the second element on this list–the second group w.r.t. the property of leftness (Step 3). The expressions in the target segment are now only applied to the members of the group that was selected in this way; i.e., the semantic models of 'top' and 'cross' are now only applied to the objects in that column (Steps 4 to 6).

[3]With more data and hence the possibility to set aside a development set, one could and should of course set such a threshold automatically.

Semantic word models are applied through a simple calculation of distance between values (of semantic model and actual scene): the closer, the better the match of word to scene. (Modulo selectivity of a feature; for a feature that occurred for all lemmata with a high specificity (small σ), good matches are expected to be closer to the prototype value than for features with a high variability.)

This method encodes parts of the utterance semantics procedurally, namely the way how certain phrases (here grouped under the label *landmark*) semantically modify other phrases (here grouped under the label *target*). This encoding makes the algorithm perhaps harder to understand than semantic composition rules tied to syntactic rules, but it also affords a level of abstraction over specific syntactic rules: our very general concepts of *landmark* and *target* cover various ways of modification (e.g. through PPs or relative clauses), adding to the robustness of the approach.

4 Evaluation

With an f-score of 0.985 (10-fold cross validation), the transformation-based learning of the segmentation performs quite well, roughly at the level of state-of-the-art POS-taggers (albeit with a much smaller tag inventory). Also evaluated via cross-validation on the corpus, the resolution component as a whole performs with an accuracy of 80.67% (using frequency-based word-semantic features; it drops to 66.95% for average-based). There were on average 7 objects in each scene in the corpus; i.e. the baseline of getting the reference right by chance is 14%. Our system significantly improves over this baseline.

We also evaluated the system in a more realistic application situation. We asked subjects to refer to certain pieces in presented scenes (via typed utterances); here, the system reached a success-rate of 66% (7 subjects, 100 scene / utterance pairs). While this is considerably lower than the corpus-based evaluation, it is still on a par with related systems using more complicated resolution methods (Roy, 2002; Gorniak and Roy, 2004). We also think these results represent the lower end of the performance range that can be expected in practical use, as in an interactive dialogue system users have time to adapt to the capabilities of the system.

5 Conclusions

We have presented a method for resolving definite, exophoric reference to objects that are visually co-present to user and system. The method combines automatically acquired models (a 'visual word semantics', a simple, but effective mapping between visual features and words; and a 'visual grammar', a semantically motivated segmentation of utterances) and hard-coded knowledge (combination procedure). To us, this combines the strengths of two approaches: statistical, where robustness and wide coverage is required, hard-coding, where few, but complex patterns are concerned.

We are currently integrating the module into a working dialogue system; in future work we will investigate the use of digital images as input format.

Acknowledgements

This work was supported by DFG through an Emmy Noether Programm Grant to the second author.

References

Eric Brill. 1993. *A Corpus-Based Approach to Language Learning*. Ph.D. thesis, University of Pennsylvania.

Peter Gorniak and Deb Roy. 2004. Grounded semantic composition for visual scenes. In *Journal of Artifical Intelligence Research*.

Lance A. Ramshaw and Mitchell P. Marcus. 1995. Text chunking using transformation-based learning. In *Proceedings of the Third Workshop on Very Large Corpora*, pages 82–94.

Terry Regier and Laura A. Carlson. 2001. Grounding spatial language in perception: An empirical and computational investigation. In *Journal of Experimental Psychology*, volume 130, pages 273–298.

Deb Roy. 2002. Learning words and syntax for a visual description task. *Computer Speech and Language*, 16(3).

David Schlangen and Raquel Fernández. 2007. Beyond repair: Testing the limits of the conversational repair system. In *Proceedings of SIGdial 2007*, pages 51–54, Antwerp, Belgium, September.

Linda G. Shapiro and George C. Stockman. 2001. *Computer Vision*. Prentice Hall, New Jersey, USA.

Alexander Siebert, David Schlangen, and Raquel Fernández. 2007. An implemented method for distributed collection and assessment of speech data. In *Proceedings of SIGdial 2007*, Antwerp, Belgium.

A Framework for Building Conversational Agents Based on a Multi-Expert Model

Mikio Nakano, Kotaro Funakoshi, Yuji Hasegawa, Hiroshi Tsujino
Honda Research Institute Japan Co., Ltd.
8-1 Honcho, Wako, Saitama 351-0188, Japan
{nakano, funakoshi, yuji.hasegawa, tsujino}@jp.honda-ri.com

Abstract

This paper presents a novel framework for building symbol-level control modules of animated agents and robots having a spoken dialogue interface. It features distributed modules called experts each of which is specialized to perform certain kinds of tasks. A common interface that all experts must support is specified, and any kind of expert can be incorporated if it has the interface. Several modules running in parallel coordinate the experts by accessing them through the interface, so that the whole system can achieve flexible control, such as interruption handling and parallel task execution.

1 Introduction

As much attention is recently paid to autonomous agents such as robots and animated agents, spoken dialogue is expected to be a natural interface between users and such agents. Our objective is to establish a framework for developing the intelligence module of such agents.

In establishing such a framework, we focus on achieving the following features. (1) *Multi-domain dialogue:* Since agents are usually expected to perform multiple kinds of tasks, they need to work in multiple domains and switch domains according to user utterances. (2) *Interruption handling:* It is crucial for human-agent interaction to be able to handle users' interrupting utterances while speaking or performing tasks. (3) *Parallel task execution:* Agents, especially robots that perform physical actions, are expected to be able to execute multiple tasks in parallel when possible. For example, robots should be able to engage in a dialogue while moving. (4) *Extensibility:* Since the agents can be used for a variety of tasks, various strategies for dialogue and task planning should be able to be incorporated.

Although a number of models for conversational agents have been proposed, no model has all of the above properties. Several multi-domain dialogue system models have been proposed and they are extensible, but it is not clear how they handle interruptions to system utterances and actions (e.g., O'Neill et al. (2004), Lin et al. (1999), and Hartikainen et al. (2004)). There are several spoken dialogue agents and robots that can handle interruptions thanks to their asynchronous control (Asoh et al., 1999; Boye et al., 2000; Blaylock et al., 2002; Lemon et al., 2002), they do not focus on making it easy to add new dialogue domains with a variety of dialogue strategies.

This paper presents a framework called RIME (Robot Intelligence based on Multiple Experts), which employs modules called *experts*.[1] Each expert is specialized for achieving certain kinds of tasks by performing physical actions and engaging in dialogues. It corresponds to the symbol-level control module of a system that can engage in tasks in a single small domain, and it employs fixed control strategies. Only some of the experts take charge in understanding user utterances and decide actions. The basic idea behind RIME is to specify a common interface of experts for coordinating them and to achieve flexible control. In RIME, several mod-

[1] RIME is an improved version of our previous model (Nakano et al., 2005), whose interruption handling was too simple and which could not achieve parallel task execution.

Proceedings of the 9th SIGdial Workshop on Discourse and Dialogue, pages 88–91,
Columbus, June 2008.

ules run in parallel for coordinating experts. They are *understander*, which is responsible for speech understanding, *action selector*, which is responsible for selecting actions, and *task planner*, which is responsible for deciding which expert should work to achieve tasks.

RIME achieves the above mentioned features. Multi-domain dialogues are possible by selecting an appropriate expert which is specialized to dialogues in a certain domain. Interruption handling is possible because each expert must have methods to detect interruptions and decide actions to handle interruptions, and coordinating modules can use these methods. Parallel task execution is possible because experts have methods for providing information to decide which experts can take charge at the same time, and the task planner utilizes that information. Extensibility is achieved because any kind of expert can be incorporated if it supports the common interface. This makes it possible for agent developers to build a variety of conversational agents.

2 Multi-Expert Model

This section explains RIME in detail. Fig. 1 depicts its module architecture.

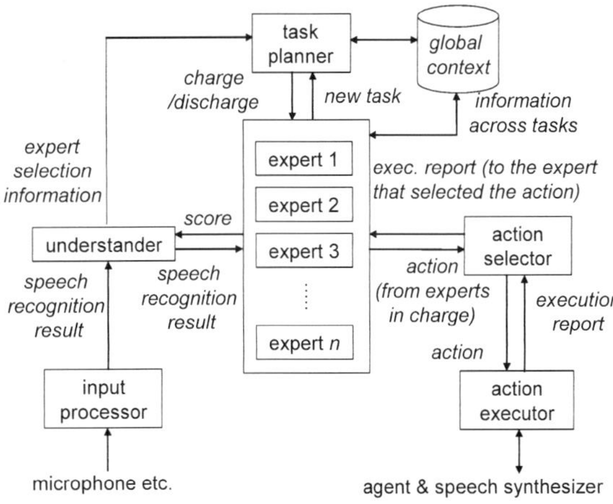

Figure 1: Architecture for RIME-Based Systems

2.1 Experts

Each expert is a kind of object in the object-oriented programming framework. In this paper, we call tasks performed by one expert *primitive tasks*. Experts should be prepared for each primitive task type. For example, if there is an expert for a primitive task type "telling someone's extension number", "telling person A's extension number" is a primitive task. By performing a series of primitive tasks, a complicated task can be performed. For example, a museum guide robot can perform "explaining object B" by executing "moving to B" and "giving an explanation on B". Among the experts, a small number of experts can perform tasks at one time. Such experts are called *being in charge*.

Each expert holds information on the progress of the primitive task. It includes task-type-independent information, such as which action in this primitive task is being performed and whether the previous robot action finished, and task-type-dependent information such as the user intention understanding results and dialogue history. The contents and the data structure for the task-type-dependent information for each expert can be designed by the system developer.

Experts are classified into *system-initiative task experts* and *user-initiative task experts*. In this paper, the *initiative* of a task means who can initiate the task. For example, the task "understanding a request for weather information" is a user-initiative task, and the task "providing weather information" is a system-initiative task.

In RIME, executing multiple tasks in parallel becomes possible by making multiple experts take charge. To check whether two experts can take charge simultaneously, we currently use two features *verbal* and *physical*. Two experts having the same feature cannot take charge simultaneously.

The interface of experts consists of methods for accessing its internal state. Below are some of the task-type-dependent methods, which need to be implemented by system developers.

The *understand* method updates the internal state based on the user speech recognition results, using domain-dependent sentence patterns for utterance understanding. This method returns a score which indicates the plausibility the user utterance should be dealt with by the expert. Domain selection techniques in multi-domain spoken dialogue systems (Komatani et al., 2006) can be applied to obtain the score. The *select-action* method outputs one action based on the content of the internal state. Here, an *action* is a multimodal command which includes a text to speak and/or a physical action command.

The action can be an empty action, which means doing nothing. The *detect-interruption* method returns a Boolean value that indicates whether the previous user utterance is an interruption to the action being performed when this expert is being in charge. The *handle-interruption* method returns the action to be performed after an interruption is detected. For example, an instruction to stop the utterance can be returned.

In the definition of these methods, experts can access a common database called *global context* to store and utilize information across domains, such as information on humans, information on the environment, and past dialogue topics.

2.2 Modules Coordinating Experts

To exploit experts, three processes, namely the *understander*, the *action selector*, and the *task planner*, work in parallel.

The understander receives output of an *input processor*, which typically performs speech recognition. Each time the understander receives a user speech recognition result from the input processor, it performs the following process. First it dispatches the speech recognition result to the experts in charge and the user-initiative experts with their *understand* methods, which then returns the scores mentioned above. The expert that returns the highest score is selected as the expert to take charge. If the selected expert is not in charge, it tells the task planner that the expert is selected as the user-initiative expert to take charge. If the selected expert is in charge, it calls the *detect-interruption* method of the expert. If *true* is returned, it tells the action selector that an interruption utterance is detected.

The action selector repeats the following process for each expert being in charge in a short cycle. When an interruption for the expert is detected, it calls the expert's *handle-interruption* method, and it then sends the returned action to the action executor, which is assumed to execute multimodal actions by controlling agents, speech synthesizers, and other modules. Otherwise, unless it is not waiting for a user utterance, it calls the expert's *select-action* methods, and then sends the returned action to the action executor. The returned action can be an empty action. Note that it is assumed that the action executor can perform two or more actions in parallel when possible.

ID	task type	initiative	feature
A	understanding weather information requests	user	verbal
B	providing weather information	agent	verbal
C	understanding extension number requests	user	verbal
D	providing extension numbers	agent	verbal
E	understanding requests for guiding to places	user	verbal
F	moving to show the way	agent	physical
G	explaining places	agent	verbal

Table 1: Experts in the Example Robotic System

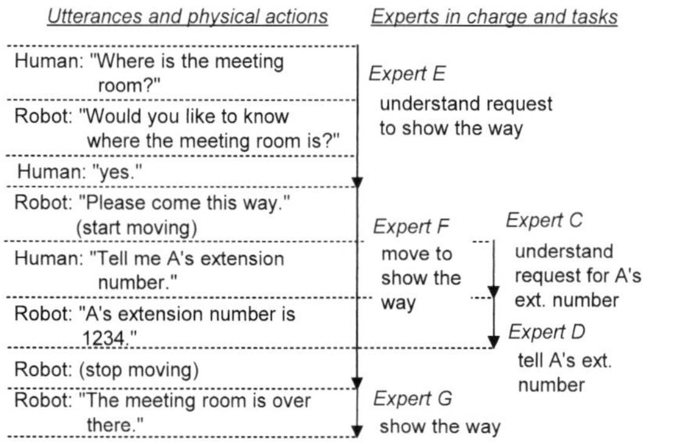

Figure 2: Expert Selection in a Parallel Task Execution Example

The task planner is responsible for deciding which experts take charge and which experts do not. It sometimes makes an expert take charge by setting a primitive task, and sometimes it discharges an expert to cancel the execution of its primitive task. To make such decisions, it receives several pieces of information from other modules. First it receives from the understander information on which expert is selected to understand a new utterance. It also receives information on the finish of the primitive task from an expert being in charge. In addition, it receives new tasks from the experts that understand human requests. The task planner also consults the global context to access the information shared by the experts and the task planner. In this paper we do not discuss the details of task planning algorithms, but we have implemented a task planner with a simple hierarchical planning mechanism.

There can be other processes whose output is written in the global context. For example, a robot and human localization process using image processing and other sensor information processing can be used.

3 Implementation as a Toolkit

The flexibility of designing experts increases the amount of effort for programming in building experts. We therefore developed RIME-TK (RIME-ToolKit), which provides libraries that facilitate building systems based on RIME. It is implemented in Java, and contains an abstract expert class hierarchy. The system developers can create new experts by extending those abstract classes. Those abstract classes have frequently used functions such as WFST-based language understanding, template-based language generation, and frame-based dialogue management. RIME-TK also contains the implementations of the understander and the action selector. In addition, it specifies the interfaces for the input processor, the action executor, and the task planner. Example implementations of these modules are also included in RIME-TK. Using RIME-TK, conversational agents can be built by creating experts, an input processor, an action executor, and a task planner.

As an example, we have built a robotic system, which is supposed to work at a reception, and can perform several small tasks such as providing extension numbers of office members and guiding to several places near the reception such as a meeting room and a restroom. Some experts in the system are listed in Table 1. Fig. 2 shows an example interaction between a human and the robotic system that includes parallel task execution and how experts are charged. The detailed explanation is omitted for the lack of the space.

By developing several other robotic systems and spoken dialogue systems (e.g., Komatani et al. (2006), Nakano et al. (2006), and Nishimura et al. (2007)), we have confirmed that RIME and RIME-TK are viable.

4 Concluding Remarks

This paper presented RIME, a framework for building conversational agents. It is different from previous frameworks in that it makes it possible to build agents that can handle interruptions and execute multiple tasks in parallel by employing experts which have a common interface. Although the current implementation is useful for building various kinds of systems, we believe that preparing more kinds of expert templates and improving expert selection for understanding utterances facilitate building a wider variety of systems.

Acknowledgments We would like to thank all people who helped us to build RIME-TK and its applications.

References

H. Asoh, T. Matsui, J. Fry, F. Asano, and S. Hayamizu. 1999. A spoken dialog system for a mobile office robot. In *Proc. Eurospeech-99*, pages 1139–1142.

N. Blaylock, J. Allen, and G. Ferguson. 2002. Synchronization in an asynchronous agent-based architecture for dialogue systems. In *Proc. Third SIGdial Workshop*, pages 1–10.

J. Boye, B. A. Hockey, and M. Rayner. 2000. Asynchronous dialogue management: Two case-studies. In *Proc. Götalog-2000*.

M. Hartikainen, M. Turunen, J. Hakulinen, E.-P. Salonen, and J. A. Funk. 2004. Flexible dialogue management using distributed and dynamic dialogue control. In *Proc. Interspeech-2004*, pages 197–200.

K. Komatani, N. Kanda, M. Nakano, K. Nakadai, H. Tsujino, T. Ogata, and H. G. Okuno. 2006. Multi-domain spoken dialogue system with extensibility and robustness against speech recognition errors. In *Proc. 7th SIGdial Workshop*, pages 9–17.

O. Lemon, A. Gruenstein, A. Battle, and S. Peters. 2002. Multi-tasking and collaborative activities in dialogue systems. In *Proc. Third SIGdial Workshop*, pages 113–124.

B. Lin, H. Wang, and L. Lee. 1999. Consistent dialogue across concurrent topics based on an expert system model. In *Proc. Eurospeech-99*, pages 1427–1430.

M. Nakano, Y. Hasegawa, K. Nakadai, T. Nakamura, J. Takeuchi, T. Torii, H. Tsujino, N. Kanda, and H. G. Okuno. 2005. A two-layer model for behavior and dialogue planning in conversational service robots. In *Proc. 2005 IEEE/RSJ IROS*, pages 1542–1547.

M. Nakano, A. Hoshino, J. Takeuchi, Y. Hasegawa, T. Torii, K. Nakadai, K. Kato, and H. Tsujino. 2006. A robot that can engage in both task-oriented and non-task-oriented dialogues. In *Proc. 2006 IEEE/RAS Humanoids*, pages 404–411.

Y. Nishimura, S. Minotsu, H. Dohi, M. Ishizuka, M. Nakano, K. Funakoshi, J. Takeuchi, Y. Hasegawa, and H. Tsujino. 2007. A markup language for describing interactive humanoid robot presentations. In *Proc. IUI-07*.

I. O'Neill, P. Hanna, X. Liu, and M. McTear. 2004. Cross domain dialogue modelling: an object-based approach. In *Proc. Interspeech-2004*, pages 205–208.

From GEMINI to DiaGen: Improving Development of Speech Dialogues for Embedded Systems

Stefan W. Hamerich
University of Hamburg
Department of Informatics
Natural Language Systems Division
Hamburg – Germany
Harman/Becker Automotive Systems
CoC Speech & Connectivity
Speech Services
Ulm – Germany
shamerich@harmanbecker.com

Abstract

In this paper DiaGen is presented, a tool that provides support in generating code for embedded dialogue applications. By aid of it, the dialogue development process is speeded up considerably. At the same time it is guaranteed that only well-formed and well-defined constructs are used. Having had its roots in the EU-funded project GEMINI, fundamental changes were necessary to adopt it to the requirements of the application environment. Additionally within this paper the basics of embedded speech dialogue systems are covered.

1 Introduction

The EU funded research project GEMINI (Generic Environment for Multilingual Interactive Natural Interfaces) aimed at the development of an Application Generation Platform (AGP) to semiautomatically generate multimodal dialogue applications for database access (Hamerich et al., 2004a). At the end of the project, two telephony applications had been successfully deployed: a banking application for a Greek bank, and a citizen care application for a German city. The former has been used by several thousand customers (Hamerich et al., 2004b).

Based on the ideas and concepts of GEMINI a new tool named DiaGen has been developed, which improves the development process for dialogue applications with regard to certain aspects.

This paper is structured as follows: First the basic ideas of the GEMINI AGP are introduced. Next the characteristics and peculiarities of embedded speech applications are explained. This is followed by a description of the concepts of GEMINI which had been a starting point for the development of DiaGen. The core of this paper follows: a detailled description of the DiaGen tool. Finally the conclusion and outlook are presented.

2 The GEMINI AGP

The GEMINI AGP provided support for the semiautomatic creation of phone-based dialogue applications. The development process had several layers. Through the different phases of a layer the application developer was guided by a wizard and had to use specialised assistants for each phase.

The first starting point was a rough abstract dialogue model, which has been enriched step by step through all phases until finally dialogue model was completed. All models are completely written in a language specifically developed for the purposes of GEMINI covering both, dialogue description and data modelling (Hamerich et al., 2003; Schubert and Hamerich, 2005).

Originally the GEMINI AGP was designed for phone-based or web-based applications. Therefore the final outcome of the AGP was VoiceXML or xHTML, according to the initial selection of the application developer.

The three layers of the platform are described in depth in (d'Haro et al., 2006).

3 Automotive Speech Dialogues

Speech dialogues for cars are embedded solutions running under real-time operating systems with very

Proceedings of the 9th SIGdial Workshop on Discourse and Dialogue, pages 92–95,
Columbus, June 2008.

low memory and CPU power (Hamerich, 2005).[1] Next to these hardware requirements customers from automotive industry demand very explicit specifications to understand the complete dialogue flow and see its connections to the graphical/haptical HMI (human machine interface) in a car. Therefore special algorithms and tools are used, to develop and run speech dialogues on such embedded systems. In consequence Harman/Becker has a proprietary dialogue description language developed especially for being used on embedded environments (Hamerich and Hanrieder, 2004). The Generic Dialogue Modelling Language (GDML) is designed as a compiled language to save memory and CPU resources. This makes sense, since dialogues within a car are still closed applications.

Speech control for cars is available to the end customer since 1996 (Heisterkamp, 2001). Today many car manufacturers offer speech control systems. Typical applications in a car are voice control of telephone, tuner and navigation system. Direct control of media files using their meta-data (e.g. ID3-Tags) by saying e.g. "play title 'Bad' by 'Michael Jackson'" is a feature currently under development (Wang and Hamerich, 2008).

In spite of several tools and libraries, dialogue development for automotive applications is mainly still manual work.

4 Porting Ideas from GEMINI to DiaGen

Since the GEMINI AGP showed that advanced speech dialogue applications can be created fast and easy it was straightforward to attempt to transfer at least some of the possibilities from the AGP into the world of embedded speech dialogues. However the following features need to be changed for the new tool:

- Speech dialogues in cars do not access a database; instead the devices are controlled directly by the speech dialogue. Therefore DiaGen does not need a database interface but should instead offer a flexible way to integrate access to external devices.

- When starting development with the AGP first a rough dialogue specification has to be provided, which for every new application needs to be given again (except the library approach is used, which makes only sense for very similar applications). It would make sense to provide a sample dialogue at the start of dialogue development for embedded applications, containing the most common interfaces and allowing faster creation of new applications from this starting point.

- When using the AGP for dialogue development, there was no consistency check for speech grammars and their connection to the dialogue. This should be improved with DiaGen.

- Since highly customised applications are demanded, code is still written by hand. Nevertheless dialogue designers are supported with several tools and libraries. Therefore the new tool should fit into the existing tool chain, but should also allow for manual editing or at least fine-tuning of the code. Since it was experienced from GEMINI that generating VoiceXML from the models coded in the GEMINI modelling language was hard work, it was decided to directly work on the runtime language for the new tool. This minimises efforts for the generation components and on the other hand allows for easy editing of code files. That means for the new tool no generator component is needed. Instead the compiler needed for the embedded dialogue descriptions should be added to DiaGen, to allow for integrated development.

- Since the creation of a phone-based dialogue system requires specialised handling for different situations (e.g. for database access, output generation, etc.) several specialised wizards have been created forming the AGP. Since development for a speech control system is quite different it does not make sense, to have several assistants. Therefore DiaGen integrates all the needed functionality into one tool.

[1] Generally embedded systems comprise other highly integrated systems as well. Since the approach for embedding speech dialogue systems described here can work on such systems as well, the term 'embedded' is used as a generalisation.

5 DiaGen

As already described above, DiaGen was developed as a new tool, based on the experiences made within the GEMINI project. The key idea of DiaGen is to ease development of speech dialogues for automotive applications. The main point here is not only to speed up coding of dialogue scripts but additionally to support the development of correct, consistent, and user-friendly dialogue applications.

The main differences between DiaGen and the GEMINI AGP are already described above. In this section the most outstanding properties of the final tool are discussed in detail.

5.1 Modelling Language

Since effort for generating runtime code from development models was a big issuee within GEMINI and it is often required to change code details even in a late phase of development, it was decided for DiaGen to work directly on GDML. This allows DiaGen to offer manual editing at any development stage.

5.2 Integration

For a GDML developer, there are daily tools to work with. These are the grammar and dialogue compiler and a testing and debugging tool. These tools all have been integrated into DiaGen. For each tool, DiaGen allows to set configuration parameters as well as to compile and debug directly in the environment.

5.3 Project Model

One of the main features of DiaGen is a complete project model, which contains all project files and runtime configuration settings. Loading this model into DiaGen allows easy compiling, testing and editing of the complete application.

The model can be extended by editing the contained files using DiaGen. Additionally DiaGen also offers the possibility to add predefined routines or methods to the model, allowing for a library usage.

Another advantage of the model is the complete coverage of variables, functions, prompts, etc. This speeds up the development process quite a lot, since the tool automatically proposes allowed argument values for a function call. And if a variable has not been defined in the current context, this can just be done by a simple click on the respective button. This feature was already available in parts with the GEMINI AGP.

5.4 Sample Application

As already mentioned in section 4 development for a new application with DiaGen starts with a sample application. This saves time since setting up a new running application with correct configuration settings by hand can be a lengthy process. If instead a complete running system is copied and stripped down, this costs time as well. Starting with a small sample application therefore is much more efficient.

The sample application can easily be updated and maintained, therefore even new configuration settings or techniques can be adopted.

5.5 Device Interface

To control devices by speech, their interface must be accessible for the dialogue. This in GDML generally is done with the concept of system calls for details see (Hamerich and Hanrieder, 2004). New system calls can be created using DiaGen or just be added to an existing DiaGen project. When a system call is needed, it can just be selected from a list, saving time for lookup. Of course all the advantages of the project model (sec. 5.3) apply for system calls and their arguments and results as well.

5.6 Grammar Tag Consistency

GDML (like VoiceXML) uses semantic grammar tags to identify user utterances. These tags are even independent of the used language making GDML dialogues complete language independent. This gives bigger flexibility and minimises efforts for porting a dialogue application to another language.

To initiate a dialogue reaction, a specified tag has to be delivered from the parser. For each tag a dialogue action inside the dialogue code itself is needed. In this case consistency of these tags in grammar and dialogue script is of highest importance. As already mentioned the GEMINI AGP did not ensure this consistency automatically. This led to high efforts when developing an application with the AGP. To minimise these efforts and disable potential errors the consistency shall be ensured automatically by DiaGen.

To do so DiaGen offers a special view of the grammar. For each grammar rule or combination of rules all possible grammar tags are shown. Selecting a tag automatically constructs a complete switch-case statement for all possible alternatives and ensures consistency between grammar and dialogue.

5.7 Usage of DiaGen

DiaGen has been developed to allow fast creation of flexible speech dialogues for automotive applications. See Figure 1 for possibilities of its context menu. It was used successfully for a proactive dynamic traffic information application based on Traffic Message Channel (TMC) messages. This application has already been described in (Hamerich, 2007). Since the tool is still in its testing phase, it is currently used for prototypical development only.

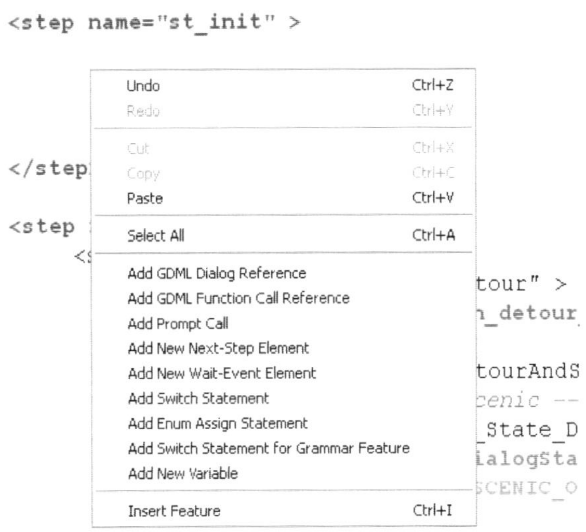

Figure 1: *Context menu of DiaGen within GDML dialog step.*

6 Conclusion

In this paper DiaGen was presented. A tool to improve the development process of embedded speech dialogues as used for automotive systems. Major improvements offered by usage of DiaGen are speed-up of coding and verified code consistency. DiaGen results partly from the experiences collected within the GEMINI project. But since GEMINI concentrated on phone-based and multimodal applications, several changes have been necessary for embedded dialogues, which have been described.

7 Future Work

As pointed out the tool is currently used to develop a pilot application. As feedback from the work on the pilot application, DiaGen is constantly being updated. At a later development stage of DiaGen it will be evaluated to be used for product development as well.

References

L.F. d'Haro, R. de Córdoba, J. Ferreiros, S.W. Hamerich, V. Schless, B. Kladis, V. Schubert, O. Kocsis, S. Igel, and J.M. Pardo. 2006. An Advanced Platform to Speed up the Design of Multilingual Dialog Applications for Multiple Modalities. *Speech Communication*, 48(6):863–887.

S.W. Hamerich and G. Hanrieder. 2004. Modelling Generic Dialog Applications for Embedded Systems. In *Proc. ICSLP*, pages 237–240, Jeju, Korea.

S.W. Hamerich, Y.-F. H. Wang, V. Schubert, V. Schless, and S. Igel. 2003. XML-Based Dialogue Descriptions in the GEMINI Project. In *Proc. 'Berliner XML-Tage 2003'*, pages 404–412, Berlin, Germany.

S.W. Hamerich, R. de Córdoba, V. Schless, L.F. d'Haro, B. Kladis, V. Schubert, O. Kocsis, S. Igel, and J.M. Pardo. 2004a. The GEMINI Platform: Semi-Automatic Generation of Dialogue Applications. In *Proc. ICSLP*, pages 2629–2632, Jeju, Korea.

S.W. Hamerich, V. Schubert, V. Schless, R. de Córdoba, J. M. Pardo, L. F. d'Haro, B. Kladis, O. Kocsis, and S. Igel. 2004b. Semi-Automatic Generation of Dialogue Applications in the GEMINI Project. In *Proc. SIGdial*, pages 31–34, Cambridge, USA.

S.W. Hamerich. 2005. Speech Dialogue Systems for Cars - an Overview. *SDV – Sprache und Datenverarbeitung*, 29(2):107–118.

S.W. Hamerich. 2007. Towards Advanced Speech Driven Navigation Systems for Cars. In *Proc. IE*, pages 247–250, Ulm, Germany.

P. Heisterkamp. 2001. Linguatronic – Product-Level Speech System for Mercedes-Benz Cars. In *Proc. HLT*, pages 1–2, San Diego, USA.

V. Schubert and S.W. Hamerich. 2005. The Dialog Application Metalanguage GDialogXML. In *Proc. EUROSPEECH*, pages 789–792, Lisbon, Portugal.

Y.-F.H. Wang and S.W. Hamerich, 2008. *Dybkjær, L. and Minker, W. (Ed.): Recent Trends in Discourse and Dialogue*, chapter Designing Speech-Controlled Media File Selection for Automotive Systems, pages 25–43. Springer, Dordrecht, Netherlands.

Quantifying Ellipsis in Dialogue: an index of mutual understanding

Marcus Colman, Arash Eshghi and Patrick G. T. Healey
Interaction, Media and Communication Research Group
Queen Mary, University of London
E1 4NS UK
{marcus, arash, ph}@dcs.qmul.ac.uk

Abstract

This paper presents a coding protocol that allows naïve users to annotate dialogue transcripts for anaphora and ellipsis. Cohen's kappa statistic demonstrates that the protocol is sufficiently robust in terms of reliability. It is proposed that quantitative ellipsis data may be used as an index of mutual-engagement. Current and potential uses of ellipsis coding are described.

1. Introduction

Spontaneously generated dialogue, whether naturally occurring or task-oriented, rarely sticks to accepted rules of grammar or even politeness. Interruptions, ungrammatical utterances and grunts or other noises are found in the majority of contributions in dialogue corpora. One reason for this is the ubiquitous use of ellipsis; the omission of words or phrases from a contribution which can be inferred or extracted from previous contributions. Ellipsis is optional; the full constituent could serve communication as well as the elliptical version. Where ellipsis occurs across speakers i.e., one participant makes (elliptical) use of another's contribution, it provides a direct index of the mutual-accessibility of the current conversational context (cf. Healey et. al. 2007; Eshghi and Healey, 2007).

In some cases elliptical contributions are obvious, as in the polar response 'yeah', signifying that a question has been heard, understood and considered; however, there are degrees of complexity that would seem to require a close understanding of what another participant is referring to. It is this issue of mutual-accessibility or 'grounding' that we propose can be investigated through the quantification of elliptical phenomena. These phenomena are, we propose, also related to the way referring expressions can contract over repeated use. (e.g. Schober and Clark, 1989; Wilkes-Gibbs and Clark, 1992). The approach taken in Clark et al.'s 'collaborative theory' is that as mutual understanding increases, dialogue contributions become shorter as referring terms become part of the common ground. Clark and Krych (2004) note that various elliptical phrases can be used to establish common ground, from continuers ('uh-huh', 'yeah') or assessments ('gosh') to establishing shared attention through deictic expressions such as 'this', 'that', 'here' and 'there'.

Healey et al. (2007) demonstrated the basic concept and viability of quantifying ellipsis phenomena as a quantitative index of mutual-accessibility of context. They showed that the frequency of use of cross-speaker elliptical expressions in online chat varies systematically depending on whether communication is 'local' i.e. within a single chat room or 'remote'. However, the coding of ellipsis in this study did not follow an explicit protocol. It relied mainly on the distinctions made by Fernandez et al. (2004) but specific measures of reliability and validity were not calculated.

Proceedings of the 9th SIGdial Workshop on Discourse and Dialogue, pages 96–99,
Columbus, June 2008.

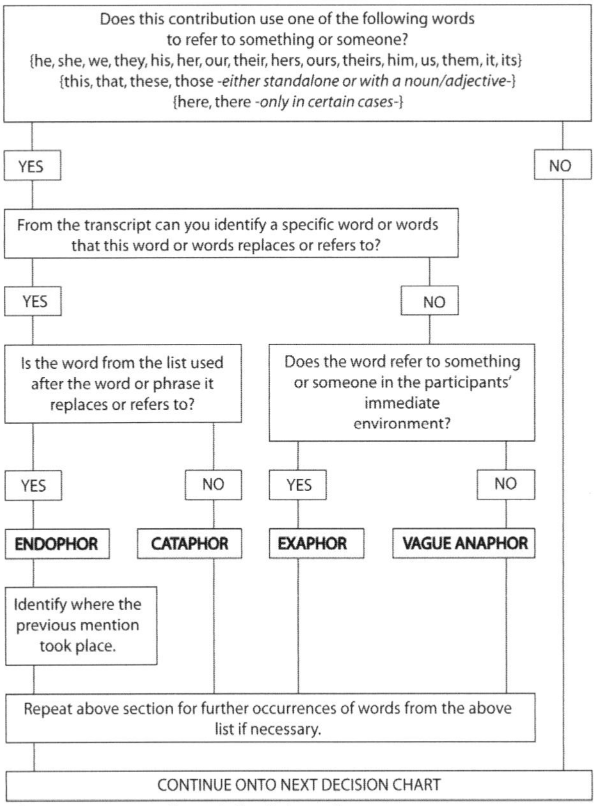

Figure 1. 'Anaphora' decision chart

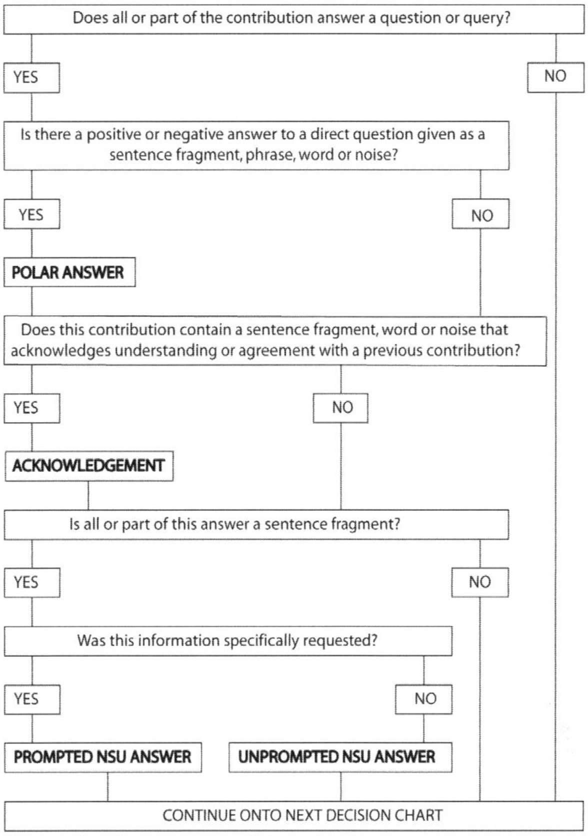

Figure 2. 'Answers' decision chart

In this paper we present an ellipsis coding protocol that provides a set of coding categories and we report the inter-rater reliability scores that have been obtained with it. In order to simplify coding and increase reliability, categories suggested by Fernandez et al. have been collapsed into broader ones. It should be pointed out that we are not, in general, trying to produce an accurate or definitive analysis of ellipsis. The protocol is rather the product of contending with the compromise between robust coding categories and linguistic elegance. The categories presented here are generally ordered in terms of occurrence in order to assist the coder. A contribution to dialogue may contain more than one type of elliptical utterance; contributions are not assigned to one mutually exclusive category. Rather, coders are able to use the protocol to label any part of a dialogue that is elliptical.

2. The Ellipsis Protocol

The protocol is designed as a tool for coding one aspect of dialogue, developed with the intention that users with no specific knowledge of linguistics can use it. As can be seen from Figures 1-4, it consists of four binary branching decision trees that are applied to each contribution in an interaction. Full instructions for use of the protocol have also been written and are available from the authors.

3. Inter-rater reliability

In order to demonstrate reliability between coders, two coders (one computer scientist, one psychologist) applied the ellipsis protocol to a sample of task oriented dialogue. This was taken from the HCRC Map Task corpus (Anderson et al, 1991); a series of dialogues in which one participant attempts to describe a route on a fictional map to another. The longest of these dialogues was chosen to be coded (transcript Q1NC1) which consisted of 446 turns and 5533 words. Cohen's kappa was calculated using the procedure outlined in Howell (1994); see Carletta (1996) for a discussion of the use of kappa in dialogue coding. Kappa in this instance was .81, which shows very high reliability, even by conservative standards (Krippendorff,

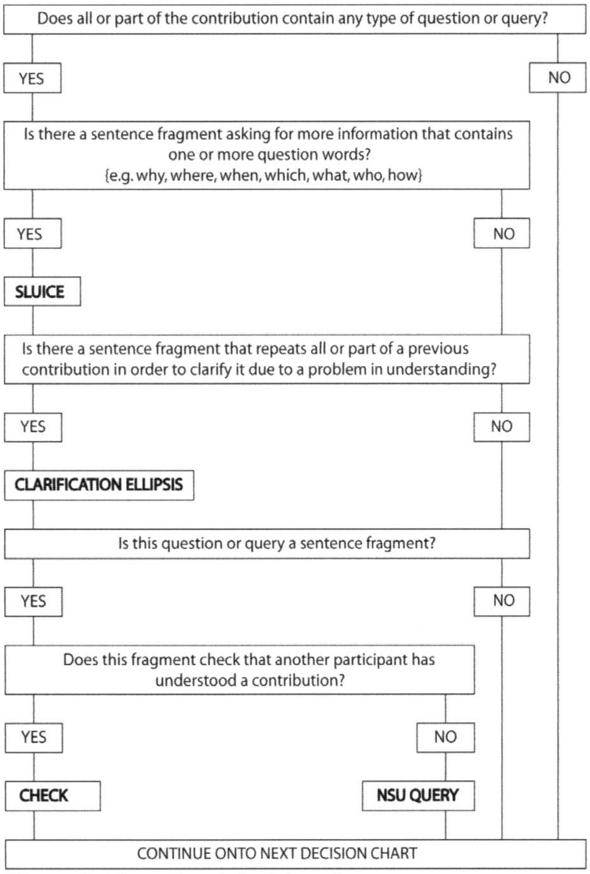

Figure 3. 'Questions' decision chart

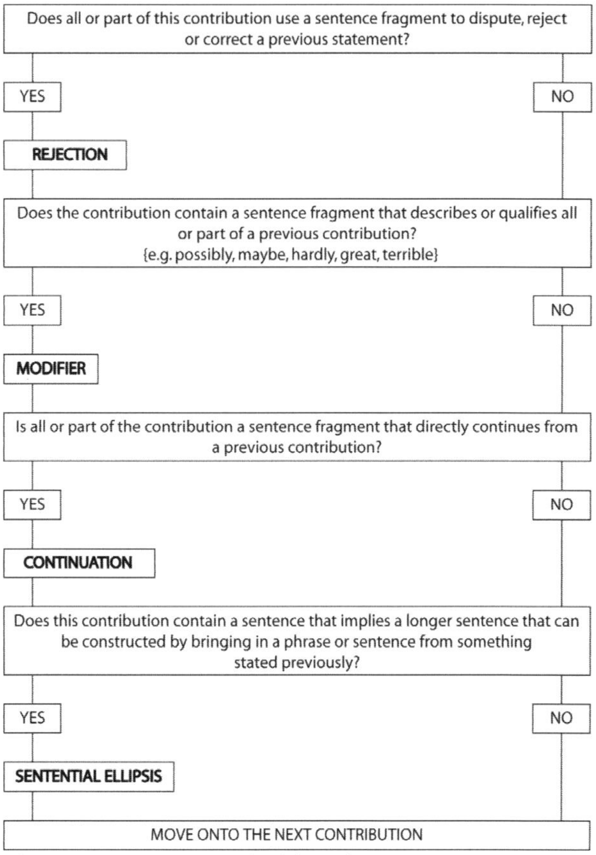

Figure 4. 'Statements' decision chart

1980). Table 1 below presents a breakdown of the instances of categories that were agreed upon.

Table 1 shows the total number and approximate percentage of agreements. Also given, '1.dis' and '2.dis' are the number of observed instances by coders one and two respectively identified but disputed for that particular category. The total number of elliptical or non-elliptical instances coded, from single words or phrases to entire turns was 624; of these, 100 (16%) were disagreed upon and 78 instances (12.5%) were agreed to contain no elliptical phenomena (no ellipsis disagreements = 50). Some categories have very low frequencies; however, previous work suggests that these categories are necessary. To some extent this table shows the limitations of the kappa statistic; coder agreement varies considerably across these categories.

	Endophor	Cataphor	Exaphor	Vague Anaphor
Total	**119**	**2**	**8**	**33**
%	**19**	**.03**	**1.3**	**5.3**
1.dis	12	1	1	20
2.dis	10	3	17	6
	Polar Answer	Acknowledge	Prompted NSU Ans.	Un-prompted NSU Ans.
Total	**113**	**78**	**1**	**7**
%	**18.1**	**12.5**	**0.2**	**1.1**
1.dis	7	15	0	1
2.dis	5	9	1	5
	Sluice	Clarification Ellipsis	Check	NSU Query
Total	**2**	**7**	**20**	**27**
%	**.03**	**1.1**	**3.2**	**4.3**
1.dis	0	0	2	5
2.dis	2	2	0	2
	Rejection	Modification	Continua-tion	Sentential Ellipsis
Total	**2**	**1**	**13**	**13**
%	**.03**	**.002**	**2.1**	**2.1**
1.dis	1	0	3	10
2.dis	4	0	3	3

Table 1. Total agreements by category

4. Discussion

Although mutual-accessibility of context is fundamental to communication, there has not been a reliable method for observing or measuring it. The ellipsis protocol presented here thus provides a useful step in this direction. It gives a standardised coding scheme that can quantify the extent to which speakers can directly access the constituents of each other's turns.

In previous work there have been several different attempts to define taxonomies of elliptical or context dependent utterances. For example, non-sentential utterances (NSUs), e.g. Schlangen and Lascarides (2003); Fernandez and Ginzburg (2002); Fernandez, Ginzburg and Lappin (2007). One issue with these previous approaches is the lack of reliability data; a statistic such as Cohen's kappa is needed in order to demonstrate that a taxonomy or coding scheme can be reliably applied between independent coders. Carletta et al. (1997) presented a reliable coding scheme for the classification of dialogue moves; although there are overlaps between their categories and ours, the questions used in the scheme are intended to establish solely the function of an utterance and importantly, not whether the utterance is elliptical. The protocol presented here achieves a high level of reliability for some of these context dependent phenomena without requiring specific prior knowledge of the relevant linguistic theory.

Further work will code a sample from the BNC (Burnard, 2000) in order to allow comparisons with previous taxonomies. The HCRC map task corpus has previously been examined in terms of various features of dialogue, e.g. Dialogue Games Analysis (Kowtko et al, 1991) and disfluencies (Lickley and Bard, 1998). Ongoing work will develop this through coding the entire HCRC map task corpus; providing data on how ellipsis varies over different conditions such as medium, familiarity and task role.

Acknowledgments

Thanks go to the HCRC group for providing the map task data. Thanks also to Jackie Folkes and Greg Mills for help and advice.

References

Anderson, A., Bader. M., Bard, E., Boyle, E., Doherty, G. M., Garrod, S., Isard, S., Kowtko, J., McAllister, J., Miller, J., Sotillo, C., Thompson, H. S. and Weinert, R. (1991). The HCRC Map Task Corpus. *Language and Speech*, 34, 351-366.

Burnard, L. (2000). *Reference Guide for the British National Corpus (World Edition)*. Oxford University Computing Services.

Carletta, J. (1996). Assessing agreement on classification tasks: the kappa statistic. *Computational Linguistics*, 22(2): 249-254.

Clark, H. H. and Krych, M. A. (2004). Speaking while monitoring addressees for understanding. *Journal of Memory and Language*, 50, 62-81.

Eshghi, A. and Healey, P. G. T. (2007). Collective states of understanding. *Proceedings of the 8th SIGdial workshop on discourse and dialogue*. pp 2-9.

Fernandez, R. and Ginzburg, J. (2002). Non-sentential utterances: a corpus study. *Traitement automatique des languages: dialogue*, 43(2), 13-42.

Fernandez, R., Ginzburg J and Lappin, S, (2004). Classifying ellipsis in dialogue: a machine learning approach. *Proceedings of the 20th international conference on computational linguistics*. pp 240-246.

Fernandez, R. , Ginzburg J and Lappin, S. (2007). Classifying non-sentential utterances in dialogue: a machine learning approach. *Computational Linguistics* 33(3), 397-427.

Healey, P. G. T., White, G., Eshghi, A. and Light, A. (2007). Communication Spaces. *Computer Supported Co-operative Work*, 2007.

Howell, D. C. (1997). *Statistical Methods for Psychology*. Duxbury Press.

Kowtko, J. C., Isard, S. D. and Doherty, G. M. (1991). Conversational games within dialogue. *Proceedings of the espirit workshop on discourse coherence*, 1991.

Krippendorff, K. (1980). *Content Analysis: an introduction to its methodology*. Beverly Hills: Sage Publications.

Lickley, R. and Bard, E. (1998). When can listeners detect disfluency in spontaneous speech? *Language and Speech*, 41.

Schlangen, D. and Lascarides, A. (2003). The interpretation of non-sentential utterances in dialogue. *Proceedings of the 4th SIGdial workshop on discourse and dialogue*, 2003.

Schober, M. F. and Clark, H. H. (1989). Understanding by addressees and overhearers. *Cognitive Psychology*, 21, 211-232.

Wilkes-Gibbs, D. and Clark, H. H. (1992). Coordinating beliefs in conversation. *Journal of Memory and Language*, 31, 183-194.

Implicit Proposal Filtering in Multi-Party Consensus-Building Conversations

Yasuhiro Katagiri
Future University – Hakodate
katagiri@fun.ac.jp

Yosuke Matsusaka
National Institute of Advanced Industrial Science and Technology
yosuke.matsusaka@aist.go.jp

Yasuharu Den
Chiba University
den@cogsci.l.chiba-u.ac.jp

Mika Enomoto
Tokyo University of Technology
menomoto@media.teu.ac.jp

Masato Ishizaki
The University of Tokyo
ishizaki@iii.u-tokyo.ac.jp

Katsuya Takanashi
Kyoto University
takanasi@ar.media.kyoto-u.ac.jp

Abstract

An attempt was made to statistically estimate proposals which survived the discussion to be incorporated in the final agreement in an instance of a Japanese design conversation. Low level speech and vision features of hearer behaviors corresponding to aiduti, noddings and gaze were found to be a positive predictor of survival. The result suggests that non-linguistic hearer responses work as implicit proposal filters in consensus building, and could provide promising candidate features for the purpose of recognition and summarization of meeting events.

1 Introduction

Non-verbal signals, such as gaze, head nods, facial expressions and bodily gestures, play significant roles in the conversation organization functions. Several projects have been collecting multi-modal conversation data (Carletta et al., 2006) for multi-party dialogues in order to develop techniques for meeting event recognitions from non-verbal as well as verbal signals. We investigate, in this paper, hearer response functions in multi-party consensus-building conversations. We focus particularly on the evaluative aspect of verbal and non-verbal hearer responses. During the course of a consensus-building discussion meeting, a series of proposals are put on the table, examined, evaluated and accepted or rejected. The examinations of proposals can take the form of explicit verbal exchanges, but they can also be implicit through accumulations of hearer responses. Hearers would express, mostly unconsciously for non-verbal signals, their interest and positive appraisals toward a proposal when it is introduced and is being discussed, and that these hearer responses would collectively contribute to the determination of final consensus making. The question we address is whether and in what degree it is possible and effective to filter proposals and estimate agreement by using verbal and non-verbal hearer responses in consensus-building discussion meetings.

2 Multi-Party Design Conversation Data

2.1 Data collection

We chose multi-party design conversations for the domain of our investigation. Different from a fixed problem solving task with a 'correct' solution, participants are given partially specified design goals and engage in a discussion to come up with an agreement on the final design plan. The condition of our data collection was as follows:

Number of participants: six for each session
Arrangement: face-to-face conversation
Task: Proposal for a new mobile phone business
Role: No pre-determined role was imposed

A compact meeting archiver equipment, AIST-MARC (Asano and Ogata, 2006), which can capture panoramic video and speaker-separated speech streams, was used to record conversations (Fig. 1). The data we examined consist of one 30 minutes conversation conducted by 5 males and 1 female. Even though we did not assign any roles, a chairperson and a clerk were spontaneously elected by the participants at the beginning of the session.

Proceedings of the 9th SIGdial Workshop on Discourse and Dialogue, pages 100–103,
Columbus, June 2008.

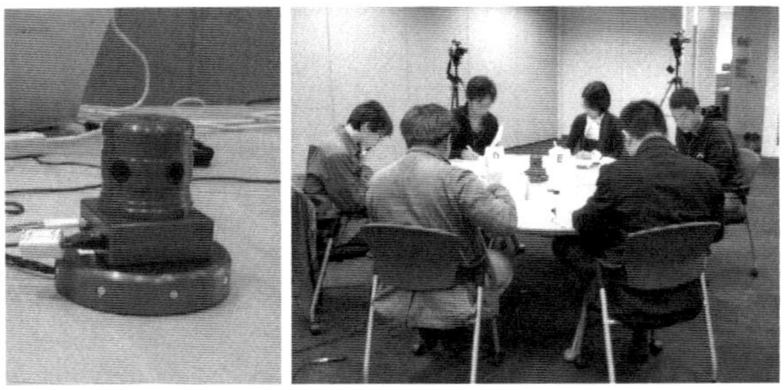

Figure 1: AIST-MARC and a recording scene

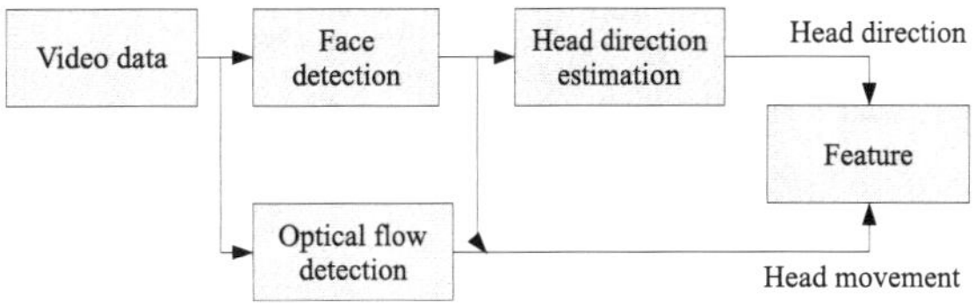

Figure 2: Image processing algorithm

2.2 Data Annotation

2.2.1 Clause units

In order to provide a clause level segmentation of a multi-channel speech stream, we extended the notion of 'clause units (CUs)', originally developed for analyzing spoken monologues in the Corpus of Spontaneous Japanese (Takanashi et al., 2003), to include reactive tokens (Clancy et al., 1996) and other responses in spoken conversations. Two of the authors who worked on the Corpus of Spontaneous Japanese independently worked on the data and resolved the differences, which created 1403 CUs consisting of 469 complete utterances, 857 reactive tokens, and 77 incomplete or fragmental utterances.

2.2.2 Proposal units

We developed a simple classification scheme of discourse segments for multi-party consensus building conversations based on the idea of 'interaction process analysis' (Bales, 1950).

Proposal: Presentation of new ideas and their evaluation. Substructure are often realized through elaboration and clarification.

Summary: Sum up multiple proposals possibly with their assessment

Orientation: Lay out a topic to be discussed and signal a transition of conversation phases, initiated mostly by the facilitator of the discussion

Miscellaneous: Other categories including opening and closing segments

The connectivity between clause units, the content of the discussion, interactional roles, relationship with adjacent segments and discourse markers were considered in the identification of proposal units. Two of the authors, one worked on the Corpus of Spontaneous Japanese and the other worked for the project of standardization of discourse tagging, independently worked on the data and resolved the differences, which resulted in 19 proposals, 8 summaries, 19 orientations and 2 miscellaneouses.

2.3 Core clause units and survived proposal units

Core clause units (CUs) were selected, out of all the clause units, based on whether the CUs have substantial content as a proposal. A CU was judged as a core CU, when the annotator would find it appropriate to express, upon hearing the CU, either an approval or a disapproval to its content if she were in the position of a participant of the conversation. Three of the authors worked on the text data excluding the reactive tokens, and the final selection was settled by majority decision. 35 core CUs were selected from 235 CUs in the total of 19 proposal PUs. Cohen's kappa agreement rate was 0.894.

Survived proposal units (PUs) were similarly selected, out of all the proposal units, based on whether the PUs were incorporated in the final agreement among all the participants. 9 survived PUs were selected from 19 proposal PUs.

3 Feature Extraction of Hearer's Behavior

For each clause unit (CU), verbal and non-verbal features concerning hearer's behavior were extracted from the audio and the video data.

3.1 Non-Verbal Features

We focused on nodding and gaze, which were approximated by vertical and horizontal head movements of participants.

An image processing algorithm (Figure 2) was applied to estimate head directions and motions (Matsusaka, 2005). Figure 3 shows a sample scene and the results of applying head direction estimation algorithm.

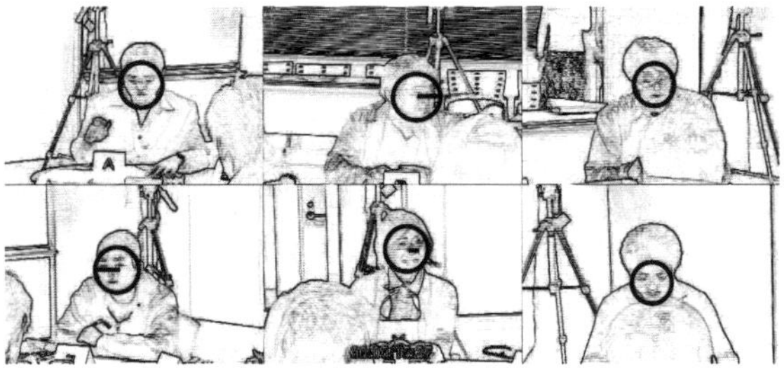

Figure 3: Sample scene with image processing results. The circles represent detected face areas, and the lines in the circles represent head directions.

For each CU, the vertical and horizontal components of head movements of 5 hearers were calculated for two regions, the region inside the CU and the 1-sec region immediately after the CU. For each of the two regions, the mean and the peak values and the relative location, in the region, of the peak were computed. These 12 non-verbal features were used for the statistical modeling.

3.2 Verbal Features

Verbal features were extracted from the audio data. For each CU, power values of 5 hearers were extracted for two regions, 'within' and 'after' CU, and for each of the two regions, the mean and the peak values and the relative location, in the region, of the peak were computed. In addition to these verbal features, we also used aiduti features of reactive tokens (RTs). The percentage of the total duration of RTs, the total number of RTs, and the number of participants who produced an RT were computed in 'within' and 'after' regions for each of the CUs. A total of 12 CU verbal features were used for the statistical modeling.

4 Experiments

4.1 Overview of the Algorithm

Statistical modeling was employed to see if it is possible to identify the proposal units (PUs) that are survived in the participants' final consensus. To this end, we, first, find the dominant clause unit (CU) in each PU, and, then, based on the verbal and non-verbal features of these CUs, we classify PUs into 'survived' and 'non-survived.'

Table 1: The optimal model for finding core-CUs

	Estimate
(Intercept)	-1.72
within/speech power/mean	-11.54
after/vertical motion/peak loc.	-4.25
after/speech power/mean	3.91
after/aiduti/percent	3.02

Table 2: Confusion matrix of core-CU prediction experiment (precision = 0.50, recall = 0.086)

	Predicted	
Observed	Non-core	Core
Non-core	431	3
Core	32	3

4.2 Finding Dominant CUs

A logistic regression model was used to model the coreness of CUs. A total of 24 verbal and non-verbal features were used as explanatory variables. Since the number of non-core CUs was much larger than that of core CUs, down-sampling of negative instances was performed. To obtain a reliable estimation, a sort of Monte Carlo simulation was adopted.

A model selection by using AIC was applied for the 35 core CUs and another 35 non-core CUs that were re-sampled from among the set of 434 complete and non-core CUs. This process was repeated 100 times, and the features frequently selected in this simulation were used to construct the optimal model. Table 1 shows the estimated coefficient for the optimal model, and Table 2 shows the accuracy based on a leave-1-out cross validation. The dominant CU in each PU was identified as the CU

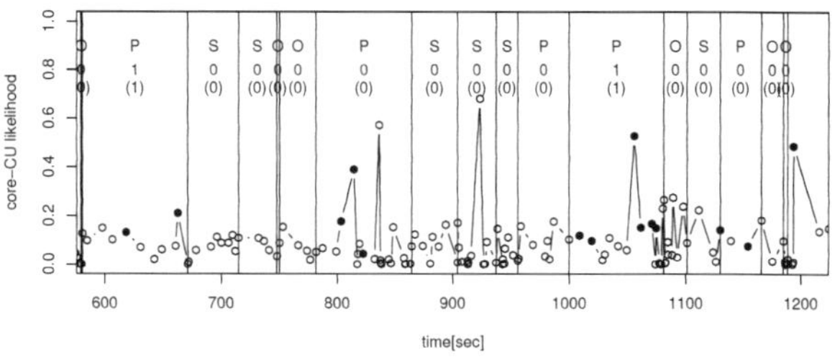

Figure 4: The predicted coreness of CUs. Dominant CUs were defined to be CUs with the highest coreness in each of the PUs. Black and white dots are CUs labeled as core and non-core.

Table 3: The optimal model for finding survived-PUs

	Estimate
within/vertical motion/peak val.	3.96
within/speech power/mean	−27.76
after/speech power/peak val.	1.49

Table 4: Result of the survived-PU prediction (precision = 0.83, recall = 0.44)

	Predicted	
Observed	Non-survived	Survived
Non-survived	37	1
Survived	4	5

with the highest predicted value in that PU. Figure 4 shows the predicted values for coreness.

4.3 Finding Survived PUs

The verbal and non-verbal features of the dominant CUs of each of the PUs were used for the modeling of the survived-PU prediction. Discriminant analysis was utilized and a model selection was applied for the 47 PUs. Table 3 shows the estimated coefficient for the optimal model, and Table 4 shows the accuracy based on a leave-1-out cross validation.

5 Discussions

The results of our estimation experiments indicate that the final agreement outcome of the discussion can be approximately estimated at the proposal level. Though it may not be easy to identify actual utterances contributing to the agreement (core-CUs), the dominant CUs in PUs were found to be effective in the identification of survived-PUs. The prediction accuracy of survived-PUs was about 89%, with the chance level of 69%, whereas that of core-CUs was about 92%, with the chance level of 86%.

In terms of hearer response features, intensity of verbal responses (*within/speech power/mean*, *after/speech power/mean*), and immediate nodding responses (*after/vertical motion/peak loc.*) were the most common contributing features in core-CU estimation. In contrast, occurrence of a strong aiduti immediately after, rather than within, the core-CU (*after/speech power/peak val.*), and a strong nodding within the core-CU (*within/vertical motion/peak val.*) appear to be signaling support from hearers to the proposal. It should be noted that identification of target hearer behaviors must be validated against manual annotations before these generalizations are established. Nevertheless, the results are mostly coherent with our intuitions on the workings of hearer responses in conversations.

6 Conclusions

We have shown that approximate identification of the proposal units incorporated into the final agreement can be obtained through the use of statistical pattern recognition techniques on low level speech and vision features of hearer behaviors. The result provides a support for the idea that hearer responses convey information on hearers' affective and evaluative attitudes toward conversation topics, which effectively functions as implicit filters for the proposals in the consensus building process.

Acknowledgments

The work reported in this paper was supported by Japan Society for the Promotion of Science Grants-in-aid for Scientific Research (B) 18300052.

References

F. Asano and J. Ogata. 2006. Detection and separation of speech events in meeting recordings. In *Proc. Interspeech*, pages 2586–2589.

R. F. Bales. 1950. A set of categories for the analysis of small group interaction. *American Sociological Review*, 15:257–263.

J. Carletta, S. Ashby, S. Bourban, M. Flynn, M. Guillemot, T. Hain, J. Kadlec, V. Karaiskos, W. Kraaij, M. Kronenthal, G. Lathoud, M. Lincoln, A. Lisowska, I. McCowan, W. Post, D. Reidsma, and P. Wellner. 2006. The AMI meeting corpus: A pre-announcement. In *Machine Learning for Multimodal Interaction*, pages 28–39.

P. M. Clancy, S. A. Thompson, R. Suzuki, and H. Tao. 1996. The conversational use of reactive tokens in English, Japanese and Mandarin. *Journal of Pragmatics*, 26:355–387.

Y. Matsusaka. 2005. Recognition of 3 party conversation using prosody and gaze. In *Proc. Interspeech*, pages 1205–1208.

K. Takanashi, T. Maruyama, K. Uchimoto, and H. Isahara. 2003. Identification of 'sentence' in. spontaneous Japanese: detection and modification of clause boundaries. In *Proc. ISCA & IEEE Workshop on Spontaneous Speech Processing and Recognition*, pages 183–186.

Optimal Dialog in Consumer-Rating Systems using a POMDP Framework

Zhifei Li
Center for Language and Speech Processing
Johns Hopkins University
Baltimore, MD 21218, USA
zhifei.work@gmail.com

Patrick Nguyen, Geoffrey Zweig
Microsoft Corporation
1 Microsoft Way,
Redmond, WA 98052, USA
{panguyen,gzweig}@microsoft.com

Abstract

Voice-Rate is an experimental dialog system through which a user can call to get product information. In this paper, we describe an optimal dialog management algorithm for Voice-Rate. Our algorithm uses a POMDP framework, which is probabilistic and captures uncertainty in speech recognition and user knowledge. We propose a novel method to learn a user knowledge model from a review database. Simulation results show that the POMDP system performs significantly better than a deterministic baseline system in terms of both dialog failure rate and dialog interaction time. To the best of our knowledge, our work is the first to show that a POMDP can be successfully used for disambiguation in a complex voice search domain like Voice-Rate.

1 Introduction

In recent years, web-based shopping and rating systems have provided a valuable service to consumers by allowing them to shop products and share their assessments of products online. The use of these systems, however, requires access to a web interface, typically through a laptop or desktop computer, and this restricts their usefulness. While mobile phones also provide some web access, their small screens make them inconvenient to use. Therefore, there arises great interests in having a spoken dialog interface through which a user can call to get product information (e.g., price, rating, review, etc.) on the fly. Voice-Rate (Zweig et al., 2007) is such a system. Here is a typical scenario under which shows the usefulness of the Voice-Rate system. A user enters a store and finds that a digital camera he has not planned to buy is on sale. Before he decides to buy the camera, he takes out his cell phone and calls Voice-Rate to see whether the price is really a bargain and what other people have said about the camera. This helps him to make a wise decision. The Voice-Rate system (Zweig et al., 2007) involves many techniques, e.g., information retrieval, review summarization, speech recognition, speech synthesis, dialog management, etc. In this paper, we mainly focus on the dialog management component.

When a user calls Voice-Rate for the information of a specific product, the system needs to identify, from a database containing millions of products, the *exact* product the user intends. To achieve this, the system first solicits the user for the product name. Using the product name as a query, the system then retrieves from its database a list of products related to the query. Ideally, the highest-ranked product should be the one intended by the user. In reality, this is often not the case due to various reasons. For example, there might be a speech recognition error or an information retrieval ranking error. Moreover, the product name is usually very ambiguous in identifying an exact product. The product name that the user says may not be exactly the same as the name in the product database. For example, while the user says *"Canon Powershot SD750"*, the exact name in the product database may be *"Canon Powershot SD750 Digital Camera"*. Even the user says the *exact* name, it is possible that the same name may be corresponding to different products in different categories, for instance books and movies.

Due to the above reasons, whenever the Voice-Rate system finds multiple products matching the user's initial speech query, it initiates a dialog procedure to identify the intended product by asking questions about the products. In the product database,

Proceedings of the 9th SIGdial Workshop on Discourse and Dialogue, pages 104–111,
Columbus, June 2008.

many attributes can be used to identify a product. For example, a digital camera has the product name, category, brand, resolution, zoom, etc. Given a list of products, different attributes may have different ability to distinguish the products. For example, if the products belong to many categories, the category attribute is very useful to distinguish the products. In contrast, if all the products belong to a single category, it makes no sense to ask a question on the category. In addition to the variability in distinguishing products, different attributes may require different knowledge from the user in order for them to answer questions about these attributes. For example, while most users can easily answer a question on *category*, they may not be able to answer a question on the *part number* of a product, though the *part number* is unique and perfect to distinguish products. Other variabilities are in the difficulty that the attributes impose on speech recognition and speech synthesis. Clearly, given a list of products and a set of attributes, what questions and in what order to ask is essential to make the dialog successful. Our goal is to *dynamically* find such important attributes at each stage/turn.

The baseline system (Zweig et al., 2007) asks questions only on product name and category. The order of questions is fixed: first ask questions on product category, and then on name. Moreover, it is deterministic and does not model uncertainly in speech recognition and user knowledge. Partially observable Markov decision process (POMDP) has been shown to be a general framework to capture the uncertainty in spoken dialog systems. In this paper, we present a POMDP-based probabilistic system, which utilizes rich product information and captures uncertainty in speech recognition and user knowledge. We propose a novel method to learn a user knowledge model from a review database. Our simulation results show that the POMDP-based system improves the baseline significantly.

To the best of our knowledge, our work is the first to show that a POMDP can be successfully used for disambiguation in a complex voice search domain like Voice-Rate.

2 Voice-Rate Dialog System Overview

Figure 1 shows the main flow in the Voice-Rate system with simplification. Specifically, when a user calls Voice-Rate for the information of a specific

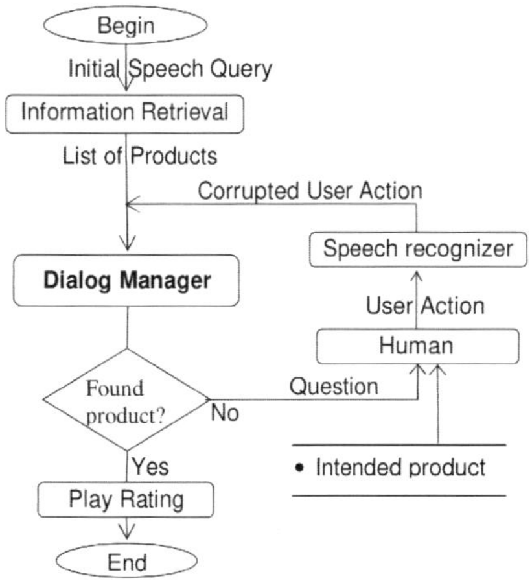

Figure 1: Flow Chart of Voice-Rate System

Step-1:	remove products that do not match the user action
Step-2:	any *category* question to ask?
	yes: ask the question and return
	no: go to step-3
Step-3:	ask a *product name* question

Table 1: Baseline Dialog Manager Algorithm

product, the system first solicits the user for the product name. Treating the user input as a *query* and the product names in the product database as *documents*, the system retrieves a list of products that match the user input based on TF-IDF measure. Then, the *dialog manager* dynamically generates questions to identify the specific intended product. Once the product is found, the system plays back its rating information. In this paper, we mainly focus on the *dialog manager* component.

Baseline Dialog Manager: Table 1 shows the baseline dialog manager. In Step-1, it removes all the products that are not consistent with the user response. For example, if the user answers "camera" when given a question on *category*, the system removes all the products that do not belong to category "camera". In Step-2 and Step-3, the baseline system asks questions about product name and product category, and product category has a higher priority.

3 Overview of POMDP

3.1 Basic Definitions

A Partially Observable Markov Decision Process (POMDP) is a general framework to handle uncertainty in a spoken dialog system. Following notations in Williams and Young (2007), a POMDP is defined as a tuple $\{S, A, T, R, O, Z, \lambda, \vec{b}_0\}$ where S is a set of states s describing the environment; A is a set of machine actions a operating on the environment; T defines a transition probability $P(s^{'}|s, a)$; R defines a reward function $r(s, a)$; O is a set of observations o, and an observation can be thought as a corrupted version of a user action; Z defines an observation probability $P(o^{'}|s^{'}, a)$; λ is a geometric discount factor; and $\vec{b}_0$ is an initial belief vector.

The POMDP operates as follows. At each time-step (a.k.a. *stage*), the environment is in some unobserved state s. Since s is not known exactly, a distribution (called a *belief vector* $\vec{b}$) over possible states is maintained where $\vec{b}(s)$ indicates the probability of being in a particular state s. Based on the current belief vector $\vec{b}$, an *optimal action selection* algorithm selects a machine action a, receives a reward r, and the environment transits to a new unobserved state $s^{'}$. The environment then generates an observation $o^{'}$ (i.e., a user action), after which the system update the belief vector $\vec{b}$. We call the process of adjusting the belief vector $\vec{b}$ at each stage *"belief update"*.

3.2 Applying POMDP in Practice

As mentioned in Williams and Young (2007), it is not trivial to apply the POMDP framework to a specific application. To achieve this, one normally needs to design the following three components:

- State Diagram Modeling
- Belief Update
- Optimal Action Selection

The *state diagram* defines the topology of the graph, which contains three kinds of elements: *system state*, *machine action*, and *user action*. To drive the transitions, one also needs to define a set of models (e.g., user goal model, user action model, etc.). The modeling assumptions are application-dependent. The state diagram, together with the models, determines the dynamics of the system.

In general, the *belief update* depends on the observation probability and the transition probability, while the transition probability itself depends on the modeling assumptions the system makes. Thus, the exact belief update formula is application-specific.

Optimal action selection is essentially an optimization algorithm, which can be defined as,

$$a^* = \arg\max_{a \in A} G(P(a)), \quad (1)$$

where A refers to a set of machine actions a. Clearly, the optimal action selection requires three sub-components: a goodness measure function G, a prediction algorithm P, and a search algorithm (i.e., the *argmax* operator). The prediction algorithm is used to predict the behavior of the system in the future if a given machine action a was taken. The search algorithm can use an exhaustive linear search or an approximated greedy search depending on the size of A (Murphy, 2000; Spaan and Vlassis, 2005).

4 POMDP Framework in Voice-Rate

In this section, we present our instantiation of POMDP in the Voice-Rate system.

4.1 State Diagram Modeling

4.1.1 State Diagram Design

Table 2 summarizes the main design choices in the state diagram for our application, i.e., identifying the intended product from a large list of products.

As in Williams and Young (2007), we incorporate both the user goal (i.e., the intended product) and the user action in the *system state*. Moreover, to efficiently update belief vector and compute optimal action, the state space is dynamically generated and pruned. In particular, instead of listing all the possible combinations between the products and the user actions, at each stage, we only generate states containing the products and the user actions that are relevant to the last machine action. Moreover, at each stage, if the belief probability of a product is smaller than a threshold, we prune out this product and all its associated system states. Note that the intended product may be pruned away due to an overly large threshold. In the simulation, we will use a development set to tune this threshold.

As shown in Table 2, five kinds of *machine actions* are defined. The questions on product names are usually long, imposing difficulty in speech synthesis/recgonition and user input. Thus, short questions (e.g., questions on category or simple attributes) are preferable. This partly motivate us to exploit rich product information to help the dialog.

Seven kinds of *user actions* are defined as shown in Table 2. Among them, the user actions "others", "not related", and "not known" are special. Specifically, to limit the question length and to ensure the

Component	Design	Comments
System State	(Product, User action)	e.g., (HP Computer, Category: computer)
Machine Action	Question on *Category*	e.g., choose category: Electronics, Movie, Book
	Question on *Product name*	e.g., choose product name: Canon SD750 digital camera, Canon Powershot A40 digital camera, Canon SD950 digital camera, Others
	Question on *Attribute*	e.g., choose memory size: 64M, 128M, 256M
	Confirmation question	e.g., you want Canon SD750 camera, yes or no?
	Play Rating	e.g., I think you want Canon SD750 digital camera, here is the rating!
User Action	Category	e.g., Movie
	Product name	e.g., Canon SD750 digital camera
	Attribute value	e.g., memory size: 64M
	Others	used when a question has too many possible options
	Yes/No	used for a confirmation question
	Not related	used if the intended product is unrelated to the question
	Not known	used if the user does not have required knowledge to answer the question

Table 2: State Diagram Design in Voice-Rate

human is able to memorize all the options, we restrict the number of options in a single question to a threshold N (e.g., 5). Clearly, given a list of products and a question, there might be more than N possible options. In such a case, we need to merge some options into the "others" class. The third example in Table 2 shows an example with the "others" option. One may exploit a clustering algorithm (e.g., an iterative greedy search algorithm) to find an optimal merge. In our system, we simply take the top-(N-1) options (ranked by the belief probabilities) and treat all the remaining options as "others".

The "not related" option is required when some candidate products are irrelevant to the question. For example, when the system asks a question regarding the attribute "cpu speed" while the products contain both books and computers, the "not related" option is required in case the intended product is a book.

Lastly, while some attributes are very useful to distinguish the products, a user may not have enough knowledge to answer a question on these attributes. For example, while there is a unique *part number* for each product, however, the user may not know the exact part number for the intended product. Thus, "not known" option is required whenever the system expects the user is unable to answer the question.

4.1.2 Models

We assume that the user does not change his goal (i.e., the intended product) along the dialog. We also assume that the user *rationally* answers the question to achieve his goal. Additionally, we assume that the speech synthesis is good enough such that the user always gets the right information that the system intends to convey. The two main models that we consider include an observation model that captures speech recognition uncertainty, and a user knowledge model that captures the variability of user knowledge required for answering questions on different attributes.

Observation Model: Since the speech recognition engine we are using returns only a one-best and its confidence value $C \in [0, 1]$. We define the observation function as follows,

$$P(\widehat{a}_u|a_u) = \begin{cases} C & \text{if } \widehat{a}_u = a_u, \\ \frac{1-C}{|A_u|-1} & \text{otherwise.} \end{cases} \quad (2)$$

where a_u is the true user action, $\widehat{a}_u$ is the speech recognition output (i.e., corrupted user action), and A_u is the set of user actions related to the last machine action.

User Knowledge Model: In most of the applications (Roy et al., 2000; Williams, 2007) where the POMDP framework got applied, it is normally assumed that the user needs only common sense to answer the questions asked by the dialog system. Our application is more complex as the product information is very rich. A user may have different difficulty in answering different questions. For example, while a user can easily answer a question on *category*, he may not be able to answer a question on the *part number*. Thus, we define a user knowledge model to capture such uncertainty. Specifically, given a question (say a_m) and an intended product (say g_u) in the user's mind, we want to know how likely the user has required knowledge to answer the question. Formally, the user knowledge model is,

$$P(a_u|g_u, a_m) = \begin{cases} P(\textit{unk}|g_u, a_m) & \text{if } a_u\text{=}\textit{unk}, \\ 1 - P(\textit{unk}|g_u, a_m) & \text{if } a_u\text{=}\textit{truth}, \\ 0 & \text{otherwise.} \end{cases} \tag{3}$$

where *unk* represents the user action "not known". Clearly, given a specific product g_u and a specific question a_m, there is exactly one correct user action (represented by *truth* in Equation 3), and its probability is $1 - P(\textit{unk}|g_u, a_m)$. Now, to obtain a user knowledge model, we only need to obtain $P(\textit{unk}|g_u, a_m)$. As shown in Table 2, there are four kinds of *question-type* machine actions a_m. We assume that the user always has knowledge to answer a question regarding the category and product name, and thus $P(\textit{unk}|g_u, a_m)$ for these types of machine actions are zero regardless of what the specific product g_u is. Therefore, we only need to consider $P(\textit{unk}|g_u, a_m)$ when a_m is a question about an attribute (say *attr*). Moreover, since there are millions of products, to deal with the data sparsity issue, we assume $P(\textit{unk}|g_u, a_m)$ does not depends on a specific product g_u, instead it depends on only the category (say *cat*) of the product g_u. Therefore,

$$P(\textit{unk}|g_u, a_m) \approx P(\textit{unk}|\textit{cat,attr}). \tag{4}$$

Now, we only need to get the probability $P(\textit{unk}|\textit{cat,attr})$ for each attribute *attr* in each category *cat*. To learn $P(\textit{unk}|\textit{cat,attr})$, one may collect data from human, which is very expensive. Instead, we learn this model from a database of online reviews for the products. Our method is based on the following intuition: *if a user cares/knows about an attribute of a product, he will mention either the **attribute name**, or the **attribute value**, or **both** in his review of this product.* With this intuition, the occurrence frequency of a given *attr* in a given category *cat* is collected from the review database, followed by proper weighting, scaling and normalization, and thus $P(\textit{unk}|\textit{cat,attr})$ is obtained.

4.2 Belief Update

Based on the model assumptions in Section 4.1.2, the belief update formula for the state $(g_u, a_u^{'})$ is,

$$\vec{b}(g_u, a_u^{'}) = k \times P(\widehat{a}_u^{'}|a_u^{'}) P(a_u^{'}|g_u, a_m) \sum_{a_u \in A(g_u)} \vec{b}(g_u, a_u) \tag{5}$$

where k is a normalization constant. The $P(\widehat{a}_u^{'}|a_u^{'})$ is the observation function as defined in Equation 2, while $P(a_u^{'}|g_u, a_m)$ is the user knowledge model as defined in Equation 3. The $A(g_u)$ represents the set of user actions a_u related to the system states for which the intended product is g_u.

In our state representation, a single product g_u is associated with several states which differ in the user action a_u, and the belief probability of g_u is the sum of the probabilities of these states. Therefore, even there is a speech recognition error or an unintentional user mistake, the true product still gets a non-zero belief probability (though the true/ideal user action a_u gets a zero probability). Moreover, the probability of the true product will get promoted through later iterations. Therefore, our system has error-handling capability, which is one of the major advantages over the deterministic baseline system.

4.3 Optimal Action Selection

As mentioned in Section 3.2, the optimal action selection involves three sub-components: a prediction algorithm, a goodness measure, and a search algorithm. Ideally, in our application, we should minimize the time required to successfully identify the intended product. Clearly, this is too difficult as it needs to predict the infinite future and needs to encode the time into a reward function. Therefore, for simplicity, we predict only one-step forward, and use the entropy as a goodness measure[1]. Formally,

[1]Due to this approximation, one may argue that our model is more like the greedy information theoretic model in Paek and Chickering (2005), instead of a POMDP model. However, we believe that our model follows the POMDP modeling framework in general, though it does not involve reinforcement learning currently.

the optimization function is as follows:

$$a^* = \arg\min_{a \in A} H(\text{Products} \mid a), \quad (6)$$

where $H(\text{Products} \mid a)$ is the entropy over the belief probabilities of the products if the machine action a was taken. When predicting the belief vector using Equation 5, we consider only the user knowledge model and ignore the observation function[2].

In the above, we consider only the *question-type* machine actions. We also need to decide when to take the *play rating* action such that the dialog will terminate. Specifically, we take the *play rating* action whenever the belief probability of the most probable product is greater than a threshold. Moreover, the threshold should depend on the number of surviving products. For example, if there are fifty surviving products and the most probable product has a belief probability greater than 0.3, it is reasonable to take the *play rating* action. This is not true if there are only four surviving products. Also note that if we set the thresholds to too small values, the system may play the rating for a *wrong* product. We will use a development set to tune these thresholds.

4.3.1 Machine Action Filtering during Search

We use an exhaustive linear search for the operator *argmin* in Equation 6. However, additional filtering during the search is required.

Repeated Question: Since the speech response from the user to a question is *probabilistic*, it is quite possible that the system will choose the same question that has been asked in previous stages[3]. Since our product information is very rich, many different questions have the similar capability to reduce entropy. Therefore, during the search, we simply ignore all the questions asked in previous stages.

"Not Related" Option: While reducing entropy helps to reduce the confusion at the *machine* side, it does not measure the "weirdness" of a question to the *human*. For example, when the intended product is a book and the candidate products contain both books and computers, it is quite possible that the optimal action, based solely on entropy reduction, is a question on the attribute "cpu speed". Clearly, such a question is very weird to the human as he is looking for a book that has nothing related to "cpu speed". Though the user may be able to choose the "not related" option correctly after thinking for a while, it degrades the dialog quality. Therefore, for a given question, whenever the system predicts that the user will have to choose the "not related" option with a probability greater than a threshold, we simply ignore such questions in the search. Clearly, if we set the threshold as zero, we essentially eliminates the "not related" option. That is, at each stage, we generate questions only on attributes that apply to all the candidate products. Since we dynamically remove products whose probability is smaller than a threshold at each stage, the valid question set dynamically expands. Specifically, at the beginning, only very general questions (e.g., questions on category) are valid, then more refined questions become valid (e.g., questions on product brand), and finally very specific questions are valid (e.g, questions on product model). This leads to very natural behavior in identifying a product, i.e., **coarse to fine**[4]. It also makes the system adapt to the user knowledge. Specifically, as the user demonstrates deeper knowledge of the products by answering the questions correctly, it makes sense to ask more refined questions about the products.

5 Simulation Results

To evaluate system performance, ideally one should ask people to call the system, and manually collect the performance data. This is very expensive. Alternatively, we develop a simulation method, which is automatic and thus allow fast evaluation of the system during development[5]. In fact, many design choices in Section 4 are inspired by the simulation.

5.1 Simulation Model

Figure 2 illustrates the general framework for the simulation. The process is very similar to that in Figure 1 except that the human user and the speech

[2]Note that we ignore the observation function only in the prediction, not in real belief update.

[3]In a regular decision tree, the answer to a question is *deterministic*. It never asks the same question as that does not lead to any additional reduction of entropy. This problem is also due to the fact we do not have an explicit reward function.

[4]While the baseline dialog manager achieves the similar behavior by *manually* enforcing the order of questions, the system here *automatically* discovers the order of questions and the question set is much more richer than that in the baseline.

[5]However, we agree that simulation is not without its limitations and the results may not precisely reflect real scenarios.

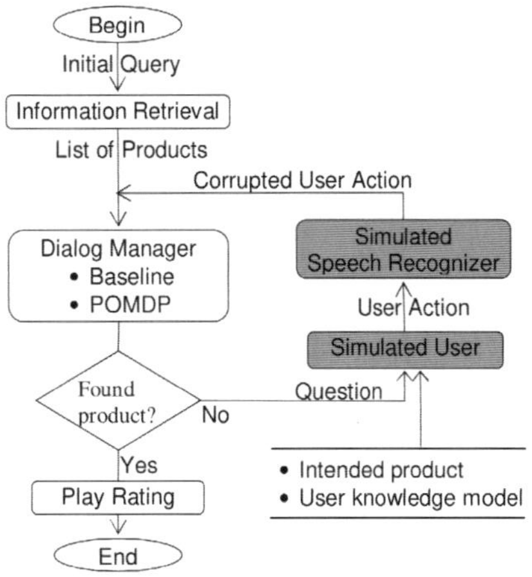

Figure 2: Flow Chart in Simulation

recognizer are replaced with a simulated component, and that the simulated user has access to a user knowledge model. In particular, we generate the user action and its corrupted version using random number generators by following the models defined in Equations 3 and 2, respectively. We use a fixed value (e.g., 0.9) for C in Equation 2.

Clearly, our goal here is not to evaluate the goodness of the user knowledge model or the speech recognizer. Instead, we want to see how the probabilistic dialog manger (i.e., POMDP) performs compared with the deterministic baseline dialog manager, and to see whether the richer attribute information helps to reduce the dialog interaction time.

5.2 Data Resources

In the system, we use three data resources: a product database, a review database, and a query-click database. The product database contains detailed information for 0.2 million electronics and computer related products. The review database is used for learning the user knowledge model. The query-click database contains 2289 pairs in the format (text query, product clicked). One example pair is (Canon Powershot A700, Canon Powershot A700 6.2MP digital camera). We divide it into a development set (1308 pairs) and a test set (981 pairs).

5.3 Results on Information Retrieval

For each initial query, the information retrieval (IR) engine returns a list of top-ranked products. Whether the intended product is in the returned list depends on the size of the list. If the intended product is in the list, the IR successfully recalled the product. Table 3 shows the correlation between the recall rate and the size of the returned list. Clearly, the larger the list size is, the larger the recall rate is. One may notice that the IR recall rate is low. This is because the query-click data set is very noisy, that is, the clicked product may be nothing to do with the query. For example, (msn shopping, Handspring Treo 270) is one of the pairs in our data set.

List Size	Recall Rate (%)
50	38.36
100	41.46
150	43.5

Table 3: Information Retrieval Recall Rates on Test set

5.4 Dialog System Configuration and Tuning

As mentioned in Section 4, several parameters in the system are configurable and tunable. Specifically, we set the max number of options in a question as 5, and the threshold for "not related" option as zero. We use the development set to tune the following parameters: the threshold of the belief probability below which the product is pruned, and the thresholds above which the most probable product is played. The parameters are tuned in a way such that no dialog error is made on the development set.

5.5 Results on Error Handling

Even the IR succeeds, the dialog system may not find the intended product successfully. In particular, the baseline system does not have error handling capability. Whenever the system makes a speech recognition error or the user mistakenly answers a question, the dialog system fails (either plays the rating for a wrong product or fails to find any product). On the contrary, our POMDP framework has error handling functionality due to its probabilistic nature. Table 5 compares the dialog error rate between the baseline and the POMDP systems. Clearly, the POMDP system performs much better to handle errors. Note that the POMDP system does not eliminate dialog failures on the test set because the **thresholds** are not perfect for the *test set*[6]. This is due to two reasons: the system may prune the intended product (*reason-1*), and the system may play the rating for a wrong product (*reason-2*).

[6]Note that the POMDP system does not have dialog failures on the *development set* as we tune the system in this way.

System	Size	Average			Max		
		Stages	Characters	Words	Stages	Characters	Words
Baseline	50	2.44	524.0	82.3	11	2927	546
	100	3.37	765.4	120.4	25	7762	1369
	150	3.90	906.4	143.0	30	9345	1668
POMDP	50	1.57	342.8	54.3	4	2659	466
	100	2.36	487.9	76.6	18	3575	597
	150	2.59	541.3	85.0	19	4898	767

Table 4: Interaction Time Results on Test Set

Size	Baseline (%)	POMDP (%)		
		Total	Reason-1	Reason-2
50	13.8	8.2	4.2	4.0
100	17.7	2.7	1.2	1.5
150	19.3	4.7	0.7	4.0

Table 5: Dialog Failure Rate on Test Set

5.6 Results on Interaction Time

It is quite difficult to measure the exact interaction time, so instead we measure it through the number of stages/characters/words required during the dialog process. Clearly, the number of characters is the one that matches most closely to the true time. Table 4 reports the average and maximum numbers. In general, the POMDP system performs much better than the baseline system. One may notice the difference in the number of stages between the baseline and the POMDP systems is not as significant as in the number of characters. This is because the POMDP system is able to exploit very short questions while the baseline system mainly uses the product name question, which is normally very long. The long question on product name also imposes difficulty in speech synthesis, user input, and speech recognition, though this is not reflected in the simulation.

6 Conclusions

In this paper, we have applied the POMDP framework into Voice-Rate, a system through which a user can call to get product information (e.g., price, rating, review, etc.). We have proposed a novel method to learn a user knowledge model from a review database. Compared with a deterministic baseline system (Zweig et al., 2007), the POMDP system is probabilistic and is able to handle speech recognition errors and user mistakes, in which case the deterministic baseline system is doomed to fail. Moreover, the POMDP system exploits richer product information to reduce the interaction time required to complete a dialog. We have developed a simulation model, and shown that the POMDP system improves the baseline system significantly in terms of both dialog failure rate and dialog interaction time. We also implement our POMDP system into a speech demo and plan to carry out tests through humans.

Acknowledgement

This work was conducted during the first author's internship at Microsoft Research; thanks to Dan Bohus, Ghinwa Choueiter, Yun-Cheng Ju, Xiao Li, Milind Mahajan, Tim Paek, Yeyi Wang, and Dong Yu for helpful discussions.

References

K. Murphy. 2000. A survey of POMDP solution techniques. Technical Report, U. C. Berkeley.

T. Paek and D. Chickering. 2005. The Markov assumption in spoken dialogue management. *In Proc of SIGdial 2005.*

N. Roy, J. Pineau, and S. Thrun. 2000. Spoken dialog management for robots. *In Proc of ACL 2000.*

M. Spaan and N. Vlassis. 2005. Perseus: randomized point-based value iteration for POMDPs. *Journal of Artificial Intelligence Research*, 24:195-220.

J. Williams. 2007. Applying POMDPs to Dialog Systems in the Troubleshooting Domain. *In Proc HLT/NAACL Workshop on Bridging the Gap: Academic and Industrial Research in Dialog Technology.*

J. Williams and S. Young. 2007. Partially Observable Markov Decision Processes for Spoken Dialog Systems. *Computer Speech and Language* 21(2): 231-422.

G. Zweig, P. Nguyen, Y.C. Ju, Y.Y. Wang, D. Yu, and A. Acero. 2007. The Voice-Rate Dialog System for Consumer Ratings. *In Proc of Interspeech 2007.*

Training and Evaluation of the HIS POMDP Dialogue System in Noise

M. Gašić, S. Keizer, F. Mairesse, J. Schatzmann, B. Thomson, K. Yu, S. Young
Machine Intelligence Laboratory
Engineering Department
Cambridge University
United Kingdom

Abstract

This paper investigates the claim that a dialogue manager modelled as a Partially Observable Markov Decision Process (POMDP) can achieve improved robustness to noise compared to conventional state-based dialogue managers. Using the Hidden Information State (HIS) POMDP dialogue manager as an exemplar, and an MDP-based dialogue manager as a baseline, evaluation results are presented for both simulated and real dialogues in a Tourist Information Domain. The results on the simulated data show that the inherent ability to model uncertainty, allows the POMDP model to exploit alternative hypotheses from the speech understanding system. The results obtained from a user trial show that the HIS system with a trained policy performed significantly better than the MDP baseline.

1 Introduction

Conventional spoken dialogue systems operate by finding the most likely interpretation of each user input, updating some internal representation of the dialogue state and then outputting an appropriate response. Error tolerance depends on using confidence thresholds and where they fail, the dialogue manager must resort to quite complex recovery procedures. Such a system has no explicit mechanisms for representing the inevitable uncertainties associated with speech understanding or the ambiguities which naturally arise in interpreting a user's intentions. The result is a system that is inherently fragile, especially in noisy conditions or where the user is unsure of how to use the system.

It has been suggested that Partially Observable Markov Decision Processes (POMDPs) offer a natural framework for building spoken dialogue systems which can both model these uncertainties and support policies which are robust to their effects (Young, 2002; Williams and Young, 2007a). The key idea of the POMDP is that the underlying dialogue state is hidden and dialogue management policies must therefore be based not on a single state estimate but on a distribution over all states.

Whilst POMDPs are attractive theoretically, in practice, they are notoriously intractable for anything other than small state/action spaces. Hence, practical examples of their use were initially restricted to very simple domains (Roy et al., 2000; Zhang et al., 2001). More recently, however, a number of techniques have been suggested which do allow POMDPs to be scaled to handle real world tasks. The two generic mechanisms which facilitate this scaling are factoring the state space and performing policy optimisation in a reduced *summary state space* (Williams and Young, 2007a; Williams and Young, 2007b).

Based on these ideas, a number of real-world POMDP-based systems have recently emerged. The most complex entity which must be represented in the state space is the user's goal. In the *Bayesian Update of Dialogue State (BUDS)* system, the user's goal is further factored into conditionally independent *slots*. The resulting system is then modelled as a dynamic Bayesian network (Thomson et al., 2008). A similar approach is also developed in

Proceedings of the 9th SIGdial Workshop on Discourse and Dialogue, pages 112–119,
Columbus, June 2008.

(Bui et al., 2007a; Bui et al., 2007b). An alternative approach taken in the *Hidden Information State (HIS)* system is to retain a complete representation of the user's goal, but partition states into equivalence classes and prune away very low probability partitions (Young et al., 2007; Thomson et al., 2007; Williams and Young, 2007b).

Whichever approach is taken, a key issue in a real POMDP-based dialogue system is its ability to be robust to noise and that is the issue that is addressed in this paper. Using the HIS system as an exemplar, evaluation results are presented for a real-world tourist information task using both simulated and real users. The results show that a POMDP system can learn noise robust policies and that N-best outputs from the speech understanding component can be exploited to further improve robustness.

The paper is structured as follows. Firstly, in Section 2 a brief overview of the HIS system is given. Then in Section 3, various POMDP training regimes are described and evaluated using a simulated user at differing noise levels. Section 4 then presents results from a trial in which users conducted various tasks over a range of noise levels. Finally, in Section 5, we discuss our results and present our conclusions.

2 The HIS System

2.1 Basic Principles

A POMDP-based dialogue system is shown in Figure 1 where s_m denotes the (unobserved or hidden) machine state which is factored into three components: the last user act a_u, the user's goal s_u and the dialogue history s_d. Since s_m is unknown, at each time-step the system computes a belief state such that the probability of being in state s_m given belief state b is $b(s_m)$. Based on this current belief state b, the machine selects an action a_m, receives a reward $r(s_m, a_m)$, and transitions to a new (unobserved) state s'_m, where s'_m depends only on s_m and a_m. The machine then receives an observation o' consisting of an N-best list of hypothesised user actions. Finally, the belief distribution b is updated based on o' and a_m as follows:

$$b'(s'_m) = kP(o'|s'_m, a_m) \sum_{s_m \in S_m} P(s'_m|a_m, s_m) b(s_m) \quad (1)$$

where k is a normalisation constant (Kaelbling et al., 1998). The first term on the RHS of (1) is called the *observation model* and the term inside the summation is called the *transition model*. Maintaining this belief state as the dialogue evolves is called *belief monitoring*.

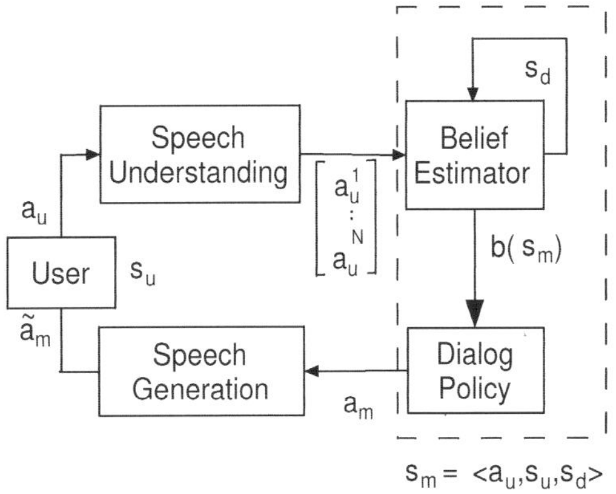

Figure 1: Abstract view of a POMDP-based spoken dialogue system

At each time step t, the machine receives a reward $r(b_t, a_{m,t})$ based on the current belief state b_t and the selected action $a_{m,t}$. Each action $a_{m,t}$ is determined by a policy $\pi(b_t)$ and building a POMDP system involves finding the policy π^* which maximises the discounted sum R of the rewards

$$R = \sum_{t=0}^{\infty} \lambda^t r(b_t, a_{m,t}) \quad (2)$$

where λ^t is a discount coefficient.

2.2 Probability Models

In the HIS system, user goals are partitioned and initially, all states $s_u \in S_u$ are regarded as being equally likely and they are placed in a single partition p_0. As the dialogue progresses, user inputs result in changing beliefs and this root partition is repeatedly split into smaller partitions. This splitting is binary, i.e. $p \rightarrow \{p', p - p'\}$ with probability $P(p'|p)$. By replacing s_m by its factors (s_u, a_u, s_d) and making reasonable independence assumptions, it can be shown (Young et al., 2007) that in partitioned form (1) becomes

$$b'(p', a'_u, s'_d) \;=\; k \cdot \underbrace{P(o'|a'_u)}_{\substack{\text{observation}\\ \text{model}}} \; \underbrace{P(a'_u|p', a_m)}_{\substack{\text{user action}\\ \text{model}}}$$

$$\cdot \sum_{s_d} \underbrace{P(s'_d|p', a'_u, s_d, a_m)}_{\substack{\text{dialogue}\\ \text{model}}} \; \underbrace{P(p'|p) b(p, s_d)}_{\substack{\text{partition}\\ \text{splitting}}} \quad (3)$$

where p is the parent of p'.

In this equation, the *observation model* is approximated by the normalised distribution of confidence measures output by the speech recognition system. The *user action model* allows the observation probability that is conditioned on a'_u to be scaled by the probability that the user would speak a'_u given the partition p' and the last system prompt a_m. In the current implementation of the HIS system, user dialogue acts take the form $act(a = v)$ where act is the dialogue type, a is an attribute and v is its value [for example, *request(food=Chinese)*]. The user action model is then approximated by

$$P(a'_u|p', a_m) \approx P(\mathcal{T}(a'_u)|\mathcal{T}(a_m)) P(\mathcal{M}(a'_u)|p') \quad (4)$$

where $\mathcal{T}(\cdot)$ denotes the *type* of the dialogue act and $\mathcal{M}(\cdot)$ denotes whether or not the dialogue act *matches* the current partition p'. The dialogue model is a deterministic encoding based on a simple grounding model. It yields probability one when the updated dialogue hypothesis (i.e., a specific combination of p', a'_u, s_d and a_m) is consistent with the history and zero otherwise.

2.3 Policy Representation

Policy representation in POMDP-systems is non-trivial since each action depends on a complex probability distribution. One of the simplest approaches to dealing with this problem is to discretise the state space and then associate an action with each discrete grid point. To reduce quantisation errors, the HIS model first maps belief distributions into a reduced *summary space* before quantising. This summary space consists of the probability of the top two hypotheses plus some status variables and the user act type associated with the top distribution. Quantisation is then performed using a simple distance metric to find the nearest grid point. Actions in summary space refer specifically to the top two hypotheses, and unlike actions in master space, they are limited to a small finite set: *greet, ask, explicit_confirm, implicit_confirm, select_confirm, offer, inform, find_alternative, query_more, goodbye*. A simple heuristic is then used to map the selected next system action back into the full *master* belief space.

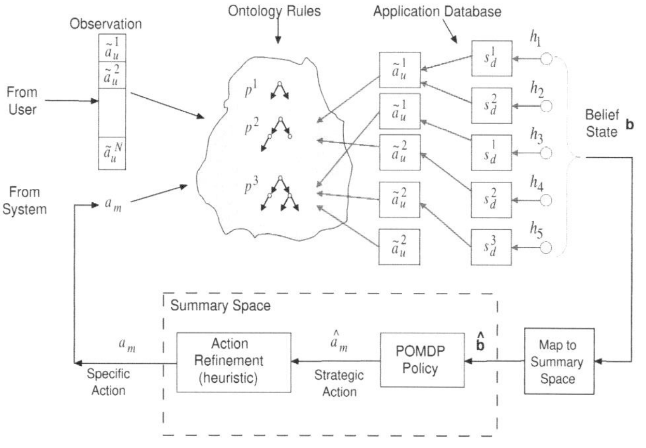

Figure 2: Overview of the HIS system dialogue cycle

The dialogue manager is able to support negations, denials and requests for alternatives. When the selected summary action is to offer the user a venue, the summary-to-master space mapping heuristics will normally offer a venue consistent with the most likely user goal hypothesis. If this hypothesis is then rejected its belief is substantially reduced and it will no longer be the top-ranking hypothesis. If the next system action is to make an alternative *offer*, then the new top-ranking hypothesis may not be appropriate. For example, if an expensive French restaurant near the river had been offered and the user asks for one nearer the centre of town, any alternative offered should still include the user's confirmed desire for an expensive French restaurant. To ensure this, all of the grounded features from the rejected hypothesis are extracted and all user goal hypotheses are scanned starting at the most likely until an alternative is found that matches the grounded features. For the current turn only, the summary-to-master space heuristics then treat this hypothesis as if it was the top-ranking one. If the system then offers a venue based on this hypothesis, and the user accepts it, then, since system outputs are appended to user inputs for the purpose of belief updating, the alternative hypothesis will move to the top, or near the top, of the ranked hypothesis list. The dialogue then typically continues with its focus on the newly offered alternative venue.

2.4 Summary of Operation

To summarise, the overall processing performed by the HIS system in a single dialogue turn (i.e. one cycle of system output and user response) is as shown in Figure 2. Each user utterance is decoded into an N-best list of dialogue acts. Each incoming act plus the previous system act are matched against the forest of user goals and partitions are split as needed. Each user act a_u is then duplicated and bound to each partition p. Each partition will also have a set of dialogue histories s_d associated with it. The combination of each p, a_u and updated s_d forms a new dialogue hypothesis h_k whose beliefs are evaluated using (3). Once all dialogue hypotheses have been evaluated and any duplicates merged, the master belief state b is mapped into summary space $\hat{b}$ and the nearest policy belief point is found. The associated summary space machine action $\hat{a}_m$ is then heuristically mapped back to master space and the machine's actual response a_m is output. The cycle then repeats until the user's goal is satisfied.

3 Training and Evaluation with a Simulated User

3.1 Policy optimisation

Policy optimisation is performed in the discrete summary space described in the previous section using on-line batch ϵ-greedy policy iteration. Given an existing policy π, dialogs are executed and machine actions generated according to π except that with probability ϵ a random action is generated. The system maintains a set of belief points $\{\hat{\boldsymbol{b}}_i\}$. At each turn in training, the nearest stored belief point $\hat{\boldsymbol{b}}_k$ to $\hat{\boldsymbol{b}}$ is located using a distance measure. If the distance is greater than some threshold, $\hat{\boldsymbol{b}}$ is added to the set of stored belief points. The sequence of points $\hat{\boldsymbol{b}}_k$ traversed in each dialogue is stored in a list. Associated with each $\hat{\boldsymbol{b}}_i$ is a function $Q(\hat{\boldsymbol{b}}_i, \hat{a}_m)$ whose value is the expected total reward obtained by choosing summary action $\hat{a}_m$ from state $\hat{\boldsymbol{b}}_i$. At the end of each dialogue, the total reward is calculated and added to an accumulator for each point in the list, discounted by λ at each step. On completion of a batch of dialogs, the Q values are updated according to the accumulated rewards, and the policy updated by choosing the action which maximises each Q value. The whole process is then repeated until the policy stabilises.

In our experiments, ϵ was fixed at 0.1 and λ was fixed at 0.95. The reward function used attempted to encourage short successful dialogues by assigning $+20$ for a successful dialogue and -1 for each dialogue turn.

3.2 User Simulation

To train a policy, a user simulator is used to generate responses to system actions. It has two main components: a *User Goal* and a *User Agenda*. At the start of each dialogue, the goal is randomly initialised with requests such as "name", "addr", "phone" and constraints such as "type=restaurant", "food=Chinese", etc. The agenda stores the dialogue acts needed to elicit this information in a stack-like structure which enables it to temporarily store actions when another action of higher priority needs to be issued first. This enables the simulator to refer to previous dialogue turns at a later point. To generate a wide spread of realistic dialogs, the simulator reacts wherever possible with varying levels of patience and arbitrariness. In addition, the simulator will relax its constraints when its initial goal cannot be satisfied. This allows the dialogue manager to learn negotiation-type dialogues where only an approximate solution to the user's goal exists. Speech understanding errors are simulated at the dialogue act level using confusion matrices trained on labelled dialogue data (Schatzmann et al., 2007).

3.3 Training and Evaluation

When training a system to operate robustly in noisy conditions, a variety of strategies are possible. For example, the system can be trained only on noise-free interactions, it can be trained on increasing levels of noise or it can be trained on a high noise level from the outset. A related issue concerns the generation of grid points and the number of training iterations to perform. For example, allowing a very large number of points leads to poor performance due to over-fitting of the training data. Conversely, having too few point leads to poor performance due to a lack of discrimination in its dialogue strategies.

After some experimentation, the following training schedule was adopted. Training starts in a noise free environment using a small number of grid points and it continues until the performance of the policy levels off. The resulting policy is then taken as an initial policy for the next stage where the noise level is increased, the number of grid points is expanded and the number of iterations is increased. This process is repeated until the highest noise level is reached. This approach was motivated by the observation that a key factor in effective reinforcement learning is the balance between exploration and exploitation. In POMDP policy optimisation which uses dynamically allocated grid points, maintaining this balance is crucial. In our case, the noise introduced by the simulator is used as an implicit mechanism for increasing the exploration. Each time exploration is increased, the areas of state-space that will be visited will also increase and hence the number of available grid points must also be increased. At the same time, the number of iterations must be increased to ensure that all points are visited a sufficient number of times. In practice we found that around 750 to 1000 grid points was sufficient and the total number of simulated dialogues needed for training was around 100,000.

A second issue when training in noisy conditions is whether to train on just the 1-best output from the simulator or train on the N-best outputs. A limiting factor here is that the computation required for N-best training is significantly increased since the rate of partition generation in the HIS model increases exponentially with N. In preliminary tests, it was found that when training with 1-best outputs, there was little difference between policies trained entirely in no noise and policies trained on increasing noise as described above. However, policies trained on 2-best using the incremental strategy did exhibit increased robustness to noise. To illustrate this, Figures 3 and 4 show the average dialogue success rates and rewards for 3 different policies, all trained on 2-best: a hand-crafted policy (hdc), a policy trained on noise-free conditions (noise_free) and a policy trained using the incremental scheme described above (increm). Each policy was tested using 2-best output from the simulator across a range of error rates. In addition, the noise-free policy was also tested on 1-best output.

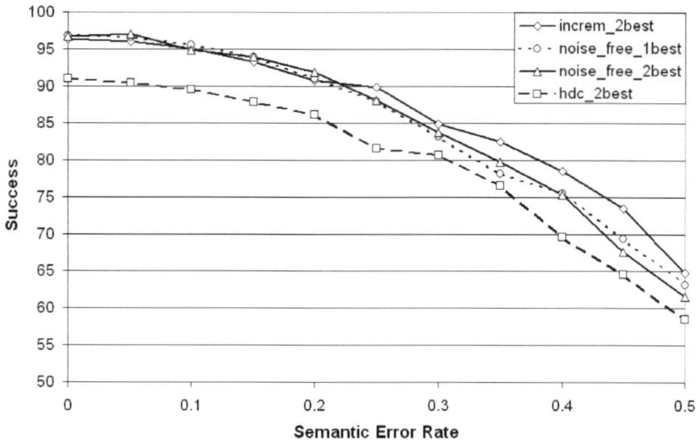

Figure 3: Average simulated dialogue success rate as a function of error rate for a hand-crafted (hdc), noise-free and incrementally trained (increm) policy.

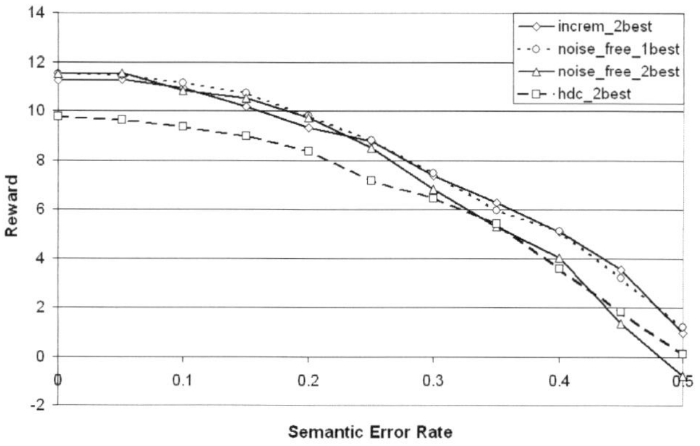

Figure 4: Average simulated dialogue reward as a function of error rate for a hand-crafted (hdc), noise-free and incrementally trained (increm) policy.

As can be seen, both the trained policies improve significantly on the hand-crafted policies. Furthermore, although the average rewards are all broadly similar, the success rate of the incrementally trained policy is significantly better at higher error rates. Hence, this latter policy was selected for the user trial described next.

4 Evaluation via a User Trial

The HIS-POMDP policy (HIS-TRA) that was incrementally trained on the simulated user using 2-best lists was tested in a user trial together with a hand-crafted HIS-POMDP policy (HIS-HDC). The strategy used by the latter was to first check the most likely hypothesis. If it contains sufficient grounded keys to match 1 to 3 database entities, then *offer* is selected. If any part of the hypothesis is inconsistent or the user has explicitly asked for another suggestion, then *find_alternative* action is selected. If the user has asked for information about an offered entity then *inform* is selected. Otherwise, an ungrounded component of the top hypothesis is identified and depending on the belief, one of the confirm actions is selected.

In addition, an MDP-based dialogue manager developed for earlier trials (Schatzmann, 2008) was also tested. Since considerable effort has been put in optimising this system, it serves as a strong baseline for comparison. Again, both a trained policy (MDP-TRA) and a hand-crafted policy (MDP-HDC) were tested.

4.1 System setup and confidence scoring

The dialogue system consisted of an ATK-based speech recogniser, a Phoenix-based semantic parser, the dialogue manager and a diphone based speech synthesiser. The semantic parser uses simple phrasal grammar rules to extract the dialogue act type and a list of attribute/value pairs from each utterance.

In a POMDP-based dialogue system, accurate belief-updating is very sensitive to the confidence scores assigned to each user dialogue act. Ideally these should provide a measure of the probability of the decoded act given the true user act. In the evaluation system, the recogniser generates a 10-best list of hypotheses at each turn along with a compact confusion network which is used to compute the inference evidence for each hypothesis. The latter is defined as the sum of the log-likelihoods of each arc in the confusion network and when exponentiated and renormalised this gives a simple estimate of the probability of each hypothesised utterance. Each utterance in the 10-best list is passed to the semantic parser. Equivalent dialogue acts output by the parser are then grouped together and the dialogue act for each group is then assigned the sum of the sentence-level probabilities as its confidence score.

4.2 Trial setup

For the trial itself, 36 subjects were recruited (all British native speakers, 18 male, 18 female). Each subject was asked to imagine himself to be a tourist in a fictitious town called Jasonville and try to find particular hotels, bars, or restaurants in that town. Each subject was asked to complete a set of pre-defined tasks where each task involved finding the name of a venue satisfying a set of constraints such as food type is Chinese, price-range is cheap, etc., and getting the value of one or more additional attributes of that venue such as the address or the phone number.

For each task, subjects were given a scenario to read and were then asked to solve the task via a dialogue with the system. The tasks set could either have one solution, several solutions, or no solution at all in the database. In cases where a subject found that there was no matching venue for the given task, he/she was allowed to try and find an alternative venue by relaxing one or more of the constraints.

In addition, subjects had to perform each task at one of three possible noise levels. These levels correspond to signal/noise ratios (SNRs) of 35.3 dB (low noise), 10.2 dB (medium noise), or 3.3 dB (high noise). The noise was artificially generated and mixed with the microphone signal, in addition it was fed into the subject's headphones so that they were aware of the noisy conditions.

An instructor was present at all times to indicate to the subject which task description to follow, and to start the right system with the appropriate noise-level. Each subject performed an equal number of tasks for each system (3 tasks), noise level (6 tasks) and solution type (6 tasks for each of the types 0, 1, or multiple solutions). Also, each subject performed one task for all combinations of system and noise level. Overall, each combination of system, noise level, and solution type was used in an equal number of dialogues.

4.3 Results

In Table 1, some general statistics of the corpus resulting from the trial are given. The semantic error rate is based on substitutions, insertions and deletions errors on semantic items. When tested after the trial on the transcribed user utterances, the semantic error rate was 4.1% whereas the semantic error rate on the ASR input was 25.2%. This means that 84% of the error rate was due to the ASR.

Tables 2 and 3 present success rates (Succ.) and average performance scores (Perf.), comparing the two HIS dialogue managers with the two MDP base-

Number of dialogues	432
Number of dialogue turns	3972
Number of words (transcriptions)	18239
Words per utterance	4.58
Word Error Rate	32.9
Semantic Error Rate	25.2
Semantic Error Rate transcriptions	4.1

Table 1: General corpus statistics.

line systems. For the success rates, also the standard deviation (std.dev) is given, assuming a binomial distribution. The success rate is the percentage of successfully completed dialogues. A task is considered to be fully completed when the user is able to find the venue he is looking for and get all the additional information he asked for; if the task has no solution and the system indicates to the user no venue could be found, this also counts as full completion. A task is considered to be partially completed when only the correct venue has been given. The results on partial completion are given in Table 2, and the results on full completion in Table 3. To mirror the reward function used in training, the performance for each dialogue is computed by assigning a reward of 20 points for full completion and subtracting 1 point for the number of turns up until a successful recommendation (i.e., partial completion).

Partial Task Completion statistics			
System	Succ. (std.dev)	#turns	Perf.
MDP-HDC	68.52 (4.83)	4.80	8.91
MDP-TRA	70.37 (4.75)	4.75	9.32
HIS-HDC	74.07 (4.55)	7.04	7.78
HIS-TRA	84.26 (3.78)	4.63	12.22

Table 2: Success rates and performance results on partial completion.

Full Task Completion statistics			
System	Succ. (std.dev)	#turns	Perf.
MDP-HDC	64.81 (4.96)	5.86	7.10
MDP-TRA	65.74 (4.93)	6.18	6.97
HIS-HDC	63.89 (4.99)	8.57	4.20
HIS-TRA	78.70 (4.25)	6.36	9.38

Table 3: Success rates and performance results on full completion.

The results show that the trained HIS dialogue manager significantly outperforms both MDP based dialogue managers. For success rate on partial completion, both HIS systems perform better than the MDP systems.

4.3.1 Subjective Results

In the user trial, the subjects were also asked for a subjective judgement of the systems. After completing each task, the subjects were asked whether they had found the information they were looking for (yes/no). They were also asked to give a score on a scale from 1 to 5 (best) on how natural/intuitive they thought the dialogue was. Table 4 shows the results for the 4 systems used. The performance of the HIS systems is similar to the MDP systems, with a slightly higher success rate for the trained one and a slightly lower score for the handcrafted one.

System	Succ. Rate (std.dev)	Score
MDP-HDC	78 (4.30)	3.52
MDP-TRA	78 (4.30)	3.42
HIS-HDC	71 (4.72)	3.05
HIS-TRA	83 (3.90)	3.41

Table 4: Subjective performance results from the user trial.

5 Conclusions

This paper has described recent work in training a POMDP-based dialogue manager to exploit the additional information available from a speech understanding system which can generate ranked lists of hypotheses. Following a brief overview of the Hidden Information State dialogue manager and policy optimisation using a user simulator, results have been given for both simulated user and real user dialogues conducted at a variety of noise levels.

The user simulation results have shown that although the rewards are similar, training with 2-best rather than 1-best outputs from the user simulator yields better success rates at high noise levels. In view of this result, we would have liked to investigate training on longer N-best lists, but currently computational constraints prevent this. We hope in the future to address this issue by developing more efficient state partitioning strategies for the HIS system.

The overall results on real data collected from the user trial clearly indicate increased robustness by the HIS system. We would have liked to be able to plot performance and success scores as a function of noise level or speech understanding error rate, but there is great variability in these kinds of complex real-world dialogues and it transpired that the trial data was insufficient to enable any statistically meaningful presentation of this form. We estimate that we need at least an order of magnitude more trial data to properly investigate the behaviour of such systems as a function of noise level. The trial described here, including transcription and analysis consumed about 30 man-days of effort. Increasing this by a factor of 10 or more is not therefore an option for us, and clearly an alternative approach is needed.

We have also reported results of subjective success rate and opinion scores based on data obtained from subjects after each trial. The results were only weakly correlated with the measured performance and success rates. We believe that this is partly due to confusion as to what constituted success in the minds of the subjects. This suggests that for subjective results to be meaningful, measurements such as these will only be really useful if made on live systems where users have a real rather than imagined information need. The use of live systems would also alleviate the data sparsity problem noted earlier.

Finally and in conclusion, we believe that despite the difficulties noted above, the results reported in this paper represent a first step towards establishing the POMDP as a viable framework for developing spoken dialogue systems which are significantly more robust to noisy operating conditions than conventional state-based systems.

Acknowledgements

This research was partly funded by the UK EPSRC under grant agreement EP/F013930/1 and by the EU FP7 Programme under grant agreement 216594 (CLASSIC project: www.classic-project.org).

References

TH Bui, M Poel, A Nijholt, and J Zwiers. 2007a. A tractable DDN-POMDP Approach to Affective Dialogue Modeling for General Probabilistic Frame-based Dialogue Systems. In *Proc 5th Workshop on Knowledge and Reasoning in Practical Dialogue Systems*, pages 34–57.

TH Bui, B van Schooten, and D Hofs. 2007b. Practical dialogue manager development using POMDPs . In *8th SIGdial Workshop on Discourse and Dialogue*, Antwerp.

LP Kaelbling, ML Littman, and AR Cassandra. 1998. Planning and Acting in Partially Observable Stochastic Domains. *Artificial Intelligence*, 101:99–134.

N Roy, J Pineau, and S Thrun. 2000. Spoken Dialogue Management Using Probabilistic Reasoning. In *Proc ACL*.

J Schatzmann, B Thomson, and SJ Young. 2007. Error Simulation for Training Statistical Dialogue Systems. In *ASRU 07*, Kyoto, Japan.

J Schatzmann. 2008. *Statistical User and Error Modelling for Spoken Dialogue Systems*. Ph.D. thesis, University of Cambridge.

B Thomson, J Schatzmann, K Weilhammer, H Ye, and SJ Young. 2007. Training a real-world POMDP-based Dialog System. In *HLT/NAACL Workshop "Bridging the Gap: Academic and Industrial Research in Dialog Technologies"*, Rochester.

B Thomson, J Schatzmann, and SJ Young. 2008. Bayesian Update of Dialogue State for Robust Dialogue Systems. In *Int Conf Acoustics Speech and Signal Processing ICASSP*, Las Vegas.

JD Williams and SJ Young. 2007a. Partially Observable Markov Decision Processes for Spoken Dialog Systems. *Computer Speech and Language*, 21(2):393–422.

JD Williams and SJ Young. 2007b. Scaling POMDPs for Spoken Dialog Management. *IEEE Audio, Speech and Language Processing*, 15(7):2116–2129.

SJ Young, J Schatzmann, K Weilhammer, and H Ye. 2007. The Hidden Information State Approach to Dialog Management. In *ICASSP 2007*, Honolulu, Hawaii.

SJ Young. 2002. Talking to Machines (Statistically Speaking). In *Int Conf Spoken Language Processing*, Denver, Colorado.

B Zhang, Q Cai, J Mao, E Chang, and B Guo. 2001. Spoken Dialogue Management as Planning and Acting under Uncertainty. In *Eurospeech*, Aalborg, Denmark.

A Frame-Based Probabilistic Framework for Spoken Dialog Management Using Dialog Examples

Kyungduk Kim, Cheongjae Lee, Sangkeun Jung and Gary Geunbae Lee
Department of Computer Science and Engineering
Pohang University of Science & Technology (POSTECH)
San 31, Hyoja-Dong, Pohang, 790-784, Republic of Korea
{getta, lcj80, hugman, gblee}@postech.ac.kr

Abstract

This paper proposes a probabilistic framework for spoken dialog management using dialog examples. To overcome the complexity problems of the classic partially observable Markov decision processes (POMDPs) based dialog manager, we use a frame-based belief state representation that reduces the complexity of belief update. We also used dialog examples to maintain a reasonable number of system actions to reduce the complexity of the optimizing policy. We developed weather information and car navigation dialog system that employed a frame-based probabilistic framework. This framework enables people to develop a spoken dialog system using a probabilistic approach without complexity problem of POMDP.

1 Introduction

A robust dialog manager is an essential part of spoken dialog systems, because many such systems have failed in practice due to errors in speech recognition. Speech recognition errors can be propagated to spoken language understanding (SLU), so the speech input must be considered error-prone from a standpoint of dialog management. Therefore robust dialog managers are necessary to develop practical spoken dialog systems.

One approach to dialog management uses the partially observable Markov decision process (POMDP) as a statistical framework, because this approach can model the uncertainty inherent in human-machine dialog (Doshi and Roy, 2007). The dialog manager uses a probabilistic, rather than deterministic, approach to manage dialog. As more information becomes available, the dialog manager updates its belief states. A POMDP-based dialog manager can learn the optimized policy that maximizes expected rewards by reinforcement learning.

But applying classic POMDP to a practical dialog system incurs a scalability problem. The computational complexity of updating belief states and optimizing the policy increases rapidly with the size of the state space in a slot-filling dialog task. To solve this scalability problem, the method of compressing states or mapping the original state space to summarized space can be used (Williams and Young, 2006; Roy et al.,2005), but these algorithms tend to approximate the state space excessively. The complexity problem of POMDP comes from updating beliefs that are out of the user's intention, and from calculating the reward of system actions that do not satisfy user's objective.

In this paper, we propose a new probabilistic framework for spoken dialog management using dialog examples. We adopted a frame-based belief state representation to reduce the complexity of belief update. Furthermore, we used an example-based approach to generate only a reasonable number of system action hypotheses in a new framework. We developed a dialog system by using our new framework in weather information service and car navigation service.

Proceedings of the 9th SIGdial Workshop on Discourse and Dialogue, pages 120–127,
Columbus, June 2008. ©2008 Association for Computational Linguistics

2 Overview

We try to address two problems of applying POMDP to slot-filling dialog management. 1) Computational complexity of belief update: it is difficult to maintain and update all belief states at every turn of dialog since there are too many dialog states in slot-filling dialog tasks. 2) Computational complexity of policy optimizing: optimizing complexity depends on both the space size of dialog states, and the number of available machine actions. In slot-filling dialog tasks, a system action can have various slot values so that the system needs to choose an action among a large number of action hypotheses.

In our new probabilistic framework (Figure 1), we try to solve these problems. Our approach uses 1) the frame-based belief state representation to solve the computational complexity problem of belief update and 2) the dialog examples to generate action hypotheses to solve the computational complexity of policy optimizing by reducing the number of system action hypotheses. First, the system groups belief states dynamically using frame-based belief state representation according to user's utterance and its SLU result. Then the system uses an example-based approach to generate only system action hypotheses that are suitable for current belief states. If there are too many hypotheses for calculating expected utility, the system prunes them away until only a reasonable number of hypotheses remains. The following describes the details of each system's component and the dialog managing process.

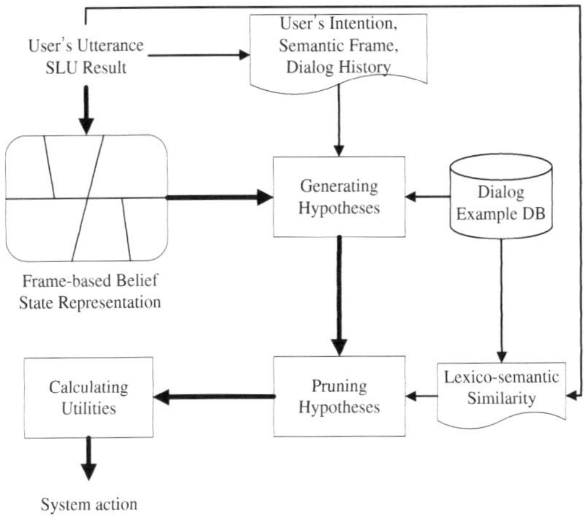

Figure 1. Overview of the system operation. Bold arrows indicate the control flow. Thin arrows indicate the data flow.

3 Frame-based Belief State Representation

We assumed that the machine's internal representation of the dialog state s_m consists of three components: user's goal s_u, user's last action a_u and dialog history s_d. This section briefly describes the basic introduction of POMDP framework and explains each component of machine's internal state in the standpoint of our frame-based probabilistic framework.

3.1 POMDP for spoken dialog management

A POMDP is defined as a tuple that consists of six substates: (S, A, P, R, Ω, O) where S is a set of state, A is a set of action, P is a transition probability $P(s'|s,a)$, R is a reward function $R(s,a,s')$, Ω is a set of observation and O is an observation model $P(o|s,a)$. The current state is not deterministic in a POMDP framework while it is determined as a specific state in a Markov decision process (MDP) framework. In a POMDP, the probability distribution over all states $s \in S$, which is referred as a belief state $b(s)$, is maintained instead of deterministic state. At each time instant t, the system chooses an action $a \in A$, and this causes the system to move from current state s to next state s' with the transition probability $P(s'|s,a)$. Then, the system is granted a reward $R(s,a)$ while the system receives an observation o with probability of $P(o|s',a)$. The system computes the belief state in the next time instance $b'(s')$ as a following:

$$b'(s') = k \cdot P(o \mid s,a) \sum_s P(s' \mid s,a) b(s)$$

where k is a normalizing factor. This process is referred as belief update.

Optimizing a POMDP policy is a process of finding a mapping function from belief states to actions that maximizes the expected reward. The system should compute a value function over belief spaces to find optimized actions. However, unlike as in a MDP, each value in a POMDP is a function of an entire probability distribution and belief spaces are very complex, so that a POMDP has a scale problem of computing the exact value function.

A POMDP for spoken dialog system is well formulated in (Williams and Young, 2007). First, a state s can be factored to three substates: (s_u, a_u, s_d)

where s_u is a user goal state, a_u is a user action, and s_d is a dialog history. A system action a_m and user action a_u can be cast as action a and observation o respectively. With some independence assumption between variables, the belief update equation can be rewritten as following:

$$\begin{aligned} b'(s') &= b(s'_u, a'_u, s'_d) \cdot \\ &= k \cdot P(\tilde{a}'_u \mid a_u) P(a_u \mid s'_u, a_m) \cdot \\ &\quad \sum_{s_u} P(s'_u \mid s_u, a_m) \cdot \sum_{s_d} P(s'_d \mid a'_u, s_d, a_m) \cdot \\ &\quad \sum_{a_u} b(s'_u, a'_u, s'_d), \end{aligned}$$

where $\tilde{a}'_u$ is an automatic speech recognizer (ASR) and SLU recognition result of user action. In our framework, belief update is done based on this equation. But applying this directly to a spoken dialog system can have a problem because the probabilities used in the equation are hard to estimate from the corpus due to the data sparseness. Therefore, we adopted Young's (2007) belief update formula that is simplified from the original equation.

3.2 User goal state

In a slot-filling dialog system, the user's goal can be represented as a fully-filled frame in which all slots of the frame contain values specified by the user's intention. Therefore, if a dialog system has W slots and each slot can have a value among V candidates, then V^W user goals can be represented as frames. This means that the number of user goals is related exponentially to the number of slots. This number of user goals is intractable in practical dialog systems.

Therefore, a method is needed to reduce the size of the state space rather than maintaining all belief states. To do this, we developed a frame-based belief state representation in which the system dynamically groups set of equivalent states to a high-level frame state. Frame state, which is a similar concept to the partition in the hidden information state (HIS) approach (Young et al, 2007) represents the indistinguishable classes of user's goals. The biggest difference between frame-based representation and partition-based representation is that the former uses only user input to split the frame state, whereas the latter uses the user input and external ontology rules such as a prior probability for belief of split partition. Therefore, the frame-based representation has relatively high domain portability because it does not need that kind of external domain dependent information.

In the frame-based belief state representation, a partially-filled frame state represents the current user's goal state for which the unfilled slot can be filled in the future, while a fully-filled frame state represents a complete user's goal state. Figure 2 describes an example of the subsumption relationship between partially filled frames and fully filled frames.

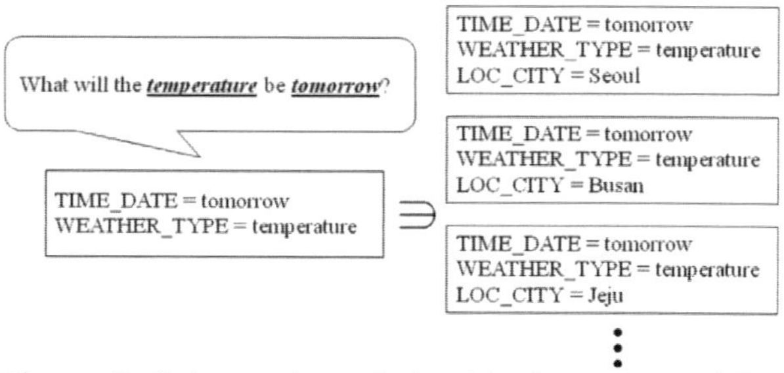

Figure 2. Subsumption relationship between partially filled frame and fully filled frame. The left frame is partially filled and three frames in the right side are fully filled.

At the start of a dialog, all states belong to the root frame state f_0. As the dialog progresses, this root frame state is split into smaller frame states whenever the value of a slot is filled by the user's input (Figure 3). First, if the user's input $[A=a]$ fills the slot of the root frame state f_0, then it splits into two frame states: f_1, which includes all user goal states with the slot A having 'a' as a value; and $\{f_0\text{-}f_1\}$, which is the relative complement of f_1. Next, if the user's input $[B=b]$ is entered to the system, each frame f_1 and $\{f_0\text{-}f_1\}$ is split into smaller frame states. The system updates not all belief states but only the beliefs of the frame states, so that the computational complexity remains relatively small.

If each user's goal has uniform distribution, the belief of frame state $b(f)$ can be calculated as follows:

$$b(f) = \frac{\#\text{ of user goals contained in frame } f}{\#\text{ of all user goals}}$$

This can be computed as follows:

$$b(f) = \prod_{s_i \in S_{filled}} \frac{1}{|V_{s_i}|} \cdot \prod_{s_j \in S_{notFilled}} \frac{|V_{s_j} - V'_{s_j}|}{|V_{s_j}|},$$

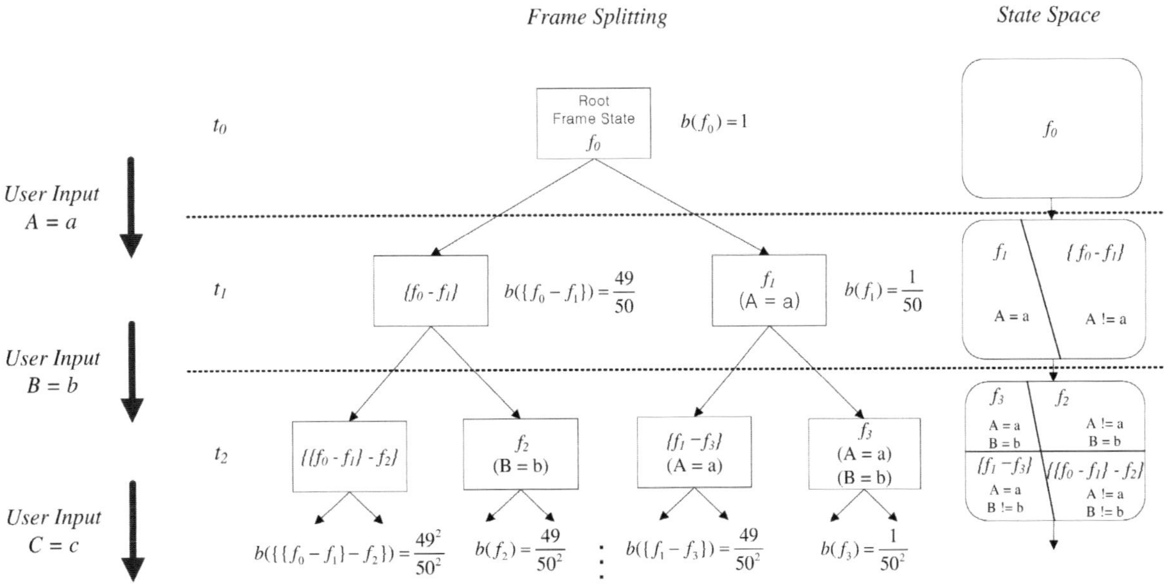

Figure 3. Splitting frame states and their beliefs with three user's inputs. f_0, f_1, f_2, … denote frame states and $b(f)$ means the belief of frame state f. A, B, C are the slot labels and a, b, c are the respective values of these slots.

where S_{filled} means the set of slots that are filled by the user's input in frame state f, and $S_{notFilled}$ means the set of empty slots. V_s denotes the set of available values for slot s, and V_s' stands for the set of values for slot s that were specified by the user in other frame states.

3.3 User action

The SLU result of current user's utterance is used for the user action. The result frame of SLU consists of a speech act, a main goal, and several named-entity component slots for each user's utterance. The speech act stands for the surface-level speech act per single utterance and the main goal slot is assigned from one of the predefined classes which classify the main application actions in a specific domain such as "search the weather (SEARCH_WEATHER)" or "search the temperature (SEARCH_TEMPERATURE)" in the weather information service domain. The tasks for filling the named-entity component slots, such as, name of the city, name of the state, are viewed as a sequence labeling task. The Figure 4 shows some examples of predefined classes for SLU semantic frame in weather information service dialog system

Our SLU module was developed based on the concept spotting approach, which aims to extract only the essential information for predefined meaning representation slots, and was implemented by applying a conditional random field model (Lee et al., 2007).

Speech Act		
YN_QUESTION	WH_QUESTION	REQUEST
REQ_QUESTION	ACCEPT	REJECT
STATEMENT	SAY	HOPE
THANK		

Main goal		
SEARCH_WEATHER	ASK_STATE_LIST	SEARCH
SEARCH_TEMPERATURE	ASK_CITY_LIST	NONE
SEARCH_RAINY_PROB		

Component slots		
TIME_DATE	LOC_CITY	LOC_STATE
WEATHER_TYPE		

Figure 4 Example predefined classes for semantic frame of SLU in weather information service dialog system.

3.4 Dialog history

Similar to the traditional frame-based dialog management approach, a frame can represent the history of the dialog. The difference between the traditional frame-based dialog manager and our framework is that traditional frame-based dialog manager maintains only one frame while our framework can maintain multiple dialog hypotheses. Moreover, each hypothesis in our framework can have a probability as in the belief state of the classic POMDP.

4 Example-based System Action Generation

4.1 Example-based system action hypothesis generation

It is impossible to consider all of the system actions as hypotheses because the number of possible actions is so large. We used an example-based approach to generate a reasonable number of system action hypotheses as hinted in (Lee et al., 2006). In this approach, the system retrieves the best dialog example from dialog example database (DEDB) which is semantically indexed from a dialog corpus. To query a semantically close example for the current situation, the system uses the user's intention (speech act and main goal), semantic frame (component slots) and discourse history as search key constraints (Lee et al., 2006). These search keys can be collected with SLU output (e.g., user intention and semantic frame) and discourse history in a dialog manager. Figure 5 describes an example of search key for DEDB on a weather information service system.

User's utterance	What will the ***temperature*** be ***tomorrow***? *Weather_Type Time_Date*
Search key constraints	Speech Act = wh_question Main Goal = search_temperature WEATHER_TYPE = 1 (filled) TIME_DATE = 1 (filled) LOC_CITY = 0 (unfilled) LOC_STATE = 0 (unfilled)
Lexico-semantic Input	What will the [WEATHER_TYPE] be [TIME_DATE]?

Figure 5. Example search key constraints for dialog example database.

For each frame state $f_1, ..., f_n$, the system generates one or more system action hypotheses by querying the DEDB respectively. Queried actions may inconsistent with the current frame state because the situation of indexed dialog examples may different from current dialog situation. Therefore, the system maps the contents of dialog example to information of current frame state. Slot values of frame state and information from content database (e.g., weather information database) are used for making the action consistent. If the system retrieves more than a threshold number of system action hypotheses using the search key constrains, then the system should prune away dialog examples to maintain only a reasonable number of hypotheses. We used lexico-semantic similarity between the user utterance and the retrieved examples to limit the number of hypotheses. To measure the lexico-semantic similarity, we first replace the slot values in the user utterance by its slot names to generate lexico-semantic input, and calculate the normalized edit distance between that input and retrieved examples (Figure 5). In the normalized edit distance, we defined following cost function $C(i,j)$ to give a weight to the term which is replaced by its slot name.

$$C(i,j) = \begin{cases} 0 \ \text{if}\ w_{1,i} = w_{2,j} \\ 1 \ \text{if}\ w_{1,i} \neq w_{2,j} \ \text{and}\ w_{1,i}, w_{2,j} \notin S_{slot\_name} \\ 1.5 \ \text{if}\ w_{1,i} \neq w_{2,j} \ \text{and}\ w_{1,i}, w_{2,j} \in S_{slot\_name} \end{cases}$$

where $w_{1,i}$ is ith word of user's utterance, $w_{2,j}$ is jth word of dialog example's utterance, and S_{slot_name} is the set of slot names. According to the lexico-semantic similarity, the system appends the top N_h-ranked hypotheses to the final action hypotheses (where N_h is the rank threshold).

Many existing systems used heuristics or rule-based approaches to reduce the number of system action hypotheses (Young et al., 2007). But these methods are not flexible enough to handle all dialog flows because a system developer should design new heuristics or rules whenever the system needs to support a new kind of dialog flow. The example-based approach, on the contrary, can instantly refine the control of dialog flows by adding new dialog examples. This is a great advantage when a system developer wants to change or refine a dialog control flow.

4.2 Calculating Expected Utilities

We adopted the principle of maximum expected utility to determine the optimized system actions among the hypotheses (Paek and Horvitz, 2004).

$$\tilde{a}_m^* = \arg\max_a EU(a \mid \xi) = \arg\max_a \sum_h P(H = h \mid \xi) u(a,h) = \arg\max_h \sum_h b(h) u(a,h)$$

where ξ denotes all information about the environment, $u(a,h)$ means the utility of taking an action when the internal state of the machine is h, which consists of three substates, (f, a_u, s_d) : f is a frame state, a_u is a user's last action, and s_d is a dialog history. The utility function $u(a,h)$ can be specific to each application. We defined a handcrafted utility function to calculate the expected utility.

5 Experiments

We performed two evaluations. 1) Real user evaluation: we measured the user satisfaction with various factors by human. 2) Simulated user evaluation: we implemented user simulator to measure the system performance with a large number of dialogs. We built dialog corpora in two domains: weather information service and car navigation.

5.1 Real user evaluation

We built a dialog corpus in weather information service to measure the performance of the dialog system using our approach by real user evaluation. This corpus consists of 99 dialogs with 503 user utterances (turns). User's utterances were annotated with the semantic frame including speech acts, main goal and component slots for training the SLU module and indexing the DEDB.

To evaluate the preliminary performance, four test volunteers among computer science people evaluated our dialog system with five different weather information-seeking tasks. The volunteers typed their utterances with a keyboard rather than using a real ASR because it is hard to control the WER. We employed a simulated ASR error channel by generating random errors to evaluate the performance of dialog management under various levels of WER. We will explain the details of our ASR channel simulator in Section 5.2. The WER is controlled by this ASR channel simulator while the volunteers were interacting with computer. To measure the user perception of task completion rate (TCR), the volunteers evaluated the system's response in each dialog to measure the success turn rate (STR) and decided whether the entire dialog was successful or not. We evaluated the performance of our dialog system based on criteria outlined in (Litman and Pan, 2004) by measuring user satisfaction, which is defined with a linear combination of three measures: TCR, Mean Recognition Accuracy (MRA), and STR.

$$\text{User Satisfaction} = \alpha\text{TCR} + \beta\text{STR} + \gamma\text{MRA}$$

In our evaluation, we set α, β and γ to 1/3, so that the maximum value of the user satisfaction is one.

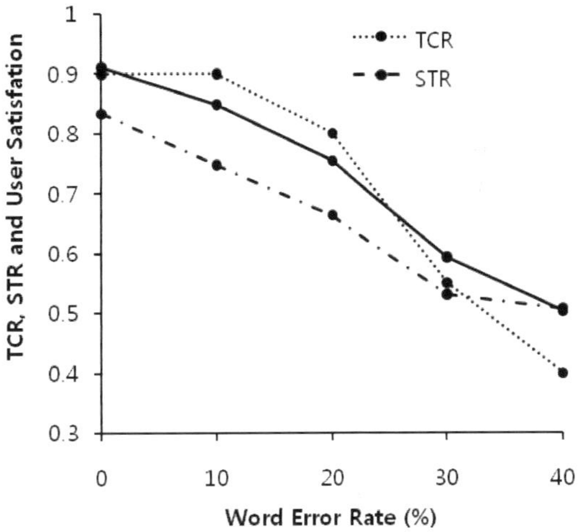

Figure 6 Dialog system performance with various word error rates in weather information seeking tasks. Dotted line is TCR; dashed line is STR; solid line is user satisfaction.

TCR, STR and user satisfaction decreased with WER. User satisfaction has relatively high value when the WER is smaller than 20% (Figure 6). If the WER is equal or over 20%, user satisfaction has small value because the TCR decreases rapidly in this range.

Generally, TCR has a higher value than STR, because although a dialog turn may fail, users still have a chance to use other expressions which can be well recognized by the system. As a result of this, even when some dialog turns fail, the task can be completed successfully.

TCR decreases rapidly when WER $\geq$20%. When WER is high, the probability of losing the information in a user utterance is also large. Especially, if words contain important meaning, i.e., values of component slots in SLU, it is difficult for the system to generate a proper response.

STR is 0.83 when WER is zero, i.e., although all user inputs are correctly recognized, the system sometimes didn't generate proper outputs. This failure can be caused by SLU errors or malfunction of the dialog manager. SLU errors can be propagated to the dialog manager, and this leads the system to generate a wrong response because SLU results are inputs of dialog manger.

If the WER is 20%, user satisfaction is relatively small because TCR decreases rapidly in this range. This means that our approach is useful in a system devoted to providing weather information, and is relatively robust to speech errors if the WER is less than 20%.

5.2 Simulated user evaluation

We built another dialog corpus in car navigation service to measure the performance of the dialog system by simulated user evaluation. This corpus consists of 123 dialogs with 510 user utterances (turns). The SLU result frame of this corpus has 7 types of speech acts, 8 types of main goals, and 5 different component slots.

The user simulator and ASR channel simulator has been used for evaluating the proposed dialog management framework. The user simulator has two components: an *Intention Simulator* and a *Surface Simulator*. The *Intention Simulator* generates the next user intention given current discourse context, and the *Surface Simulator* generates user sentence to express the generated intention.

ASR channel simulator simulates the speech recognition errors including substitution, deletion, and insertions errors. It uses the phoneme confusion matrix to estimate the probability distribution for error simulation. ASR channel simulator distorts the generated user utterance from Surface Simulator. By simulating user intentions, surface form of user sentence and ASR channel, we can test the robustness of the proposed dialog system in both speech recognition and speech understanding errors.

We defined a final state of dialog to automatically measure TCR of a simulated dialog. If a dialog flow reaches the final state, the evaluator regards that the dialog was successfully completed. TCRs and average dialog lengths were measured under various WER conditions that were generated by ASR channel simulator. Until the SLU result is an actual input of the dialog manager, we also measured the SLU accuracy. If a SLU result is same as a user's intention of the Intention Simulator, then the evaluator considers that the result is correct. Unlike in the real user evaluation, the dialog system could be evaluated with relatively large amount of simulated dialogs in the simulated user evaluation. 5000 simulated dialogs were generated for each WER condition.

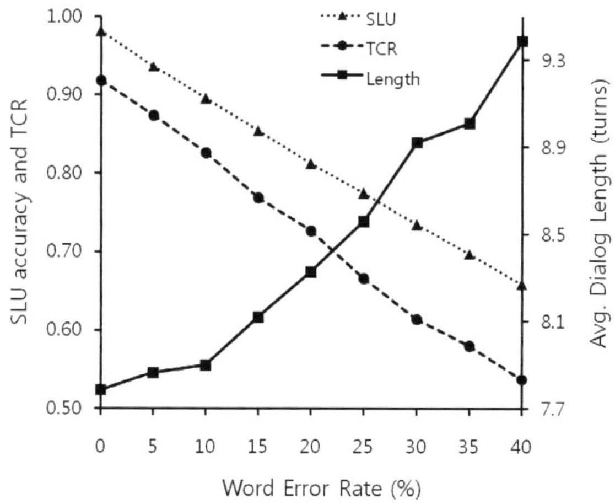

Figure 7 TCR, SLU accuracy, and average dialog length of the dialog system under various WER conditions.

We found that the SLU accuracy and TCR linearly decreased with the WER. Similar in the human evaluation, TCR is about 0.9 when WER is zero, and it becomes below 0.7 when WER is higher than 20%. Average dialog length, on contrary, increased with WER, and it has similar values when WER is less than 10% although it increased relatively rapidly when WER is higher than 15%.

6 Conclusions

This paper proposed a new probabilistic method to manage the human-machine dialog by using the frame-state belief state representation and the example-based system action hypothesis generation. The frame-based state representation reduces the computational complexity of belief update by grouping the indistinguishable user goal states. And the system generates the system action hypotheses with the example-based approach in order to refine the dialog flows easily. In addition, this approach employed the POMDP formalism to maintain belief distribution over dialog states so that the system can be robust to speech recognition errors by considering the uncertainty of user's input.

A prototype system using our approach has been implemented and evaluated by real and simulated user. According to the preliminary evaluation, our framework can be a useful approach to manage a spoken dialog system.

We plan to progress the research on adopting a formalized online search to determine the optimal system action (Ross and Chaib-draa, 2007). With the online searching, system doesn't need to behave the useless computation because this approach searches only possible path. We expect that this property of the online searching show the synergetic effect on dialog management if it combines with example-based approach.

Similar to example-based approach, the case-based reasoning approach (Eliasson, 2006) can be helpful for our future research. Some properties such as using previous cases to process current case can be shared with our approach. We think that some other properties including the concept of online learning can be useful for making our approach concrete

Acknowledgments

This research was supported by the MKE (Ministry of Knowledge Economy), Korea, under the ITRC (Information Technology Research Center) support program supervised by the IITA (Institute for Information Technology Advancement) (IITA-2008-C1090-0801-0045)

References

Changki Lee, Jihyun Eun, Minwoo Jeong, and Gary Geunbae Lee, Y. Hwang, M. Jang, "A multi-strategic concept-spotting approach for robust understanding of spoken Korean," *ETRI Journal*, vol. 29, No.2, pp. 179-188, 2007.

Cheongjae Lee, Sangkeun Jung, Jihyun Eun, Minwoo Jeong and Gary Geunbae Lee, "A situation-based dialogue management using dialogue examples," in *Proceedings of International conference on Acoustics, Speech, and Signal Processing*, Toulouse, 2006.

Diane J. Litman and Shimei Pan, "Empirically evaluating an adaptable spoken dialogue system," in *Proceedings of the 8th International Conference on Spoken Language Processing,* pp. 2145-2148, 2004.

Finale Doshi and Nicholas Roy, "Efficient Model Learning for Dialog Management," in *Proceeding of the ACM/IEEE international conference on Human-robot interaction*, Washington DC, 2007.

Jason D. Williams and Steve Young, "Scaling POMDPs for dialog management with composite summary point-based value iteration (CSPBVI)," in *Proceedings of AAAI Workshop on Statistical and Empirical Approaches for Spoken Dialogue Systems*, Boston, 2006.

Jason D. Williams and Steve Young, " Partially Observable Markov Decision Processes for Spoken Dialog Systems." *Computer Speech and Language* 21(2): 231-422, 2007

Karolina Eliasson, "The Use of Case-Based Reasoning in a Human-Robot Dialog System", *Licentiate of Engineering Thesis of Linköping Institute of Technology at Linköping University*, 2006

Nicholas Roy, Geoffrey Gordon, and Sebastian Thrun, "Finding approximate pomdp solutions through belief compression," *Journal of Artificial Intelligence Research*, vol. 23, pp.1–40, 2005.

Sptéphane Ross, Brahim Chaib-draa, "AEMS: An Anytime Online Search Algorithm for Approximate Policy Refinement in Large POMDPs", in *Proceedings of the 20th International Joint Conference on Artificial Intelligence*, 2007

Steve Young, Jost Schatzmann, Karl Weilhammer and Hui Ye, "The hidden information state approach to dialog management," in *Proceedings of International Conference on Acoustics, Speech, and Signal Processing*, Honolulu, 2007.

Tim Paek and Eric Horvitz, "Optimizing automated call routing by integrating spoken dialog models with queuing models," in *Proceedings of HLT-NAACL*, pp. 41-48, Boston, 2004.

Invited Talk

Speaking More Like You: Lexical, Acoustic/Prosodic, and Discourse Entrainment in Spoken Dialogue Systems

Julia Hirschberg
Department of Computer Science
Columbia University
julia@cs.columbia.edu

Abstract

When people engage in conversation, they adapt the way they speak to the speaking style of their conversational partner in a variety of ways. For example, they may adopt a certain way of describing something based upon the way their conversational partner describes it, or adapt their pitch range or speaking rate to a conversational partner's. They may even align their turn-taking style or use of cue phrases to match their partner's. These types of entrainment have been shown to correlate with various measures of task success and dialogue naturalness. While there is considerable evidence for lexical entrainment from laboratory experiments, much less is known about other types of acoustic-prosodic and discourse-level entrainment and little work has been done to examine entrainments in multiple modalities for the same dialogue. We will discuss work on entrainment in multiple dimensions in the Columbia Games Corpus. Our goal is to understand how the different varieties of entrainment correlate with one another and to determine which types of entrainment will be both useful and feasible for Spoken Dialogue Systems.

Proceedings of the 9th SIGdial Workshop on Discourse and Dialogue, page 128,
Columbus, June 2008.

Discourse Level Opinion Relations: An Annotation Study

Swapna Somasundaran
Dept. of Computer Science
University of Pittsburgh
Pittsburgh, PA 15260
swapna@cs.pitt.edu

Josef Ruppenhofer
Intelligent Systems Program
University of Pittsburgh
Pittsburgh, PA 15260
josefr@cs.pitt.edu

Janyce Wiebe
Dept. of Computer Science
University of Pittsburgh
Pittsburgh, PA 15260
wiebe@cs.pitt.edu

Abstract

This work proposes *opinion frames* as a representation of discourse-level associations that arise from related opinion targets and which are common in task-oriented meeting dialogs. We define the opinion frames and explain their interpretation. Additionally we present an annotation scheme that realizes the opinion frames and via human annotation studies, we show that these can be reliably identified.

1 Introduction

There has been a great deal of research in recent years on opinions and subjectivity. Opinions have been investigated at the phrase, sentence, and document levels. However, little work has been carried out at the level of discourse.

Consider the following excerpt from a dialog about designing a remote control for a television (the opinion *targets* - what the opinions are about - are shown in *italics*).

(1) D:: And I thought **not too** *edgy and like a box*, **more** kind of *hand-held* **not** as *computery*, yeah, **more** *organic shape* I think. *Simple designs*, like the last one we just saw, **not too** *many buttons* . . .

Speaker *D* expresses an opinion in favor of a design that is simple and organic in shape, and against an alternative design which is not. Several individual opinions are expressed in this passage. The first is a negative opinion about the design being too edgy and box-like, the next is a positive opinion toward a hand-held design, followed by a negative opinion toward a computery shape, and so on. While we believe that recognizing individual expressions of opinions, their properties, and components is important, we believe that discourse interpretation is needed as well. It is by understanding the passage as a discourse that we see *edgy*, *like a box*, *computery*, and *many buttons* as descriptions of the type of design *D* does not prefer, and *hand-held*, *organic shape*, and *simple designs* as descriptions of the type he does. These descriptions are not in general synonyms/antonyms of one another; for example, there are hand-held "computery" devices and simple designs that are edgy. The unison/opposition among the descriptions is due to how they are used in the discourse.

This paper focuses on such relations between the targets of opinions in discourse. Specifically, we propose *opinion frames*, which consist of two opinions which are related by virtue of having united or opposed targets. We believe that recognizing opinion frames will provide more information for NLP applications than recognizing their individual components alone. Further, if there is uncertainty about any one of the components, we believe opinion frames are an effective representation incorporating discourse information to make an overall coherent interpretation (Hobbs, 1979; Hobbs, 1983).

To our knowledge, this is the first work to extend a manual annotation scheme to relate opinions in the discourse. In this paper, we present opinion frames, and motivate their usefulness through examples. Then we provide an annotation scheme for capturing these opinion frames. Finally we perform fine-grained annotation studies to measure the human reliability in recognizing of these opinion frames.

Proceedings of the 9th SIGdial Workshop on Discourse and Dialogue, pages 129–137,
Columbus, June 2008.

Opinion frames are presented in Section 2, our annotation scheme is described in Section 3, the inter-annotator agreement studies are presented in Section 4, related work is discussed in Section 5, and conclusions are in Section 6.

2 Opinion Frames

2.1 Introduction

The components of opinion frames are individual opinions and the relationships between their targets.

We address two types of opinions, *sentiment* and *arguing*. Following (Wilson and Wiebe, 2005; Somasundaran et al., 2007), sentiment includes positive and negative evaluations, emotions, and judgments, while arguing includes arguing *for* or *against* something, and arguing *that* something should or should not be done. In our examples, the lexical anchors revealing the opinion type (as the words are interpreted in context) are indicated in **bold face**. In addition, the text span capturing the target of the opinion (again, as interpreted in context) is indicated in *italics*.

(2) D:: ... this kind of rubbery material, *it's* a **bit more bouncy**, like you said they get chucked around a lot. A **bit more durable** and *that* can also be **ergonomic** and *it* kind of feels **a bit different from all the other remote controls**.

Speaker *D* expresses his preference for the rubbery material for the remote. He reiterates his opinion with a number of positive evaluations like **bit more bouncy**, **bit more durable**, **ergonomic** and so on.

All opinions in this example are related to the others via opinion frames by virtue of having the same targets, i.e., the opinions are essentially about the same things (the rubbery material for the remote). For example, the opinions **ergonomic** and **a bit different from all the other remote controls** are related in a frame of type *SPSPsame*, meaning the first opinion is a *S(entiment)* with polarity *P(ositive)*; the second also is a *S(entiment)* with polarity *P(ositive)*; and the targets of the opinions are in a same (target) relation.

The specific target relations addressed in this paper are the relations of either being the same or being alternatives to one another. While these are not the only possible relations, they are not infrequent, and they commonly occur in task-oriented dialogs such as those in our data.

SPSPsame, SNSNsame, APAPsame, ANANsame, SPAPsame, APSPsame, SNANsame, ANSNsame, SPSNalt, SNSPalt, APANalt, ANAPalt, SPANalt, SNAPalt, APSNalt, ANSPalt
SPSNsame, SNSPsame, APANsame, ANAPsame, SPANsame, APSNsame, SNAPsame, ANSPsame, SPSPalt, SNSNalt, APAPalt, ANANalt, SPAPalt, SNANalt, APSPalt, ANSNalt

Table 1: Opinion Frames

With four opinion type - polarity pairs (*SN*, *SP*, *AN*, *AP*), for each of two opinion slots, and two possible target relations, we have 4 * 4 * 2 = 32 types of frame, listed in Table 1.

In the remainder of this section, we elaborate further on the *same* target relation (in 2.2) the *alternative* target relation (in 2.3) and explain a method by which these relationships can be propagated (in 2.4). Finally, we illustrate the usefulness of opinion frames in discourse interpretation (in 2.5).

2.2 *Same* Targets

Our notion of sameness for targets includes cases of anaphora and ellipses, lexically similar items, as well as less direct relations such as part-whole, subset, inferable, and instance-class.

Looking at the opinion frames for Example 2 in more detail, we separately list the opinions, followed by the relations between targets.

Opinion Span - target Span	Type
O1 **bit more bouncy** - *it's* [t1]	SP
O2 **bit more durable** - ellipsis [t2]	SP
O3 **ergonomic** - *that* [t3]	SP
O4 **a bit different from all the other remote** - *it* [t4]	SP

Target - target	Rel
t1 - t2	same
t1 - t3	same
t3 - t4	same

Ellipsis occurs with **bit more durable**. [t2] represents the (implicit) target of that opinion, and [t2] has a *same* relation to [t1], the target of the **bit more bouncy** opinion. (Note that the interpretation of the first target, [t1], would require anaphora resolution of its target span with a previous noun phrase, *rubbery material*.)

Let us now consider the following passage, in which a meeting participant analyzes two leading remotes on the market.[1]

(3) D:: These are two **leading** *remote controls* at the moment. You know *they*'re **grey**, *this one*'s got **loads of buttons**, it's **hard to tell** from here what *they* actually do, and *they* **don't look very exciting at all**.

Opinion Span - target Span	Rel
O1 **leading** - *remote controls* [t1]	SP
O2 **grey** - *they* [t2]	SN
O3 **loads of buttons** - *this one* [t3]	SN
O4 **hard to tell** - *they* [t4]	SN
O5 **don't look very exciting at all** - *they* [t5]	SN

Target - target	Rel
t1 - t2	same
t2 - t3	same
t3 - t4	same
t5 - t1	same

Target [t2] is the set of two leading remotes, and [t3], which is in a *same* relation with [t2], is one of those remotes. Target [t4], which is also in a *same* relation with [t3], is an aspect of that remote, namely its buttons. Thus, opinion O3 is directly about one of the remotes, and indirectly about the set of both remotes. Similarly, opinion O4 is directly about the buttons of one of the remotes, and indirectly about that remote itself.

2.3 *Alternative* Targets

The *alt(ernative)* target relation arises when multiple choices are available, and only one can be selected. For example, in the domain of TV remote controls, the set of all shapes are alternatives to one another, since a remote control may have only one shape at a time. In such scenarios, a positive opinion regarding one choice may imply a negative opinion toward the rest of the choices, and vice versa.

As an example, let us now consider the following passage (some intervening utterances have been removed for clarity).

(4) C:: ... shapes **should be** *curved*, so round shapes[2] **Nothing** *square-like*.
C:: ... So we **shouldn't have too** *square corners* and that kind of thing.
B:: Yeah okay. **Not** ***the old box look***.

Opinion Span - target Span	Rel
O1 **should be** - *curved* [t1]	AP
O2 **Nothing** - *square-like* [t2]	AN
O3 **shouldn't have** - *square corners* [t3]	AN
O4 **too** - *square corners* [t3]	SN
O5 **Not** - *the old box look* [t4]	AN
O6 **the old box look** - *the old box look* [t4]	SN

Target - target	Rel
t1 -t2	alternatives
t2 - t3	same
t3 - t4	same

There is an *alt* relation between, for example, [t1] and [t2]. Thus, we have an opinion frame between *O1* and *O2*, whose type is *APANalt*. From this frame, we understand that a positive opinion is expressed toward something and a negative opinion is expressed toward its alternative.

2.4 Link Transitivity

When individual targets are linked, they form a chain-like structure. Due to this, a connecting path may exist between targets that were not directly linked by the human annotators. This path may be traversed to create links between new pairs of targets - which in turn results in new opinion frame relations. For instance, in Example 4, the frame with direct relation is *O1O2 APANalt*. By following the *alt* link from [t1] to [t2] and the *same* link from [t2] to [t3], we have an *alt* link between [t1] and [t3], and the additional frames *O1O3 APANalt* and *O1O4 APSNalt*. Repeating this process would finally link speaker *C's* opinion O1 with *B's* opinion O6, yielding a *APSNalt* frame.

2.5 Interpretation

This section illustrates two motivations for opinion frames: they may unearth additional information over and above the individual opinions stated in the text, and they may contribute toward arriving at a coherent interpretation (Hobbs, 1979; Hobbs, 1983) of the opinions in the discourse.

Through opinion frames, opinions regarding something not explicitly mentioned in the local context and not even lexically related can become relevant, providing more information about someone's opinions. This is particularly interesting when *alt* relations are involved, as opinions towards one alternative imply opinions of opposite polarity toward the remaining options. For instance in Example 4

[1] In the other examples in this paper, the source (holder) of the opinions is the speaker. The **leading** opinion in this example is an exception: its source is implicit; it is a consensus opinion that is not necessarily shared by the speaker (i.e., it is a *nested source* (Wiebe et al., 2005)).

[2] In the context of the dialogs, the annotators read the "so round shapes" as a summary statement. Had the "so" been interpreted as Arguing, the round shapes would have been annotated as a target (and linked to *curved*).

above, if we consider only the explicitly stated opinions, there is only one (positive) opinion about the curved shape, namely *O1*. However, the speaker expresses several other opinions which reinforce his positivity toward the curved shape. These are in fact opinion frames in which the other opinion has the opposite polarity as *O1* and the target relation is *alt* (for example frames such as *O1O3 APANalt* and *O1O4 APSNalt*).

In the dialog, notice that speaker *B* agrees with *C* and exhibits his own reinforcing opinions. These would be similarly linked via targets resulting in frames like *O1O6 APSNalt*.

Turning to our second point, arriving at a coherent interpretation obviously involves disambiguation. Suppose that some aspect of an individual opinion, such as polarity, is unclear. If the discourse suggests certain opinion frames, this may in turn resolve the underlying ambiguity. For instance in Example 2, we see that out of context, the polarities of **bouncy** and **different from other remotes** are unclear (bounciness and being different may be negative attributes for another type of object). However, the polarities of two of the opinions are clear (**durable** and **ergonomic**). There is evidence in this passage of discourse continuity and *same* relations, such as the pronouns, the lack of contrastive cue phrases, and so on. This evidence suggests that the speaker expresses similar opinions throughout the passage, making the opinion frame *SPSPsame* more likely throughout. Recognizing the frames would resolve the polarity ambiguities of **bouncy** and **different**.

Example 2 is characterized by opinion frames in which the opinions reinforce one other. Interestingly, interplays among different opinion types may show the same type of reinforcement. As we analyzed above, Example 4 is characterized by mixtures of opinion types, polarities, and target relations. However, the opinions are still unified in the intention to argue for a particular type of shape. There is evidence in this passage suggesting reinforcing frames: the negations are applied to targets that are alternative to the desired option, and the passage is without contrastive discourse cues. If we are able to recognize the best overall set of opinion frames for the passage, the polarity ambiguities will be resolved.

On the other hand, evidence for non-reinforcing opinions would suggest other frames, potentially resulting in different interpretations of polarity and relations among targets. Such non-reinforcing associations between opinions and often occur when the speaker is ambivalent or weighing pros and cons. Table 1 lists the frames that occur in reinforcing scenarios in the top row, and the frames that occur in non-reinforcing scenarios in the bottom row.

3 Annotation Scheme

Our annotation scheme began with the definition and basics of the opinion annotation from previous work (Wilson and Wiebe, 2005; Somasundaran et al., 2007). We then add to it the attributes and components that are necessary to make an Opinion Frame.

First, the text span that reveals the opinion expression is identified. Then, the text spans corresponding to the targets are marked, if there exist any (we also allow span-less targets). Then, the type and polarity of the opinion in the context of the discourse is marked. Finally the targets that are related (again in the context of the discourse) are linked. Specifically, the components that form the Annotation of the frame are as follows:

Opinion Span: This is a span of text that reveals the opinion.

Type: This attribute specifies the opinion type as either *Arguing* or *Sentiment*.

Polarity: This attribute identifies the valence of an opinion and can be one of: *positive, negative, neutral, both, unknown.*

Target Span: This is a span of text that captures what an opinion is about. This can be a proposition or an entity.

Target Link: This is an attribute of a target and records all the targets in the discourse that the target is related to.

Link Type: The link between two targets is specified by this attribute as either *same* or *alternative*.

In addition to these definitions, our annotation manual has guidelines detailing how to deal with grammatical issues, disfluencies, etc. Appendix A illustrates how this annotation scheme is applied to the utterances of Example 4.

Links between targets can be followed in either direction to construct chains. In this work, we consider target relations to be commutative, i.e., Link(t1,t2) => Link(t2,t1). When a newly annotated target is similar (or opposed) to a set of targets already participating in *same* relations, then the *same* (or *alt*) link is made only to one of them - the one that looks most natural. This is often the one that is closest.

4 Annotation Studies

Construction of an opinion frame is a stepwise process where first the text spans revealing the opinions and their targets are selected, the opinion text spans are classified by type and polarity and finally the targets are linked via one of the possible relations. We split our annotation process into these 3 intuitive stages and use an evaluation that is most applicable for the task at that stage.

Two annotators (both co-authors on the paper) underwent training at each stage, and the annotation manual was revised after each round of training. In order to prevent errors incurred at earlier stages from affecting the evaluation of later stages, the annotators produced a consensus version at the end of each stage, and used that consensus annotation as the starting point for the next annotation stage. In producing these consensus files, one annotator first annotated a document, and the other annotator reviewed the annotations, making changes if needed. This prevented any discussion between the annotators from influencing the tagging task of the next stage.

In the following subsections, we first introduce the data and then present our results for annotation studies for each stage, ending with discussion.

4.1 Data

The data used in this work is the AMI meeting corpus (Carletta et al., 2005) which contains multimodal recordings of group meetings. We annotated meetings from the scenario based meetings, where four participants collaborate to design a new TV remote control in a series of four meetings. The meetings represent different project phases, namely project kick-off, functional design, conceptual design, and detailed design. Each meeting has rich transcription and segment (turn/utterance) information for each speaker. Each utterance consists of one or more sentences. At each agreement stage we used approximately 250 utterances from a meeting for evaluation. The annotators also used the audio and video recordings in the annotation of meetings.

Gold	Exact	Lenient	Subset
ANN-1	53	89	87
ANN-2	44	76	74

Table 2: Inter-Annotator agreement on Opinion Spans

4.2 Opinion Spans and Target Spans

In this step, the annotators selected text spans and labeled them as *opinion* or *target* We calculated our agreement for text span retrieval similar to Wiebe et al. (2005). This agreement metric corresponds to the Precision metric in information retrieval, where annotations from one annotator are considered the gold standard, and the other annotator's annotations are evaluated against it.

Table 2 shows the inter-annotator agreement (in percentages). For the first row, the annotations produced by Annotator-1 (ANN-1) are taken as the gold standard and, for the second row, the annotations from annotator-2 form the gold standard. The "Exact" column reports the agreement when two text spans have to match exactly to be considered correct. The "Lenient" column shows the results if an overlap relation between the two annotators' retrieved spans is also considered to be a hit. Wiebe et al. (2005) use this approach to measure agreement for a (somewhat) similar task of subjectivity span retrieval in the news corpus. Our agreement numbers for this column is comparable to theirs. Finally, the third column, "Subset", shows the agreement for a more strict constraint, namely, that one of the spans must be a subset of the other to be considered a match. Two opinion spans that satisfy this relation are ensured to share all the opinion words of the smaller span.

The numbers indicate that, while the annotators

Gold	Exact	Lenient	Subset
ANN-1	54	73	71
ANN-2	54	75	74

Table 3: Inter-Annotator agreement on Target Spans

Gold	Exact	Lenient	Subset
ANN-1	74	87	87
ANN-2	76	90	90

Table 4: Inter-Annotator agreement on Targets with Perfect Opinion spans

do not often retrieve the exact same span, they reliably retrieve approximate spans. Interestingly, the agreement numbers between Lenient and Subset columns are close. This implies that, in the cases of inexact matches, the spans retrieved by the two annotators are still close. They agree on the opinion words and differ mostly on the inclusion of function words (e.g. articles) and observation of syntactic boundaries.

In similar fashion, Table 3 gives the inter-annotator agreement for target span retrieval. Additionally, Table 4 shows the inter-annotator agreement for target span retrieval when opinions that do not have an exact match are filtered out. That is, Table 4 shows results only for targets of the opinions on which the annotators perfectly agree. As targets are annotated with respect to the opinions, this second evaluation removes any effects of disagreements in the opinion detection task. As seen in Table 4, this improves the inter-coder agreement.

4.3 Opinion Type and Polarity

In this step, the annotators began with the consensus opinion span and target span annotations. We hypothesized that given the opinion expression, determining whether it is Arguing or Sentiment would not be difficult. Similarly, we hypothesized that target information would make the polarity labeling task clearer.

As every opinion instance is tagged with a type

	Type Tagging	Polarity Tagging
Accuracy	97.8%	98.5%
κ	0.95	0.952

Table 5: Inter-Annotator agreement on Opinion Types and Polarity

and polarity, we use Accuracy and Cohen's Kappa (κ) metric (Cohen, 1960). The κ metric measures the inter-annotator agreement above chance agreement. The results, in Table 5, show that κ both for type and polarity tagging is very high. This confirms our hypothesis that Sentiment and Arguing can be reliably distinguished once the opinion spans are known. Our polarity detection task shows an improvement in κ over a similar polarity assignment task by Wilson et al. (2005) for the news corpus (κ of 0.72). We believe this improvement can partly be attributed to the target information available to our annotators.

4.4 Target Linking

As an intuitive first step in evaluating target linking, we treat target links in the discourse similarly to anaphoric chains and apply methods developed for co-reference resolution (Passonneau, 2004) for our evaluation. Passonneau's method is based on Krippendorf's α metric (Krippendorff, 2004) and allows for partial matches between anaphoric chains. In addition to this, we evaluate links identified by both annotators for the type (*same / alternative*) labeling task with the help of the κ metric.

Passonneau (2004) reports that in her co-reference task on spoken monologs, α varies with the difficulty of the corpus (from 0.46 to 0.74). This is true in our case too. Table 6 shows our agreement for the four types of meetings in the AMI corpus: the kickoff meeting (a), the functional design (b), the conceptual design (c) and the detailed design (d).

Of the meetings, the kickoff meeting (a) we use has relatively clear discussions. The conceptual design meeting (c) is the toughest, as as participants are expressing opinions about a hypothetical (desirable) remote. In our detailed design meeting (d), there are two final designs being evaluated. On analyzing the chains from the two annotators, we discovered that one annotator had maintained two separate chains for the two remotes as there is no explicit linguistic indication (within the 250 utterances) that these two are alternatives. The second annotator, on the other hand, used the knowledge that the goal of the meeting is to design a single TV remote to link them as alternatives. Thus by changing just two links in the second annotator's file to account for this, our α for this meeting went up from 0.52

Meeting:	a	b	c	d
Target linking (α)	0.79	0.74	0.59	0.52
Relation Labeling (κ)	1	1	0.91	1

Table 6: Inter-Annotator agreement on Target relation identification

to 0.70. We plan to further explore other evaluation methodologies that account for severity of differences in linking and are more relevant for our task. Nonetheless, the resulting numbers indicate that there is sufficient information in the discourse to provide for reliable linking of targets.

The high κ for the relation type identification shows that once the presence of a link is detected, it is not difficult to determine if the targets are similar or alternatives to each other.

4.5 Discussion

Our agreement studies help to identify the aspects of opinion frames that are straightforward, and those that need complex reasoning. Our results indicate that while the labeling tasks such as opinion type, opinion polarity and target relation type are relatively reliable for humans, retrieval of opinions spans, target spans and target links is more difficult.

A common cause of annotation disagreement is different interpretation of the utterance, particularly in the presence of disfluencies and restarts. For example consider the following utterance where a participant is evaluating the drawing of another participant on the white board.

(5) *It's a baby shark* , **it looks to me**, . . .

One annotator interpreted this "it looks to me" as an arguing for the belief that it was indeed a drawing of a baby shark *(positive Arguing)*. The second annotator on the other hand looked at it as a *neutral* viewpoint/evaluation (*Sentiment*) being expressed regarding the drawing. Thus even though both annotators felt an opinion is being expressed, they differed on its type and polarity.

There are some opinions that are inherently on the borderline of Sentiment and Arguing. For example, consider the following utterance where there is an appeal to importance:

(6) **Also important** for you all is um the *production cost must be maximal twelve Euro and fifty cents.*

Here, "also important" might be taken as an assessment of the high value of adhering to the budget (relative to other constraints), or simply as an argument for adhering to the budget.

One potential source of problems to the target-linking process consists of cases where the same item becomes involved in more than one opposition. For instance, in the example below, speaker *D* initially sets up an alternative between speech recognition and buttons as a possible interface for navigation. But later, speaker *A* re-frames the choice as between having speech recognition only and having both options. Connecting up all references to speech recognition as a target respects the co-reference but it also results in incorrect conclusions: the speech recognition is an alternative to having both speech recognition and buttons.

(7) A:: One thing is **interesting** is talking about *speech recognition* in a remote control...
D:: ... So that we don't need any button on the remote control it would be all based on speech.
A:: ... I think *that* **would not work so well**. **You wanna** have *both options*.

5 Related Work

Evidence from the surrounding context has been used previously to determine if the current sentence should be subjective/objective (Riloff et al., 2003; Pang and Lee, 2004)) and adjacency pair information has been used to predict congressional votes (Thomas et al., 2006). However, these methods do not explicitly model the relations between opinions. Additionally, in our scheme opinions that are not in the immediate context may be allowed to influence the interpretation of a given opinion via target chains.

Polanyi and Zaenen (2006), in their discussion on contextual valence shifters, have also observed the phenomena described in this work - namely that a central topic may be divided into subtopics in order to perform evaluations, and that discourse structure can influence the overall interpretation of valence.

Snyder and Barzilay (2007) combine an agreement model based on contrastive RST relations with a local *aspect* (or target) model to make a more informed overall decision for sentiment classification. The contrastive cue indicates a change in the sentiment polarity. In our scheme, their aspects would be related as *same* and their high contrast relations would result in frames such as *SPSNsame*, *SNSPsame*. Additionally, our frame relations would link sentiments across non-adjacent clauses, and make connections via *alt* target relations.

Considering the discourse relation annotations in the PDTB (Prasad et al., 2006), there can be alignment between discourse relations (like contrast) and our opinion frames when the frames represent dominant relations between two clauses. However, when the relation between opinions is not the most prominent one between two clauses, the discourse relation may not align with the opinion frames. And when an opinion frame is between two opinions in the same clause, there would be no discourse relation counterpart at all. Further, opinion frames assume particular intentions that are not necessary for the establishment of ostensibly similar discourse relations. For example, we may not impose an opinion frame even if there are contrastive cues. (Please refer to Appendix B for examples)

With regard to meetings, the most closely related work includes the dialog-related annotation schemes for various available corpora of conversation (Dhillon et al. (2003) for ICSI MRDA; Carletta et al. (2005) for AMI) As shown by Somasundaran et al. (2007), dialog structure information and opinions are in fact complementary. We believe that, like discourse relations, dialog information will additionally help in arriving at an overall coherent interpretation.

6 Conclusion and Future work

This is the first work that extends an opinion annotation scheme to relate opinions via target relations. We first introduced the idea of opinion frames as a representation capturing discourse level relations that arise from related opinion targets and which are common in task-oriented dialogs such as our data. We built an annotation scheme that would capture these relationships. Finally, we performed extensive inter-annotator agreement studies in order to find the reliability of human judgment in recognizing frame components. Our results and analysis provide insights into the complexities involved in recognizing discourse level relations between opinions.

Acknowledgments

This research was supported in part by the Department of Homeland Security under grant N000140710152.

References

J. Carletta, S. Ashby, and et al. 2005. The AMI Meetings Corpus. In *Proceedings of Measuring Behavior Symposium on "Annotating and measuring Meeting Behavior"*.

J. Cohen. 1960. A coefficient of agreement for nominal scales. *Educational and Psychological Measurement*, 20:37–46.

R. Dhillon, S. Bhagat, H. Carvey, and E. Shriberg. 2003. Meeting recorder project: Dialog act labeling guide. Technical report, ICSI Tech Report TR-04-002.

J. Hobbs. 1979. Coherence and coreference. *Cognitive Science*, 3:67–90.

J. Hobbs, 1983. *Why is Discourse Coherent?*, pages 29–70. Buske Verlag.

K. Krippendorff. 2004. *Content Analysis: An Introduction to Its Methodology, 2nd Edition*. Sage Publications, Thousand Oaks, California.

B. Pang and L. Lee. 2004. A sentimental education: Sentiment analysis using subjectivity summarization based on minimum cuts. In *ACl 2004*.

R. J. Passonneau. 2004. Computing reliability for coreference annotation. In *LREC*.

L. Polanyi and A. Zaenen, 2006. *Contextual Valence Shifters*, chapter 1. Computing Attitude and Affect in Text: Theory and Applications. Springer.

R. Prasad, N. Dinesh, A. Lee, A. Joshi, and B. Webber. 2006. Annotating attribution in the Penn Discourse TreeBank. In *Workshop on Sentiment and Subjectivity in Text*. ACL.

E. Riloff, J. Wiebe, and T. Wilson. 2003. Learning subjective nouns using extraction pattern bootstrapping. In *CoNLL 2003*.

B. Snyder and R. Barzilay. 2007. Multiple aspect ranking using the good grief algorithm. In *HLT 2007: NAACL*.

S. Somasundaran, J. Ruppenhofer, and J. Wiebe. 2007. Detecting arguing and sentiment in meetings. In *SIGdial Workshop on Discourse and Dialogue 2007*.

M. Thomas, B. Pang, and L. Lee. 2006. Get out the vote: Determining support or opposition from congressional floor-debate transcripts. In *EMNLP 2006*.

J. Wiebe, T. Wilson, and C Cardie. 2005. Annotating expressions of opinions and emotions in language. *Language Resources and Evaluation*, pages 164–210.

T. Wilson and J. Wiebe. 2005. Annotating attributions and private states. In *Proceedings of ACL Workshop on Frontiers in Corpus Annotation II: Pie in the Sky*.

T. Wilson, J. Wiebe, and P. Hoffmann. 2005. Recognizing contextual polarity in phrase-level sentiment analysis. In *HLT-EMNLP 2005*.

A Annotation Example

C:: ... shapes **should be** *curved*, so round shapes. **Nothing** *square-like*.
C:: ... So we **shouldn't have too** *square corners* and that kind of thing.
B:: Yeah okay. **Not** ***the old box look***.

Span	Attributes
O1 **should be**	type=Arguing; Polarity=pos; target=t1
t1 *curved*	Link,type=(t2,alt)
O2 **Nothing**	type=Arguing; Polarity=neg; target=t2
t2 *square-like*	Link,type=(t1,alt),(t3,same)
O3 **shouldn't have**	type=Arguing; Polarity=neg; target=t3
O4 **too**	type=Sentiment; Polarity=neg; target=t3
t3 *square corners*	Link,type=(t2,same),(t4,same)
O5 **Not**	type=Arguing; Polarity=neg; target=t4
t4 *the old box look*	Link,type=(t3,same)
O6 **the old box look**	type=Sentiment; Polarity=neg; target=t4

B Comparison between Opinion Frames and Discourse Relations

Opinion frames can align with discourse relations between clauses only when the frames represent the dominant relation between two clauses (1); but not when the opinions occur in the same clause (2); or when the relation between opinions is not the most prominent (3); or when two distinct targets are neither same nor alternatives (4).

(1) **Non-reinforcing opinion frame (SNSP-same); Contrast discourse relation**
D :: And so what I have found and after a lot of work actually I draw for you this *schema* that can be maybe **too technical** for you but is **very important** for me you know.

(2) **Reinforcing opinion frame (SPSPsame); no discourse relation**
Thirty four percent said it takes too long to learn to use a remote control, they **want** something that's *easier to use* straight away, *more intuitive* perhaps.

(3) **Reinforcing opinion frame (SPSPsame); Reason discourse relation**
She even likes my manga, actually the quote is: "I **like** *it*, because you **like** *it*, honey." (source: web)

(4) **Unrelated opinions; Contrast discourse relation**
A :: Yeah, what I have to say about means. *The smart board* is **okay**. *Digital pen* is **horrible**. I dunno if you use it. But if you want to download it to your computer, it's doesn't work. No.

Argumentative Human Computer Dialogue for Automated Persuasion

Pierre Andrews* and **Suresh Manandhar*** and **Marco De Boni****

* Department of Computer Science
University of York
York YO10 5DD
UK
{pandrews,suresh}@cs.york.ac.uk

** Unilever Corporate Research
Bedford MK44 1LQ
UK
Marco.De-Boni@unilever.com

Abstract

Argumentation is an emerging topic in the field of human computer dialogue. In this paper we describe a novel approach to dialogue management that has been developed to achieve persuasion using a textual argumentation dialogue system. The paper introduces a layered management architecture that mixes task-oriented dialogue techniques with chatbot techniques to achieve better persuasiveness in the dialogue.

1 Introduction

Human computer dialogue is a wide research area in Artificial Intelligence. Computer dialogue is now used at production stage for applications such as tutorial dialogue – that helps teaching students (Freedman, 2000) – task-oriented dialogue – that achieves a particular, limited task, such as booking a trip (Allen et al., 2000) – and chatbot dialogue (Levy et al., 1997) – that is used within entertainment and help systems.

None of these approaches use persuasion as a mechanism to achieve dialogue goals. However, research towards the use of persuasion in Human Computer Interactions has spawned around the field of natural argumentation (Norman and Reed, 2003). Similarly research on Embodied Conversational Agents (ECA) (Bickmore and Picard, 2005) is also attempting to improve the persuasiveness of agents with persuasion techniques; however, it concentrates on the visual representation of the interlocutor rather than the dialogue management. Previous research on human computer dialogue has rarely focused on persuasive techniques (Guerini, Stock, and Zancanaro, 2004, initiated some research in that field). Our dialogue management system applies a novel method, taking advantage of persuasive and argumentation techniques to achieve persuasive dialogue.

According to the *cognitive dissonance* theory (Festinger, 1957), people will try to minimise the discrepancy between their behaviour and their beliefs by integrating new beliefs or distorting existing ones. In this paper, we approach persuasion as a process shaping user's beliefs to eventually change their behaviour.

The presented dialogue management system has been developed to work on known limitations of current dialogue systems:

The *impression of lack of control* is an issue when the user is interacting with a purely task-oriented dialogue system (Farzanfar et al., 2005). The system follows a plan to achieve the particular task, and the user's dialogue moves are dictated by the planner and the plan operators.

The *lack of empathy* of computers is also a problem in human-computer interaction for applications such as health-care, where persuasive dialogue could be applied (Bickmore and Giorgino, 2004). The system does not respond to the user's personal and emotional state, which sometimes lowers the user's implication in the dialogue. However, existing research (Klein, Moon, and Picard, 1999) shows that a system that gives appropriate response to the user's emotion can lower frustration.

In human-human communication, these limitations reduce the effectiveness of persuasion

Proceedings of the 9th SIGdial Workshop on Discourse and Dialogue, pages 138–147,
Columbus, June 2008.

(Stiff and Mongeau, 2002). Even if the response towards the computer is not always identical to the one to humans, it seems sensible to think that persuasive dialogue systems can be improved by applying known findings from human-human communication.

The dialogue management architecture described in this paper (see Figure 1) addresses these dialogue management issues by using a novel layered approach to dialogue management, allowing the mixing of techniques from task-oriented dialogue management and chatbot techniques (see Section 4).

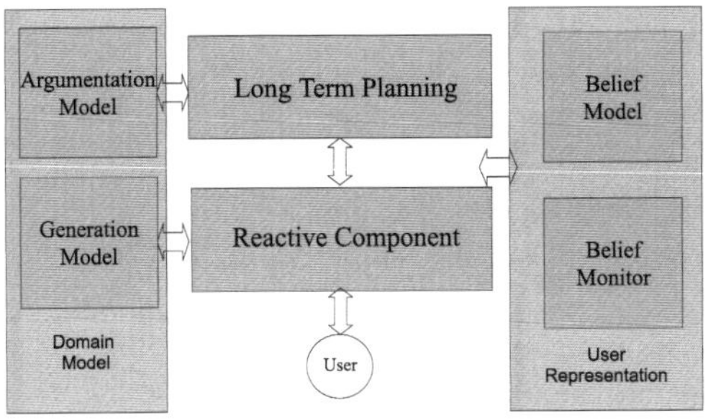

Figure 1: Layered Management Architecture

The use of a planner guarantees the consistency of the dialogue and the achievement of persuasive goals (see Section 4.2). Argumentative dialogue can be seen as a form of task-oriented dialogue where the system's task is to persuade the user by presenting the arguments. Thus, the dialogue manager first uses a task-oriented dialogue methodology to create a dialogue plan that will determine the content of the dialogue. The planning component's role is to guarantee the consistency of the dialogue and the achievement of the persuasive goals.

In state-of-the-art task-oriented dialogue management systems, the planner provides instructions for a surface realizer (Green and Lehman, 2002), responsible of generating the utterance corresponding to the plan step. Our approach is different to allow more reactivity to the user and give a feeling of control over the dialogue. In this layered approach, the reactive component provides a direct reaction to the user input, generating one or more utterances for a given plan step, allowing for reactions to user's counter arguments as well as backchannel and chitchat phases without cluttering the plan.

Experimental results show that this layered approach allows the user to feel more comfortable in the dialogue while preserving the dialogue consistency provided by the planner. Eventually, this translates into a more persuasive dialogue (see Section 6).

2 Related Work

Persuasion through dialogue is a novel field of Human Computer Interaction. Reiter, Robertson, and Osman (2003),Reed (1998) and Carenini and Moore (2000) apply persuasive communication principles to natural language generation, but only focus on monologue.

The 3-tier planner for tutoring dialogue by Zinn, Moore, and Core (2002) provides a dialogue management technique close to our approach: a top-tier generates a dialogue plan, the middle-tier generates refinements to the plan and the bottom-tier generates utterances. Mazzotta, de Rosis, and Carofiglio (2007) also propose a planning framework for user-adapted persuasion where the plan operators are mapped to natural language (or ECA) generation. However, these planning approaches do not include a mechanism to react to user's counter arguments that are difficult to plan beforehand. This paper propose a novel approach that could improve the user's comfort in the dialogue as well as its persuasiveness.

3 Case Study

Part of the problem in evaluating persuasive dialogue is using an effective evaluation framework. Moon (1998) uses the Desert Survival Scenario to evaluate the difference of persuasion and trust in interaction between humans when face-to-face or when mediated by a computer system (via an instant messaging platform).

The Desert Survival Scenario (Lafferty, Eady, and Elmers, 1974) is a negotiation scenario used in team training. The team is put in a scenario where they are stranded in the desert after a plane crash. They have to negotiate a ranking of the most eligible items (knife, compass, map, etc.) that they should keep for their survival.

For the evaluation of the dialogue system, a similar scenario is presented to the participants. The user has to choose an initial preferred ranking of items and then engages in a discussion with the dialogue system that tries to persuade the user to change the ranking. At the end of the dialogue, the user has the opportunity to either change or keep the ranking.

The architecture of the dialogue system is described throughout this paper using examples from the Desert Scenario. The full evaluation protocol is described in Section 5 and 6.

4 Dialogue Management Architecture

The following sections provide a description of the dialogue management architecture introduced in Figure 1.

4.1 Argumentation Model

The Argumentation model represents the different arguments (conclusions and premises) that can be proposed by the user or by the system. Figure 2 gives a simplified example of the Desert Scenario model.

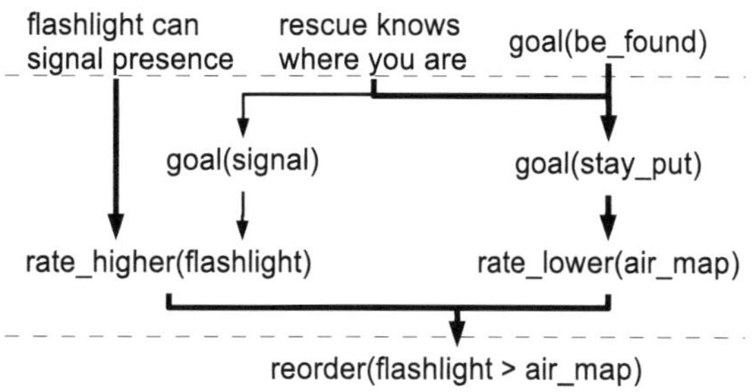

Figure 2: Argumentation Model Sample

This model shows the different facts that are known by the system and the relations between them. Arrows represent the *support* relation between two facts. For example, *rescue_knows_where_you_are* is a support to the fact ***goal**(signal)* (the user goal is to signal presence to the rescue) as well as a support to ***goal**(stay_put)* (the user goal is to stay close to the wreckage). This relational model is comparable to the argumentation framework proposed by Dung (1995), but stores more information about each argument for reasoning within the planning and reactive component (see Section 4.2).

Each fact in this model represents a belief to be introduced to the user. For example, when the dialogue tries to achieve the goal ***reorder**(flashlight > air_map)*: the system wants the user to believe that the "flashlight" item should be ranked higher than the "air_map" item. The argumentation model describes the argumentation process that is required to introduce this new belief: the system first has to make sure the user believes in ***rate_lower**(air_map)* and ***rate_higher**(flashlight)*.

Lower level facts (see Figure 2) are the goal facts of the dialogue, the ones the system chooses as dialogue goals, according to known user beliefs and the system's goal beliefs (e.g. according to the ranking the system is trying to defend). The facts in the middle of the hierarchy are intermediate facts that need to be asserted during the dialogue. The top-level facts are world knowledge: facts that require minimum defense and can be easily grounded in the dialogue.

4.2 Planning Component

The planning component's task is to find a plan using the argumentation model to introduce the required facts in the user's belief to support the persuasive goals. The plan is describes a path in the argumentation model beliefs hierarchy that translates to argumentation segments in the dialogue.

In our current evaluation method, the goal of the dialogue is to change the user's beliefs about the items so that the user eventually changes the ranking. At the beginning of the dialogue, the ranking of the system is chosen and persuasive goals are computed for the dialogue. These persuasive goals correspond to the lower level facts in the argumentation model – like "***reorder**(flashlight > air_map)*" in our previous example. The available planning operators are:

***use_world**(fact)* describes a step in the dialogue that introduces a simple fact to the user.

ground**(fact)* describes a step in the dialogue that grounds a fact in the user beliefs. Grounding a fact is a different task from the ***use_world operator as it will need more support during the dialogue.

***do_support**([fact0, fact1, ...], fact2)* describes a complex support operation. The system will initiate a dialogue segment supporting *fact2* with the facts *fact1* and *fact0*, etc. that have previously been introduced in the user beliefs.

The planning component can also use two non-argumentative operators, *do_greetings* and *do_farewells*, that are placed respectively at the beginning and the end of the dialogue plan to open and close the session.

Here is an example plan using the two arguments described in Figure 2 to support the goal ***reorder****(flashlight > air map)*:

Step 1 *do_greetings*

Step 2 *use_world*(goal(be_found))
ground(rescue_knows_where_you_are)
ground(can(helpatnight, item(flashlight)))

Step 3 *do_support*([can(helpatnight, item(flashlight))], rate_higher(item(flashlight)))
do_support([rescue_knows_where_you_are, goal(be_found)], goal(stay_put))

Step 4 *do_support*([goal(stay_put)], rate_lower(item(air_map)))

Step 5 *do_support*(..., reorder(item(flashlight), item(air_map)))

Step 6 *do_farewells*

The plan is then interpreted by the reactive component that is responsible for realizing each step in a dialogue segment.

4.3 The Reactive Component

The reactive component's first task is to realize the operators chosen by the planning component into dialogue utterance(s). However, it should not be mistaken for a surface language realizer. The reactive component's task, when realizing the operator, is to decide how to present the particular argumentation operator and its parameters to the user according to the dialogue context and the user's reaction to the argument. This reactive process is described in the following sections.

4.3.1 Realization and Reaction Strategies

Each step of the plan describes the general topic of a dialogue segment[1]. A dialogue segment is a set of utterances from the system and from the user that are related to a particular argument. For example, in the Desert Scenario, the operator ***ground****(can(helpatnight, item(flashlight)))* may result in the following set of utterances:

S(ystem) I think the flashlight could be useful as it could help us at night,

U(ser) How is that? We are not going to move during the night.

S well, if we want to collect water, it will be best to do things at night and not under the burning sun.

U I see. It could be useful then.

In this example, the ground operator has been realized by the reactive component in two different utterances to react to the user's interaction.

The goal of the reactive component is to make the user feel that the system understands what has been said. It is also important to avoid replanning as it tries to defend the arguments chosen in the plan.

As described in Section 4.2, the planner relies on the argumentation model to create a dialogue plan. Encoding all possible defenses and reactions to the user directly in this model will explode the search space of the planner and require careful authoring to avoid planning inconsistencies[2]. In addition, predicting at the planning level what counter arguments a user is likely to make requires a prior knowledge of the user's beliefs. At the beginning of a one-off dialogue, it is not possible to make prior assumptions on the user's beliefs; the system has a shallow knowledge of the user's beliefs and will discover them as the dialogue goes.

Hence, it is more natural to author a reactive dialogue that will respond to the user's counter arguments as they come and extends the user beliefs model as it goes. In our architecture if the user is disagreeing with an argument, the plan is not revised directly; if possible, the reactive component selects new, contextually appropriate, supporting facts for the current plan operator. It can do this multiple consecutive *local repairs* if the user needs more convincing and the domain model provides enough defenses. This allows for a simpler planning framework.

[1] i.e. it is not directly interpreted as an instruction to generate one unique utterance.

[2] a new plan could go against the previously used arguments.

In addition, when available, and even if the user agrees with the current argument, the reactive component can also choose from a set of "dialogue smoothing" or backchannel utterances to make the dialogue feel more natural. Here is an example from the Desert Scenario:

S `We don't have much water, we need to be rescued as soon as possible.`
*(from plan step: **user_world**(goal(be_found)))*

U `right`

S `I am glad we agree.`*(backchannel)*

S `There is a good chance that the rescue team already knows our whereabouts. We should be optimistic and plan accordingly, don't you think?`
(from plan step:
***use_world**(rescue_knows_where_you_are))*

4.3.2 Detecting user reactions

The reactive component needs to detect if the user is agreeing to its current argument or resisting the new fact that is presented. Because the dialogue management system was developed from the perspective of a system that could be easily ported to different domains, choice was made to use a domain independent and robust agreement/disagreement detection.

The agreement/disagreement detection is based on an utterance classifier. The classifier is a cascade of binary Support Vector Machines (SVM) (Vapnik, 2000) trained on the ICSI Meeting corpus (Janin et al., 2003). The corpus contains 8135 spurts[3] annotated with agreement/disagreement information Hillard, Ostendorf, and Shriberg (2003).

A multi-class SVM classifier is trained on *local features* of the spurts such as a) the length of the spurt, b) the first word of the spurt, c) the bigrams of the spurts, and d) part of speech tags. The classification achieves an accuracy of 83.17% with an N-Fold 4 ways split cross validation. Additional results and comparison with state-of-the-art are available in Appendix A.

During the dialogue, the classifier is applied on each of the user's utterances, trying to determine if the user is agreeing or disagreeing with the system. According to this labelling, the strategies described in section 4.3.1 and 4.3.3 are applied.

4.3.3 Revising the plan

The reactive component will attempt *local repairs* to the plan by defending the argumentation move chosen by the planning component. However, there are cases when the user will still not accept an argument. In these cases, imposing the belief to the user is counter-productive and the current goal belief should be dropped from the plan.

For each utterance chosen by the reactive component, the belief model of the user is updated to represent the system knowledge of the user's beliefs. Every time the user agrees to an utterance from the system, the belief model is extended with a new belief; in the previous example, when the user says *"I see, it could be useful then."*, the system detects an agreement (see the Section 4.3.2) and extends the user's beliefs model with the belief: ***can**(helpatnight, item(flashlight))*. The agreement is then followed by a *local repair*, since the user doesn't disagree with the statement made, the system also extends the belief model with beliefs relevant to the content of the local repair, thus learning more about the user's belief model.

As a result of this process, when the system decides to revise the plan, the planning component does not start from the same beliefs state as previously. In effect, the system is able to learn user's beliefs based on the agreement/disagreement with the user, it can therefore make a more effective use of the argumentation hierarchy to find a better plan to achieve the persuasive goals.

Still, there are some cases when the planning component will be unable to find a new plan from the current belief state to the goal belief state – this can happen when the planner has exhausted all its argumentative moves for a particular sub-goal. In these cases, the system has to make concessions and drop the persuasive goals that it cannot fulfil. By dropping goals, the system will lower the final persuasiveness, but guarantees not coercing the user.

4.3.4 Generation

Utterance generation is made at the reactive component level. In the current version of the dialogue management system, the utterance generation

[3]speech utterances that have no pauses longer than .5 seconds.

is based on an extended version of Alicebot AIML [4].

AIML is an XML language that provides a pattern/template generation model mainly used for chatbot systems. An AIML bot defines a set of categories that associate a *topic*, the context of the previous bot utterance (called *that* in the AIML terminology), a *matching pattern* that will match the last user utterance and a *generation template*. The *topic*, *matching* and *that* field define matching patterns that can contain * wildcards accepting any token(s) of the user utterance (e.g. *HELLO* * would match any utterance starting by "Hello"). They are linked to a *generation template* that can reuse the tokens matched by the patterns wildcards to generate an utterance tailored to the user input and the dialogue context.

For the purpose of layered dialogue management, the AIML language has been extended to include more features: 1) A new pattern slot has been introduced to link a set of categories to a particular argumentation operator; 2) Utterances generations are linked to the belief they are trying to introduce to the user and if an agreement is detected, this belief is added to the user belief model.

For example, a set of matching categories for the Desert Scenario could be:

Plan operator: `use_world(goal(survive))`

- **Category 1** :
  - **Pattern** `*`
  - **Template** `Surviving is our priority, do you want to hear about my desert survival insights?`
- **Category 2** :
  - **Pattern** `* insights`
  - **That** `* survival insights`
  - **Template** `I mean, I had a few ideas ...common knowledge I suppose.`
- **Category 3** :
  - **Pattern** `*`
  - **That** `* survival insights`
  - **Template** `Well, we are in this together.  Let me tell you of what I think of desert survival, ok?`

[4] `http://www.alicebot.org/`

These three categories can be used to match the user reaction during the dialogue segment corresponding to the plan operator: ***use_world****(goal(survive))*. *Category 1* is used as the initiative taking generation. It will be the first one to be used when the system comes from a previously finished step. *Categories 2-3* are all "defenses" that support *Category 1*. They will be used to react to the user if no agreement is detected from the last utterances. For example, if the user says *"what kind of survival insights??"* as a reply to the generation from *Category 1*, a disagreement is detected and the reactive component will have a contextualised answer as given by *category 2* whose `that` pattern matches the last utterance from the system, the `pattern` pattern matches the user utterance.

The dialogue management system uses 187 categories tailored to the Desert Scenario as well as 3737 general categories coming from the Alice chatbot and used to generate the dialogue smoothing utterances. Developing domain specific reactions is a tedious and slow process that was iteratively achieved with Wizard of OZ experiments with real users. In these experiments, users were told they were going to have a dialogue with another human in the Desert Scenario context. The dialogue system manages the whole dialogue, except for the generation phase that is mediated by an expert that can either choose the reaction of the system from an existing set of utterances, or type a new one.

5 Persuasiveness Metric

Evaluating a behavior change would require a long-term observation of the behavior that would be dependent to external elements (Bickmore and Picard, 2005). To evaluate our system, an evaluation protocol measuring the change in the beliefs underlying the behavior was chosen. As explained in Section 3, the Desert Scenario is used as a base for the evaluation. Each participant is told that he is stranded in the desert. The user gives a preferred initial ranking R_i of the items (knife, compass, map, etc.). The user then engages in a dialogue with the system. The system then attempts to change the user's ranking to a different ranking R_s through persuasive dialogue. At the end of the dialogue, the user can change this choice to arrive at a final ranking R_f.

The persuasiveness of the dialogue can be measured as the evolution of the distance between the user ranking (R_i, R_f) and the system ranking (R_s). The Kendall τ distance (Kendall, 1938) is used to compute the pairwise disagreement between two rankings. The change of the Kendall τ distance during the dialogue gives an evaluation of the persuasiveness of the dialogue: $P_{ersuasiveness} = K\tau(R_i, R_s) - K\tau(R_f, R_s)$. In the current evaluation protocol, the R_s is always the reverse of the R_i, so $K\tau(R_i, R_s)$ is always the maximum distance possible: $\frac{n \times (n-1)}{2}$ where n is the number of items to rank. The minimum Kendall tau distance is 0. If the system was persuasive enough to make the user invert the initial ranking, $P_{ersuasiveness}$ of the system is maximum and equal to: $\frac{n \times (n-1)}{2}$. If the system does not succeed in changing the user ranking, then $P_{ersuasiveness}$ is zero.

6 Evaluation Results and Discussion

16 participants have been recruited from a variety of ages (from 20 to 59) and background. They were all told to use a web application that describes the Desert Scenario (see Section 3) and proposes to undertake two instant messaging chats with two human users[5]. However, both discussions are managed by different versions of the dialogue system, following a similar protocol:

- one version of the dialogue is managed by a *limited* version of the dialogue system, with no reactive component. This version is similar to a purely task-oriented system, planning and revising the plan directly on dialogue failures,
- the second version is the *full* dialogue system as described in this paper.

Each participant went through one dialogue with each system, in a random order. This comparison shows that the dialogue flexibility provided by the reactive component allows a more persuasive dialogue. In addition, when faced with the second dialogue, the participant has formed more beliefs about the scenario and is more able to counter argue.

[5]The evaluation is available Online at http://www.cs.york.ac.uk/aig/eden

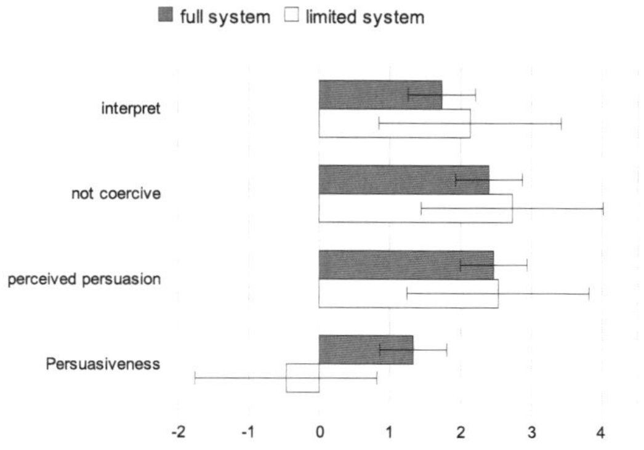

Figure 3: Comparative Results. *interpret, not coercive, perceived persuasion* are on a scale of $[0 - 4]$ (see Appendix B). $P_{ersuasiveness}$ is on a scale of $[-10, 10]$.

Figure 3 reports the independent $P_{ersuasiveness}$ metric results as well as interesting answers to a questionnaire that the participants filled after each dialogue (see the Appendix B for detailed results and questionnaire).

Over all the dialogues, the *full* system is **18%** more persuasive than the *limited* system. This is measured by the $P_{ersuasiveness}$ metric introduced in Section 5. With the *full* system, the participants did an average of **1.33 swaps of items towards** the system's ranking. With the *limited* system, the participants did an average of **0.47 swaps of items away** from the system's ranking. However, the answers to the self evaluated *perceived persuasion* question show that the participants did not see any significant difference in the ability to persuade of the *limited* and the *full* systems.

According to the question *interpret*, the participants found that the *limited* system understood better what they said. This last result might be explained by the behavior of the systems: the *limited* system drops an argument at every user disagreement, making the user believe that the disagreement was understood. The *full* system tries to defend the argument; if possible with a contextually tailored support, however, if this is not available, it may use a generic support, making the user believe he was not fully understood.

Our interpretation of the fact that the discrepancy between user self evaluation of the interaction with the system and the measured persuasion is that, even if the *full* system is more argumentative, the user didn't feel coerced[6]. These results show that a more persuasive dialogue can be achieved without deteriorating the user perception of the interaction.

7 Conclusion

Our dialogue management system introduces a novel approach to dialogue management by using a layered model mixing the advantages of state-of-the-art dialogue management approaches. A planning component tailored to the task of argumentation and persuasion searches the ideal path in an argumentation model to persuade the user. To give a reactive and natural feel to the dialogue, this task-oriented layer is extended by a reactive component inspired from the chatbot dialogue management approach. The Desert Scenario evaluation, providing a simple and independent metric for the persuasiveness of the dialogue system provided a good protocol for the evaluation of the dialogue system. This one showed to be 18% more persuasive than a purely task-oriented system that was not able to react to the user interaction as smoothly.

Our current research on the dialogue management system consists in developing another evaluation domain where a more complex utterance generation can be used. This will allow going further than the simple template based system, offering more diverse answers to the user and avoiding repetitions; it will also allow us to experiment textual persuasion tailored to other parameters of the user representation, such as the user personality.

References

Allen, J. F., G. Ferguson, B. W. Miller, E. K. Ringger, and T. Sikorski. 2000. *Dialogue Systems: From Theory to Practice in TRAINS-96*, chapter 14.

Bickmore, T. and T. Giorgino. 2004. Some novel aspects of health communication from a dialogue systems perspective. In *AAAI Fall Symposium*.

Bickmore, T. W. and R. W. Picard. 2005. Establishing and maintaining long-term human-computer relationships. *ACM Trans. Comput.-Hum. Interact.*, 12(2):293–327.

Carenini, G. and J. Moore. 2000. A strategy for generating evaluative arguments. In *International Conference on Natural Language Generation*.

Dung, P. M. 1995. On the acceptability of arguments and its fundamental role in nonmonotonic reasoning, logic programming and n-person games. *Artif. Intell.*, 77(2):321–357.

Farzanfar, R., S. Frishkopf, J. Migneault, and R. Friedman. 2005. Telephone-linked care for physical activity: a qualitative evaluation of the use patterns of an information technology program for patients. *J. of Biomedical Informatics*, 38(3):220–228.

Festinger, Leon. 1957. *A Theory of Cognitive Dissonance*. Stanford University Press.

Freedman, R. 2000. Plan-based dialogue management in a physics tutor. In *Proceedings of ANLP '00*.

Galley, M., K. Mckeown, J. Hirschberg, and E. Shriberg. 2004. Identifying agreement and disagreement in conversational speech: use of bayesian networks to model pragmatic dependencies. In *Proceedings of ACL'04*.

Green, N. and J. F. Lehman. 2002. An integrated discourse recipe-based model for task-oriented dialogue. *Discourse Processes*, 33(2):133–158.

Guerini, M., O. Stock, and M. Zancanaro. 2004. Persuasive strategies and rhetorical relation selection. In *Proceedings of ECAI-CMNA*.

Hillard, D., M. Ostendorf, and E. Shriberg. 2003. Detection of agreement vs. disagreement in meetings: training with unlabeled data. In *Proceedings of NAACL'03*.

Janin, A., D. Baron, J. Edwards, D. Ellis, D. Gelbart, N. Morgan, B. Peskin, T. Pfau, E. Shriberg, A. Stolcke, and C. Wooters. 2003. The ICSI meeting corpus. In *Proceedings of ICASSP'03*.

Kendall, M. G. 1938. A new measure of rank correlation. *Biometrika*, 30(1/2):81–93.

Klein, J., Y. Moon, and R. W. Picard. 1999. This computer responds to user frustration. In *CHI'99*.

Lafferty, J. C., Eady, and J. Elmers. 1974. *The desert survival problem*.

Levy, D., R. Catizone, B. Battacharia, A. Krotov, and Y. Wilks. 1997. Converse:a conversational companion. In *Proceedings of 1st International Workshop on Human-Computer Conversation*.

Mazzotta, I., F. de Rosis, and V. Carofiglio. 2007. Portia: A user-adapted persuasion system in the healthy-eating domain. *Intelligent Systems, IEEE*, 22(6).

Moon, Y. 1998. The effects of distance in local versus remote human-computer interaction. In *Proceedings of SIGCHI'98*.

Norman, Timothy J. and Chris Reed. 2003. *Argumentation Machines : New Frontiers in Argument and Computation (Argumentation Library)*. Springer.

Reed, C. 1998. *Generating Arguments in Natural Language*. Ph.D. thesis, University College London.

Reiter, E., R. Robertson, and L. M. Osman. 2003. Lessons from a failure: generating tailored smoking cessation letters. *Artif. Intell.*, 144(1-2):41–58.

Stiff, J. B. and P. A. Mongeau. 2002. *Persuasive Communication*, second edition.

Vapnik, V. N. 2000. *The Nature of Statistical Learning Theory*.

Zinn, C., J. D. Moore, and M. G. Core. 2002. A 3-tier planning architecture for managing tutorial dialogue. In *Proceedings of ITS '02*.

[6] The answers to the *not coercive* question do not show any significant difference in the perception of coercion of the two system.

A Agreement/Disagreement Classification

	Setup 1	Setup 2
Galley et al., global features	86.92%	84.07%
Galley et al., local features	85.62%	83.11%
Hillard et al.	82%	NA
SVM	**86.47%**	**83.17%**

Table 1: Accuracy of different agreement/disagreement classification approaches.

The accuracy of state-of-the-art techniques (Hillard, Ostendorf, and Shriberg (2003) and Galley et al. (2004)) are reported in Table 1 and compared to our SVM classifier. Two experimental setups were used:

Setup 1 reproduces Hillard, Ostendorf, and Shriberg (2003) training/testing split between meetings;

Setup 2 reproduces the N-Fold, 4 ways split used by Galley et al. (2004).

The SVM results are arguably lower than Galley et al. system with labeled dependencies. However, this is because our system only relies on local features of each utterance, while Galley et al. (2004) use *global features* (i.e. features describing relations between consecutive utterances) suggest that adding global features would also improve the SVM classifier.

B Evaluation Questionnaire

In the evaluation described in section 6, the participants were asked to give their level of agreement with each statement on the scale: Strongly disagree (0), Disagree (1), Neither agree nor disagree (2), Agree (3), Strongly Agree(4). Table 2 provides a list of questions with the average agreement level and the result of a paired t-test between the two system results.

label	**question**	***full* system**	***limited* system**	**ttest**
interpret	"In the conversation, the other user interpreted correctly what you said"	1.73	2.13	0.06
perceived persuasion	"In the conversation, the other user was persuasive"	2.47	2.53	0.44
not coercive	"The other user was not forceful in changing your opinion"	2.4	2.73	0.15
sluggish	"The other user was sluggish and slow to reply to you in this conversation"	1.27	1.27	0.5
understand	"The other user was easy to understand in the conversation"	3.2	3.13	0.4
pace	"The pace of interaction with the other user was appropriate in this conversation"	2.73	3.07	0.1
friendliness	"The other user was friendly"	2.93	2.87	0.4
length	length of the dialogue	12min 19s	08min 33s	0.07
persuasiveness	$P_{ersuasiveness}$	1.33	-0.47	0.05

Table 2: Results from the evaluation questionnaire.

Modeling Vocal Interaction for Text-Independent Participant Characterization in Multi-Party Conversation

Kornel Laskowski
Cognitive Systems Labs
Universität Karlsruhe
Karlsruhe, Germany
kornel@ira.uka.de

Mari Ostendorf
Dept. of Electrical Engineering
University of Washington
Seattle WA, USA
mo@ee.washington.edu

Tanja Schultz
Cognitive Systems Labs
Universität Karlsruhe
Karlsruhe, Germany
tanja@ira.uka.de

Abstract

An important task in automatic conversation understanding is the inference of social structure governing participant behavior. We explore the dependence between several social dimensions, including assigned role, gender, and seniority, and a set of low-level features descriptive of talkspurt deployment in a multiparticipant context. Experiments conducted on two large, publicly available meeting corpora suggest that our features are quite useful in predicting these dimensions, excepting gender. The classification experiments we present exhibit a relative error rate reduction of 37% to 67% compared to choosing the majority class.

1 Introduction

An important task in automatic conversation understanding is the inference of social structure governing participant behavior; in many conversations, the maintenance or expression of that structure is an implicit goal, and may be more important than the propositional content of what is said.

There are many social dimensions along which participants may differ (Berger, Rosenholtz and Zelditch, 1980). Research in social psychology has shown that such differences among participants entail systematic differences in observed turn-taking and floor-control patterns (e.g. (Bales, 1950), (Tannen, 1996), (Carletta, Garrod and Fraser-Krauss, 1998)), and that participant types are not independent of the types and sizes of conversations in which they appear. In the present work, we consider the dimensions of assigned role, gender, and seniority level. We explore the predictability of these dimensions from a set of low-level speech activity features, namely the *probabilities* of initiating and continuing talkspurts in specific multiparticipant contexts, estimated from entire conversations. For our purposes, talkspurts (Norwine and Murphy, 1938) are contiguous intervals of speech, with internal pauses no longer than 0.3 seconds. Features derived from talkspurts are not only easier to compute than higher-level lexical, prosodic, or dialogue act features, they are also applicable to scenarios in which only privacy-sensitive data (Wyatt et al, 2007) is available. At the current time, relatively little is known about the predictive power of talkspurt timing in the context of large multi-party corpora.

As stated, our primary goal is to quantify the dependence between specific types of speech activity features and specific social dimensions; however, doing so offers several additional benefits. Most importantly, the existence of significant dependence would suggest that multiparticipant speech activity detectors (Laskowski, Fügen and Schultz, 2007) relying on models conditioned on such attributes may outperform those relying on general models. Furthermore, conversational dialogue systems deployed in multi-party scenarios may be perceived as more human-like, by humans, if their talkspurt deployment strategies are tailored to the personalities they are designed to embody.

Computational work which is most similar to that presented here includes the inference of static dominance (Rienks and Heylen, 2005) and influence (Rienks et al., 2006) rankings. In that work, the authors employed several speech activity features differing from ours in temporal scale and normaliza-

Proceedings of the 9th SIGdial Workshop on Discourse and Dialogue, pages 148–155,
Columbus, June 2008. ©2008 Association for Computational Linguistics

tion. Notably, their features are not probabilities which are directly employable in a speech activity detection system. In addition, several higher-level features were included, such as topic changes, participant roles, and rates of phenomena such as turns and interruptions, and these were shown to yield the most robust performance. Our aim is also similar to that in (Vinciarelli, 2007) on radio shows, where the proposed approach relies on the relatively fixed temporal structure of production broadcasts, a property which is absent in spontaneous conversation. Although (Vinciarelli, 2007) also performs single-channel speaker diarization, he does not explore behavior during vocalization overlap.

Aside from the above, the focus of the majority of existing research characterizing participants is the detection of dynamic rather than static roles (i.e. (Banerjee and Rudnicky, 2004), (Zancanaro et al, 2006), (Rienks et al., 2006)). From a mathematical perspective, the research presented here is a continuation of our earlier work on meeting types (Laskowski, Ostendorf and Schultz, 2007), and we rely on much of that material in the presentation which follows.

2 Characterizing Participants

Importantly, we characterize participants in entire *groups*, rather than characterizing each participant independently. Doing so allows us to apply constraints on the group as a whole, eliminating the need for hypothesis recombination (in the event that more than one participant is assigned a role which was meant to be unique). Additionally, treating groups holistically allows for modeling the interactions between specific pairs of participant types.

For each conversation or meeting[1] of K participants, we compute a feature vector $\mathbf{F}$, in which all one-participant and two-participant speech activity features are found in a particular order, typically imposed by microphone channel or seating assignment (the specific features are described in Section 4). The goal is to find the most likely group assignment of participant labels that account for the observed $\mathbf{F}$. In (Laskowski, Ostendorf and Schultz, 2007), it was shown that meeting types in a large meeting corpus can be successfully inferred from $\mathbf{F}$ using this approach; here, we employ the same framework to classify participant types in the K-length vector $\mathbf{g}$, for the group as a whole:

$$\begin{aligned} \mathbf{g}^* &= \arg\max_{\mathbf{g} \in \mathcal{G}} P(\mathbf{g} \,|\, \mathbf{F}) \\ &= \arg\max_{\mathbf{g} \in \mathcal{G}} \underbrace{P(\mathbf{g})}_{\text{MM}} \underbrace{P(\mathbf{F} \,|\, \mathbf{g})}_{\text{BM}} , \end{aligned} \tag{1}$$

where MM and BM are the membership and behavior models, respectively, and $\mathcal{G}$ is the set of all possible assignments of $\mathbf{g}$.

In the remainder of this section, we define the participant characteristics we explore, which include assigned role, gender, and seniority. We treat these as separate tasks, applying the same classification framework. We also show how our definitions provide search space constraints on Equation 1.

2.1 Conversations with Unique Roles

Given a meeting of K participants, we consider a set of roles $\mathcal{R} = \{R_1, R_2, \cdots, R_K\}$ and assign to each participant k, $1 \leq k \leq K$, exactly one role in $\mathcal{R}$. An example group assignment is the vector $\mathbf{r}_1$ of length K, where $\mathbf{r}_1[k] = R_k$. The set $\mathbb{R}$ of group assignment alternatives $\mathbf{r} \in \mathbb{R}$ is given by permutations $\alpha : \mathbb{R} \mapsto \mathbb{R}$, where $\alpha \in \mathbb{S}_K$, the *symmetric group on K symbols*[2]. The number of elements in $\mathbb{R}$ is identically the number of unique permutations in $\mathbb{S}_K$, a quantity known as its *order* $|\mathbb{S}_K| = K!$.

To identify the most likely group assignment $\mathbf{r}^* = \alpha^*(\mathbf{r}_1)$ given the set $\mathbf{F}$ of observables, we iterate over the $K!$ elements of $\mathbb{S}_K$ using

$$\alpha^* = \arg\max_{\alpha \in \mathbb{S}_K} P(\mathbf{F} \,|\, \alpha(\mathbf{r}_1)) , \tag{2}$$

where we have elided the prior $P(\alpha)$ assuming that it is uniform. Following the application of Equation 2, the most likely role of participant k is given by $\alpha^*(\mathbf{r}_1)[k]$.

Alternately, we may be interested in identifying only a subset of the roles in $\mathcal{R}$, namely a leader, or a manager. In this case, participant roles are drawn from $\mathcal{L} = \{L, \neg L\}$, under the constraint that exactly one participant is assigned the role L. The set $\mathbb{L}$ of

[1] "Conversation" and "meeting" will be used interchangeably in the current work.

[2] For an overview of group theoretic notions and notation, we refer the reader to (Rotman, 1995).

alternative group assignments has K indicator vector members $\mathbf{l}_j$, $1 \leq j \leq K$, where $\mathbf{l}_j[k]$ is L for $k = j$ and $\neg L$ otherwise.[3] We iterate over the indicator vectors to obtain

$$j^* = \arg\max_{j \in \{1, \cdots, K\}} P(\mathbf{F} \mid \mathbf{l}_j), \quad (3)$$

assuming uniform priors $P(\mathbf{l}_j)$. Following the application of Equation 3, j^* is the index of the most likely L participant.

We note that this framework for unique role classification is applicable to classifying unique ranks, without first having to collapse them into non-unique rank classes as was necessary in (Rienks et al., 2006).

2.2 Conversations with Non-Unique Roles

The second type of inference we consider is for dimensions in which roles are not unique, i.e. where participants are in principle drawn independently from a set of alternatives. This naturally includes dimensions such as gender, seniority, age, etc.

As an example, we treat the case of gender. Participant genders are drawn independently from $\mathcal{H} = \{♀, ♂\}$. The set of group assignment alternatives $\mathbf{h}$ is given by the Cartesian product $\mathcal{H}^K$, of 2^K unique elements. We search for the most likely group assignment $\mathbf{h}^*$, given the observables $\mathbf{F}$, by iterating over these elements using

$$\mathbf{h}^* = \arg\max_{\mathbf{h} \in \mathcal{H}^K} P(\mathbf{h}) \, P(\mathbf{F} \mid \mathbf{h}). \quad (4)$$

Once $\mathbf{h}^*$ is found, the gender of each participant k is available in $\mathbf{h}^*[k]$.

A similar scenario is found for seniority, when it is not uniquely ranked. We assume a set of N_S mutually exclusive seniority levels $S_i \in \mathcal{S} = \{S_1, S_2, \cdots, S_{N_S}\}$, $1 \leq i \leq N_S$. During search, each participant's seniority level is drawn independently from $\mathcal{S}$, leading to group assignments $\mathbf{s} \in \mathcal{S}^K$, of which there are N_S^K. As for gender, we iterate over these to find

$$\mathbf{s}^* = \arg\max_{\mathbf{s} \in \mathcal{S}^K} P(\mathbf{s}) \, P(\mathbf{F} \mid \mathbf{s}). \quad (5)$$

The seniority of participant k, following the application of Equation 5, is $\mathbf{s}^*[k]$.

[3] For completeness, we note that each $\mathbf{l}_j$ corresponds to a permutation $\beta : \mathbb{L} \mapsto \mathbb{L}$ of $\mathbf{l}_1$, and that $\beta \in \langle \tau \rangle$, the *cyclic subgroup generated by* τ, where τ is the permutation $(1, 2, \cdots, K)$.

3 Data

In the current work, we use two different corpora of multi-party meetings. The first, the scenario subset of the AMI Meeting Corpus (Carletta, 2007), consists of meetings involving $K = 4$ participants who play different specialist roles in a product design team. We have observed the recommended division of this data into: AMITRAINSET of 98 meetings; AMIDEVSET of 20 meetings; and AMIEVALSET, also of 20 meetings. Although each participant takes part in approximately 4 meetings, the 3 sets are disjoint in participants. We use only the provided word alignments of these meetings. The corpus is accompanied by metadata which specifies the gender and assigned role of each participant.

The second corpus consists of the `Bed`, `Bmr`, and `Bro` meeting types in the ICSI Meeting Corpus (Janin et al., 2003). Each meeting is identified by one of {`Bed`, `Bmr`, `Bro`}, as well as a numerical identifier d. We have divided these meetings into: ICSITRAINSET, consisting of the 33 meetings for which $d \bmod 4 \in \{1, 2\}$; ICSIDEVSET, consisting of the 18 meetings for which $d \bmod 4 \equiv 3$; and ICSIEVALSET, consisting of the 16 meetings for which $d \bmod 4 \equiv 0$. These three sets are not disjoint in participants, and the number of instrumented participants K varies from meeting to meeting, between 3 and 9. The corpus is accompanied by metadata specifying the gender, age, and education level of each participant. We use only the forced alignments of these meetings, available in the accompanying MRDA Corpus (Shriberg et al, 2004).

4 Features

Our observation space is the complete K-participant vocal interaction on-off pattern description for a meeting $\mathcal{C}$, a discretized version of which we denote as $\mathbf{q}_t \in \{0, 1\}^K$ for $1 \leq t \leq T$, where T is the duration of $\mathcal{C}$ in terms of the number of 100 ms frames. Details regarding the discretization (and subsequent feature computation) can be found in (Laskowski, Ostendorf and Schultz, 2007).

We compute from $\mathbf{q}_t$ the following features[4] which are the elements of $\mathbf{F}$: f_k^{VI}, the probabil-

[4] Feature type superscripts indicate talkspurt initiation (I) or continuation (C), for either single-participant vocalization (V) or vocalization overlap (O).

ity that participant k initiates vocalization at time t when no-one else was speaking at $t-1$; f_k^{VC}, the probability that participant k continues vocalization at time t when no-one else was speaking at $t-1$; $f_{k,j}^{OI}$, the probability that participant k initiates vocalization at time t when participant j was speaking at $t-1$; and $f_{k,j}^{OC}$ the probability that participant k continues vocalization at time t when participant j was speaking at $t-1$. Values of the features, which are time-independent probabilities, are estimated using a variant of the Ising model (cf. (Laskowski, Ostendorf and Schultz, 2007)). Additionally, we compute a feature f_k^V, the probability that participant k vocalizes at time t, and single-participant averages of the two-participant features: $\langle f_{k,j}^{OI}\rangle_j$, $\langle f_{j,k}^{OI}\rangle_j$, $\langle f_{k,j}^{OC}\rangle_j$, and $\langle f_{j,k}^{OC}\rangle_j$. The complete feature vector for a conversation of K participants then consists of $7K$ one-participant features, and $2(K^2-K)$ two-participant features.

We note that multiple phenomena contribute to the overlap features. The features $f_{k,j}^{OI}$ are based on counts from interruptions, backchannels, and precise floor handoffs. The features $f_{k,j}^{OC}$ are based on counts from interruptions, attempts to hold the floor, and backchannels. Both feature types also contain counts incurred during schism, when the conversation splits into two sub-conversations.

5 Models

Since K may change from meeting to meeting, the size of the feature vector $\mathbf{F}$ must be considered variable. We therefore factor the behavior model, assuming that all features are mutually independent and that each is described by its own univariate Gaussian model $N(\mu,\sigma^2)$. These parameters are maximum likelihood estimates from the f_k and $f_{k,j}$ values in a training set of conversations. In most of these experiments, where the number of classes is small, no parameter smoothing is needed.

For the cases where the group prior is not uniform and participant types are not unique, the membership model assumes independent participant types and has the general form

$$P(\mathbf{g}) = \prod_{k=1}^{K} P(\mathbf{g}[k]), \quad (6)$$

where $P(\mathbf{g}[k])$ is the probability that the k-th participant is type $\mathbf{g}[k]$. This model is used for gender ($P(\mathbf{h})$) and seniority ($P(\mathbf{s})$). The probabilities of specific types are maximum likelihood estimates from the training data.

6 Assigned Role Classification

6.1 Classifying Unique Roles

For unique role classification, we use the AMI Meeting Corpus. All meetings consist of $K=4$ participants, and each participant is assigned one of four roles: project manager (PM), marketing expert (ME), user interface designer (UI), or industrial designer (ID).

As mentioned in Section 2.1, classifying the unique role of all participants, jointly, involves enumerating over the possible permutations of $\{\text{PM},\text{ME},\text{UI},\text{ID}\}$. We use AMITRAINSET to train the behavior model, and then classify AMIDEVSET using Equation 2, one feature type at a time, to identify the best 3 feature types for this task; development experiments suggest that classification rates level off after a small handful of the best performing feature types is included. Those feature types were found to be f_k^{VI}, $\langle f_{k,j}^{OI}\rangle_j$, and $f_{k,j}^{OI}$, capturing the probability of initiating a talkspurt in silence, of initiating a talkspurt when someone else is speaking, and of initiating a talkspurt when a participant in a specific other role is speaking, respectively. On AMIEVALSET, these feature types lead to single-feature-type 4-way classification rates of 41%, 29%, and 53%, respectively. When all three types are used together ($3K+K^2$ features in total), the rate is 53%. Accuracy when all feature types are used is 46%, indicating that some feature types are detrimental to this task.

The confusion matrix for classification using the three best feature types is shown in Table 1. The matrix shows that association between the reference assignment of PM, as well as of UI, and the hypothesized assignment based on the three feature types mentioned is statistically significant. On the other hand, assignment of ID and ME does not deviate significantly from chance.

6.2 Finding the Manager

Using the same data as above, we explore the simplified task of finding a specific participant type. We

Ref	Hyp			
	ID	ME	PM	UI
ID	**8**	6	4	2
ME	5	**8**	4	3
PM	3	4	++**12**	− 1
UI	4	2	−− 0	++**14**

Table 1: Confusion matrix for role classification on AMIEVALSET; reference assignment is found in the rows, hypothesized assignment in columns. Correctly classified roles, along the diagonal, are highlighted in bold. Statistical significance of association at the $p < 0.005$ level per class, using a 2×2 χ^2-test, is shown using "++" and "−−", for above chance and below chance values, respectively; the same is true of "+" and "−", for significance at the $0.005 \leq p < 0.05$ level.

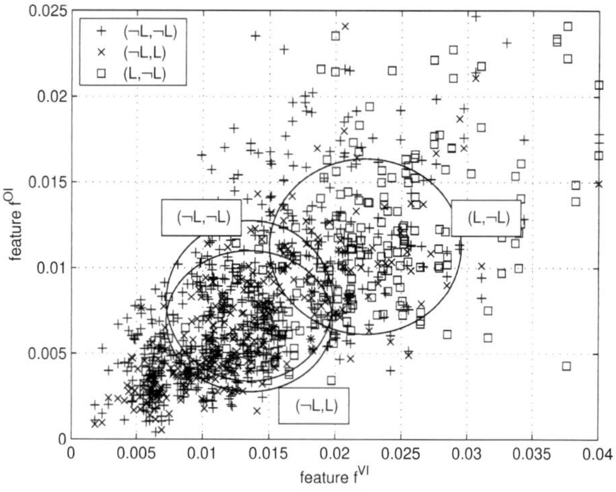

Figure 1: Distribution of $(f_k^{VI}, f_{k,j}^{OI})$ pairs for each of $(\neg L, \neg L)$, $(\neg L, L)$, and $(L, \neg L)$. Ellipses are centered on AMITRAINSET means and encompass one standard deviation.

equate the project manager role with L, and the remaining roles with $\neg L$. This is justified by the AMI meeting scenario, in which participant groups take a product design from start to prototype, and in which the project manager is expected to make the group run smoothly.

The behavior model, trained on AMITRAINSET, is applied using Equation 3 to determine the most likely index j^* of the leader L, given the observed $\mathbf{F}$, from among the $K = 4$ alternatives. To select the best 3 feature types, we once again use AMIDEVSET; these turn out to be the same as those for role classification, namely f_k^{VI}, $\langle f_{k,j}^{OI} \rangle_j$, and $f_{k,j}^{OI}$. Using these three feature types individually, we are able to identify the leader PM in 12 of the 20 meetings in AMIEVALSET. When all three are used together, the identification rate is 60%. However, when all feature types are used, the identification rate climbs to 75%. Since all participants are equally likely to be the leader, the baseline for comparison is random guessing (25% accuracy).

Figure 1 shows the distribution of two of the selected features, f_k^{VI} and $f_{k,j}^{OI}$, for the data in AMITRAINSET; we also show the first standard deviation of the single-Gaussian diagonal-covariance models induced. We first note that f_k^{VI} and $f_{k,j}^{OI}$ are correlated, i.e. that the probability of beginning a talkspurt in silence is correlated with the probability of beginning a talkspurt when someone else is speaking. L consistently begins more talkspurts, both in silence and during other people's speech. It is also interesting that $\neg L$ is slightly less likely to initiate a talkspurt when L is already speaking than when another $\neg L$ is. This suggests that $\neg L$ participants consistently observe the L-status of the already speaking party when contemplating talkspurt production. Finally, we note that neither the probability of continuing a talkspurt f_k^{VC} (related to talkspurt duration) nor f_k^{V} (related to overall amount of talk) are by themselves good $L/\neg L$ discriminators.

7 Gender Classification

Gender classification is an example of a task with a Cartesian search space. For these experiments, we use the AMI Meeting Corpus and the ICSI Meeting Corpus. In both corpora, gender is encoded in the first letter of each participant's unique identifier. The ratio of male to female occurrences is $2 : 1$ in AMITRAINSET, and $4 : 1$ in ICSITRAINSET. Choosing the majority class leads to gender classification rates of 65% and 81% on AMIEVALSET and ICSIEVALSET, respectively.

We enumerate alternative group assignments using Equation 4. Somewhat surprisingly, no single feature type leads to AMIEVALSET or ICSIEVALSET classification rates higher than those obtained by hypothesizing all participants to be male. On AMIDEVSET, one feature type $(f_{k,j}^{OI})$ yields negligibly better accuracy, but does not generalize to the corresponding evaluation data. Furthermore, the association between reference gender labels and hypothesized gender labels, on both evaluation sets, does not appear to be statistically significant at the $p < 0.05$ level. This finding that males and females do not differ significantly in their deployment of talkspurts is likely a consequence of the social structure of the particular groups studied. The fact that AMI roles are acted may also have an effect.

8 Seniority Classification

As a second example of non-unique roles, we attempt to classify participant seniority. For these experiments, we use the ICSI Meeting corpus, in which each participant's education level appears as an optional, self-reported attribute. We have manually clustered these attributes into $N_S = 3$ mutually exclusive seniority categories.[5] Each participant's seniority is drawn independently from $\mathcal{S} = \{\text{GRAD}, \text{PHD}, \text{PROF}\}$; a breakdown for ICSITRAINSET is shown in Table 2. Choosing the majority class ($P(\text{PHD}) = 0.444$ on ICSITRAINSET) yields a classification accuracy of 45% on ICSIEVALSET. We note that in this data, education level is closely correlated with age group.

Seniority	Number of		
	spkrs	occur	meets
GRAD	15	81	33
PHD	13	87	29
PROF	3	28	28
all	31	196	33

Table 2: Breakdown by seniority $\mathcal{S}$ in ICSITRAINSET by the number of unique participants (spkrs), the number of occurrences (occur), and the number of meetings (meets) in which each seniority occurs.

8.1 Classifying Participant Types Independently of Conversation Types

We first treat the problem of classifying participant seniority levels independently of the type of conversation being studied. We identify the most likely seniority assignment for all participants using Equation 5. The best three feature types, determined using ICSIDEVSET, are f_k^V, $f_{k,j}^{OI}$, and $f_{k,j}^{OC}$ (representing the probability of speaking, of beginning a talkspurt when a specific seniority participant is already speaking, and of continuing a talkspurt when a specific seniority participant is speaking), yielding single-feature-type classification rates of 52%, 59%, and 59%, respectively. When used together, these three feature types produce the confusion matrix shown in Table 3 and a rate of 61%, better than when all feature types are used (58%). This represents a 28% relative error reduction over chance. As can be seen in the table, association between the reference and hypothesized seniority assignments is statistically significant on unseen data. It is also evident that confusion between GRAD and PROF is lower than between more proximate seniority levels.

Ref	Hyp		
	GRAD	PHD	PROF
GRAD	++**11**	26	3
PHD	− 2	++**41**	− 3
PROF	0	−− 6	++**10**

Table 3: Confusion matrix for seniority classification on ICSIEVALSET; reference assignment is found in the rows, hypothesized assignment in columns. Highlighting and use of "++", "+", "−", and "−−" as in Table 1.

Figure 2 shows the distribution of $(f_k^V, f_{k,j}^{OC})$ pairs in ICSITRAINSET, together with the first standard deviation, for each combination of the already speaking seniority participant and the seniority participant initiating a new talkspurt (except for (PROF, PROF), since there is at most one PROF in each ICSITRAINSET meeting).

As is clear from the figure, PROF participants in this data talk more than either of the two other seniority types. The figure also demonstrates a difference of behavior during speech overlap. The four ellipses describing GRAD behavior when overlapping with any of the other three classes, as well as PHD behavior when overlapping with GRAD participants, are relatively broad and indicate the absence of strong tendency or preference. However, PHD participants are more likely to continue vocalizing in overlap with other PHD participants, and even more likely to continue through overlap with PROF partic-

[5] GRAD includes "`Grad`", as well as "`Undergrad`", "`B.A.`", and "`Finished BA in 2001`", due to their small number of exemplars; PHD includes "`PhD`" and "`Postdoc`"; and PROF includes "`Professor`" only.

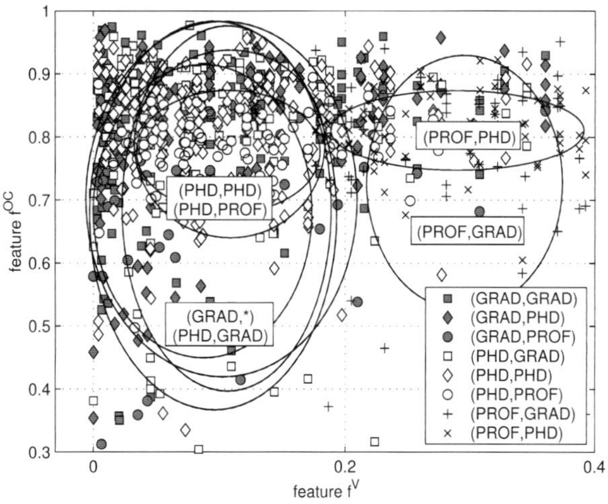

Figure 2: Distribution of $(f_k^V, f_{k,j}^{OC})$ feature value pairs for each of the (k, j) participant pairs (GRAD, GRAD), (GRAD, PHD), (GRAD, PROF), (PHD, GRAD), (PHD, PHD), (PHD, PROF), (PROF, GRAD), and (PROF, PHD). Ellipses are centered on ICSITRAINSET means and encompass one standard deviation.

ipants. A similar trend is apparent for PROF participants: the mean likelihood that they continue vocalizing in overlap with GRAD participants lies below $\mu - \sigma$ (bottom 17%) of their model with PHD participants. We believe that the senior researchers in this data are consciously minimizing their overlap with students, who talk less, to make it easier for the latter to speak up.

8.2 Conditioning on Conversation Type

We now repeat the experiments in the previous section, but condition the behavior and membership models on meeting type t:

$$\mathbf{s}^* = \arg\max_{\mathbf{s} \in \mathcal{S}^K} \sum_{t \in \mathcal{T}} P(t)\ P(\mathbf{s} \mid t)\ P(\mathbf{F} \mid \mathbf{s}, t), \quad (7)$$

where $t \in \mathcal{T} = \{\texttt{Bed}, \texttt{Bmr}, \texttt{Bro}\}$.

Performance using maximum likelihood estimates for the behavior model $P(\mathbf{F} \mid \mathbf{s}, t)$ results in a seniority classification rate on ICSIEVALSET of 61%, i.e. no improvement over conversation-type-independent classification. We suspect this is due to the smaller amounts of training material. To verify this assumption, we smooth the maximum likelihood estimates, $\mu_{S_i,t}, \sigma^2_{S_i,t}$, towards the maximum likelihood conversation-type-independent estimates, μ_{S_i}, σ_{S_i}, using

$$\hat{\mu}_{S_i,t} = \alpha \mu_{S_i,t} + (1 - \alpha)\, \mu_{S_i}, \quad (8)$$

$$\hat{\sigma}^2_{S_i,t} = \alpha \sigma_{S_i,t} + (1 - \alpha)\, \sigma^2_{S_i}, \quad (9)$$

where the value of $\alpha = 0.7$ was selected using ICSIDEVSET. This leads to a rate of 63% on ICSIEVALSET. Furthermore, if instead of estimating the prior on conversation type $P(t)$ from the training data, we use our meeting type estimates from (Laskowski, Ostendorf and Schultz, 2007), the classification rate increases to 67%. A control experiment in which the true type t_{test} of each test meeting is known, i.e. $P(t) = 1$ if $t_{test} = t$ and 0 otherwise, shows that the maximum accuracy achievable under optimal $P(t)$ estimation is 73%.

9 Conclusions

We have explored several socially meaningful partitions of participant populations in two large multiparty meeting corpora. These include assigned role, leadership (embodied by a manager position), gender, and seniority. Our proposed classifier, which can represent participants in groups rather than independently, is able to leverage the observed differences between specific pairs of participant classes. Using only low-level features capturing when participants choose to vocalize relative to one another, it attains relative error rate reductions on unseen data of 37%, 67%, and 40% over chance on classifying role, leadership, and seniority, respectively. We have also shown that the same classifier, using the same features, cannot discriminate between genders in either corpus.

A comparison of the proposed feature types and their performance on the tasks we have explored is shown in Table 4. Consistently, the most useful feature types appear to be the probability of initiating a talkspurt in silence, and the probability of initiating a talkspurt when a participant of a specific type is already speaking. Additionally, on the ICSI Meeting Corpus, the probability of speaking appears to be dependent on seniority, and the probability of continuing to vocalize in overlap with another participant appears to depend on the seniority of the latter. Finally, we note that, for seniority classification on the unseen ICSIEVALSET, the top 3 feature types outperform the best single feature type, indicating a degree of feature type complementarity; this is also true for L-detection on AMIEVALSET when all feature types, as opposed to the single best feature type, are used.

Feature Type	AMI $\mathcal{R}$	AMI $\mathcal{L}$	AMI $\mathcal{H}$	ICSI $\mathcal{H}$	ICSI $\mathcal{S}$	ICSI $\mathcal{S}\|t^*$
f_k^V	44	—	—	—	*52	*57
f_k^{VI}	*41	*60	—	—	52	56
f_k^{VC}	34	—	—	—	—	62
$\langle f_{j,k}^{OI} \rangle_j$	44	—	—	—	47	56
$\langle f_{k,j}^{OI} \rangle_j$	*29	*60	—	—	49	59
$f_{k,j}^{OI}$	*53	*60	64	—	*59	*59
$\langle f_{j,k}^{OC} \rangle_j$	24	—	—	—	—	57
$\langle f_{k,j}^{OC} \rangle_j$	—	—	—	—	54	59
$f_{k,j}^{OC}$	—	—	—	—	*59	*63
top 3*	53	60	—	—	61	67
all	46	75	43	47	58	57
priors	25	25	65	81	45	45

Table 4: Comparative classification performance for 3 experiments on AMIEVALSET and 3 experiments on ICSIEVALSET, per feature type; $\mathcal{R}$, $\mathcal{L}$, $\mathcal{H}$, and $\mathcal{S}$ as defined in Section 2. Also shown is performance on the best three feature types (selected using development data) and all feature types, as well as that when choosing the majority class ("prior"), informed by training data priors; for $\mathcal{R}$ and $\mathcal{L}$ classification, "prior" performance is equal to random guessing. "—" indicates that a feature type, by itself, did not perform above the corresponding "prior" rate; top-3 feature type selection indicated by "*".

Our results not only suggest new, easy-to-compute, low-level features for the automatic classification of participants into socially meaningful types, but also offer scope for informing turn-taking or talkspurt-deployment policies in conversational agents deployed in multi-party settings. Additionally, they suggest that implicit models of certain equivalence classes may lead to improved performance on other tasks, such as multi-participant vocal activity detection.

Acknowledgments

We would like to thank Jean Carletta for helpful comments during the final preparation of this manuscript, and Liz Shriberg for access to the ICSI MRDA Corpus.

References

R. Bales. 1950. *Interaction Process Analysis.* Addison-Wesley Press, Inc.

S. Banerjee and A. Rudnicky. 2004. Using simple speech based features to detect the state of a meeting and the roles of the meeting participants. *Proc. INTERSPEECH*, pp.2189-2192.

J. Berger, S. Rosenholtz, M. Zelditch Jr. 1980. Status Organizing Processes. *Annual Review of Sociology*, **6**:479-508.

J. Carletta, S. Garrod, and H. Fraser-Krauss. 1998. Communication and placement of authority in workplace groups — The consequences for innovation. *Small Group Research*, **29**(5):531-559.

J. Carletta. 2007. Unleashing the killer corpus: Experiences in creating the multi-everything AMI Meeting Corpus. *Language Resources and Evaluation Journal*, **41**(2):181–190.

A. Janin, D. Baron, J. Edwards, D. Ellis, D. Gelbart, N. Morgan, B. Peskin, T. Pfau, E. Shriberg, A. Stolcke, and C. Wooters. 2003. The ICSI Meeting Corpus. *Proc. ICASSP*, pp.364–367.

K. Laskowski, M. Ostendorf, and T. Schultz. 2007. Modeling vocal interaction for text-independent classification of conversation type. *Proc. SIGdial*, pp.194-201.

K. Laskowski, C. Fügen, and T. Schultz. 2007. Simultaneous multispeaker segmentation for automatic meeting recognition. *Proc. EUSIPCO*, pp.1294-1298.

A. Norwine and O. Murphy. 1938. Characteristic time intervals in telephonic conversation. *Bell System Technical Journal*, **17**:281-291.

R. Rienks and D. Heylen. 2005. Dominance detection in meetings using easily obtainable features. *Proc. MLMI.*

R. Rienks, D. Zhang, D. Gatica-Perez, and W. Post. 2006. Detection and application of influence rankings in small-group meetings. *Proc. ICMI.*

J. Rotman. 1995. *An Introduction to the Theory of Groups.* Springer-Verlag New York, Inc.

E. Shriberg, R. Dhillon, S. Bhagat, J. Ang, and H. Carvey. 2004. The ICSI Meeting Recorder Dialog Act (MRDA) Corpus. *Proc. SIGdial*, pp.97–100.

D. Tannen. 1996. *Gender & Discourse.* Oxford University Press, USA.

A. Vinciarelli. 2007. Speakers role recognition in multiparty audio recordings using social network analysis and duration distribution modeling. *IEEE Trans. Multimedia*, **9**(6):1215-1226.

D. Wyatt, J. Bilmes, T. Choudhury, and H. Kautz. 2007. A privacy-sensitive approach to modeling multi-person conversations. *Proc. IJCAI*, pp.1769–1775.

M. Zancanaro, B. Lepri, and F. Pianesi. 2006. Automatic detection of group functional roles in face to face interactions. *Proc. ICMI.*

Modelling and Detecting Decisions in Multi-party Dialogue

Raquel Fernández, Matthew Frampton, Patrick Ehlen, Matthew Purver, and **Stanley Peters**
Center for the Study of Language and Information
Stanford University
{raquel|frampton|ehlen|mpurver|peters}@stanford.edu

Abstract

We describe a process for automatically detecting decision-making sub-dialogues in transcripts of multi-party, human-human meetings. Extending our previous work on *action item identification*, we propose a structured approach that takes into account the different roles utterances play in the decision-making process. We show that this structured approach outperforms the accuracy achieved by existing decision detection systems based on flat annotations, while enabling the extraction of more fine-grained information that can be used for summarization and reporting.

1 Introduction

In collaborative and organized work environments, people share information and make decisions extensively through multi-party conversations, usually in the form of meetings. When audio or video recordings are made of these meetings, it would be valuable to extract important information, such as the decisions that were made and the trains of reasoning that led to those decisions. Such a capability would allow work groups to keep track of courses of action that were shelved or rejected, and could allow new team members to get quickly up to speed. Thanks to the recent availability of substantial meeting corpora—such as the ISL (Burger et al., 2002), ICSI (Janin et al., 2004), and AMI (McCowan et al., 2005) Meeting Corpora—current research on the structure of decision-making dialogue and its use for automatic decision detection has helped to bring this vision closer to reality (Verbree et al., 2006; Hsueh and Moore, 2007b).

Our aim here is to further that research by applying a simple notion of dialogue structure to the task of automatically detecting decisions in multi-party dialogue. A central hypothesis underlying our approach is that this task is best addressed by taking into account the roles that different utterances play in the decision-making process. Our claim is that this approach facilitates both the detection of regions of discourse where decisions are discussed and adopted, and also the identification of important aspects of the decision discussions themselves, thus opening the way to better and more concise reporting.

In the next section, we describe prior work on related efforts, including our own work on action item detection (Purver et al., 2007). Sections 3 and 4 then present our decision annotation scheme, which distinguishes several types of decision-related dialogue acts (DAs), and the corpus used as data (in this study a section of the AMI Meeting Corpus). Next, in Section 5, we describe our experimental methodology, including the basic conception of our classification approach, the features we used in classification, and our evaluation metrics. Section 6 then presents our results, obtained with a hierarchical classifier that first trains individual *sub-classifiers* to detect the different types of decision DAs, and then uses a *super-classifier* to detect decision regions on the basis of patterns of these DAs, achieving an F-score of 58%. Finally, Section 7 presents some conclusions and directions for future work.

2 Related Work

Recent years have seen an increasing interest in research on decision-making dialogue. To a great extent, this is due to the fact that decisions have

Proceedings of the 9th SIGdial Workshop on Discourse and Dialogue, pages 156–163,
Columbus, June 2008. ©2008 Association for Computational Linguistics

been shown to be a key aspect of meeting speech. User studies (Lisowska et al., 2004; Banerjee et al., 2005) have shown that participants regard decisions as one of the most important outputs of a meeting, while Whittaker et al. (2006) found that the development of an automatic decision detection component is critical to the re-use of meeting archives. Identifying decision-making regions in meeting transcripts can thus be expected to support development of a wide range of applications, such as automatic meeting assistants that process, understand, summarize and report the output of meetings; meeting tracking systems that assist in implementing decisions; and group decision support systems that, for instance, help in constructing group memory (Romano and Nunamaker, 2001; Post et al., 2004; Voss et al., 2007).

Previously researchers have focused on the interactive aspects of argumentative and decision-making dialogue, tackling issues such as the detection of agreement and disagreement and the level of emotional involvement of conversational participants (Hillard et al., 2003; Wrede and Shriberg, 2003; Galley et al., 2004; Gatica-Perez et al., 2005). From a perhaps more formal perspective, Verbree et al. (2006) have created an argumentation scheme intended to support automatic production of argument structure diagrams from decision-oriented meeting transcripts. Only Hsueh and Moore (2007a; 2007b), however, have specifically investigated the automatic detection of decisions.

Using the AMI Meeting Corpus, Hsueh and Moore (2007b) attempt to identify the dialogue acts (DAs) in a meeting transcript that are "decision-related". The authors define these DAs on the basis of two kinds of manually created summaries: an extractive summary of the whole meeting, and an abstractive summary of the decisions made in the meeting. Those DAs in the extractive summary that support any of the decisions in the abstractive summary are then manually tagged as decision-related DAs. They trained a Maximum Entropy classifier to recognize this single DA class, using a variety of lexical, prosodic, dialogue act and topical features. The F-score they achieved was 0.35, which gives a good indication of the difficulty of this task.

In our previous work (Purver et al., 2007), we attempted to detect a particular kind of decision common in meetings, namely *action items*—public commitments to perform a given task. In contrast to the approach adopted by Hsueh and Moore (2007b), we proposed a hierarchical approach where individual classifiers were trained to detect distinct action item-related DA classes (*task description*, *timeframe*, *ownership* and *agreement*) followed by a super-classifier trained on the hypothesized class labels and confidence scores from the individual classifiers that would detect clusters of multiple classes. We showed that this structured approach produced better classification accuracy (around 0.39 F-score on the task of detecting action item regions) than a flat-classifier baseline trained on a single action item DA class (around 0.35 F-score).

In this paper we extend this approach to the more general task of detecting decisions, hypothesizing that—as with action items—the dialogue acts involved in decision-making dialogue form a rather heterogeneous set, whose members co-occur in particular kinds of patterns, and that exploiting this richer structure can facilitate their detection.

3 Decision Dialogue Acts

We are interested in identifying the main conversational units in a decision-making process. We expect that identifying these units will help in detecting regions of dialogue where decisions are made (*decision sub-dialogues*), while also contributing to identification and extraction of specific decision-related bits of information.

Decision-making dialogue can be complex, often involving detailed discussions with complicated argumentative structure (Verbree et al., 2006). Decision sub-dialogues can thus include a great deal of information that is potentially worth extracting. For instance, we may be interested in knowing what a decision is about, what alternative proposals were considered during the decision process, what arguments were given for and against each of them, and last but not least, what the final resolution was.

Extracting these and other potential decision components is a challenging task, which we do not intend to fully address in this paper. This initial study concentrates on three main components we believe constitute the backbone of decision sub-dialogues. A typical decision sub-dialogue consists of three main components that often unfold in sequence. (a)

key	DDA class	description
I	*issue*	utterances introducing the issue or topic under discussion
R	*resolution*	utterances containing the decision that is adopted
RP	– *proposal*	– utterances where the decision adopted is proposed
RR	– *restatement*	– utterances where the decision adopted is confirmed or restated
A	*agreement*	utterances explicitly signalling agreement with the decision made

Table 1: Set of decision dialogue act (DDA) classes

A topic or issue that requires some sort of conclusion is initially raised. (b) One or more proposals are considered. And (c) once some sort of agreement is reached upon a particular resolution, a decision is adopted.

Dialogue act taxonomies often include tags that can be decision-related. For instance, the DAMSL taxonomy (Core and Allen, 1997) includes the tags `agreement` and `commit`, as well as a tag `open-option` for utterances that "suggest a course of action". Similarly, the AMI DA scheme[1] incorporates tags like `suggest`, `elicit-offer-or-suggestion` and `assess`. These tags are however very general and do not capture the distinction between decisions and more general suggestions and commitments.[2] We therefore devised a decision annotation scheme that classifies utterances according to the role they play in the process of formulating and agreeing on a decision. Our scheme distinguishes among three main decision dialogue act (DDA) classes: *issue* (*I*), *resolution* (*R*), and *agreement* (*A*). Class *R* is further subdivided into *resolution proposal* (*RP*) and *resolution restatement* (*RR*). A summary of the classes is given in Table 1.

Annotation of the *issue* class includes any utterances that introduce the topic of the decision discussion. For instance, in example (1) below, the utterances *"Are we going to have a backup?"* and *"But would a backup really be necessary?"* are tagged as *I*. The classes *RP* and *RR* are used to annotate those utterances that specify the resolution adopted—i.e. the decision made. Annotation with the class *RP* includes any utterances where the resolution is initially proposed (like the utterance *"I think maybe we could just go for the kinetic energy..."*). Sometimes decision discussions include utterances that sum up the resolution adopted, like the utterance *"Okay, fully kinetic energy"* in (1). This kind of utterance is tagged with the class *RR*. Finally, the *agreement* class includes any utterances in which participants agree with the (proposed) resolution, like the utterances *"Yeah"* and *"Good"* as well as *"Okay"* in dialogue (1).

(1) A: Are we going to have a backup?
   Or we do just–
B: But would a backup really be necessary?
A: I think maybe we could just go for the
   kinetic energy and be bold and innovative.
C: Yeah.
B: I think– yeah.
A: It could even be one of our selling points.
C: Yeah *–laugh–*.
D: Environmentally conscious or something.
A: Yeah.
B: Okay, fully kinetic energy.
D: Good.[3]

Note that an utterance can be assigned to more than one of these classes. For instance, the utterance *"Okay, fully kinetic energy"* is annotated both as *RR* and *A*. Similarly, each decision sub-dialogue may contain more than one utterance corresponding to each class, as we saw above for *issue*. While we do not a priori require each of these classes to be present for a set of utterances to be considered a decision sub-dialogue, all annotated decision sub-dialogues in our corpus include the classes *I*, *RP* and *A*. The annotation process and results are described in detail in the next section.

[1]A full description of the AMI Meeting Corpus DA scheme is available at `http://mmm.idiap.ch/private/ami/annotation/dialogue_acts_manual_1.0.pdf`, after free registration.

[2]Although they can of course be used to aid the identification process—see Section 5.3.

[3]This example was extracted from the AMI dialogue ES2015c and has been modified slightly for presentation purposes.

4 Data: Corpus & Annotation

In this study, we use 17 meetings from the AMI Meeting Corpus (McCowan et al., 2005), a publicly available corpus of multi-party meetings containing both audio recordings and manual transcriptions, as well as a wide range of annotated information including dialogue acts and topic segmentation. Conversations are all in English, but they can include native and non-native English speakers. All meetings in our sub-corpus are driven by an elicitation scenario, wherein four participants play the role of *project manager*, *marketing expert*, *interface designer*, and *industrial designer* in a company's design team. The overall sub-corpus makes up a total of 15,680 utterances/dialogue acts (approximately 920 per meeting). Each meeting lasts around 30 minutes.

Two authors annotated 9 and 10 dialogues each, overlapping on two dialogues. Inter-annotator agreement on these two dialogues was similar to (Purver et al., 2007), with *kappa* values ranging from 0.63 to 0.73 for the four DDA classes. The highest agreement was obtained for class *RP* and the lowest for class *A*.[4]

On average, each meeting contains around 40 DAs tagged with one or more of the DDA subclasses in Table 1. DDAs are thus very sparse, corresponding to only 4.3% of utterances. When we look at the individual DDA sub-classes this is even more pronounced. Utterances tagged as *issue* make up less than 0.9% of utterances in a meeting, while utterances annotated as *resolution* make up around 1.4%—1% corresponding to *RP* and less than 0.4% to *RR* on average. Almost half of DDA utterances (slightly over 2% of all utterances on average) are tagged as belonging to class *agreement*.

We compared our annotations with the annotations of Hsueh and Moore (2007b) for the 17 meetings of our sub-corpus. The overall number of utterances annotated as decision-related is similar in the two studies: 40 *vs*. 30 utterances per meeting on average, respectively. However, the overlap of the annotations is very small leading to negative *kappa* scores. As shown in Figure 1, only 12.22% of utterances tagged with one of our DDA classes correspond to an utterance annotated as decision-related by Hsueh & Moore. While presumably this is a consequence of our different definitions for DDAs, it seems also partially due to the fact that sometimes we disagreed about where decisions were being made. Most of the overlap is found with utterances tagged as *resolution* (*RP* or *RR*). Around 32% of utterances tagged as *resolution* overlap with AMI DDAs, while the overlap with utterances annotated as *issue* and *agreement* is substantially lower—around 7% and 1.5%, respectively. This is perhaps not surprising given their definition of a "decision-related" DA (see Section 2). Classes like *issue* and especially *agreement* shape the interaction patterns of decision-sub-dialogues, but are perhaps unlikely to appear in an extractive summary.[5]

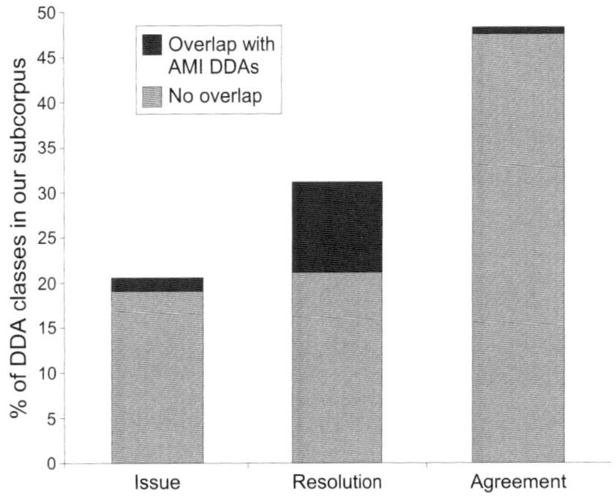

Figure 1: Overlap with AMI annotations

5 Experiments

5.1 Classifiers

Our hierarchical approach to decision detection involves two steps:

1. We first train one independent *sub-classifier* for the identification of each of our DDA classes, using features derived from the properties of the utterances in context (see below).

2. To detect decision sub-dialogues, we then train a *super-classifier*, whose features are the hypothesized class labels and confidence scores

[4]The annotation guidelines we used are available online at `http://godel.stanford.edu/twiki/bin/view/Calo/CaloDecisionDiscussionSchema`

[5]Although, as we shall see in Section 6.2, they contribute to improve the detection of decision sub-dialogues and of other DDA classes.

from the sub-classifiers, over a suitable window.[6]

The super-classifier is then able to "correct" the DDA classes hypothesized by the sub-classifiers on the basis of richer contextual information: if a DA is classified as positive by a sub-classifier, but negative by the super-classifier, then this sub-classification is "corrected", i.e. it is changed to negative. Hence this hierarchical approach takes advantage of the fact that within decision sub-dialogues, our DDAs can be expected to co-occur in particular types of patterns.

We use the linear-kernel support vector machine classifier SVMlight (Joachims, 1999) in all classification experiments.

5.2 Evaluation

In all cases we perform 17-fold cross-validation, each fold training on 16 meetings and testing on the remaining one.

We can evaluate the performance of our approach at three levels: the accuracy of the sub-classifiers in detecting each of the DDA classes, the accuracy obtained in detecting DDA classes after the output of the sub-classifiers has been corrected by the super-classifier, and the accuracy of the super-classifier in detecting decision sub-dialogues. For the DDA identification task (both uncorrected and corrected) we use the same lenient-match metric as Hsueh and Moore (2007b), which allows a margin of 20 seconds preceding and following a hypothesized DDA.[7] We take as reference the results they obtained on detecting their decision-related DAs.

For the evaluation of the decision sub-dialogue detection task, we follow (Purver et al., 2007) and use a windowed metric that divides the dialogue into 30-second windows and evaluates on a per window basis. As a baseline for this task, we compare the performance of our hierarchical approach to a flat classification approach, first using the flat annotations of Hsueh and Moore (2007a) that only include a single DDA class, and second using our annotations, but for the binary classification of whether an utterance is decision-related or not, without distinguishing among our DDA sub-classes.

[6] The width of this window is estimated from the training data and corresponds to the average length in utterances of a decision sub-dialogue—25 in our sub-corpus.

[7] Note that here we only give credit for hypotheses based on a 1–1 mapping with the gold-standard labels.

5.3 Features

To train the DDA sub-classifiers we extracted utterance features similar to those used by Purver et al. (2007) and Hsueh and Moore (2007b): lexical unigrams and durational and locational features from the transcripts; prosodic features extracted from the audio files using Praat (Boersma, 2001); general DA tags and speaker information from the AMI annotations; and contextual features consisting of the same set of features from immediately preceding and following utterances. Table 2 shows the full feature set.

Lexical	unigrams after text normalization
Utterance	length in words, duration in seconds, percentage of meeting
Prosodic	pitch & intensity min/max/mean/dev, pitch slope, num of voice frames
DA	AMI dialogue act class
Speaker	speaker id & AMI speaker role
Context	features as above for utterances u +/- 1... u +/- 5

Table 2: Features for decision DA detection

6 Results

6.1 Baseline

On the task of detecting decision-related DAs, Hsueh and Moore (2007b) report an F-score of 0.33 when only lexical features are employed. Using a combination of different features allows them to boost the score to 0.35. Although the differences both in definition and prior distribution between their DAs and our DDA classes make direct comparisons unstraightforward (see Sec. 4), we consider this result a baseline for the DDA detection task.

As a baseline system for the decision sub-dialogue detection task, we use a flat classifier trained on the word unigrams of the current utterance (lexical features) and the unigrams of the immediately preceding and following utterances (+/-1-utterance context). Table 3 shows the accuracy per 30-second window obtained when a flat classifier is applied to AMI annotations and to our own annotations, respectively.[8] In general, the flat classifiers yield high recall (over 90%) but rather low precision (below 35%).

[8] Note that the task of detecting decision sub-dialogues is not directly addressed by (Hsueh and Moore, 2007b).

As can be seen, using our DA annotations (CALO DDAs) with all sub-classes merged into a single class yields better results than using the AMI DDA flat annotations. The reasons behind this result are not entirely obvious. In principle, our annotated DDAs are by definition less homogeneous than the AMI DDAs, which could lead to a lower performance in a simple binary approach. It seems however that the regions that contain our DDAs are easier to detect than the regions that contain AMI DDAs.

Flat classifier	Re	Pr	F1
AMI DDAs	.97	.21	.34
CALO DDAs	.96	.34	.50

Table 3: Flat classifiers with lexical features and +/–1-utterance context

6.2 Hierarchical Results

Performance of the hierarchical classifier with lexical features and +/- 1-utterance context is shown in Table 4. The results of the super-classifier can be compared directly to the baseline flat classifier of Table 3. We can see that the use of the super-classifier to detect decision sub-dialogues gives a significantly improved performance over the flat approach. This is despite low sub-classifier performance, especially for the classes with very low frequency of occurrence like *RR*. Precision for decision sub-dialogue detection improves around 0.5 points ($p < 0.05$ on an paired t-test), boosting F-scores to 0.55 ($p < 0.05$). The drop in recall from 0.96 to 0.91 is not statistically significant.

	sub-classifiers				super
	I	RP	RR	A	classifier
Re	.25	.44	.09	.88	.91
Pr	.21	.24	.14	.18	.39
F1	.23	.31	.11	.30	.55

Table 4: Hierarchical classifier with lexical features and +/–1-utterance context

We investigated whether we could improve results further by using additional features, and found that we could. The best results obtained with the hierarchical classifier are shown in Table 5. We applied feature selection to the features shown in Table 2 using *information gain* and carried out several trial classifier experiments. Like Purver et al. (2007) and (Hsueh and Moore, 2007b), we found that lexical features increase classifier performance the most.

As DA features, we used the AMI DA tags `elicit-assessment`, `suggest` and `assess` for classes *I* and *A*; and tags `suggest`, `fragment` and `stall`, for classes *RP* and *RR*. Only the DA features for the *Resolution* sub-classes (*RP* and *RR*) gave significant improvements ($p < 0.05$). Utterance and speaker features were found to improve the recall of the sub-classes significantly ($p < 0.05$), and the precision of the super-classifier ($p < 0.05$). As for prosodic information, we found minimum and maximum intensity to be the most generally predictive, but although these features increased recall, they caused precision and F-scores to decrease.

When we experimented with contextual features (i.e. features from utterances before and after the current dialogue act), we only found lexical contextual features to be useful. With the current dataset, for classes *I*, *RP* and *RR*, the optimal amount of lexical contextual information turned out to be +/- 1 utterances, while for class *A* increasing the amount of lexical contextual information to +/-5 utterances yielded better results, boosting both precision and F-score ($p < 0.05$). Speaker, utterance, DA and prosodic contextual features gave no improvement.

The scores on the left hand side of Table 5 show the best results obtained with the sub-classifiers for each of the DDA classes. We found however that the super-classifier was able to improve over these results by correcting the hypothesized labels on the basis of the DDA patterns observed in context (see the corrected results on Table 5). In particular, precision increased from 0.18 to 0.20 for class *I* and from 0.28 to 0.31 for class *RP* (both results are statistically significant, $p < 0.05$). Our best F-score for class *RP* (which is the class with the highest overlap with AMI DDAs) is a few points higher than the one reported in (Hsueh and Moore, 2007b)—0.38 *vs.* 0.35, respectively.

Next we investigated the contribution of the class *agreement*. Although this class is not as informative for summarization and reporting as the other DDA classes, it plays a key role in the interactive process that shapes decision sub-dialogues. Indeed, including this class helps to detect other more contentful DDA classes such as *issue* and *resolution*.

	sub-classifiers				corr. sub-classifiers				corr. sub. w/o A			super	super
	I	RP	RR	A	I	RP	RR	A	I	RP	RR	w/o A	with A
Re	.45	.49	.18	.55	.43	.48	.18	.55	.43	.48	.18	.91	.88
Pr	.18	.28	.14	.30	.20	.31	.14	.30	.18	.30	.14	.36	.43
F1	.25	.36	.16	.39	.28	.38	.16	.39	. 26	.37	.16	.52	.58

Table 5: Hierarchical classifier with uncorrected and corrected results for sub-classifiers, with and w/o class A; lexical, utterance, and speaker features; +/–1-utt lexical context for I-RP-RR and +/–5-utt lexical context for A.

Table 5 also shows the results obtained with the hierarchical classifier when class *A* is ignored. In this case the small correction observed in the precision of classes *I* and *RP* w.r.t. the original output of the sub-classifiers is not statistically significant. The performance of the super-classifier (sub-dialogue detection) also decreases significantly in this condition: 0.43 *vs.* 0.36 precision and 0.58 *vs.* 0.52 F-score ($p < 0.05$).

6.3 Robustness to ASR output

Finally, since the end goal is a system that can automatically extract decisions from raw audio and video recordings of meetings, we also investigated the impact of ASR output on our approach. We used SRI's Decipher (Stolcke et al., 2008)[9] to produce word confusion networks for our 17 meeting sub-corpus and then ran our detectors on the WCNs' best path. Table 6 shows a comparison of F-scores. The two scores shown for the super-classifier correspond to using the best feature set *vs.* using only lexical features. When ASR output is used, the results for the DDA classes decrease between 6 and 11 points. However, the performance of the super-classifier does not experience a significant degradation (the drop in F-score from 0.58 to 0.51 is not statistically significant). The results obtained with the hierarchical detector are still significantly higher than those achieved by the flat classifier (0.51 *vs.* 0.50, $p < 0.05$).

F1	I	RP	RR	A	super	flat
WCNs	.22	.30	.08	.28	.51/.51	.50
Manual	.28	.38	.16	.39	.58/.55	.50

Table 6: Comparison of F-scores obtained with WCNs and manual transcriptions

[9]Stolcke et al. (2008) report a word error rate of 26.9% on AMI meetings.

7 Conclusions & Future Work

We have shown that our earlier approach to action item detection can be successfully applied to the more general task of detecting decisions. Although this is indeed a hard problem, we have shown that results for automatic decision-detection in multi-party dialogue can be improved by taking account of dialogue structure and applying a hierarchical approach. Our approach consists in distinguishing between the different roles utterances play in the decision-making process and uses a hierarchical classification strategy: individual sub-classifiers are first trained to detect each of the DDA classes; then a super-classifier is used to detect patterns of these classes and identify decisions sub-dialogues. As we have seen, this structured approach outperforms the accuracy achieved by systems based on flat classifications. For the task of detecting decision sub-dialogues we achieved 0.58 F-score in initial experiments—a performance that proved to be rather robust to ASR output. Results for the individual sub-classes are still low and there is indeed a lot of room for improvement. In future work, we plan to increase the size of our data-set, and possibly extend our set of DDA classes, by for instance including a *disagreement* class, in order to capture additional properties of the decision-making process.

We believe that our structured approach can help in constructing more concise and targeted reports of decision sub-dialogues. An immediate further extension of the current work will therefore be to investigate the automatic production of useful descriptive summaries of decisions.

Acknowledgements We are thankful to the three anonymous SIGdial reviewers for their helpful comments and suggestions. This material is based upon work supported by the Defense Advanced Research Projects Agency (DARPA) under Contract No. FA8750-07-D-0185/0004. Any opinions, findings and conclusions or recommendations expressed in this material are those of the authors and do not necessarily reflect the views of DARPA.

References

Satanjeev Banerjee, Carolyn Rosé, and Alex Rudnicky. 2005. The necessity of a meeting recording and playback system, and the benefit of topic-level annotations to meeting browsing. In *Proceedings of the 10th International Conference on Human-Computer Interaction.*

Paul Boersma. 2001. Praat, a system for doing phonetics by computer. *Glot International*, 5(9–10).

Susanne Burger, Victoria MacLaren, and Hua Yu. 2002. The ISL Meeting Corpus: The impact of meeting type on speech style. In *Proceedings of the 7th International Conference on Spoken Language Processing (INTERSPEECH - ICSLP)*, Denver, Colorado.

Mark Core and James Allen. 1997. Coding dialogues with the DAMSL annotation scheme. In D. Traum, editor, *Proceedings of the 1997 AAAI Fall Symposium on Communicative Action in Humans and Machines.*

Michel Galley, Kathleen McKeown, Julia Hirschberg, and Elizabeth Shriberg. 2004. Identifying agreement and disagreement in conversational speech: Use of Bayesian networks to model pragmatic dependencies. In *Proceedings of the 42nd Annual Meeting of the Association for Computational Linguistics (ACL).*

Daniel Gatica-Perez, Ian McCowan, Dong Zhang, and Samy Bengio. 2005. Detecting group interest level in meetings. In *IEEE International Conference on Acoustics, Speech, and Signal Processing (ICASSP).*

Dustin Hillard, Mari Ostendorf, and Elisabeth Shriberg. 2003. Detection of agreement vs. disagreement in meetings: Training with unlabeled data. In *Companion Volume of the Proceedings of HLT-NAACL 2003 - Short Papers*, Edmonton, Alberta, May.

Pei-Yun Hsueh and Johanna Moore. 2007a. What decisions have you made?: Automatic decision detection in meeting conversations. In *Proceedings of NAACL/HLT*, Rochester, New York.

Pey-Yun Hsueh and Johanna Moore. 2007b. Automatic decision detection in meeting speech. In *Proceedings of MLMI 2007*, Lecture Notes in Computer Science. Springer-Verlag.

Adam Janin, Jeremy Ang, Sonali Bhagat, Rajdip Dhillon, Jane Edwards, Javier Marcías-Guarasa, Nelson Morgan, Barbara Peskin, Elizabeth Shriberg, Andreas Stolcke, Chuck Wooters, and Britta Wrede. 2004. The ICSI meeting project: Resources and research. In *Proceedings of the 2004 ICASSP NIST Meeting Recognition Workshop.*

Thorsten Joachims. 1999. Making large-scale SVM learning practical. In B. Schölkopf, C. Burges, and A. Smola, editors, *Advances in Kernel Methods – Support Vector Learning.* MIT Press.

Agnes Lisowska, Andrei Popescu-Belis, and Susan Armstrong. 2004. User query analysis for the specification and evaluation of a dialogue processing and retrieval system. In *Proceedings of the 4th International Conference on Language Resources and Evaluation.*

Iain McCowan, Jean Carletta, W. Kraaij, S. Ashby, S. Bourban, M. Flynn, M. Guillemot, T. Hain, J. Kadlec, V. Karaiskos, M. Kronenthal, G. Lathoud, M. Lincoln, A. Lisowska, W. Post, D. Reidsma, and P. Wellner. 2005. The AMI Meeting Corpus. In *Proceedings of Measuring Behavior 2005, the 5th International Conference on Methods and Techniques in Behavioral Research*, Wageningen, Netherlands.

Wilfried M. Post, Anita H.M. Cremers, and Olivier Blanson Henkemans. 2004. A research environment for meeting behaviour. In *Proceedings of the 3rd Workshop on Social Intelligence Design.*

Matthew Purver, John Dowding, John Niekrasz, Patrick Ehlen, Sharareh Noorbaloochi, and Stanley Peters. 2007. Detecting and summarizing action items in multi-party dialogue. In *Proceedings of the 8th SIGdial Workshop on Discourse and Dialogue*, Antwerp, Belgium.

Nicholas C. Romano, Jr. and Jay F. Nunamaker, Jr. 2001. Meeting analysis: Findings from research and practice. In *Proceedings of the 34th Hawaii International Conference on System Sciences.*

Andreas Stolcke, Xavier Anguera, Kofi Boakye, Özgür Çetin, Adam Janin, Matthew Magimai-Doss, Chuck Wooters, and Jing Zheng. 2008. The icsi-sri spring 2007 meeting and lecture recognition system. In *Proceedings of CLEAR 2007 and RT2007.* Springer Lecture Notes on Computer Science.

Daan Verbree, Rutger Rienks, and Dirk Heylen. 2006. First steps towards the automatic construction of argument-diagrams from real discussions. In *Proceedings of the 1st International Conference on Computational Models of Argument*, volume 144, pages 183–194. IOS press.

Lynn Voss, Patrick Ehlen, and the DARPA CALO MA Project Team. 2007. The CALO Meeting Assistant. In *Proceedings of NAACL-HLT*, Rochester, NY, USA.

Steve Whittaker, Rachel Laban, and Simon Tucker. 2006. Analysing meeting records: An ethnographic study and technological implications. In *MLMI 2005, Revised Selected Papers.*

Britta Wrede and Elizabeth Shriberg. 2003. Spotting "hot spots" in meetings: Human judgements and prosodic cues. In *Proceedings of the 9th European Conference on Speech Communication and Technology*, Geneva, Switzerland.

User Simulation as Testing for Spoken Dialog Systems

Hua Ai*
Intelligent Systems Program
University of Pittsburgh
210 S. Bouquet St., Pittsburg, PA 15260
Hua@cs.pitt.edu

Fuliang Weng
Research and Technology Center
Robert Bosch LLC
4009 Miranda Ave., Palo Alto, CA 94304
Fuliang.weng@us.bosch.com

Abstract

We propose to use user simulation for testing during the development of a sophisticated dialog system. While the limited behaviors of the state-of-the-art user simulation may not cover important aspects in the dialog system testing, our proposed approach extends the functionality of the simulation so that it can be used at least for the early stage testing before the system reaches stable performance for evaluation involving human users. The proposed approach includes a set of evaluation measures that can be computed automatically from the interaction logs between the user simulator and the dialog system. We first validate these measures on human user dialogs using user satisfaction scores. We also build a regression model to estimate the user satisfaction scores using these evaluation measures. Then, we apply the evaluation measures on a simulated dialog corpus trained from the real user corpus. We show that the user satisfaction scores estimated from the simulated corpus are not statistically different from the real users' satisfaction scores.

1 Introduction

Spoken dialog systems are being widely used in daily life. The increasing demands of such systems require shorter system development cycles and better automatic system developing techniques. As a result, machine learning techniques are applied to learn dialog strategies automatically, such as reinforcement learning (Singh et al., 2002; Williams & Young, 2007), supervised learning (Henderson et al., 2005), etc. These techniques require a significant amount of training data for the automatic learners to sufficiently explore the vast space of possible dialog states and strategies. However, it is always hard to obtain training corpora that are large enough to ensure that the learned strategies are reliable. User simulation is an attempt to solve this problem by generating synthetic training corpora using computer simulated users. The simulated users are built to mimic real users' behaviors to some extent while allowing them to be programmed to explore unseen but still possible user behaviors. These simulated users can interact with the dialog systems to generate large amounts of training data in a low-cost and time-efficient manner. Many previous studies (Scheffler, 2002; Pietquin, 2004) have shown that the dialog strategies learned from the simulated training data outperform the hand-crafted strategies. There are also studies that use user simulation to train speech recognition and understanding components (Chung, 2004).

While user simulation is largely used in dialog system training, it has only been used in limited scope for testing specific dialog system components in the system evaluation phase (López-Cózar et al., 2003; Filisko and Seneff, 2006). This is partly because the state-of-the-art simulated users have quite limited abilities in mimicking human users' behaviors and typically over-generate possible dialog behaviors. This is not a major problem when using simulated dialog corpus as the training corpus for dialog strategy learning because the over-generated simulation behaviors would only provide the machine learners with a broader dialog state space to explore (Ai et al., 2007). However, realistic user behaviors are highly desired in the testing phase because the systems are evaluated and adjusted based on the analysis of the dialogs generated in this phase. Therefore, we would ex-

* This study was conducted when the author was an intern at Bosch RTC.

Proceedings of the 9th SIGdial Workshop on Discourse and Dialogue, pages 164–171,
Columbus, June 2008.

pect that these user behaviors are what we will see in the final evaluation with human users. In this case, any over-generated dialog behaviors may cause the system to be blamed for untargeted functions. What is more, the simulated users cannot provide subjective user satisfaction feedback which is also important for improving the systems.

Since it is expensive and time-consuming to test every version of the system with a significant amount of paid subjects, the testing during the development is typically constrained to a limited number of users, and often, to repeated users who are colleagues or developers themselves. Thus, the system performance is not always optimized for the intended users.

Our ultimate goal is to supplement human testing with simulated users during the development to speed up the system development towards desired performance. This would be especially useful in the early development stage, since it would avoid conducting tests with human users when they may feel extremely frustrated due to the malfunction of the unstable system.

As a first attempt, we try to extend the state-of-the-art user simulation by incorporating a set of new but straightforward evaluation measures for automatically assessing the dialog system performance. These evaluation measures focus on three basic aspects of task-oriented dialog systems: understanding ability, efficiency, and the appropriateness of the system actions. They are first applied on a corpus generated between a dialog system and a group of human users to demonstrate the validity of these measures with the human users' satisfaction scores. Results show that these measures are significantly correlated with the human users' satisfactions. Then, a regression model is built to predict the user satisfaction scores using these evaluation measures. We also apply the regression model on a simulated dialog corpus trained from the above real user corpus, and show that the user satisfaction scores estimated from the simulated dialogs do not differ significantly from the real users' satisfaction scores. Finally, we conclude that these evaluation measures can be used to assess the system performance based on the estimated user satisfaction.

2 User Simulation Techniques

Most user simulation models are trained from dialog corpora generated by human users. Earlier models predict user actions based on simple relations between the system actions and the following user responses. (Eckert et al., 1997) first suggest a bigram model to predict the next user's action based on the previous system's action. (Levin et al., 2000) add constraints to the bigram model to accept the expected dialog acts only. However, their basic assumption of making the next user's action dependent only on the system's previous action is oversimplified. Later, many studies model more comprehensive user behaviors by adding user goals to constrain the user actions (Scheffler, 2002; Pietquin, 2004). These simulated users mimic real user behaviors in a statistical way, conditioning the user actions on the user goals and the dialog contexts. More recent research defines agenda for simulated users to complete a set of settled goals (Schatzmann et al., 2007). This type of simulated user updates the agenda and the current goal based on the changes of the dialog states.

In this study, we build a simulated user similar to (Schatzmann et al., 2007) in which the simulated user keeps a list of its goals and another agenda of actions to complete the goals. In our restaurant selection domain, the users' tasks are to find a desired restaurant based on several constraints specified by the task scenarios. We consider these restaurant constraints as the goals for the simulated user. At the beginning of the dialog, the simulated user randomly generates an agenda for the list of the ordered goals corresponding to the three constraints in requesting a restaurant. An agenda contains multiple ordered items, each of which consists of the number of constraints and the specific constraints to be included in each user utterance. During the dialog, the simulated user updates its list of goals by removing the constraints that have been understood by the system. It also removes from its agenda the unnecessary actions that are related to the already filled goals while adding new actions. New actions are added according to the last system's question (such as requesting the user to repeat the last utterance) as well as the simulated user's current goals. The actions that address the last system's question are given higher priorities then other actions in the agenda. For example, if the dialog system fails to understand the last user utterance and thus requests a clarification, the simulated user will satisfy the system's request before moving on to discuss a new constraint. The simulated user updated the agenda with the new actions after each user turn.

The current simulated user interacts with the system on the word level. It generates a string of words by instantiating its current action using predefined templates derived from previously collected corpora with real users. Random lexical errors are added to simulate a spoken language understanding performance with a word error rate of 15% and a semantic error rate of 11% based on previous experience (Weng et al., 2006).

3 System and Corpus

CHAT (Conversational Helper for Automotive Tasks) is a spoken dialog system that supports navigation, restaurant selection and mp3 player applications. The system is specifically designed for users to interact with devices and receive services while performing other cognitive demanding, or primary tasks such as driving (Weng et al., 2007). CHAT deploys a combination of off-the-shelf components, components used in previous language applications, and components specifically developed as part of this project. The core components of the system include a statistical language understanding (SLU) module with multiple understanding strategies for imperfect input, an information-state-update dialog manager (DM) that handles multiple dialog threads and mixed initiatives (Mirkovic and Cavedon, 2005), a knowledge manager (KM) that controls access to ontology-based domain knowledge, and a content optimizer that connects the DM and the KM for resolving ambiguities from the users' requests, regulating the amount of information to be presented to the user, as well as providing recommendations to users. In addition, we use Nuance 8.5[1] with dynamic grammars and classbased n-grams, for speech recognition, and Nuance Vocalizer 3.0 for text-to-speech synthesis (TTS). However, the two speech components, i.e., the recognizer and TTS are not used in the version of the system that interacts with the simulated users.

The CHAT system was tested for the navigation domain, the restaurant selection and the MP3 music player. In this study, we focus on the dialog corpus collected on the restaurant domain only. A small number of human users were used as dry-run tests for the system development from November, 2005 to January, 2006. We group the adjacent dry-runs to represent system improvement stages on a weekly basis. Table 1 shows the improvement stages, the dry-run dates which each stage includes, and the number of subjects tested in each stage. A final evaluation was conducted during January 19-31, 2006, without any further system modifications. This final evaluation involved 20 paid subjects who were recruited via internet advertisement.

Only the users in the final evaluation completed user satisfaction surveys after interacting with the system. In the survey, users were asked to rate the conversation from 6 perspectives, each on a 5-point scale: whether the system was easy to use, whether the system understood the user well, whether the interaction pattern was natural, whether the system's actions were appropriate, whether the system acted as expected, and whether the user was willing to use the system on a regular base. A user satisfaction score was computed as the average of the 6 ratings.

Stage	Dry-run Dates	Users
1	11/21/05, 11/22/05	2
2	11/30/05, 12/1/05, 12/2/05	3
3	12/7/05, 12/8/05	2
4	12/13/05, 12/14/05, 12/15/05	5
5	12/19/05, 12/20/05, 12/21/05	4
6	12/27/05, 12/28/05	2
7	1/4/06, 1/5/06	2
8	1/10/06, 1/11/06, 1/13/06	4
9	1/16/06, 1/17/06	3

Table 1: Dry-runs

Nine tasks of restaurant selections were used in both dry-runs and the final evaluation using 12 constraints in total (e.g., cuisine type, price level, location). These 12 constraints are spread across the nine tasks evenly with three constraints per task. In addition, each task is carefully worded based on the task-constrained and language-unconstrained guideline. In other words, we want the users to form an intended mental context while trying to prevent them from copying the exact phrasing in the task description. During the dry-runs, the users randomly pick three to four tasks to

[1] See http://www.nuance.com for details.

Utterances	Constraints Understood by the System	Action Types & Understanding Status
User1: I'm looking for a five star Thai [Italian] restaurant accept credit cards		Action: req_info Slots conveyed: 3 slots
System1: There are 7 restaurants that have a five star rating, accept credit cards, and serve Thai food in my database. Here are the first few: TeJUS, Slam Corner Cate, Setha's Restaurant. Should I continue?	service level=five star cuisine type=Thai payment type=credit card	Action: pro_info Slots accepted: 3 slots Completely matched: 2 slots
User2: I need to look for Italian restaurant		Action: rereq_info Slot conveyed: 1 slot
System2: Are you looking for a restaurant that serves Italian food?	service level=five star cuisine type=Italian (unconfirmed) payment type=credit card	Action: exp_confirm Slot updated: 1 slot Completely matched: 2.5 slot
User3: yes		Action: exp_confirm Slot conveyed: 1 slot
System3: I found 38 restaurants that serve Italian food, accept credit cards and have a five star rating, for example, Toto Café ...	service level=five star cuisine type=Italian (confirmed) payment type=credit card	Action: pro_info Slots accepted: 3 slots Completely matched: 3 slots
User4: I'm done.		Action: close_dialog

Table 2: A Sample Dialog with Annotations.

test the system, while in the final evaluation each user is required to complete all of the 9 tasks. As a result of the final evaluation in the restaurant domain with 2500 restaurants, we reached a task completion rate of 94% with a word recognition rate of 85%, and a semantic accuracy rate of 89%.

4 Evaluation Measures

In this section, we describe in detail the evaluation measures covering three basic aspects of task-oriented dialog systems: understanding ability, efficiency, and the appropriateness of the system actions.

4.1 Understanding Ability Measures

Human-human dialog is a process to reach mutual understandings between the dialog partners by exchanging information through the dialog. This information exchanging process also takes place in the interaction between users and spoken dialog systems. In a task-oriented conversation, the dialog system's major task is to understand the users' needs in order to provide the right service. In the information-state update framework, the system continuously updates its information-states during the dialog while the users are conveying their requirements. If a misunderstanding occurs, there would be a mismatch between the users' requirements and the system's understandings. Thus, the error recovery dialog is needed to fix the mismatches. The error recovery dialog can be initiated either by the system by asking the user to rephrase or to repeat the previous utterance, or by the user to restate the previous request.

We use the percent of agreement between the system's and the user's understandings (**understandingAgreement**) to measure how well the system understands the user. The computation of this measure is illustrated through the example dialog in Table 2. In this table, the first column shows the system utterances and the user utterances received by the system. The correct words are shown in square brackets immediately after the misunderstood words (E.g., in Utterance "User1"). The second column represents semantic content from the users' utterances in the form of constraint-value pairs based on the system's understandings. This information can be automatically retrieved from the system logs. The third column includes the action types of the current system/user utterances. Since the dialog manager is an information-updating dialog manager that manages information in the format of slots, this column also shows the number of slots that are exchanged in the utterance and the number of matched slots. In our task domain, the user can request information (**req_info**), request the same information again (**rereq_info**), answer an explicit confirmation (**exp_confirm**), and close a dialog (**close_dialog**). The system can provide information (**pro_info**) or explicitly confirms (**exp_confirm**) the information. Another available system action that is not shown in this example is to ask the user to repeat/rephrase (**rephrase**), where the user can respond by providing the information again (**repro_info**).

In our experiment, we measure the understandings between the users and the system by comparing the values of the constraints that are specified by the users with their values understood by the system. In this dialog, the user specified all constraints in the first utterance:

Service level = Five star
Cuisine type = Italian
Payment type = Credit card

The first system utterance shows that the system understood two constraints but misunderstood the cuisine type, thus the percent agreement of mutual understandings is 2/3 at this time. Then, the user restated the cuisine type and the second system utterance confirmed this information. Since the system only asks for explicit information when its confidence is low, we count the system's understanding on the cuisine type as a 50% match with the user's. Therefore, the total percent agreement is 2.5/3. The user then confirmed that the system had correctly understood all constraints. Therefore, the system provided the restaurant information in the last utterance. The system's understanding matches 100% with the user's at this point.

The percent agreement of system/user understandings over the entire dialog is calculated by averaging the percent agreement after each turn. In this example, understandingAgreement is (2/3 + 2.5/3 + 1)/3 =83.3%. We hypothesize that the higher the understandingAgreement is, the better the system performs, and thus the more the user is satisfied. The matches of understandings can be calculated automatically from the user simulation and the system logs. However, since we work with human users' dialogs in the first part of this study, we manually annotated the semantic contents (e.g., cuisine name) in the real user corpus.

Previous studies (E.g., Walker et al., 1997) use a corpus level semantic accuracy measure (**semanticAccuracy**) to capture the system's understanding ability. SemanticAccuracy is defined in the standard way as the total number of correctly understood constraints divided by the total number of constraints mentioned in the entire dialog. The understandingAgreement measure we introduce here is essentially the averaged per-sentence semantic accuracy, which emphasizes the utterance level perception rather than a single corpus level average. The intuition behind this new measure is that it is better for the system to always understand something to keep a conversation going than for the system to understand really well sometimes but really bad at other times. We compute both measures in our experiments for comparison.

4.2 Efficiency Measure

Efficiency is another important measure of the system performance. A standard efficiency measure is the number of dialog turns. However, we would like to take into account the user's dialog strategy because how the user specifies the restaurant selection constraints has a certain impact on the dialog pace. Comparing two situations where one user specifies the three constraints of selecting a restaurant in three separate utterances, while another user specifies all the constraints in one utterance, we will find that the total number of dialog turns in the second situation is smaller assuming perfect understandings. Thus, we propose to use the ratio between the number of turns in the perfect understanding situation and the number of turns in practice (**efficiencyRatio**) to measure the system efficiency. The larger the efficiencyRatio is, the closer the actual number of turns is to the perfect understanding situation. In the example in Table 2, because the user chose to specify all the constraints in one utterance, the dialog length would be 2 turns in perfect understanding situation (excluding the last user turn which is always "I'm done"). However, the actual dialog length is 6 turns. Thus, the efficiencyRatio is 2/6.

Since our task scenarios always contain three constraints, we can calculate the length of the error-free dialogs based on the user's strategy. When the user specifies all constraints in the first utterance, the ideal dialog will have only 2 turns; when the user specifies two constraints in one utterance and the other constraints in a separate utterance, the ideal dialog will have 4 turns; when the user specifies all constraints one by one, the ideal dialog will have 6 turns. Thus, in the simulation environment, the length of the ideal dialog can be calculated from the simulated users' agenda. Then, the efficiencyRatio can be calculated automatically. We manually computed this measure for the real users' dialogs.

Similarly, in order to compare with previous studies, we also investigate the total number of dialog turns (**dialogTurns**) proposed as the efficiency measure (E.g., Möller et al., 2007).

4.3 Action Appropriateness Measure

This measure aims to evaluate the appropriateness of the system actions. The definition of appropriateness can vary on different tasks and different system design requirements. For example, some systems always ask users to explicitly confirm their utterances due to high security needs. In this case, an explicit confirmation after each user utterance is an appropriate system action. However, in other cases, frequent explicit confirmations may be considered as inappropriate because they may irritate the users. In our task domain, we define the only inappropriate system action to be providing information based on misunderstood user requirements. In this situation, the system is not aware of its misunderstanding error. Instead of conducting an appropriate error-recovering dialog, the system provides wrong information to the user which we hypothesize will decrease the user's satisfaction.

We use the percentage of appropriate system actions out of the total number of system actions (**percentAppropriate**) to measure the appropriateness of system actions. In the example in Table 2, only the first system action is inappropriate in all 3 system actions. Thus, the percent system action appropriateness is 2/3. Since we can detect the system's misunderstanding and the system's action in the simulated dialog environment, this measure can be calculated automatically for the simulated dialogs. For the real user corpus, we manually coded the inappropriate system utterances.

Note that the definition of appropriate action we use here is fairly loose. This is partly due to the simplicity of our task domain and the limited possible system/user actions. Nevertheless, there is also an advantage of the loose definition: we do not bias towards one particular dialog strategy since our goal here is to find some general and easily measurable system performance factors that are correlated with the user satisfaction.

5 Investigating Evaluation Measures on the Real User Corpus

In this section, we first validate the proposed measures using real users' satisfaction scores, and then show the differentiating power of these measures through the improvement curves plotted on the dry-run data.

5.1 Validating Evaluation Measures

To validate the evaluation measures introduced in Section 4, we use Pearson's correlation to examine how well these evaluation measures can predict the user satisfaction scores. Here, we only look at the dialog corpus in final evaluation because only these users filled out the user satisfaction surveys. For each user, we compute the average value of the evaluation measures across all dialogs generated by that user.

Evaluation Measure	Correlation	P-value
understandingAgreement	0.354	0.05
semanticAccuracy	*0.304*	*0.08*
efficiencyRatio	0.406	0.02
dialogTurns	*-0.321*	*0.05*
percentAppropriate	0.454	0.01

Table3: Correlations with User Satisfaction Scores.

Table 3 lists the correlation between the evaluation measures and the user satisfaction scores, as well as the p-value for each correlation. The correlation describes a linear relationship between these measures and the user satisfaction scores. For the measures that describe the system's understanding abilities and the measures that describe the system's efficiency, our newly proposed measures show higher correlations with the user satisfaction scores than their counterparts. Therefore, in the rest of the study, we drop the two measures used by the previous studies, i.e., semanticAccuracy and dialogTurns.

We observe that the user satisfaction scores are significantly positively correlated with all the three proposed measures. These correlations confirms our expectations: user satisfaction is higher when the system's understanding matches better with the users' requirements; when the dialog efficiency is closer to the situation of perfect understanding; or when the system's actions are mostly appropriate. We suggest that these measures can serve as indicators for user satisfaction.

We further use all the measures to build a regression model to predict the user satisfaction score. The prediction model is:

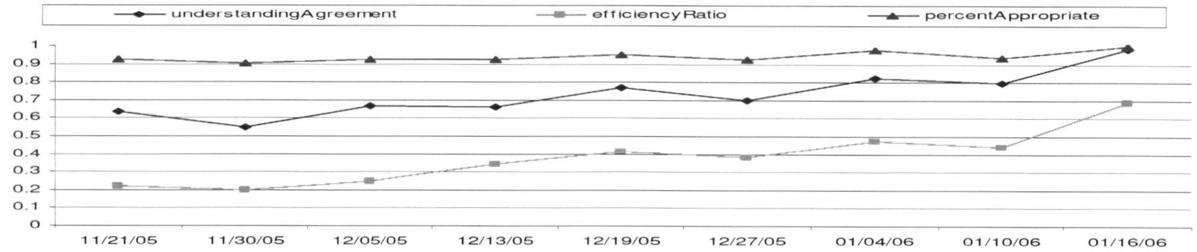

Figure 1: The Improvement Curves on Dry-run Data

User Satisfaction
= 6.123*percentAppropriate
+2.854*efficiencyRatio --- (1)
+0.864*understandingAgreement - 4.67

The R-square is 0.655, which indicates that 65.5% of the user satisfaction scores can be explained by this model. While this prediction model has much room for improvement, we suggest that it can be used to estimate the users' satisfaction scores for simulated users in the early system testing stage to quickly assess the system's performance. Since the weights are tuned based on the data from this specific application, the prediction model may not be used directly for other domains.

5.2 Assessing the Differentiating Power of the Evaluation Measures

Since this set of evaluation measures intends to evaluate the system's performance in the development stage, we would like the measures to be able to reflect small changes made in the system and to indicate whether these changes show the right trend of increased user satisfaction in reality. A set of good evaluation measures should be sensible to subtle system changes.

We assess the differentiating power of the evaluation measures using the dialog corpus collected during the dry-runs. The system was tested on a weekly basis as explained in Table 1. For each improvement stage, we compute the values for the three evaluation measures averaging across all dialogs from all users. Figure 1 shows the three improvement curves based on these three measures. The x-axis shows the first date of each improvement stage; the y-axis shows the value of the evaluation measures. We observe that all three curves show the right trends that indicate the system's improvements over the development stages.

6 Applying the Evaluation Measures on the Simulated Corpus

We train a goal and agenda driven user simulation model from the final evaluation dialog corpus with the real users. The simulation model interacts with the dialog system 20 times (each time the simulation model represents a different simulated user), generating nine dialogs on all of the nine tasks each time. In each interaction, the simulated users generate their agenda randomly based on a uniform distribution. The simulated corpus consists of 180 dialogs from 20 simulated users, which is of the same size as the real user corpus. The values of the evaluation measures are computed automatically at the end of each simulated dialog.

We compute the estimated user satisfaction score using Equation 1 for each simulated user. We then compare the user satisfaction scores of the 20 simulated users with the satisfaction scores of the 20 real users. The average and the standard deviation of the user satisfaction scores for real users are (3.79, 0.72), and the ones for simulated users are (3.77, 1.34). Using two-tailed t-test at significance level $p<0.05$, we observe that there are no statistically significant differences between the two pools of scores. Therefore, we suggest that the user satisfaction estimated from the simulated dialog corpus can be used to assess the system performance. However, these average scores only offer us one perspective in comparing the real with the simulated user satisfaction. In the future, we would like to look further into the differences between the distributions of these user satisfaction scores.

7 Conclusions and Future Work

User simulation has been increasingly used in generating large corpora for using machine learning techniques to automate dialog system design. However, user simulation has not been used much in testing dialog systems. There are two major concerns: 1. we are not sure how well the state-of-the-art user simulation can mimic realistic user behaviors; 2. we do not get important feedback on user satisfaction when replacing human users with simulated users. In this study, we suggest that while the simulated users might not be mature to use in the final system evaluation stage, they can be used in the early testing stages of the system development cycle to make sure that the system is functioning in the desired way. We further propose a set of evaluation measures that can be extracted from the simulation logs to assess the system performance. We validate these evaluation measures on human user dialogs and examine the differentiating power of these measures. We suggest that these measures can be used to guide the development of the system towards improving user satisfaction. We also apply the evaluation measures on a simulation corpus trained from the real user dialogs. We show that the user satisfaction scores estimated on the simulated dialogs do not significantly differ statistically from the real users' satisfaction scores. Therefore, we suggest that the estimated user satisfaction can be used to assess the system performance while testing with simulated users.

In the future, we would like to confirm our proposed evaluation measures by testing them on dialog systems that allows more complicated dialog structures and systems on other domains.

Acknowledgments

The authors would like to thank Zhongchao Fei, Zhe Feng, Junkuo Cao, and Baoshi Yan for their help during the simulation system development and the three anonymous reviewers for their insightful suggestions. All the remaining errors are ours.

References

H. Ai, J. Tetreault, and D. Litman. 2007. *Comparing User Simulation Models for Dialog Strategy Learning*. In Proc. NAACL-HLT (short paper session).

G. Chung. 2004. *Developing a Flexible Spoken Dialog System Using Simulation*. In Proc. of ACL 04.

W. Eckert, E. Levin, and R. Pieraccini. 1997. *User Modeling for Spoken Dialogue System Evaluation*. In Proc. of IEEE workshop on ASRU.

E. Filisko and S. Seneff. 2006. *Learning Decision Models in Spoken Dialogue Systems Via User Simulation.* In Proc. of AAAI Workshop on Statistical and Empirical Approaches for Spoken Dialogue Systems.

J. Henderson, O. Lemon, and K. Georgila. 2005. *Hybrid Reinforcement/Supervised Learning for Dialogue Policies from COMMUNICATOR data.* In IJCAI workshop on Knowledge and Reasoning in Practical Dialogue Systems.

E. Levin, R. Pieraccini, and W. Eckert. 2000. *A Stochastic Model of Human-Machine Interaction For learning Dialogue Strategies.* IEEE Trans. On Speech and Audio Processing, 8(1):11-23.

R. López-Cózar, A. De la Torre, J. C. Segura and A. J. Rubio. (2003). *Assessment of dialogue systems by means of a new simulation technique*. Speech Communication (40): 387-407.

D. Mirkovic and L. Cavedon. 2005. *Practical multi-domain, multi-device dialogue management,* PACLING'05: 6th Meeting of the Pacific Association for Computational Linguistics.

Sebastian Möller, Jan Krebber and Paula Smeele. 2006. *Evaluating the speech output component of a smart-home system*. Speech Communication (48): 1-27.

O. Pietquin, O. 2004. *A Framework for Unsupervised Learning of Dialog Strategies*. Ph.D. diss., Faculte Polytechnique de Mons.

K. Scheffler. 2002. *Automatic Design of Spoken Dialog Systems*. Ph.D. diss., Cambridge University.

S. Singh, D. Litman, M. Kearns, and M. Walker. 2002. *Optimizing DialogueManagement with Reinforcement Learning: Experiments with the NJFun System.* Journal of Artificial Intelligence Research (JAIR), vol. 16.

J. Schatzmann, B. Thomson, K. Weilhammer, H. Ye, and Young. S. 2007. *Agenda-Based User Simulation for Bootstrapping a POMDP Dialogue System.* In Proc. of NAACL-HLT (short paper session).

F. Weng, S. Varges, B. Raghunathan, F. Ratiu, H. Pon-Barry, B. Lathrop, Q. Zhang, H. Bratt, T. Scheideck, R. Mishra, K. Xu, M. Purvey, A. Lien, M. Raya, S. Peters, Y. Meng, J. Russell, L. Cavedon, E. Shriberg, and H. Schmidt. 2006. *CHAT: A Conversational Helper for Automotive Tasks.* In Proc. of Interspeech.

F. Weng, B. Yan, Z. Feng, F. Ratiu, M. Raya, B. Lathrop, A. Lien, S. Varges, R. Mishra, F. Lin, M. Purver, H. Bratt, Y. Meng, S. Peters, T. Scheideck, B. Raghunathan and Z. Zhang. 2007. *CHAT to your destination.* In Proc. Of 8th SIGdial workshop on Discourse and Dialogue.

J. Williams and S. Young. 2006. *Partially Observable Markov Decision Processes for Spoken Dialog Systems*. Computer Speech and Language.

M. Walker, D. Litman, C. Kamm, and A. Abella. 1997. *PARADISE: A Framework for Evaluating Spoken Dialogue Agents*. In Proceedings of the 35th ACL.

An Evaluation Understudy for Dialogue Coherence Models

Sudeep Gandhe and **David Traum**
Institute for Creative Technologies
University of Southern California
13274 Fiji way, Marina del Rey, CA, 90292
{gandhe,traum}@ict.usc.edu

Abstract

Evaluating a dialogue system is seen as a major challenge within the dialogue research community. Due to the very nature of the task, most of the evaluation methods need a substantial amount of human involvement. Following the tradition in machine translation, summarization and discourse coherence modeling, we introduce the the idea of evaluation understudy for dialogue coherence models. Following (Lapata, 2006), we use the information ordering task as a testbed for evaluating dialogue coherence models. This paper reports findings about the reliability of the information ordering task as applied to dialogues. We find that simple n-gram co-occurrence statistics similar in spirit to BLEU (Papineni et al., 2001) correlate very well with human judgments for dialogue coherence.

1 Introduction

In computer science or any other research field, simply building a system that accomplishes a certain goal is not enough. It needs to be thoroughly evaluated. One might want to evaluate the system just to see to what degree the goal is being accomplished or to compare two or more systems with one another. Evaluation can also lead to understanding the shortcomings of the system and the reasons for these. Finally the evaluation results can be used as feedback in improving the system.

The best way to evaluate a novel algorithm or a model for a system that is designed to aid humans in processing natural language would be to employ it in a real system and allow users to interact with it. The data collected by this process can then be used for evaluation. Sometimes this data needs further analysis - which may include annotations, collecting subjective judgments from humans, etc. Since human judgments tend to vary, we may need to employ multiple judges. These are some of the reasons why evaluation is time consuming, costly and sometimes prohibitively expensive.

Furthermore, if the system being developed contains a machine learning component, the problem of costly evaluation becomes even more serious. Machine learning components often optimize certain free parameters by using evaluation results on held-out data or by using n-fold cross-validation. Evaluation results can also help with feature selection. This need for repeated evaluation can forbid the use of data-driven machine learning components.

For these reasons, using an automatic evaluation measure as an understudy is quickly becoming a common practice in natural language processing tasks. The general idea is to find an automatic evaluation metric that correlates very well with human judgments. This allows developers to use the automatic metric as a stand-in for human evaluation. Although it cannot replace the finesse of human evaluation, it can provide a crude idea of progress which can later be validated. e.g. BLEU (Papineni et al., 2001) for machine translation, ROUGE (Lin, 2004) for summarization.

Recently, the discourse coherence modeling community has started using the information ordering task as a testbed to test their discourse coherence models (Barzilay and Lapata, 2005; Soricut and Marcu, 2006). Lapata (2006) has proposed an au-

Proceedings of the 9th SIGdial Workshop on Discourse and Dialogue, pages 172–181,
Columbus, June 2008.

tomatic evaluation measure for the information ordering task. We propose to use the same task as a testbed for dialogue coherence modeling. We evaluate the reliability of the information ordering task as applied to dialogues and propose an evaluation understudy for dialogue coherence models.

In the next section, we look at related work in evaluation of dialogue systems. Section 3 summarizes the information ordering task and Lapata's (2006) findings. It is followed by the details of the experiments we carried out and our observations. We conclude with a summary future work directions.

2 Related Work

Most of the work on evaluating dialogue systems focuses on human-machine communication geared towards a specific task. A variety of evaluation metrics can be reported for such task-oriented dialogue systems. Dialogue systems can be judged based on the performance of their components like WER for ASR (Jurafsky and Martin, 2000), concept error rate or F-scores for NLU, understandability for speech synthesis etc. Usually the core component, the dialogue model - which is responsible for keeping track of the dialogue progression and coming up with an appropriate response, is evaluated indirectly. Different dialogue models can be compared with each other by keeping the rest of components fixed and then by comparing the dialogue systems as a whole. Dialogue systems can report subjective measures such as user satisfaction scores and perceived task completion. SASSI (Hone and Graham, 2000) prescribes a set of questions used for eliciting such subjective assessments. The objective evaluation metrics can include dialogue efficiency and quality measures.

PARADISE (Walker et al., 2000) was an attempt at reducing the human involvement in evaluation. It builds a predictive model for user satisfaction as a linear combination of some objective measures and perceived task completion. Even then the system needs to train on the data gathered from user surveys and objective features retrieved from logs of dialogue runs. It still needs to run the actual dialogue system and collect objective features and perceived task completeion to predict user satisfaction.

Other efforts in saving human involvement in evaluation include using simulated users for testing (Eckert et al., 1997). This has become a popular tool for systems employing reinforcement learning (Levin et al., 1997; Williams and Young, 2006). Some of the methods involved in user simulation are as complex as building dialogue systems themselves (Schatzmann et al., 2007). User simulations also need to be evaluated as how closely they model human behavior (Georgila et al., 2006) or as how good a predictor they are of dialogue system performance (Williams, 2007).

Some researchers have proposed metrics for evaluating a dialogue model in a task-oriented system. (Henderson et al., 2005) used the number of slots in a frame filled and/or confirmed. Roque et al. (2006) proposed hand-annotating information-states in a dialogue to evaluate the accuracy of information state updates. Such measures make assumptions about the underlying dialogue model being used (e.g., form-based or information-state based etc.).

We are more interested in evaluating types of dialogue systems that do not follow these task-based assumptions: systems designed to imitate human-human conversations. Such dialogue systems can range from chatbots like Alice (Wallace, 2003), Eliza (Weizenbaum, 1966) to virtual humans used in simulation training (Traum et al., 2005). For such systems, the notion of task completion or efficiency is not well defined and task specific objective measures are hardly suitable. Most evaluations report the subjective evaluations for appropriateness of responses. Traum et. al. (2004) propose a coding scheme for response appropriateness and scoring functions for those categories. Gandhe et. al. (2006) propose a scale for subjective assessment for appropriateness.

3 Information Ordering

The information ordering task consists of choosing a presentation sequence for a set of information bearing elements. This task is well suited for text-to-text generation like in single or multi-document summarization (Barzilay et al., 2002). Recently there has been a lot of work in discourse coherence modeling (Lapata, 2003; Barzilay and Lapata, 2005; Soricut and Marcu, 2006) that has used information ordering to test the coherence models. The information-bearing elements here are sentences rather than high-level concepts. This frees the models from having to depend on a hard to get training corpus which has been hand-authored for concepts.

Most of the dialogue models still work at the higher abstraction level of dialogue acts and intentions. But with an increasing number of dialogue systems finding use in non-traditional applications such as simulation training, games, etc.; there is a need for dialogue models which do not depend on hand-authored corpora or rules. Recently Gandhe and Traum (2007) proposed dialogue models that do not need annotations for dialogue-acts, semantics and hand-authored rules for information state updates or finite state machines.

Such dialogue models focus primarily on generating an appropriate coherent response given the dialogue history. In certain cases the generation of a response can be reduced to selection from a set of available responses. For such dialogue models, maintaining the information state can be considered as a secondary goal. The element that is common to the information ordering task and the task of selecting next most appropriate response is the ability to express a preference for one sequence of dialogue turns over the other. We propose to use the information ordering task to test dialogue coherence models. Here the information bearing units will be dialogue turns.[1]

There are certain advantages offered by using information ordering as a task to evaluate dialogue coherence models. First the task does not require a dialogue model to take part in conversations in an interactive manner. This obviates the need for having real users engaging in the dialogue with the system. Secondly, the task is agnostic about the underlying dialogue model. It can be a data-driven statistical model or information-state based, form based or even a reinforcement learning system based on MDP or POMDP. Third, there are simple objective measures available to evaluate the success of information ordering task.

Recently, Purandare and Litman (2008) have used this task for modeling dialogue coherence. But they only allow for a binary classification of sequences as either coherent or incoherent. For comparing different dialogue coherence models, we need the ability for finer distinction between sequences of information being put together. Lapata (2003) proposed Kendall's τ, a rank correlation measure, as one such candidate. In a recent study they show that Kendall's τ correlates well with human judgment (Lapata, 2006). They show that human judges can reliably provide coherence ratings for various permutations of text. (Pearson's correlation for inter-rater agreement is 0.56) and that Kendall's τ is a good indicator for human judgment (Pearson's correlation for Kendall's τ with human judgment is 0.45 ($p < 0.01$)).

Before adapting the information ordering task for dialogues, certain questions need to be answered. We need to validate that humans can reliably perform the task of information ordering and can judge the coherence for different sequences of dialogue turns. We also need to find which objective measures (like Kendall's τ) correlate well with human judgments.

4 Evaluating Information Ordering

One of the advantages of using information ordering as a testbed is that there are objective measures available to evaluate the performance of information ordering task. Kendall's τ (Kendall, 1938), a rank correlation coefficient, is one such measure. Given a reference sequence of length n, Kendall's τ for an observed sequence can be defined as,

$$\tau = \frac{\text{\# concordant pairs} - \text{\# discordant pairs}}{\text{\# total pairs}}$$

Each pair of elements in the observed sequence is marked either as concordant - appearing in the same order as in reference sequence or as discordant otherwise. The total number of pairs is $C_2^n = n(n-1)/2$. τ ranges from -1 to 1.

Another possible measure can be defined as the fraction of n-grams from reference sequence, that are preserved in the observed sequence.

$$b_n = \frac{\text{\# n-grams preserved}}{\text{\# total n-grams}}$$

In this study we have used, b_2, fraction of bigrams and b_3, fraction of trigrams preserved from the reference sequence. These values range from 0 to 1. Table 1 gives examples of observed sequences and

[1] These can also be at the utterance level, but for this paper we will use dialogue turns.

Observed Sequence	b_2	b_3	τ
[0, 1, 2, 3, 4, 5, 6, 7, 8, 9]	1.00	1.00	1.00
[8, 9, 0, 1, 2, 3, 4, 5, 6, 7]	0.89	0.75	0.29
[4, 1, 0, 3, 2, 5, 8, 7, 6, 9]	0.00	0.00	0.60
[6, 9, 8, 5, 4, 7, 0, 3, 2, 1]	0.00	0.00	-0.64
[2, 3, 0, 1, 4, 5, 8, 9, 6, 7]	0.56	0.00	0.64

Table 1: Examples of observed sequences and their respective b_2, b_3 & τ values. Here the reference sequence is [0,1,2,3,4,5,6,7,8,9].

respective b_2, b_3 and τ values. Notice how τ allows for long-distance relationships whereas b_2, b_3 are sensitive to local features only. [2]

5 Experimental Setup

For our experiments we used segments drawn from 9 dialogues. These dialogues were two-party human-human dialogues. To ensure applicability of our results over different types of dialogue, we chose these 9 dialogues from different sources. Three of these were excerpts from role-play dialogues involving negotiations which were originally collected for a simulation training scenario (Traum et al., 2005). Three are from SRI's Amex Travel Agent data which are task-oriented dialogues about air travel planning (Bratt et al., 1995). The rest of the dialogues are scripts from popular television shows. Fig 6 shows an example from the air-travel domain. Each excerpt drawn was 10 turns long with turns strictly alternating between the two speakers.

Following the experimental design of (Lapata, 2006) we created random permutations for these dialogue segments. We constrained our permutations so that the permutations always start with the same speaker as the original dialogue and turns strictly alternate between the speakers. With these constraints there are still $5! \times 5! = 14400$ possible permutations per dialogue. We selected 3 random permutations for each of the 9 dialogues. In all, we have a total of 27 dialogue permutations. They are arranged in 3 sets, each set containing a permutation for all 9 dialogues. We ensured that not all permutations in a given set are particularly very good or very bad. We used Kendall's τ to balance the permutations across the given set as well as across the given dialogue.

Unlike Lapata (2006) who chose to remove the pronouns and discourse connectives, we decided not do any pre-processing on the text like removing disfluencies or removing cohesive devices such as anaphora, ellipsis, discourse connectives, etc. One of the reason is such pre-processing if done manually defeats the purpose of removing humans from the evaluation procedure. Moreover it is very difficult to remove certain cohesive devices such as discourse deixis without affecting the coherence level of the original dialogues.

6 Experiment 1

In our first experiment, we divided a total of 9 human judges among the 3 sets (3 judges per set). Each judge was presented with 9 dialogue permutations. They were asked to assign a single coherence rating for each dialogue permutation. The ratings were on a scale of 1 to 7, with 1 being very incoherent and 7 being perfectly coherent. We did not provide any additional instructions or examples of scale as we wanted to capture the intuitive idea of coherence from our judges. Within each set the dialogue permutations were presented in random order.

We compute the inter-rater agreement by using Pearson's correlation analysis. We correlate the ratings given by each judge with the average ratings given by the judges who were assigned the same set. For inter-rater agreement we report the average of 9 such correlations which is 0.73 (std dev = 0.07). Artstein and Poesio (2008) have argued that Krippendorff's α (Krippendorff, 2004) can be used for inter-rater agreement with interval scales like the one we have. In our case for the three sets α values were 0.49, 0.58, 0.64. These moderate values of alpha indicate that the task of judging coherence is indeed a difficult task, especially when detailed instructions or examples of scales are not given.

In order to assess whether Kendall's τ can be used as an automatic measure of dialogue coherence, we perform a correlation analysis of τ values against the average ratings by human judges. The Pearson's correlation coefficient is 0.35 and it is statistically not significant (P=0.07). Fig 1(a) shows the relationship between coherence judgments and τ values. This experiment fails to support the suitability

[2]For more on the relationship between b_2, b_3 and τ see row 3,4 of table 1 and figure 4.

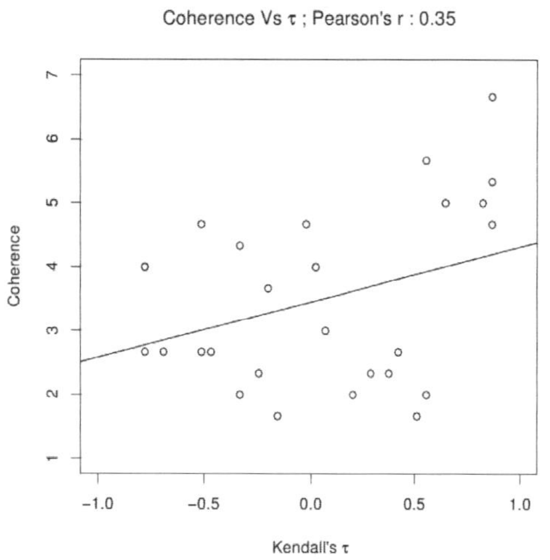

(a) Kendall's τ does not correlate well with human judgments for dialogue coherence.

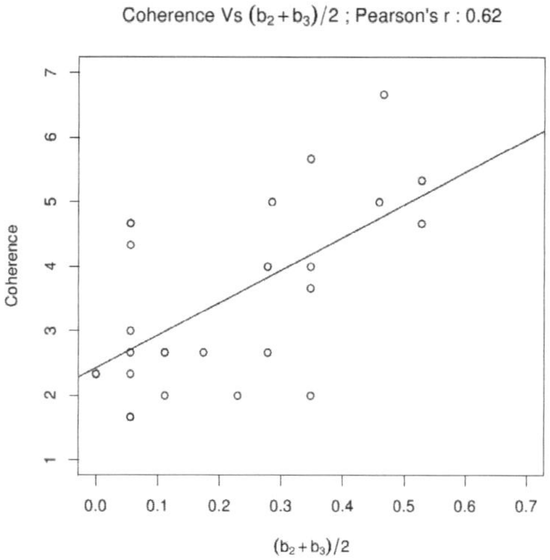

(b) Fraction of bigram & trigram counts correlate well with human judgments for dialogue coherence.

Figure 1: Experiment 1 - single coherence rating per permutation

of Kendall's τ as an evaluation understudy.

We also analyzed the correlation of human judgments against simple n-gram statistics, specifically $(b_2 + b_3)/2$. Fig 1(b) shows the relationship between human judgments and the average of fraction of bigrams and fraction of trigrams that were preserved in the permutation. The Pearson's correlation coefficient is 0.62 and it is statistically significant ($P<0.01$).

7 Experiment 2

Since human judges found it relatively hard to assign a single rating to a dialogue permutation, we decided to repeat experiment 1 with some modifications. In our second experiment we asked the judges to provide coherence ratings at every turn, based on the dialogue that preceded that turn. The dialogue permutations were presented to the judges through a web interface in an incremental fashion turn by turn as they rated each turn for coherence (see Fig 5 in the appendix for the screenshot of this interface). We used a scale from 1 to 5 with 1 being completely incoherent and 5 as perfectly coherent. [3] A total of 11 judges participated in this experiment with the first set being judged by 5 judges and the remaining two sets by 3 judges each.

For the rest of the analysis, we use the average coherence rating from all turns as a coherence rating for the dialogue permutation. We performed the inter-rater agreement analysis as in experiment 1. The average of 11 correlations is 0.83 (std dev = 0.09). Although the correlation has improved, Krippendorff's α values for the three sets are 0.49, 0.35, 0.63. This shows that coherence rating is still a hard task even when judged turn by turn.

We assessed the relationship between the average coherence rating for dialogue permutations with Kendall's τ (see Fig 2(a)). The Pearson's correlation coefficient is 0.33 and is statistically not significant ($P=0.09$).

Fig 2(b) shows high correlation of average coherence ratings with the fraction of bigrams and trigrams that were preserved in permutation. The Pearson's correlation coefficient is 0.75 and is statistically significant ($P<0.01$).

Results of both experiments suggest that, $(b_2 + b_3)/2$ correlates very well with human judgments and can be used for evaluating information ordering when applied to dialogues.

8 Experiment 3

We wanted to know whether information ordering as applied to dialogues is a valid task or not. In this experiment we seek to establish a higher baseline for

[3] We believe this is a less complex task than experiment 1 and hence a narrower scale is used.

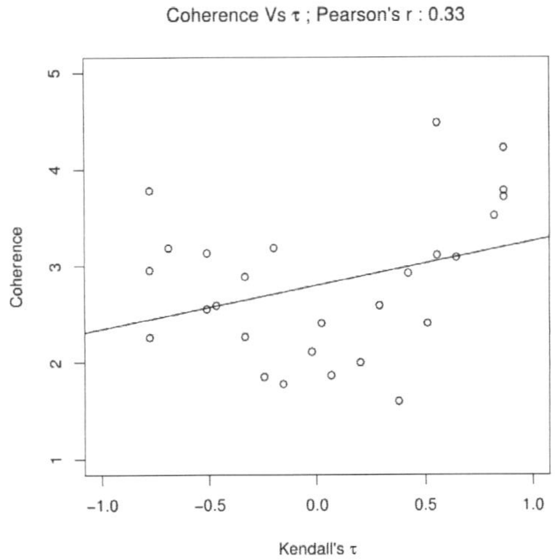

(a) Kendall's τ does not correlate well with human judgments for dialogue coherence.

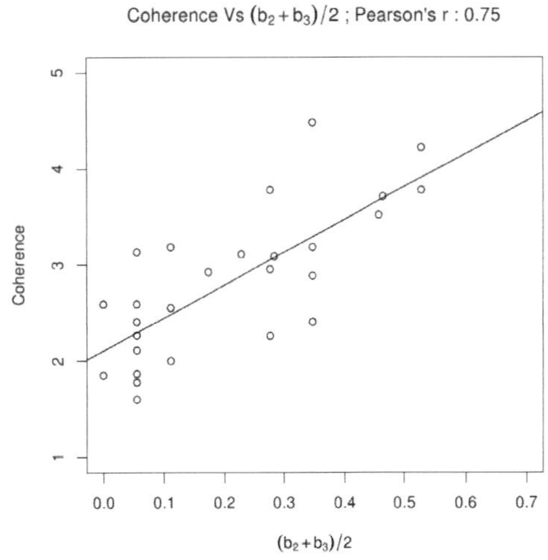

(b) Fraction of bigram & trigram counts correlate well with human judgments for dialogue coherence.

Figure 2: Experiment 2 - turn-by-turn coherence rating

the task of information ordering in dialogues. We presented the dialogue permutations to our human judges and asked them to reorder the turns so that the resulting order is as coherent as possible. All 11 judges who participated in experiment 2 also participated in this experiment. They were presented with a drag and drop interface over the web that allowed them to reorder the dialogue permutations. The reordering was constrained to keep the first speaker of the reordering same as that of the original dialogue and the re-orderings must have strictly alternating turns. We computed the Kendall's τ and fraction of bigrams and trigrams $(b_2 + b_3)/2$ for these re-orderings. There were a total of $11 \times 9 = 99$ reordered dialogue permutations. Fig 3(a) and 3(b) shows the frequency distribution of τ and $(b_2 + b_3)/2$ values respectively.

Humans achieve high values for the reordering task. For Kendall's τ, the mean of the reordered dialogues is 0.82 (std dev = 0.25) and for $(b_2 + b_3)/2$, the mean is 0.71 (std dev = 0.28). These values establish an upper baseline for the information ordering task. These can be compared against the random baseline. For τ random performance is 0.02 [4] and for $(b_2 + b_3)/2$ it is 0.11. [5]

9 Discussion

Results show that $(b_2 + b_3)/2$ correlates well with human judgments for dialogue coherence better than Kendall's τ. τ encodes long distance relationships in orderings where as $(b_2 + b_3)/2$ only looks at local context. Fig 4 shows the relationship between these two measures. Notice that most of the orderings have τ values around zero (i.e. in the middle range for τ), whereas majority of orderings will have a low value for $(b_2 + b_3)/2$. τ seems to overestimate the coherence even in the absence of immediate local coherence (See third entry in table 1). It seems that local context is more important for dialogues than for discourse, which may follow from the fact that dialogues are produced by two speakers who must react to each other, while discourse can be planned by one speaker from the beginning. Traum and Allen (1994) point out that such social obligations to respond and address the contributions of the other should be an important factor in building dialogue systems.

The information ordering paradigm does not take into account the content of the information-bearing items, e.g. the fact that turns like "yes", "I agree",

[4]Theoretically this should be zero. The slight positive bias is the result of the constraints imposed on the re-orderings - like only allowing the permutations that have the correct starting speaker.

[5]This value is calculated by considering all 14400 permutations as equally likely.

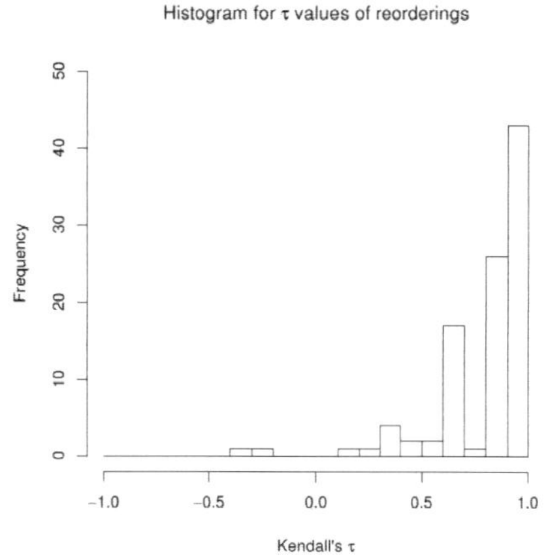

(a) Histogram of Kendall's τ for reordered sequences

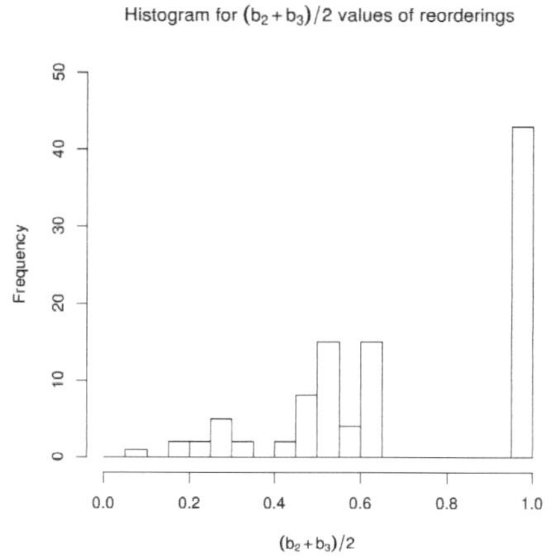

(b) Histogram of fraction of bigrams & trigrams values for reordered sequences

Figure 3: Experiment 3 - upper baseline for information ordering task (human performance)

"okay" perform the same function and should be treated as replaceable. This may suggest a need to modify some of the objective measures to evaluate the information ordering specially for dialogue systems that involve more of such utterances.

Human judges can find the optimal sequences with relatively high frequency, at least for short dialogues. It remains to be seen how this varies with longer dialogue lengths which may contain sub-dialogues that can be arranged independently of each other.

10 Conclusion & Future Work

Evaluating dialogue systems has always been a major challenge in dialogue systems research. The core component of dialogue systems, the dialogue model, has usually been only indirectly evaluated. Such evaluations involve too much human effort and are a bottleneck for the use of data-driven machine learning models for dialogue coherence. The information ordering task, widely used in discourse coherence modeling, can be adopted as a testbed for evaluating dialogue coherence models as well. Here we have shown that simple n-gram statistics that are sensitive to local features correlate well with human judgments for coherence and can be used as an evaluation understudy for dialogue coherence models. As with any evaluation understudy, one must be careful while using it as the correlation with human judgments is not perfect and may be inaccurate in some cases – it can not completely replace the need for full evaluation with human judges in all cases (see (Callison-Burch et al., 2006) for a critique of BLUE along these lines).

In the future, we would like to perform more experiments with larger data sets and different types of dialogues. It will also be interesting to see the role cohesive devices play in coherence ratings. We would like to see if there are any other measures or certain modifications to the current ones that correlate better with human judgments. We also plan to employ this evaluation metric as feedback in building dialogue coherence models as is done in machine translation (Och, 2003).

Acknowledgments

The effort described here has been sponsored by the U.S. Army Research, Development, and Engineering Command (RDECOM). Statements and opinions expressed do not necessarily reflect the position or the policy of the United States Government, and no official endorsement should be inferred. We would like to thank Radu Soricut, Ron Artstein, and the anonymous SIGdial reviewers for helpful comments.

References

Ron Artstein and Massimo Poesio. 2008. Inter-coder agreement for computational linguistics. In *To appear in Computational Linguistics*.

Regina Barzilay and Mirella Lapata. 2005. Modeling local coherence: An entity-based approach. In *Proc. ACL-05*.

Regina Barzilay, Noemie Elhadad, and Kathleen McKeown. 2002. Inferring strategies for sentence ordering in multidocument summarization. *JAIR*, 17:35–55.

Harry Bratt, John Dowding, and Kate Hunicke-Smith. 1995. The sri telephone-based atis system. In *Proceedings of the Spoken Language Systems Technology Workshop*, January.

Chris Callison-Burch, Miles Osborne, and Philipp Koehn. 2006. In *proceedings of EACL-2006*.

Wieland Eckert, Esther Levin, and Roberto Pieraccini. 1997. User modeling for spoken dialogue system evaluation. In *Automatic Speech Recognition and Understanding*, pages 80–87, Dec.

Sudeep Gandhe and David Traum. 2007. Creating spoken dialogue characters from corpora without annotations. In *Proceedings of Interspeech-07*.

Sudeep Gandhe, Andrew Gordon, and David Traum. 2006. Improving question-answering with linking dialogues. In *International Conference on Intelligent User Interfaces (IUI)*, January.

Kalliroi Georgila, James Henderson, and Oliver Lemon. 2006. User simulation for spoken dialogue systems: Learning and evaluation. In *proceedings of Interspeech*.

James Henderson, Oliver Lemon, and Kallirroi Georgila. 2005. Hybrid reinforcement/supervised learning for dialogue policies from communicator data. In *proceedings of IJCAI workshop*.

Kate S. Hone and Robert Graham. 2000. Towards a tool for the subjective assessment of speech system interfaces (SASSI). *Natural Language Engineering: Special Issue on Best Practice in Spoken Dialogue Systems*.

Daniel Jurafsky and James H. Martin. 2000. *SPEECH and LANGUAGE PROCESSING: An Introduction to Natural Language Processing, Computational Linguistics, and Speech Recognition*. Prentice-Hall.

Maurice G. Kendall. 1938. A new measure of rank correlation. *Biometrika*, 30:81–93.

Klaus Krippendorff. 2004. *Content Analysis, An Introduction to Its Methodology 2nd Edition*. Sage Publications.

Mirella Lapata. 2003. Probabilistic text structuring: Experiments with sentence ordering. In *Proceedings of the 41st Annual Meeting of the Association for Computational Linguistics*, Sapporo, Japan.

Mirella Lapata. 2006. Automatic evaluation of information ordering. *Computational Linguistics*, 32(4):471–484.

Esther Levin, Roberto Pieraccini, and Wieland Eckert. 1997. Learning dialogue strategies within the markov decision process framework. In *Automatic Speech Recognition and Understanding*, pages 72–79, Dec.

Chin-Yew Lin. 2004. ROUGE: a package for automatic evaluation of summaries. In *Proceedings of the Workshop on Text Summarization Branches Out*.

Franz Josef Och. 2003. Minimum error rate training for statistical machine translation. In *In ACL 2003: Proc. of the 41st Annual Meeting of the Association for Computational Linguistics*, July.

Kishore A. Papineni, Salim Roukos, Todd Ward, and Wei-Jing Zhu. 2001. BLEU: a method for automatic evaluation of machine translation. In *Technical Report RC22176 (W0109-022), IBM Research Division*, September.

Amruta Purandare and Diane Litman. 2008. Analyzing dialog coherence using transition patterns in lexical and semantic features. In *Proceedings 21st International FLAIRS Conference*, May.

Antonio Roque, Hua Ai, and David Traum. 2006. Evaluation of an information state-based dialogue manager. In *Brandial 2006: The 10th Workshop on the Semantics and Pragmatics of Dialogue*.

Jost Schatzmann, Blaise Thomson, Karl Weilhammer, Hui Ye, and Steve Young. 2007. Agenda-based user simulation for bootstrapping a pomdp dialogue system. In *proceedings of HLT/NAACL*, Rochester, NY.

Radu Soricut and Daniel Marcu. 2006. Discourse generation using utility-trained coherence models. In *Proc. ACL-06*.

David R. Traum and James F. Allen. 1994. Discourse obligations in dialogue processing. In *proceedings of the 32nd Annual Meeting of the Association for Computational Linguistics (ACL-94)*, pages 1–8.

David R. Traum, Susan Robinson, and Jens Stephan. 2004. Evaluation of multi-party virtual reality dialogue interaction. In *In Proceedings of Fourth International Conference on Language Resources and Evaluation (LREC)*, pages 1699–1702.

David Traum, William Swartout, Jonathan Gratch, and Stacy Marsella. 2005. Virtual humans for non-team interaction training. In *AAMAS-05 Workshop on Creating Bonds with Humanoids*, July.

M. Walker, C. Kamm, and D. Litman. 2000. Towards developing general models of usability with PARADISE. *Natural Language Engineering: Special Issue on Best Practice in Spoken Dialogue Systems*.

Richard Wallace. 2003. *Be Your Own Botmaster, 2nd Edition*. ALICE A. I. Foundation.

Joseph Weizenbaum. 1966. Eliza–a computer program for the study of natural language communication between man and machine. *Communications of the ACM*, 9(1):36–45, January.

Jason D. Williams and Steve Young. 2006. Partially observable markov decision processes for spoken dialog systems. *Computer Speech and Language*, 21:393–422.

Jason D. Williams. 2007. A method for evaluating and comparing user simulations: The cramer-von mises divergence. In *IEEE Workshop on Automatic Speech Recognition and Understanding (ASRU)*.

Appendix

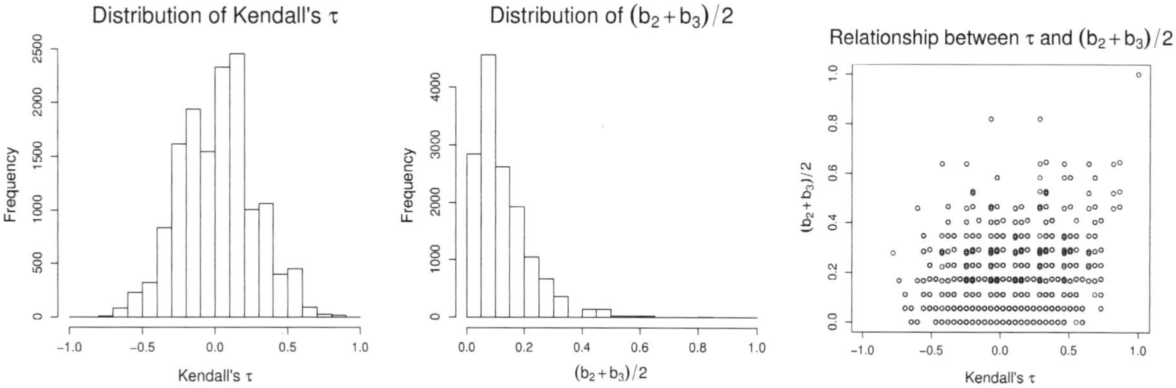

(a) (b) (c)

Figure 4: Distributions for Kendall's τ, $(b_2 + b_3)/2$ and the relationship between them for all possible dialogue permutations with 10 turns and earlier mentioned constraints.

Speaker	Text	Coherence Rating
JACK	Yeah this is Bauer.	
TONY	Jack, this is Tony. You guys are around 10 minutes from the airport?	★★★★☆
JACK	Do everything you have to.	★☆☆☆☆
TONY	No, not yet. We're still working on it. Look- you'll link up with the assault team, they're set outside the emergency room. They're sweeping the ground now, they're starting to lock it down.	★★★☆☆
JACK	Okay, that sounds alright. Tony, contacted Kim yet?	★★★★☆
TONY	No, I haven't. I just called the sheriff's station, they sent out search teams. I just don't understand why she hasn't tried contacted us yet.	★★★★★
JACK	Yeah, that's seems about right. Look- you got a complete tail number on the aircraft yet?	★★☆☆☆
TONY	Believe me; I'm putting every resource we can spare on it.	★★★☆☆
JACK	She knows she can't go back to Los Angeles, and right now the LAPD's looking for her as a murder suspect. She's not gonna reach out to us- do you understand? We've got to find her. We've got to find her.	★★★☆☆
TONY	Okay.	★★★★☆

Figure 5: Screenshot of the interface used for collecting coherence rating for dialogue permutations.

Agent	AAA at American Express may I help you?
User	yeah this is BBB BBB I need to make some travel arrangements
Agent	ok and what do you need to do?
User	ok on June sixth from San Jose to Denver, United
Agent	leaving at what time?
User	I believe there's one leaving at eleven o'clock in the morning
Agent	leaves at eleven a.m. and arrives Denver at two twenty p.m. out of San Jose
User	ok
Agent	yeah that's United flight four seventy
User	that's the one

Doctor	hello i'm doctor perez
	how can i help you
Captain	uh well i'm with uh the local
	i'm i'm the commander of the local company
	and uh i'd like to talk to you about some options you have for relocating your clinic
Doctor	uh we're not uh planning to relocate the clinic captain
	what uh what is this about
Captain	well have you noticed that there's been an awful lot of fighting in the area recently
Doctor	yes yes i have
	we're very busy
	we've had many more casual+ casualties many more patients than than uh usual in the last month
	but uh what what is this about relocating our clinic
	have have uh you been instructed to move us
Captain	no
	but uh we just have some concerns about the increase in fighting xx
Doctor	are you suggesting that we relocate the clinic
	because we had no plans
	we uh we uh we're located here and we've been uh
	we are located where the patients need us
Captain	yeah but
	yeah actually it is a suggestion that you would be a lot safer if you moved away from this area
	we can put you in an area where there's n+ no insurgents
	and we have the area completely under control with our troops
Doctor	i see captain
	is this a is this a suggestion from your commander
Captain	i'm uh the company commander

Figure 6: Examples of the dialogues used to elicit human judgments for coherence

A Framework for Model-based Evaluation of Spoken Dialog Systems

Sebastian Möller
Deutsche Telekom Laboratories
Technische Universität Berlin
10587 Berlin, Germany
sebastian.moeller@telekom.de

Nigel G. Ward
Computer Science Department
University of Texas at El Paso
El Paso, Texas 79968, USA
nigelward@acm.org

Abstract

Improvements in the quality, usability and acceptability of spoken dialog systems can be facilitated by better evaluation methods. To support early and efficient evaluation of dialog systems and their components, this paper presents a tripartite framework describing the evaluation problem. One part models the behavior of user and system during the interaction, the second one the perception and judgment processes taking place inside the user, and the third part models what matters to system designers and service providers. The paper reviews available approaches for some of the model parts, and indicates how anticipated improvements may serve not only developers and users but also researchers working on advanced dialog functions and features.

1 Introduction

Despite the utility of many spoken dialog systems today, the user experience is seldom satisfactory. Improving this is a matter of great intellectual interest and practical importance. However improvements can be difficult to evaluate effectively, and this may be limiting the pace of innovation: today, valid and reliable evaluations still require subjective experiments to be carried out, and these are expensive and time-consuming. Thus, the needs of system developers, of service operators, and of the final users of spoken dialog systems argue for the development of additional evaluation methods.

In this paper we focus on the prospects for an *early* and *model-based* evaluation of dialog systems. Doing evaluation as early as possible in the design and development process is critical for improving quality, reducing costs and fostering innovation. Early evaluation renders the process more efficient and less dependent on experience, hunches and intuitions. With the help of such models predicting the outcome of user tests, the need for subjective testing can be reduced, restricting it to that subset of the possible systems which have already been vetted in an automatic or semi-automatic way.

Several approaches have already been presented for semi-automatic evaluation. For example, the PARADISE framework (Walker et al., 1997) predicts the effects of system changes, quantified in terms of interaction parameters, on an average user judgment. Others (Araki and Doshita, 1997; López-Cózar et al., 2003; Möller et al., 2006) have developed dialog simulations to aid system optimization. However the big picture has been missing: there has been no clear view of how these methods relate to each other, and how they might be improved and joined to support efficient early evaluation.

The remainder of this paper is organized as follows. Section 2 gives a brief review of different evaluation purposes and terminology, and outlines a new tripartite decomposition of the evaluation problem. One part of our framework models the behavior of user and system during the interaction, and describes the impact of system changes on the interaction flow. The second part models the perception and judgment processes taking place inside the user, and tries to predict user ratings on various perceptual dimensions. The third part models what matters to system designers and service providers for

Proceedings of the 9th SIGdial Workshop on Discourse and Dialogue, pages 182–189,
Columbus, June 2008.

a specific application. Sections 3, 4, and 5 go into specifics on the three parts of the framework, discussing which components are already available or conceivable. Finally, Section 6 discusses the potential impact of the approach, and Section 7 lists the issues to be resolved in future work.

2 Performance, Quality, Usability and Acceptability Evaluation

Developers tend to use indices of *performance* to assess their systems. The performance indicates the "ability of a system to provide the function it has been designed for" (Möller, 2005). The function and an appropriate measure for quantifying the degree of fulfillment may easily be determined for certain components — e.g. word accuracy for a speech recognizer or concept error rate for a speech understanding module — but it is harder to specify for other components, such as a dialog manager or an output generation module. However, definitive measures of component quality are not always necessary: what matters for such a module is its contribution to the quality of the entire interaction, as it is perceived by the user.

We follow the definition of the term *quality* as introduced by Jekosch (2000) and now accepted for telephone-based spoken dialog services by the International Telecommunication Union in ITU-T Rec. P.851 (2003): "Result of judgment of the perceived composition of an entity with respect to its desired composition". Quality thus involves a perception process and a judgment process, during which the perceiving person compares the perceptual event with a (typically implicit) reference. It is the comparison with a reference which associates a user-specific value to the perceptual event. The perception and the comparison processes take place in a particular context of use. Thus, both perception and quality should be regarded as "events" which happen in a particular personal, spatial, temporal and functional context.

Usability is one sub-aspect of the quality of the system. Following the definition in ISO 9241 Part 11 (1998), usability is considered as the "extent to which a product can be used by specified users to achieve specified goals with effectiveness, efficiency and satisfaction in a specified context of use". Usability is degraded when interaction problems occur. Such problems influence the perceptual event of the user interacting with the system, and consequently the quality s/he associates with the system as a whole. This may have consequences for the *acceptability* or the system or service, that is, how readily a customer will use the system or service. This can be quantified, for example as the ratio of the potential user population to the size of the target group.

It is the task of any evaluation to quantify aspects of system performance, quality, usability or acceptability. The exact target depends on the purpose of the evaluation (Paek, 2007). For example, the system developer might be most interested in quantifying the performance of the system and its components; s/he might further need to know how the performance affects the quality perceived by the user. In contrast, the service operator might instead be most interested in the acceptability of the service. S/he might further want to know about the satisfaction of the user, influenced by the usability of the system, and also by other (e.g. hedonic) aspects like comfort, joy-of-use, fashion, etc. Different evaluation approaches may be complementary, in the sense that metrics determined for one purpose may be helpful for other purposes as well. Thus, it is useful to describe the components of different evaluation approaches in a single framework.

Figure 1 summarizes our view of the evaluation landscape. At the lower left corner is what we can change (the dialog system), at the right is what the service operator might be interested in (a metric for the value of the system). In between are three components of a model of the processes taking place in the evaluation. The behavior model describes how system and user characteristics determine the flow of the interaction and translate this to quantitative descriptors. The perception and judgment model describes how the interaction influences the perceptual and quality events felt by the user, and translates these to observable user judgments. Finally the value model associates a certain value to the quality judgments, depending on the application. The model properties have been grouped in three layers: aspects of the user and his/her behavior, aspects of the system in its context-of-use, and the work of an external observer (expert) carrying out the evalua-

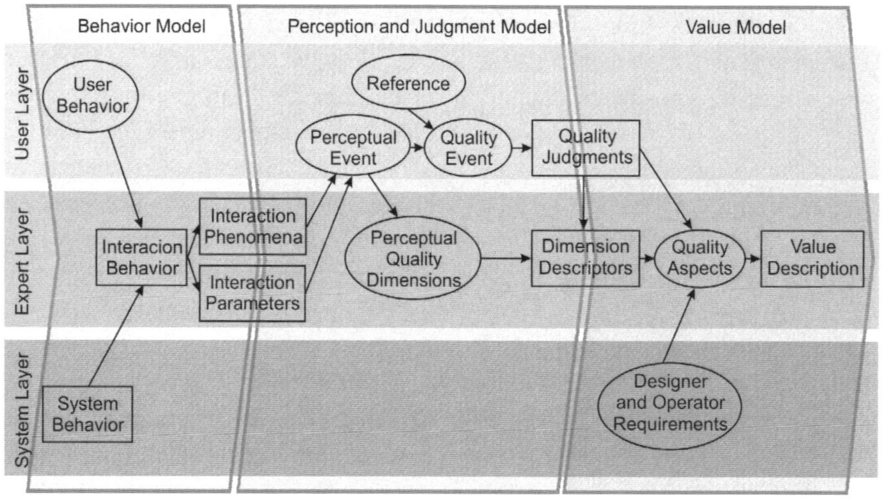

Figure 1: Tripartite view of a model-based evaluation. Observable properties are in boxes, inferred or hidden properties are in ovals. The layers organize the properties as mostly user-related, mostly system-related, and mostly expert-related, and mostly system-related.

tion. They have further been classified as to whether they are observable (boxes) or hidden from the evaluator (ovals).

The next three sections go through the three parts of the model left-to-right, explaining the needs, current status, and prospects.

3 Behavior Model

The behavior model translates the characteristics of the system and the user into predicted interaction behavior. In order to be useful, the representations of this behavior must be concise.

One way to describe dialog behavior is with *interaction parameters* which quantify the behavior of the user and/or the system during the interaction. Such parameters may be measured instrumentally or given by expert annotation. In an attempt to systematize best practice, the ITU-T has proposed a common set of interaction parameters suitable for the evaluation of telephone-based spoken dialog systems in ITU-T Suppl. 24 (2005). These parameters have been developed bottom-up from a collection of evaluation reports over the last 15 years, and include metrics related to dialog and communication in general, meta-communication, cooperativity, task, and speech-input performance (Möller, 2005). Unfortunately, it as is yet unclear which of these parameters relate to quality from a user's point-of-view. In addition, some metrics are missing which address critical aspects for the user, e.g. parameters for the quality and attractiveness of the speech output.

Another manageable way to describe system behavior is to focus on *interaction phenomena*. Several schemes have been developed for classifying such phenomena, such as system errors, user errors, points of confusion, dead time, and so on (Bernsen et al., 1998; Ward et al., 2005; Oulasvirta et al., 2006). Patterns of interaction phenomena may be reflected in interaction parameter values, and may be identified on that basis. Otherwise, they have to be determined by experts and/or users, by means of observation, interviews, thinking-aloud, and other techniques from usability engineering. (Using this terminology we can understand the practice of usability testing as being the identification of interaction phenomena, also known as "usability events" or "critical incidences", and using these to estimate specific quality aspects or the overall value of the system.)

Obtaining the interaction parameters and classifying the interaction phenomena can be done, obviously, from a corpus of user-system interactions. The challenge for early evaluation is to obtain these without actually running user tests. Thus, we would like to have a *system behavior model* and a *user behavior model* to simulate *interaction behavior*, and to map from system parameters and user properties to interaction parameters or phenomena. The value of such models for a developer is clear: they could enable estimation of how a change in the system (e.g. a change in the vocabulary) might affect the interaction properties. In addition to the desired effects, the side-effects of system changes are also important. Predicting such side-effects will substantially decrease the risk and uncertainty involved in dialogue design, thereby decreasing the gap between research and commercial work on dialog system usability (Heisterkamp, 2003; Pieraccini and Huerta, 2005).

Whereas modeling system behavior in response to user input is clearly possible (since in the last resort it is possible to fully implement the system), user behavior can probably not be modeled in closed form, because it unavoidably relates to the intricacies of the user and reflects the time-flow of the interaction. Thus, it seems necessary to employ a simulation of the interaction, as has been proposed by Araki and Doshita (1997) and López-Cózar et al. (2003), among others.

One embodiment of this idea is the MeMo workbench (Möller et al., 2006), which is based on the idea of running models of the system and of the user in a dedicated usability testing workbench. The system model is a description of the possible tasks (system task model) plus a description of the system's interaction behavior (system interaction model). The user model is a description of the tasks a user would want to carry out with the system (user task model) plus a description of the steps s/he would take to reach the goal when faced with the system (user interaction model). Currently the workbench uses simple attribute-value descriptions of tasks the system is able to carry out. From these, user-desired tasks may be derived, given some background knowledge of the domain and possible tasks. The system interaction model is described by a state diagram which models interactions as paths through a number of dialog states. The system designer provides one or several 'intended paths' through the interaction, which lead easily and/or effectively to the task goal.

The user's interaction behavior will strongly depend on the system output in the previous turn. Thus, it is reasonable to build the user interaction model on top of the system interaction model: The user mainly follows the 'intended path', but at certain points deviations from this path are generated in a probabilistic rule-based manner. For example, the user might deviate from the intended path, because s/he does not understand a long system prompt, or because s/he is irritated by a large number of options. Each deviation from the intended path has an associated probability; these are calculated from system characteristics (e.g. prompt length, number of options) and user characteristics (e.g. experience with dialog systems, command of foreign languages, assumed task and domain knowledge).

After the models have been defined, simulations of user-system interactions can be generated. These interactions are logged and annotated on different levels in order to detect interaction problems. Usability predictions are obtained from the (simulated) interaction problems. The simulations can also support reinforcement learning or other methods for automatically determining the best dialog strategy.

Building user interaction models by hand is costly. As an alternative to explicitly defining rules and probabilities, simulations can be based on data sets of actual interactions, augmented with annotations such as indications of the dialog state, current subtask, inferred user state, and interaction phenomena. Annotations can be generated by the dialog participants themselves, e.g. by re-listening after the fact (Ward and Tsukahara, 2003), or by top communicators, decision-makers, trend-setters, experts in linguistics and communication, and the like. Machine learning techniques can help by providing predictions of how users tend to react in various situations from lightly annotated data.

4 Perception and Judgment Model

Once the interaction behavior is determined, the evaluator needs to know about the impact it has on the quality perceived by the user. As pointed out in Section 2, the perception and judgments processes take place in the human user and are thus hidden from the observer. The evaluator may, however, ask the user to describe the *perceptual event* and/or the *quality event*, either qualitatively in an open form or quantitatively on rating scales. Provided that the experiment is properly planned and carried out, user *quality judgments* can be considered as direct quality measurements, reflecting the user's quality perception.

Whereas user judgments on quality will reflect the internal *reference* and thus depend heavily on the specific context and application, it may be assumed that the characteristics of the perceptual event are more universal. For example, it is likely that samples of observers and/or users would generally agree on whether a given system could be characterized as responsive, smooth, or predictable, etc. regardless of what they feel about the importance of each such quality aspect. We may take advantage of this by defining a small set of universal *perceptual quality dimensions*, that together are sufficient for predicting system value from the user's point-of-view.

In order to quantify the quality event and to identify perceptual quality dimensions, psychometric measurement methods are needed, e.g. interaction experiments with appropriate measurement scales. Several attempts have been made to come up with a common questionnaire for user perception measurement related to spoken dialog systems, for example the SASSI questionnaire (Hone and Graham, 2000) for systems using speech input, and the ITU-standard augmented framework for questionnaires (ITU-T Rec. P.851, 2003) for systems with both speech-input and speech-output capabilities. Studies of the validity and the reliability of these questionnaires (Möller et al., 2007) show that both SASSI and P.851 can cover a large number of different quality and usability dimensions with a high validity, and mainly with adequate reliability, although the generalizability of these results remains to be shown.

On the basis of batteries of user judgments obtained with these questionnaires, *dimension descriptors* of the perceptual quality dimensions can be extracted by means of factor analysis. A summary of such multidimensional analyses in Möller (2005b) reveals that users' perceptions of quality and usability can be decomposed into around 5 to 8 dimensions. The resulting dimensions include factors such as overall acceptability, task effectiveness, speed, cognitive effort, and joy-of-use. It should be noted that most such efforts have considered task-oriented systems, where effectiveness, efficiency, and success are obviously important, however these dimensions may be less relevant to systems designed for other purposes, for example tutoring or "edutainment" (Bernsen et al., 2004), and additional factors may be needed for such applications.

In order to describe the impact of the interaction flow on user-perceived quality, or on some of its sub-dimensions, we would ideally model the human perception and judgment processes. Such an approach has the clear advantage that the resulting model would be generic, i.e. applicable to different systems and potentially for different user groups, and also analytic, i.e. able to explain why certain interaction characteristics have a positive or negative impact on perceived quality. Unfortunately, the perception and judgment processes involved in spoken-dialog interaction are not yet well understood, as compared, for example, to those involved in listening to transmitted speech samples and judging their quality. For the latter, models are available which estimate quality with the help of peripheral auditory perception models and a signal-based comparison of representations of the perceptual event and the assumed reference (Rix et al., 2006). They are able to estimate user judgments on "overall quality" with an average correlation of around 0.93, and are widely used for planning, implementing and monitoring telephone networks.

For interactions with spoken dialog systems, the situation is more complicated, as the perceptual events depend on the interaction between user and systems, and not on one speech signal alone. A way out is not to worry about the perception processes, and instead to use simple linear regression models for predicting an average user judgment from various interaction parameters. The most widely used framework designed to support this sort of early evaluation is PARADISE (Walker et al., 1997). The target variable of PARADISE is an average of several user judgments (labeled "user satisfaction") of different system and interaction aspects, such as system voice, perceived system understanding, task ease, interaction pace, or the transparency of the interaction. The interaction parameters are of three types, those relating to efficiency (including elapsed time and the number of turns), those relating to "dialog quality" (including mean recognition score and the number of timeouts and rejections), and a measure of effectiveness (task success). The model can be trained on data, and the results are readily interpretable: they can indicate which features of the interaction are most critical for improving user satisfaction.

PARADISE-style models can be very helpful tools for system developers. For example, a recent investigation showed that the model can be used to effectively determine the minimum acceptable recognition rate for a smart-home system, leading to the same critical threshold as that obtained from user judgments (Engelbrecht and Möller, 2007). However, experience also shows that the PARADISE framework does not reliably give valid predictions of *individual* user judgments, typically covering only around 40-50% of the variance in the data it is trained on. The generality is also limited: cross-system extrapolation works sometimes but other times has low accuracy (Walker et al., 2000; Möller, 2005). These limitations are easy to understand in terms of Figure 1: over-ambitious attempts to directly relate interaction parameters to a measure of overall system value seem unlikely to succeed in general. Thus it seems wise to limit the scope of the perception and judgment component to the prediction of values on the perceptual quality dimensions.

In any case, there are several ways in which such models could be improved. One issue is that a linear combination of factors is probably not generally adequate. For example, parameters like the number of turns required to execute a specific task will have a non-zero optimum value, at least for inexperienced users. An excessively low number of turns will be as sure a sign of interaction problems as an excessively large number. Such non-linear effects cannot be handled by linear models which only support relationships like "the-more-the-better" or "the-less-the-better". Non-linear algorithms may overcome these limitations. A second issue is that of temporal context: instead of using a single input vector of interaction parameters for each dialog, it may be possible to apply a sequence of feature vectors, one for each exchange (user-system utterance pair). The features may consist not only of numeric measures but also of categories encoding interaction phenomena. Using this input one could then perhaps use a neural network or Hidden-Markov Model to predict various user judgments at the end of the interaction.

5 Value Model

Even if a model can predict user judgments of "overall quality" with high validity and reliability, this is not necessarily a good indicator of the acceptability of a service. For example, systems with a sophisticated and smooth dialog flow may be unacceptable for frequent users because what counts for them is effectiveness and efficiency only. Different users may focus on different quality dimensions in different contexts, and weight them according to the task, context of use, price, etc.

A first step towards addressing this problem is to define *quality aspects* that a system developer or service operator might be concerned about. There can be many such, but in usability engineering they are typically categorized into "effectiveness", "efficiency" and "satisfaction". A more detailed taxonomy of quality aspects can be found in Möller (2005). On the basis of this or other taxonomizations, value prediction models can be developed. For example, a system enabling 5-year old girls to "talk to Barbie" might ascribe little importance to task completion, speech recognition accuracy, or efficiency, but high importance to voice quality, responsiveness, and unpredictability. The value model will derive a *value description* which takes such a weighting into account. A model for systems enabling police officers on patrol to obtain information over the telephone would have very different weights.

Unfortunately, there appear to be no published descriptions of value prediction models, perhaps because they are very specific or even proprietary, depending on a company's business logic and customer base. Such models probably need not be very complex: it likely will suffice to ascribe weights to the perceptual quality dimensions, or to quality aspects derived from system developer and/or service operator requirements. Appropriate weights may be uncovered in stakeholder workshops, where designers, vendors, usability experts, marketing strategists, user representatives and so on come together and discuss what they desire or expect.

6 Broader Impacts

We have presented a tripartite evaluation framework which shows the relationship between user and system characteristics, interaction behavior, perceptual and quality events, their descriptions, and the final value of the system or service. In doing so, we have mainly considered the needs of system developers. However, an evaluation framework that supports judgments of perceived quality could provide additional benefits for users. We can imagine user-specific value models, representing what is important to specified user groups. These could be solicited for an entire group, or inferred from each user's own personal history of interactions and decisions, e.g, through a personalization database available to the service operator. The models could also be used to support system selection, or to inform real-time system customization or adaptation.

Better evaluation will also support the needs of the research community. With the help of model-based evaluation, it will become easier for researchers not only to do evaluation more efficiently, but also to to produce more meaningful evaluation results; saying not just "this feature was useful" but also providing quantitative statements of how much the feature affects various interaction parameters, and from that how much it impacts the various quality dimensions, and ultimately the value itself. This will make evaluation more meaningful and make it easy for others to determine when an innovation is worth adopting, speeding technology transfer.

One might worry that a standardized framework might only be useful for evaluating incremental improvements, thereby discouraging work on radically different dialog design concepts. However well-designed evaluation components should enable this framework to work for systems of any type, meaning that it may be easier to explore new regions of the design space. In particular it may enable more accurate prediction of the value of design innovations which in isolation may not be effective, but which in combination may be.

7 Future Work

Although examples of some model components are available today, notably several interaction simulations and the PARADISE framework for predicting user judgments from interaction parameters, these are limited. To realize a complete and generally useful evaluation model will require considerable work, for example, on:

- *User behavior model*: Of the three components, perhaps the greatest challenges are in the development of user behavior models. We need to develop methods which produce simulated behavior which is realistic (congruent to the behavior of real users), and/or which produce interaction parameters and/or quality indicators comparable to those obtained by subjective interaction experiments. It is yet unclear whether realistic user behavior can also be generated for more advanced systems and domains, such as computer games, collaborative problem solving systems, or educational systems. We also need to develop models that accurately represent the behavior patterns of various user groups.

- *Interaction parameters*: Several quality aspects are still not reflected in the current parameter sets, e.g. indices for the quality of speech output. Some approaches are described in Möller and Heimansberg (2006), but the predictive power is still too limited. In addition, many parameters still have to be derived by expert annotation. It may be possible to automatically infer values for some parameters from properties of the user's and system's speech signals, and such analyses may be a source for new parameters, covering new quality aspects.

- *Perceptual* and *quality events* and *reference*: These items are subject of ongoing research in related disciplines, such as speech quality assessment, sound quality assessment, and product sound design. Ideas for better, more realistic modeling may be derived from cooperations with these disciplines.

- *Quality judgments* and *dimension descriptors*: In addition to the aspects covered by the SASSI and P.851 questionnaires, psychologists have defined methods for assessing cognitive load, affect, affinity towards technology, etc. Input from such questionnaires may provide a better basis for developing value models.

Although a full model may be out of reach for the next decade, a more thorough understanding of human behavior, perception and judgment processes is not only of intrinsic interest but promises benefits enough to make this a goal worth working towards.

Acknowledgments

This work was supported in part by NSF Grant No. 0415150.

References

M. Araki, and S. Doshita. 1997. Automatic Evaluation Environment for Spoken Dialogue Systems. *Dialogue Processing in Spoken Language Systems, ECAI'96 Workshop Proceedings*, Springer Lecture Notes in Artificial Intelligence No. 1236, 183-194, Springer, Berlin.

N. O. Bernsen, H. Dybkjær, and L. Dybkjær. 1998. *Designing Interactive Speech Systems: From First Ideas to User Testing*. Springer, Berlin.

N. O. Bernsen, L. Dybkjær, L., and S. Kiilerich. 2004. Evaluating Conversation with Hans Christian Andersen. *Proc. 4th Int. Conf. on Language Resources and Evaluation (LREC 2004)*, 3, pp. 1011-1014, Lisbon.

K.-P. Engelbrecht, and S. Möller. 2007. Using Linear Regression Models for the Prediction of Data Distributions. *Proc. 8th SIGdial Workshop on Discourse and Dialogue*, Antwerp, pp. 291-294.

P. Heisterkamp. 2003. "Do not attempt to light with match!": Some Thoughts on Progress and Research Goals in Spoken Dialog Systems. *Proc. 8th Europ. Conf. on Speech Communication and Technology (Eurospeech 2003 – Switzerland)*.

K. S. Hone, and R. Graham. 2000. Towards a Tool for the Subjective Assessment of Speech System Interfaces (SASSI). *Natural Language Engineering*, 3(3-4): 287-303.

ITU-T Rec. P.851. 2003. *Subjective Quality Evaluation of Telephone Services Based on Spoken Dialogue Systems*. International Telecommunication Union, Geneva.

ITU-T Suppl. 24 to P-Series Rec. 2005. *Parameters Describing the Interaction with Spoken Dialogue Systems*. International Telecommunication Union, Geneva.

ISO Standard 9241 Part 11. 1998. *Ergonomic Requirements for Office Work with Visual Display Terminals (VDTs) – Part 11: Guidance on Usability*. International Organization for Standardization, Geneva.

U. Jekosch. 2000. *Sprache hören und beurteilen: Ein Ansatz zur Grundlegung der Sprachqualitätsbeurteilung*. Habilitation thesis (unpublished), Universität/Gesamthochschule, Essen.

R. López-Cózar, A. De la Torre, J. Segura, and A. Rubio. 2003. Assessment of Dialog Systems by Means of a New Simulation Technique. *Speech Communication*, 40: 387-407.

S. Möller, P. Smeele, H. Boland, and J. Krebber. 2007. Evaluating Spoken Dialogue Systems According to De-Facto Standards: A Case Study. *Computer Speech and Language*, 21: 26-53.

S. Möller, R. Englert, K.-P. Engelbrecht, V. Hafner, A. Jameson, A. Oulasvirta, A. Raake, and N. Reithinger. 2006. MeMo: Towards Automatic Usability Evaluation of Spoken Dialogue Services by User Error Simulations. *Proc. 9th Int. Conf. on Spoken Language Processing (Interspeech 2006 – ICSLP)*, Pittsburgh PA, pp. 1786-1789.

S. Möller, and J. Heimansberg. 2006. Estimation of TTS Quality in Telephone Environments Using a Reference-free Quality Prediction Model. *Proc. 2nd ISCA/DEGA Tutorial and Research Workshop on Perceptual Quality of Systems*, Berlin, pp. 56-60.

S. Möller. 2005. *Quality of Telephone-Based Spoken Dialogue Systems*. Springer, New York NY.

S. Möller. 2005b. Perceptual Quality Dimensions of Spoken Dialogue Systems: A Review and New Experimental Results. *Proc. 4th European Congress on Acoustics (Forum Acusticum Budapest 2005)*, Budapest, pp. 2681-2686.

A. Oulasvirta, S. Möller, K.-P. Engelbrecht, and A. Jameson. 2006. The Relationship of User Errors to Perceived Usability of a Spoken Dialogue System. *Proc. 2nd ISCA/DEGA Tutorial and Research Workshop on Perceptual Quality of Systems*, Berlin, pp. 61-67.

T. Paek. 2007. Toward Evaluation that Leads to Best Practices: Reconciling Dialog Evaluation in Research and Industry. *Bridging the Gap: Academic and Industrial Research in Dialog Technologies Workshop Proceedings*, Rochester, pp. 40-47.

R. Pieraccini, J. Huerta. 2005. Where Do We and Commercial Spoken Dialog Systems. *Proc. 6th SIGdial Workshop on Discourse and Dialogue*, Lisbon, pp. 1-10.

A. W. Rix, J. G. Beerends, D.-S. Kim, P. Kroon, and O. Ghitza. 2006. Objective Assessment of Speech and Audio Quality – Technology and Applications. *IEEE Trans. Audio, Speech, Lang. Process*, 14: 1890-1901.

M. Walker, C. Kamm, and D. Litman. 2000. Towards Developing General Models of Usability with PARADISE. *Natural Language Engineering*, 6: 363-377.

M. A. Walker, D. J. Litman, C. A. Kamm, and A. Abella. 1997. PARADISE: A Framework for Evaluating Spoken Dialogue Agents. *Proc. of the ACL/EACL 35th Ann. Meeting of the Assoc. for Computational Linguistics*, Madrid, Morgan Kaufmann, San Francisco CA, pp. 271-280.

N. Ward, A. G. Rivera, K. Ward, and D. G. Novick. 2005. Root Causes of Lost Time and User Stress in a Simple Dialog System. *Proc. 9th European Conf. on Speech Communication and Technology (Interspeech 2005)*, Lisboa.

N. Ward, and W. Tsukahara. 2003. A Study in Responsiveness in Spoken Dialogue. *International Journal of Human-Computer Studies*, 59: 603-630.

The Effect of Dialogue System Output Style Variation on Users' Evaluation Judgments and Input Style

Ivana Kruijff-Korbayová and **Olga Kukina**
Department of Computational Linguistics
Saarland University, Germany
{korbay|olgak}@coli.uni-sb.de

Abstract

A dialogue system can present itself and/or address the user as an active agent by means of linguistic constructions in personal style, or suppress agentivity by using impersonal style. We compare system evaluation judgments and input style alignment of users interacting with an in-car dialogue system generating output in personal vs. impersonal style. Although our results are consistent with earlier findings obtained with simulated systems, the effects are weaker.

1 Introduction

One of the goals in developing dialogue systems that users find appealing and natural is to endow the systems with natural and contextually appropriate output. This encompasses a broad range of research issues. The one we address in this paper pertains to *style in the interpersonal dimension*: does using personal vs. impersonal style of system output have an effect on dialogue system users, in particular, on their judgments about the system and on the way they formulate their input to the system?

We define the personal/impersonal style dichotomy as reflecting primarily a distinction with respect to agentivity: personal style involves the explicit realization of an agent, whereas impersonal style avoids it. In the simplest way it is manifested by the presence of explicit reference to the dialogue participants (typically by means of personal pronouns) vs. its absence, respectively. More generally, active voice and finite verb forms are typical for personal style, whereas impersonal style often, though not exclusively, employs passive constructions or infinite verb forms:

(1) Typical personal style constructions:
  a. I found 20 albums.
  b. You have 20 albums.
  c. Please search for albums by The Beatles.

(2) Typical impersonal style constructions:
  a. 20 albums have been found.
  b. There are 20 albums.
  c. The database contains 20 albums.
  d. 20 albums found.

The designer of a dialogue system has the choice to make it manifest (its own and the user's) agentivity linguistically through the use of personal constructions or not.

Previous experiments with simulated systems have shown that a natural language interface with a synthesized voice should not say "I" (Nass and Brave, 2005) and that users align the style of their input to that of the system output (Brennan and Ohaeri, 1994). (See Section 2 for more detail.)

The dialogue system SAMMIE developed in the TALK project (Becker et al., 2007) can use either personal or impersonal output style. In personal style, it generates constructions making explicit reference to the agent (both the user and the system itself), such as (1a–1c); in impersonal style, it avoids explicit reference to any agent, as in (2a–2d). The system can be set either to use one style consistently throughout a dialogue session, or to align to the user's style, i.e., mimic the user's style on a turn-by-turn basis.

Inspired by the earlier results obtained with simulated systems (Nass and Brave, 2005; Brennan and

Proceedings of the 9th SIGdial Workshop on Discourse and Dialogue, pages 190–197,
Columbus, June 2008.

Ohaeri, 1994), we ran an experiment to test the effects of style manipulation in the SAMMIE system. In this paper, we compare two versions of the system, one using consistently the personal output style and the other the impersonal style. We designed our experiment to test (i) whether the users' judgments of the system's usability and performance differ among the system versions using the personal vs. impersonal style, and (ii) whether users align to the system style.

In Section 2 we review previous experiments concerning the effect of system output style on users' judgments and style. We describe our own experiment in Section 3, present the results in Section 4, and provide a discussion and conclusions in Section 5.

2 Previous Work

(Nass and Brave, 2005) address the issue whether a voice interface should say "I" by investigating several dimensions of user attitudes to their simulated system with a synthetic vs. recorded voice. Generally, agents that use "I" are perceived more like a person than those that do not. However, systems tend to be more positively rated when consistent with respect to such parameters as personality, gender, ontology (human vs. machine), etc. A system with a recorded voice is perceived as more human-like and thus entitled to the use of "I", whereas a synthetic-voice interface is not perceived as human enough to use "I" to refer to itself (Nass et al., 2006).

Another question is whether system output style influences users' input formulation, as would be expected due to the phenomenon of *alignment*, which is generally considered a basic principle in natural language dialogue (Garrod and Pickering, 2004).[1]

Experiments targeting human-human conversation show that in spite of the variety of linguistic expressions available, speakers in spontaneous dialogues tend to express themselves in similar ways at lexical and syntactic levels. For example, the surface form of a question can affect the format of the answer: the question "What time do you close?" will more likely get the response "Five o'clock" than"At five o'clock". On the other hand, "At five o'clock" is a more probable answer to "At what time do you close?" (Levelt and Kelter, 1982). There is evidence that alignment happens automatically as a result of priming, e.g., (Hadelich et al., 2004) for lexical alignment.

Lexical and syntactic alignment is present in human-computer interaction, too. (Brennan, 1996) suggested that users adopt system's terms to avoid errors, expecting the system to be inflexible. However, recent experiments show that alignment in human-computer interaction is also automatic and its strength is comparable to that in human-human communication (Branigan et al., 2003; Pearson et al., 2006).

Early results concerning users' alignment to system output style in the interpersonal dimension are reported in (Brennan and Ohaeri, 1994): They distinguish three styles: anthropomorphic (the system refers to itself using first person pronouns, like in (1a) above, fluent (complete sentences, but no self-reference) and telegraphic, like (2d). They found no difference in users' perception of the system's intelligence across the different conditions. However, they observed that the anthropomorphic group was more than twice as likely to refer to the computer using the second person pronoun "you" and it used more indirect requests and conventional politeness then the other groups. They concluded that the anthropomorphic style is undesirable for dialogue systems because it encourages more complex user input which is harder to recognize and interpret.

The described experiments used either the Wizard-of-Oz paradigm (Brennan, 1996) or preprogrammed system output (Branigan et al., 2003; Nass and Brave, 2005) and involved written communication. Such methods allow one to test assumptions about idealized human-computer interaction. The purpose of our experiment was to test whether similar effects arise in an interaction with an actual dialogue system, which may be plagued, among other factors, by speech recognition problems.

3 Experiment

Dialogue System We used the SAMMIE in-car system developed in the TALK project (Becker et al., 2006; Becker et al., 2007). SAMMIE provides a mul-

[1] This dialogue phenomenon goes under a variety of terms in the literature, besides alignment, e.g., accommodation, adaptation, convergence, entrainment or shaping (used, e.g., by (Brennan and Ohaeri, 1994)).

timodal interface to an MP3 player through speech and haptic input with a button which can be turned, pushed down and pushed sideways in four directions. System output is by speech and a graphical display. The user can perform a range of tasks: control the MP3 player (play/stop/pause playing song, next/previous/go-to track, turn shuffle mode on/off), search and browse by looking for various fields in the MP3 database (song, artist, album, etc.), search and select playlists, edit them or construct new ones. The SAMMIE system was designed with the aim to support natural, intuitive mixed-initiative interaction. Input can be given through any modality at any point and is not restricted to answers to system queries: the user can initiate new tasks as well as give any information relevant to the current task at any time. A sample interaction is shown below (Becker et al., 2006).

(3) U: Show me the Beatles albums.

S: I have these four Beatles albums. [shows a list of album names]

U: Which songs are on this one? [selects the Red Album]

S: The Red Album contains these songs [shows a list of the songs]

U: Play the third one.

S: [song "From Me To You" plays]

The SAMMIE system has a German and an English version which both provide the same functionality. The experiment employed the German version. See (Kruijff-Korbayová et al., 2008) for a description of the natural language generation module.

Setup Figure 1 shows a picture of the experiment setup. To simulate the driving situation, we used the "3D-Fahrschule" software.[2] The driving simulator visuals were projected on a wall-sized back-projection screen. The graphical interface of the SAMMIE system was shown on a display next to the steering wheel. Participants wore headphones with a microphone for the spoken input and output. The button for manual input was positioned to the right of their chair. The experimenter was sitting in an adjacent room and could see and hear everything happening in the experiment lab. The subjects could not see the experimenter, but heard her instructions, including the task assignments, from loudspeakers. If necessary, the subjects were able to talk to the experimenter.

Figure 1: Experiment setup

Participants A total of 28 participants were paid to take part in the experiment. All were native German speakers, 22 female and 6 male, 22 students of the Saarland University and 6 employees. All but two participants had a driver's license and 20 participants reported driving more than 500km a year. 10 participants had previous experience with a driving simulation and 6 had used a dialogue system before. Each participant was assigned to one style condition, 14 to personal and 14 to impersonal style. To ensure as even a distribution as possible, there were 11 female and 3 male participants in each style condition, one of whom was a non-driver. There were 4 employees in impersonal style condition and 2 in the personal one.

Procedure Each participant was welcomed by the experimenter, seated in the experiment lab, and given brief written instructions concerning the driving simulator, the SAMMIE system and the evaluation procedure. The participants were instructed to use mainly spoken input to accomplish the tasks, although they were allowed to use manual input, too.

The participants first made a ca. 2-minute drive to get familiar with the driving simulator. Then they were asked to chose a destination city (Amsterdam, Madrid or London) and drive there on a highway. During the driving, the experimenter successively

[2] http://www.3d-fahrschule.de/index.htm

read to the participant 2 trial tasks and 11 experimental tasks to be solved using the SAMMIE system.

The tasks involved exploring the contents of a database of about 25 music albums and were of four types: (1) finding some specified title(s); (2) selecting some title(s) satisfying certain constraints; (3) manipulating the playlists by adding or removing songs and (4) free-use of the system.

The experimental tasks were presented to each participant in randomized order apart from the free use of the system, which was always the last task. To avoid priming by the style of the task formulation, and to help the participants memorize the task, the experimenter (E) repeated each task assignment twice to the participant, once in personal and once in impersonal style, as shown in the example below.

(4) E: *Bitte frage das System nach den Liedern von "Pur". Du willst also wissen welche Lieder von "Pur" es gibt.*
E: Please ask the the system about the songs by "Pur". You would like to know which songs by "Pur" there are.

The time the participants spent completing the individual tasks was not constrained. It took them about 40 minutes to complete all the tasks.

Afterwards, each participant was asked to fill in a questionnaire about their attitudes towards the system, consisting of questions with a 6-point scale ranging from 1 (low grade) to 6 (high grade). The questions were a subset of those used in (Nass and Brave, 2005) and (Mutschler et al., 2007), for example: *How do you assess the system in general:* technical (1) – human-like (6); *Communication with the system seemed to you:* boring (1) – exciting (6); *In terms of usability, the system is:* inefficient (1) —efficient(6).

Upon completing the questionnaire, the participant was paid and discharged.

Collected data The questionnaire responses have been tabulated and the dialogues of the subjects with the system have been recorded and transcribed.[3] The utterances of the participants (on average 95 per session) were subsequently manually annotated with the following features for further analysis:

[3]We did not record the data from the driving simulator.

- Construction type:

  Personal (+/-) Is the utterance a complete sentence in active voice or imperative form

  Impersonal (+/-) Is the utterance expressed by passive voice, infinite verb form (e.g., "Lied abspielen" (*lit.* "song play")), or expletive "es-gibt" ("there-is") construction

  Telegraphic (+/-) Is the utterance expressed by a phrase, e.g., "weiter" ("next")

- Personal pronouns: (+/-) Does the utterance contain a first or second person pronoun

- Politeness marking: (+/-) Does the utterance contain a politeness marker, such as "bitte" ("please"), "danke" ("thanks") and verbs in subjunctive mood (eg. "ich hätte gerne")

4 Results

4.1 Style and Users' Attitudes

The first issue addressed in the experiment was whether the users have different judgments of the personal vs. impersonal version of the system. Since the system used a synthetic voice, the judgments were expected to be more positive in the impersonal style condition (Nass and Brave, 2005). Based on factor analysis performed on attitudinal data from the user questionnaires we created the six indices listed below. All indices were meaningful and reliable

1. General satisfaction with the communication with the system was composed of 3 pairs of adjectives describing communication with the system: disappointing/motivating, uninteresting/interesting and boring/exciting (Cronbach's α=0.86; t(26)=0.29, p=0.39 (one-tailed))
2. Ease of communication with the system comprised 5 parameters: naturalness of the communication with the system, formality/informality and indifference/sympathy of the system's communicative style, participants feelings during the conversation: tensed/relaxed and pleasant/unpleasant (α=0.83; t(26)=0.00, p=0.5 (one-tailed))
3. Usability of the system consisted of 1 pair of adjectives referring to the success

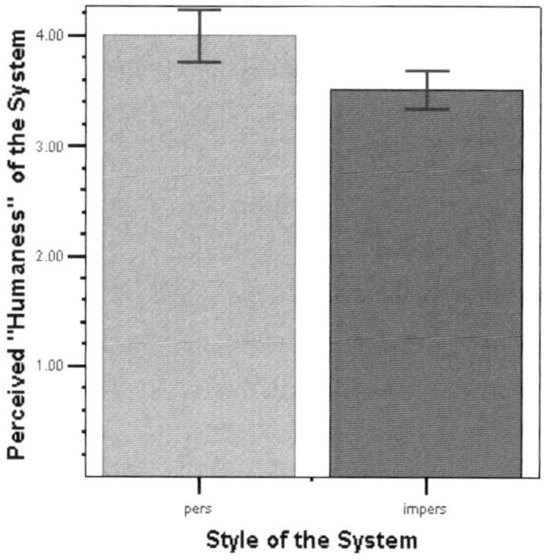

Figure 2: Perceived humanness of the system depending on system output style

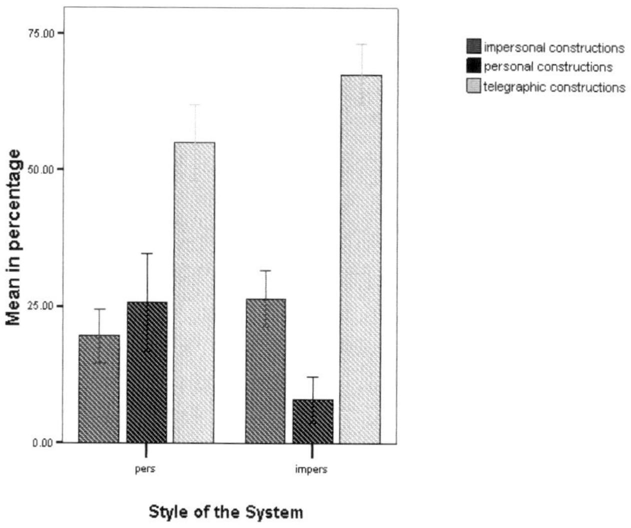

Figure 3: Distribution chart for syntactic construction types in user utterances depending on system output style

of communication with the system: unsuccessful/successful, and 4 pairs of adjectives describing the usability of the system: unpractical/practical, inefficient/efficient, complicated/simple, inconvenient/convenient (α=0.76; t(26)=0.08, p=0.47 (one-tailed))

4. Clarity of the system's speech comprised 2 pairs of adjectives describing the system's speech: unpredictable/predictable and confusing/clear (α=0.88; t(25)=0.87, p=0.2 (one-tailed))
5. Perceived "humanness" of the system was composed of 3 parameters: perceived technicality/humanness, perceived unfriendliness/friendliness and attributed conservatism/innovation (α=0.69; t(25)=1.64, p=0.06 (one-tailed))
6. System's perceived flexibility and creativity comprised 3 parameters: rigidness/flexibility of system's speech, perceived creativity of the system and intelligence attributed to the system (α=0.78; t(26)=0.40, p=0.35 (one-tailed))

We did not find any significant influence of system output style on users' attitudes. The only index with a weak tendency in the predicted direction is *perceived humanness of the system* (t(25)=1.64, p=.06 (one-tailed); see Figure 2). This goes in line with the earlier observation that an interface that refers to itself by means of a personal pronoun is perceived to be more human-like than one that does not (Nass and Brave, 2005).

4.2 Style and Alignment

The next issue we investigated was whether the users formulated their input differently with the personal vs. impersonal system version. For each dialogue session, we calculated the percentage of utterances containing the feature of interest relative to the total number of user utterances in the session.

First we analyzed the distribution of personal, impersonal and telegraphic constructions across the personal and impersonal style conditions. (The reason we separated telegraphic constructions is because they seem to be neutral with respect to style.) We compared the means of the obtained numbers between the two style conditions. Figure 3 shows the distribution of the types of syntactic constructions across the system output style conditions.

1. We expected the participants to use more personal constructions with the personal style version of the system. Independent samples t-test showed a significant result in the predicted direction (t(19)=1.8, p=0.05 (one-tailed); see Figure 3).

2. We expected to find the reverse effect with regard to the proportion of impersonal verb forms: participants using the personal style

version of the system were expected to have less infinite, passive and "es-gibt" forms than those in the impersonal style condition. However, we did not find any significant difference between the two style conditions ($t(26)=1.0$, $p=0.17$ (one-tailed)).

3. According to expectation we also did not find any significant difference in the proportion of telegraphic constructions per style condition ($t(26)=1.4$, $p=0.09$ (one-tailed)).

4. In the impersonal style condition we found a significantly lower proportion of verb-containing utterances than utterances in telegraphic form ($t(13)=3.5$, $p=0.00$ (one-tailed)). But in the personal style condition there was no statistically significant difference ($t(13)=0.7$, $p=0.25$ (one-tailed)).

Next we analyzed the distribution of first and second person pronouns across style conditions. We expected to find more personal pronouns in personal than in impersonal style condition (Brennan and Ohaeri, 1994). However, the results showed no statistically significant difference ($t(26)=0.67$, $p=0.25$ (one-tailed)).

Another prediction based on (Brennan and Ohaeri, 1994) was to find more politeness markers in the personal style. However, the analysis showed that participants in the personal style condition did not use significantly more politeness markers than those in the impersonal style condition ($t(20)=1.06$, $p=0.15$ (one-tailed)).

Finally, (Brennan and Ohaeri, 1994) predicted that personal style, being more flexible, might cause more speech recognition problems than input in impersonal style. We checked whether participants in the personal style condition had a higher rate of unrecognized utterances than those in the impersonal style condition and found no significant difference ($t(26)=0.60$, $p = 0.28$ (one-tailed)).

To summarize, we observed a significant difference in the number of personal constructions across style conditions, in accordance with the expectation based on style alignment in terms of agentivity. But we did not find a significant difference in the distribution of impersonal constructions across style conditions. Not surprisingly, there was also no significant difference in the distribution of telegraphic constructions. An unexpected finding was the higher proportion of telegraphic constructions than verb-containing ones within the impersonal style condition. However, the personal style condition showed no significant effect. Contrary to expectations, we also did not find any significant effect of style-manipulation on the number of personal pronouns, nor on the number of politeness markers.

4.3 Style Alignment over Time

Since alignment can also be seen as a process of gradual adjustment among dialogue participants in the course of their interaction, we were interested in whether participants tended to converge to using particular constructions as their session with the system progressed. For each participant we divided the transcribed conversation in two halves. Using paired samples t-test, we compared the proportion of personal, impersonal and telegraphic constructions in the first and second halves of the conversations for both style conditions.

In the personal style condition, we found no significant change in the usage of construction types between the first and the second half of the dialogue. In the impersonal style condition, we did not find any significant difference in the distribution of impersonal and telegraphic constructions either. However, we found a significant change in the number of personal constructions ($t(13)=2.5$, $p=0.02$ (one-tailed)): The participants cut down on the use of personal constructions in the second half.

5 Discussion and Conclusions

We presented the results of an experiment with the in-car multimodal dialogue system SAMMIE, aimed to test whether we obtain effects similar to earlier findings concerning the influence of system output style in the interpersonal dimension on the users' subjective judgments of a system (Nass and Brave, 2005) as well as their formulation of input (Brennan and Ohaeri, 1994). Although our results are not conclusive, they point at a range of issues for further research.

Regarding users' attitudes to the system, we found no significant difference among the styles. This is similar to (Brennan and Ohaeri, 1994) who found no difference in intelligence attributed to the system by the users, but it is at odds with the earlier finding that a synthetic voice interface was judged to be more useful when avoiding self-reference by personal pronouns (Nass and Brave, 2005).

Whereas (Brennan and Ohaeri, 1994) used a flight reservation dialogue system, (Nass and Brave, 2005) used a phone-based auction system which read out an introduction and five object descriptions. There are two points to note: First, the subjects were exposed to system output that was a read out continuous text rather than turns in an interaction. This may have reinforced the activation of particular style features. Second, the auction task may have sensibilized the subjects to the distinction between subjective (the system's) vs. objective information presentation, and thus make them more sensitive to whether the system presents itself as an active agent or not.

Regarding the question whether users align their style to that of the system, where previous experiments showed strong effects of alignment (Brennan and Ohaeri, 1994), our experiment shows some effects, but some of the results seem conflicting. On the one hand, subjects interacting with the personal style version of the system used more personal constructions than those interacting with the impersonal style version. However, subjects in either condition did not show any significant difference with respect to the use of impersonal constructions or telegraphic forms. We also found a higher proportion of telegraphic constructions than verb-containing ones within the impersonal style condition, but no such difference in the personal style. Finally, when we consider alignment over time, we find no change in construction usage in the personal style, whereas we find a decrease in the use of personal constructions in the impersonal style.

That there is no difference in the use of telegraphic constructions across conditions is not surprising. Being just phrasal sentence fragments, these constructions are neutral with respect to style. But why does there seem to be an alignment effect for personal constructions and not for others? One way of explaining this is that (some of) the constructions that we counted as impersonal are common in both styles. Besides their deliberate use as means to avoid explicit reference to oneself, the constructions typical for impersonal style also have their normal, neutral usage, and therefore, some of the utterances that we have classified as impersonal style might just be neutral formulations, rather than cases of distancing or "de-agentivization". However, we could not test this hypothesis, because we have not found a way to reliably distinguish between neutral and marked, truly impersonal utterances. This is an issue requiring further work.

The difference between our results concerning alignment and those of (Brennan and Ohaeri, 1994) is not likely to be due to a difference in the degree of interactivity (as with (Nass and Brave, 2005)). We now comment on other differences between our systems, which might have contributed to the differences in results.

One aspect where we differ concerns our distinction between personal and impersonal style, both in the implementation of the SAMMIE system and in the experiment: We include the presence/absence of agentivity not only in the system's reference to itself (akin to (Nass and Brave, 2005) and (Brennan and Ohaeri, 1994)), but also in addressing the user. This concept of the personal/impersonal distinction was inspired by such differences observed in a study of instructional texts in several languages (Kruijff et al., 1999), where the latter dimension is predominant. The present experiment results make it pertinent that more research into the motives behind expressing or suppressing agentivity in both dimensions is needed.

Apart from the linguistic design of the system's output, other factors influence users' behavior and perception of the system, and thus might confound experiment results, e.g., functionality, design, ergonomics, speech synthesis and speech recognition.

Earlier experiments reported in (Nass and Brave, 2005) suggest that a system with synthesized speech should be more positively rated when it does not refer to itself as an active agent by personal constructions. Whereas the system used by (Brennan and Ohaeri, 1994) used written interaction, we used the MARY text-to-speech synthesis system (Schröder and Trouvain, 2003) with an MBROLA diphone synthesizer, which produces an acceptable though not outstanding output quality. But as discussed earlier, contrary to (Nass and Brave, 2005) we have not observed a difference in the users' attitudes depending on style. It thus remains an open issue what effect speech output quality has on on the users' attitudes and alignment behavior.

Regarding a possible influence of speech recognition on our results, we performed a post-hoc analysis (Kruijff-Korbayová et al., 2008), which did not reveal significant differences in user attitudes or alignment behavior depending on better or worse speech recognition performance experienced by the users. A future experiment should address the possibility of an interaction between system style and speech recognition performance as both factors might be influencing the user simultaneously.

One radical difference between our experiment and the earlier ones is that the users of our system are occupied by the driving task, and therefore only have a limited cognitive capacity left to devote to the interaction with the system. This may make them less susceptible to the subtleties of style manipulation than would be the case if they were free of other tasks. A possible future experiment could address this issue by including a non-driving condition.

Finally, as we pointed out in the introduction, the SAMMIE system can also be used in an style-alignment mode, where it mimics the user's style on turn-to-turn basis. We plan to present experimental results comparing the alignment-mode with the fixed personal/impersonal style in a future publication.

Acknowledgments

This work was carried out in the TALK project (www.talk-project.org) funded by the EU as project No. IST-507802 within the 6th Framework Program.

References

T. Becker, N. Blaylock, C. Gerstenberger, I. Kruijff-Korbayová, A. Korthauer, M. Pinkal, M. Pitz, P. Poller, and J. Schehl. 2006. Natural and intuitive multimodal dialogue for in-car applications: The SAMMIE system. In *Proceedings of ECAI, PAIS Special section.*

T. Becker, N. Blaylock, C. Gerstenberger, A. Korthauer, M. Pitz, P. Poller, J. Schehl, F. Steffens, R. Stegmann, and J. Steigner. 2007. Deliverable D5.3: In-car showcase based on TALK libraries. Technical report, TALK Project, EU FP6, IST-507802.

H. Branigan, M. Pickering, J. Pearson, J. F. McLean, and C. Nass. 2003. Syntactic alignment between computer and people: the role of belief about mental states. In *Proceedings of the Annual Conference of the Cognitive Science Society.*

S. Brennan and J.O. Ohaeri. 1994. Effects of message style on user's attribution toward agents. In *Proceedings of CHI'94 Conference Companion Human Factors in Computing Systems*, pages 281–282. ACM Press.

S. Brennan. 1996. Lexical entrainment in spontaneous dialogue. In *Proceedings of the International Symposium on Spoken Dialogue (ISSD-96)*, pages 41–44.

S. Garrod and M. Pickering. 2004. Why is conversation so easy? *TRENDS in Cognitive Sciences*, 8.

K. Hadelich, H. Branigan, M. Pickering, and M. Crocker. 2004. Alignment in dialogue: Effects of feedback on lexical overlap within and between participants. In *Proceedings of the AMLaP Conference*. Aix en Provence, France.

G.J.M. Kruijff, I. Kruijff-Korbayová, J. Bateman, D. Dochev, N. Gromova, T. Hartley, E. Teich, S. Sharoff, L. Sokolova, and K. Staykova. 1999. Deliverable TEXS2: Specification of elaborated text structures. Technical report, AGILE Project, EU INCO COPERNICUS PL961104.

I. Kruijff-Korbayová, C. Gerstenberger, O. Kukina, and J. Schehl. 2008. Generation of output style variation in the SAMMIE dialogue system. In *Proceedings of INLG'08*, Salt Fork Resort, Ohio.

W.J.M. Levelt and S. Kelter. 1982. Surface form and memory in question answering. *Cognitive Psychology*, 14:78–106.

H. Mutschler, F. Steffens, and A. Korthauer. 2007. Deliverable D6.4: Final report on multimodal experiments Part I: Evaluation of the SAMMIE system. Technical report, TALK Project, EU FP6, IST-507802.

C. Nass and S. Brave, 2005. *Should voice interfaces say "I"? Recorded and synthetic voice interfaces' claims to humanity*, chapter 10, pages 113–124. The MIT Press, Cambridge.

C. Nass, S. Brave, and L. Takayama. 2006. Socializing consistency: from technical homogeneity to human epitome. In *P. Zhang & D. Galletta (Eds.), Human-computer interaction in management information systems: Foundations*, pages 373–390. Armonk, NY: M. E. Sharpe.

J. Pearson, J. Hu, H. Branigan, M. J. Pickering, and C. I. Nass. 2006. Adaptive language behavior in HCI: how expectations and beliefs about a system affect users' word choice. In *CHI '06: Proceedings of the SIGCHI conference on Human Factors in computing systems*, pages 1177–1180, New York, NY, USA. ACM.

M. Schröder and J. Trouvain. 2003. The German text-to-speech synthesis system MARY: A tool for research, development and teaching. *International Journal of Speech Technology*, 6:365–377.

Making Grammar-Based Generation Easier to Deploy in Dialogue Systems

David DeVault and **David Traum** and **Ron Artstein**
USC Institute for Creative Technologies
13274 Fiji Way
Marina del Rey, CA 90292
{devault,traum,artstein}@ict.usc.edu

Abstract

We present a development pipeline and associated algorithms designed to make grammar-based generation easier to deploy in implemented dialogue systems. Our approach realizes a practical trade-off between the capabilities of a system's generation component and the authoring and maintenance burdens imposed on the generation content author for a deployed system. To evaluate our approach, we performed a human rating study with system builders who work on a common large-scale spoken dialogue system. Our results demonstrate the viability of our approach and illustrate authoring/performance trade-offs between hand-authored text, our grammar-based approach, and a competing shallow statistical NLG technique.

1 Introduction

This paper gives an overview of a new example-based generation technique that is designed to make grammar-based generation easier to deploy in dialogue systems. Dialogue systems present several specific requirements for a practical generation component. First, the generator needs to be fast enough to support real-time interaction with a human user. Second, the generator must provide adequate coverage for the meanings the dialogue system needs to express. What counts as "adequate" can vary between systems, since the high-level purpose of a dialogue system can affect priorities regarding output fluency, fidelity to the requested meaning, variety of alternative outputs, and tolerance for generation failures. Third, developing the necessary resources for the generation component should be relatively straightforward in terms of time and expertise required. This is especially important since dialogue systems are complex systems with significant development costs. Finally, it should be relatively easy for the dialogue manager to formulate a generation request in the format required by the generator.

Together, these requirements can reduce the attractiveness of grammar-based generation when compared to simpler template-based or canned text output solutions. In terms of speed, off-the-shelf, wide-coverage grammar-based realizers such as FUF/SURGE (Elhadad, 1991) can be too slow for real-time interaction (Callaway, 2003).

In terms of adequacy of coverage, in principle, grammar-based generation offers significant advantages over template-based or canned text output by providing productive coverage and greater variety. However, realizing these advantages can require significant development costs. Specifying the necessary connections between lexico-syntactic resources and the flat, domain-specific semantic representations that are typically available in implemented systems is a subtle, labor-intensive, and knowledge-intensive process for which attractive methodologies do not yet exist (Reiter et al., 2003).

One strategy is to hand-build an application-specific grammar. However, in our experience, this process requires a painstaking, time-consuming effort by a developer who has detailed linguistic knowledge as well as detailed domain knowledge, and the resulting coverage is inevitably limited.

Wide-coverage generators that aim for applicabil-

Proceedings of the 9th SIGdial Workshop on Discourse and Dialogue, pages 198–207,
Columbus, June 2008.

ity across application domains (White et al., 2007; Zhong and Stent, 2005; Langkilde-Geary, 2002; Langkilde and Knight, 1998; Elhadad, 1991) provide a grammar (or language model) for free. However, it is harder to tailor output to the desired wording and style for a specific dialogue system, and these generators demand a specific input format that is otherwise foreign to an existing dialogue system. Unfortunately, in our experience, the development burden of implementing the translation between the system's available meaning representations and the generator's required input format is quite substantial. Indeed, implementing the translation might require as much effort as would be required to build a simple custom generator; cf. (Callaway, 2003; Busemann and Horacek, 1998). This development cost is exacerbated when a dialogue system's native meaning representation scheme is under revision.

In this paper, we survey a new example-based approach (DeVault et al., 2008) that we have developed in order to mitigate these difficulties, so that grammar-based generation can be deployed more widely in implemented dialogue systems. Our development pipeline requires a system developer to create a set of training examples which directly connect desired output texts to available application semantic forms. This is achieved through a streamlined authoring task that does not require detailed linguistic knowledge. Our approach then processes these training examples to automatically construct all the resources needed for a fast, high-quality, run-time grammar-based generation component. We evaluate this approach using a pre-existing spoken dialogue system. Our results demonstrate the viability of the approach and illustrate authoring/performance trade-offs between hand-authored text, our grammar-based approach, and a competing shallow statistical NLG technique.

2 Background and Motivation

The generation approach set out in this paper has been developed in the context of a research program aimed at creating interactive virtual humans for social training purposes (Swartout et al., 2006). Virtual humans are embodied conversational agents that play the role of people in simulations or games. They interact with human users and other virtual humans using spoken language and non-verbal behavior such as eye gaze, gesture, and facial displays.

Figure 1: Doctor Perez.

The case study we present here is the generation of output utterances for a particular virtual human, Doctor Perez (see Figure 1), who is designed to teach negotiation skills in a multi-modal, multiparty, non-team dialogue setting (Traum et al., 2005; Traum et al., 2008). The human trainee who talks to the doctor plays the role of a U.S. Army captain named Captain Kirk. We summarize Doctor Perez's generation requirements as follows.

In order to support compelling real-time conversation and effective training, the generator must be able to identify an utterance for Doctor Perez to use within approximately 200ms on modern hardware.

Doctor Perez has a relatively rich internal mental state including beliefs, goals, plans, and emotions. As Doctor Perez attempts to achieve his conversational goals, his utterances need to take a variety of syntactic forms, including simple declarative sentences, various modal constructions relating to hypothetical actions or plans, yes/no and wh-questions, and abbreviated dialogue forms such as elliptical clarification and repair requests, grounding, and turn-taking utterances. Doctor Perez currently uses about 200 distinct output utterances in the course of his dialogues.

Doctor Perez is designed to simulate a non-native English speaker, so highly fluent output is not a necessity; indeed, a small degree of disfluency is even desirable in order to increase the realism of talking to a non-native speaker.

Finally, in reasoning about user utterances, dialogue management, and generation, Doctor Perez

addressee	captain-kirk		
dialogue-act	addressee	captain-kirk	
	type	assign-turn	
	actor	doctor-perez	
speech-act	actor	doctor-perez	
	addressee	captain-kirk	
	action	assert	
	content	type	state
		polarity	negative
		time	present
		attribute	resourceAttribute
		value	medical-supplies
		object-id	market

(a) Attribute-value matrix

addressee	captain-kirk
dialogue-act.addressee	captain-kirk
dialogue-act.type	assign-turn
dialogue-act.actor	doctor-perez
speech-act.actor	doctor-perez
speech-act.addressee	captain-kirk
speech-act.action	assert
speech-act.content.type	state
speech-act.content.polarity	negative
speech-act.content.time	present
speech-act.content.attribute	resourceAttribute
speech-act.content.value	medical-supplies
speech-act.content.object-id	market

(b) Corresponding frame

Figure 2: An example of Doctor Perez's representations for utterance semantics: Doctor Perez tells the captain that there are no medical supplies at the market.

exploits an existing semantic representation scheme that has been utilized in a family of virtual humans. This scheme uses an attribute-value matrix (AVM) representation to describe an utterance as a set of core speech acts and other dialogue acts. Speech acts generally have semantic contents that describe propositions and questions about states and actions in the domain, as well as other features such as polarity and modality. See (Traum, 2003) for some more details and examples of this representation. For ease of interprocess communication, and certain kinds of statistical processing, this AVM structure is linearized so that each non-recursive terminal value is paired with a path from the root to the final attribute. Thus, the AVM in Figure 2(a) is represented as the "frame" in Figure 2(b).

Because the internal representations that make up Doctor Perez's mental state are under constant development, the exact frames that are sent to the generation component change frequently as new reasoning capabilities are added and existing capabilities are reorganized. Additionally, while only hundreds of frames currently arise in actual dialogues, the number of potential frames is orders of magnitude larger, and it is difficult to predict in advance which frames might occur.

In this setting, over a period of years, a number of different approaches to natural language generation have been implemented and tested, including hand-authored canned text, domain specific hand-built grammar-based generators (e.g., (Traum et al., 2003)), shallow statistical generation techniques, and the grammar-based approach presented in this paper. We now turn to the details of our approach.

3 Technical Approach

Our approach builds on recently developed techniques in statistical parsing, lexicalized syntax modeling, generation with lexicalized grammars, and search optimization to automatically construct all the resources needed for a high-quality run-time generation component.

The approach involves three primary steps: specification of training examples, grammar induction, and search optimization. In this section, we present the format that training examples take and then summarize the subsequent automatic processing steps. Due to space limitations, we omit the full details of these automatic processing steps, and refer the reader to (DeVault et al., 2008) for additional details.

3.1 Specification of Training Examples

Each training example in our approach specifies a target output utterance (string), its syntax, and a set of links between substrings within the utterance and system semantic representations. Formally, a training example takes the form $(u, \text{syntax}(u), \text{semantics}(u))$. We will illustrate this format using the training example in Figure 3.

In this example, the generation content author

Utterance — we don't have medical supplies here captain

Syntax

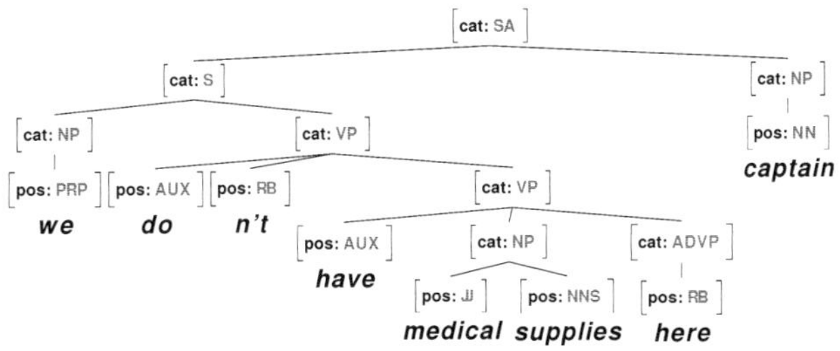

Semantics

we do n't	speech-act.action = assert speech-act.content.polarity = negative
have	speech-act.content.attribute = resourceAttribute
medical supplies . .	speech-act.content.value = medical-supplies
here	speech-act.content.object-id = market
captain	addressee = captain-kirk dialogue-act.addressee = captain-kirk speech-act.addressee = captain-kirk

Figure 3: A generation training example for Doctor Perez.

suggests the output utterance u = *we don't have medical supplies here captain*. Each utterance u is accompanied by $\mathrm{syntax}(u)$, a syntactic analysis in Penn Treebank format (Marcus et al., 1994). In this example, the syntax is a hand-corrected version of the output of the Charniak parser (Charniak, 2001; Charniak, 2005) on this sentence; we discuss this hand correction in Section 4.

To represent the meaning of utterances, our approach assumes that the system provides some set $M = \{m_1, ..., m_j\}$ of semantic representations. The meaning of any individual utterance is then identified with some subset of M. For Doctor Perez, M comprises the 232 distinct key-value pairs that appear in the system's various generation frames. In this example, the utterance's meaning is captured by the 8 key-value pairs indicated in the figure.

Our approach requires the generation content author to link these 8 key-value pairs to contiguous surface expressions within the utterance. The technique is flexible about which surface expressions are chosen (e.g. they need not correspond to constituent boundaries); however, they do need to be compatible with the way the syntactic analysis tokenizes the utterance, as follows. Let $t(u) = \langle t_1, ..., t_n \rangle$ be the terminals in the syntactic analysis, in left-to-right order. Formally, $\mathrm{semantics}(u) = \{(s_1, M_1), ..., (s_k, M_k)\}$, where $t(u) = s_1 @ \cdots @ s_k$ (with @ denoting concatenation), and where $M_i \subseteq M$ for all $i \in 1..k$. In this example, the surface expression *we don't*, which tokenizes as $\langle \mathrm{we}, \mathrm{do}, \mathrm{n't} \rangle$, is connected to key-values that indicate a negative polarity assertion.

This training example format has two features that are crucial to our approach. First, the semantics of an utterance is specified *independently* of its syntax. This greatly reduces the amount of linguistic expertise a generation content author needs to have. It also allows making changes to the underlying syntax without having to re-author the semantic links.

Second, the assignment of semantic representations to surface expressions must span the *entire utterance*. No words or expressions can be viewed as "meaningless". This is essential because, otherwise, the semantically motivated search algorithm used in generation has no basis on which to include those particular expressions when it constructs its output utterance. Many systems, including Doctor Perez, lack some of the internal representations that would be necessary to specify semantics down to the lexical level. An important feature of our approach is that it allows an arbitrary semantic granularity to be employed, by mapping the representations available in the system to appropriate multi-word chunks.

3.2 Automatic Grammar Induction and Search Optimization

The first processing step is to induce a productive grammar from the training examples. We adopt the probabilistic tree-adjoining grammar (PTAG) formalism and grammar induction technique of (Chiang, 2003). We induce our grammar from training examples such as Figure 3 using heuristic rules to assign derivations to the examples, as in (Chiang, 2003). Once derivations have been assigned, subtrees within the training example syntax are incrementally detached. This process yields the reusable linguistic resources in the grammar, as well as the statistical model needed to compute operation probabilities when the grammar is later used in generation. Figure 5 in the Appendix illustrates this process by presenting the linguistic resources inferred from the training example of Figure 3.

Our approach uses this induced grammar to treat generation as a search problem: given a desired semantic representation $M' \subseteq M$, use the grammar to incrementally construct an output utterance u that expresses M'. We treat generation as anytime search by accruing multiple goal states up until a specified timeout (200ms for Doctor Perez) and returning a list of alternative outputs ranked by their derivation probabilities.

The search space created by a grammar induced in this way is too large to be searched exhaustively in most applications. The second step of automated processing, then, uses the training examples to learn an effective search policy so that good output sentences can be found in a reasonable time frame. The solution we have developed employs a beam search strategy that uses weighted features to rank alternative grammatical expansions at each step. Our algorithm for selecting features and weights is based on the search optimization algorithm of (Daumé and Marcu, 2005), which decides to update feature weights when mistakes are made during search on training examples. We use the boosting approach of (Collins and Koo, 2005) to perform feature selection and identify good weight values.

4 Empirical Evaluation

In the introduction, we identified run-time speed, adequacy of coverage, authoring burdens, and NLG request specification as important factors in the selection of a technology for a dialogue system's NLG component. In this section, we evaluate our technique along these four dimensions.

Hand-authored utterances. We collected a sample of 220 instances of frames that Doctor Perez's dialogue manager had requested of the generation component in previous dialogues with users. Some frames occurred more than once in this sample.

Each frame was associated with a single hand-authored utterance. Some of these utterances arose in human role plays for Doctor Perez; some were written by a script writer; others were authored by system builders to provide coverage for specific frames. All were reviewed by a system builder for appropriateness to the corresponding frame.

Training. We used these 220 (frame, utterance) examples to evaluate both our approach and a shallow statistical method called *sentence retriever* (discussed below). We randomly split the examples into 198 training and 22 test examples; we used the same train/test split for our approach and sentence retriever.

To train our approach, we constructed training examples in the format specified in Section 3.1. Syntax posed an interesting problem, because the Charniak parser frequently produces erroneous syntactic analyses for utterances in Doctor Perez's domain, but it was not obvious how detrimental these errors would be to overall generated output. We therefore constructed two alternative sets of training examples – one where the syntax of each utterance was the uncorrected output of the Charniak parser, and another where the parser output was corrected by hand (the syntax in Figure 3 above is the corrected version). Hand correction of parser output requires considerable linguistic expertise, so uncorrected output represents a substantial reduction in authoring burden. The connections between surface expressions and frame key-value pairs were identical in both uncorrected and corrected training sets, since they are independent of the syntax. For each training set, we trained our generator on the 198 training examples. We then generated a single (highest-ranked) utterance for each example in both the test and training sets. The generator sometimes failed to find a successful utterance within the 200ms timeout; the success rate of our generator was 95% for training examples and 80% for test examples. The successful utterances were rated by our judges.

Sentence retriever is based on the cross-language information retrieval techniques described in (Leuski et al., 2006), and is currently in use for Doctor Perez's NLG problem. Sentence retriever does not exploit any hierarchical syntactic analysis of utterances. Instead, sentence retriever views NLG as an information retrieval task in which a set of training utterances are the "documents" to be retrieved, and the frame to be expressed is the query. At run-time, the algorithm functions essentially as a classifier: it uses a relative entropy metric to select the highest ranking training utterance for the frame that Doctor Perez wishes to express. This approach has been used because it is to some extent robust against changes in internal semantic representations, and against minor deficiencies in the training corpus, but as with a canned text approach, it requires each utterance to be hand-authored before it can be used in dialogue. We trained sentence retriever on the 198 training examples, and used it to generate a single (highest-ranked) utterance for each example in both the test and training sets. Sentence retriever's success rate was 96% for training examples and 90% for test examples. The successful utterances were rated by our judges.

Figure 7 in the Appendix illustrates the alternative utterances that were produced for a frame present in the test data but not in the training data.

Run-time speed. Both our approach and sentence retriever run within the available 200ms window.

Adequacy of Coverage. To assess output quality, we conducted a study in which 5 human judges gave overall quality ratings for various utterances Doctor Perez might use to express specific semantic frames. In total, judges rated 494 different utterances which were produced in several conditions: hand-authored (for the relevant frame), generated by our approach, and sentence retriever.

We asked our 5 judges to rate each of the 494 utterances, in relation to the specific frame for which it was produced, on a single 1 ("very bad") to 5 ("very good") scale. Since ratings need to incorporate accuracy with respect to the frame, our judges had to be able to read the raw system semantic representations. This meant we could only use judges who were deeply familiar with the dialogue system; however, the main developer of the new generation algorithms (the first author) did not participate as a judge. Judges were blind to the conditions under which utterances were produced. The judges rated the utterances using a custom-built application which presented a single frame together with 1 to 6 candidate utterances for that frame. The rating interface is shown in Figure 6 in the Appendix. The order of candidate utterances for each frame was randomized, and the order in which frames appeared was randomized for each judge.

The judges were instructed to incorporate both fluency and accuracy with respect to the frame into a single overall rating for each utterance. While it is possible to have human judges rate fluency and accuracy independently, ratings of fluency alone are not particularly helpful in evaluating Doctor Perez's generation component, since for Doctor Perez, a certain degree of disfluency can contribute to believability (as noted in Section 2). We therefore asked judges to make an overall assessment of output quality for the Doctor Perez character.

The judges achieved a reliability of $\alpha = 0.708$ (Krippendorff, 1980); this value shows that agreement is well above chance, and allows for tentative conclusions. Agreement between subsets of judges ranged from $\alpha = 0.802$ for the most concordant pair of judges to $\alpha = 0.593$ for the most discordant pair. We also performed an ANOVA comparing three conditions (generated, retrieved and hand-authored utterances) across the five judges; we found significant main effects of condition ($F(2, 3107) = 55, p < 0.001$) and judge ($F(4, 3107) = 17, p < 0.001$), but no significant interaction ($F(8, 3107) = 0.55, p > 0.8$). We therefore conclude that the individual differences among the judges do not affect the comparison of utterances across the different conditions, so we will report the rest of the evaluation on the mean ratings per utterance.

Due to the large number of factors and the differences in the number of utterances corresponding to each condition, we ran a small number of planned comparisons. The distribution of ratings across utterances is not normal; to validate our results we accompanied each t-test by a non-parametric Wilcoxon rank sum test, and significance always fell in the same general range. We found a significant difference between generated

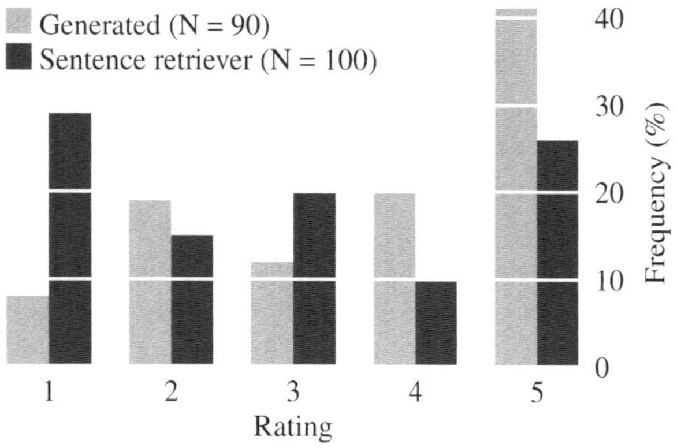

Figure 4: Observed ratings of generated (uncorrected syntax) vs. retrieved sentences for test examples.

output for all examples, retrieved output for all examples, and hand-authored utterances ($F(2, 622) = 16, p < 0.001$); however, subsequent t-tests show that all of this difference is due to the fact that hand-authored utterances (mean rating 4.4) are better than retrieved ($t(376) = 3.7, p < 0.001$) and generated ($t(388) = 5.9, p < 0.001$) utterances, whereas the difference between generated (mean rating 3.8) and retrieved (mean rating 4.0) is non-significant ($t(385) = 1.6, p > 0.1$).

Figure 4 shows the observed rating frequencies of sentence retriever (mean 3.0) and our approach (mean 3.6) on the test examples. While this data does not show a significant difference, it suggests that retriever's selected sentences are most frequently either very bad or very good; this reflects the fact that the classification algorithm retrieves highly fluent hand-authored text which is sometimes semantically very incorrect. (Figure 7 in the Appendix provides such an example, in which a retrieved sentence has the wrong polarity.) The quality of our generated output, by comparison, appears more graded, with very good quality the most frequent outcome and lower qualities less frequent. In a system where there is a low tolerance for very bad quality output, generated output would likely be considered preferable to retrieved output.

In terms of generation failures, our approach had poorer coverage of test examples than sentence retriever (80% vs. 90%). Note however that in this study, our approach only delivered an output if it could completely cover the requested frame. In the future, we believe coverage could be improved, with perhaps some reduction in quality, by allowing outputs that only partially cover requested frames.

In terms of output variety, in this initial study our judges rated only the highest ranked output generated or retrieved for each frame. However, we observed that our generator frequently finds several alternative utterances of relatively high quality (see Figure 7); thus our approach offers another potential advantage in output variety.

Authoring burdens. Both canned text and sentence retriever require only frames and corresponding output sentences as input. In our approach, syntax and semantic links are additionally needed. We compared the use of corrected vs. uncorrected syntax in training. Surprisingly, we found no significant difference between generated output trained on corrected and uncorrected syntax ($t(29) = 0.056, p > 0.9$ on test items, $t(498) = -1.1, p > 0.2$ on all items). This is a substantial win in terms of reduced authoring burden for our approach.

If uncorrected syntax is used, the additional burden of our approach lies only in specifying the semantic links. For the 220 examples in this study, one system builder specified these links in about 6 hours. We present a detailed cost/benefit analysis of this effort in (DeVault et al., 2008).

NLG request specification. Both our approach and sentence retriever accept the dialogue manager's native semantic representation for NLG as input.

Summary. In exchange for a slightly increased authoring burden, our approach yields a generation component that generalizes to unseen test problems relatively gracefully, and does not suffer from the frequent very bad output or the necessity to author every utterance that comes with canned text or a competing statistical classification technique.

5 Conclusion and Future Work

In this paper we have presented an approach to specifying domain-specific, grammar-based generation by example. The method reduces the authoring burden associated with developing a grammar-based NLG component for an existing dialogue system. We have argued that the method delivers relatively high-quality, domain-specific output without requiring that content authors possess detailed linguistic knowledge. In future work, we will study the performance of our approach as the size of the training set grows, and assess what specific weaknesses or problematic disfluencies, if any, our human rating study identifies in output generated by our technique. Finally, we intend to evaluate the performance of our generation approach within the context of the complete, running Doctor Perez agent.

Acknowledgments

Thanks to Arno Hartholt, Susan Robinson, Thomas Russ, Chung-chieh Shan, and Matthew Stone. This work was sponsored by the U.S. Army Research, Development, and Engineering Command (RDECOM), and the content does not necessarily reflect the position or the policy of the Government, and no official endorsement should be inferred.

References

Stephen Busemann and Helmut Horacek. 1998. A flexible shallow approach to text generation. In *Proceedings of INLG*, pages 238–247.

Charles B. Callaway. 2003. Evaluating coverage for large symbolic NLG grammars. *Proceedings of the International Joint Conferences on Artificial Intelligence*.

Eugene Charniak. 2001. Immediate-head parsing for language models. In *ACL '01: Proceedings of the 39th Annual Meeting on Association for Computational Linguistics*, pages 124–131, Morristown, NJ, USA. Association for Computational Linguistics.

Eugene Charniak. 2005. ftp://ftp.cs.brown.edu/pub/nlparser/parser05Aug16.tar.gz.

David Chiang. 2003. Statistical parsing with an automatically extracted tree adjoining grammar. In Rens Bod, Remko Scha, and Khalil Sima'an, editors, *Data Oriented Parsing*, pages 299–316. CSLI Publications, Stanford.

Michael Collins and Terry Koo. 2005. Discriminative reranking for natural language parsing. *Computational Linguistics*, 31(1):25–70.

Hal Daumé, III and Daniel Marcu. 2005. Learning as search optimization: approximate large margin methods for structured prediction. In *ICML '05: Proceedings of the 22nd international conference on Machine learning*, pages 169–176, New York, NY, USA. ACM.

David DeVault, David Traum, and Ron Artstein. 2008. Practical grammar-based NLG from examples. In *Fifth International Natural Language Generation Conference (INLG)*.

Michael Elhadad. 1991. FUF: the universal unifier user manual version 5.0. Technical Report CUCS-038-91.

Klaus Krippendorff, 1980. *Content Analysis: An Introduction to Its Methodology*, chapter 12, pages 129–154. Sage, Beverly Hills, CA.

Irene Langkilde and Kevin Knight. 1998. Generation that exploits corpus-based statistical knowledge. In *COLING-ACL*, pages 704–710.

I. Langkilde-Geary. 2002. An empirical verification of coverage and correctness for a general-purpose sentence generator.

Anton Leuski, Ronakkumar Patel, David Traum, and Brandon Kennedy. 2006. Building effective question answering characters. In *The 7th SIGdial Workshop on Discourse and Dialogue*.

Mitchell P. Marcus, Beatrice Santorini, and Mary Ann Marcinkiewicz. 1994. Building a large annotated corpus of english: The penn treebank. *Computational Linguistics*, 19(2):313–330.

E. Reiter, S. Sripada, and R. Robertson. 2003. Acquiring correct knowledge for natural language generation. *Journal of Artificial Intelligence Research*, 18:491–516.

William Swartout, Jonathan Gratch, Randall W. Hill, Eduard Hovy, Stacy Marsella, Jeff Rickel, and David Traum. 2006. Toward virtual humans. *AI Mag.*, 27(2):96–108.

David Traum, Michael Fleischman, and Eduard Hovy. 2003. Nl generation for virtual humans in a complex social environment. In *Working Notes AAAI Spring Symposium on Natural Language Generation in Spoken and Written Dialogue*, March.

David Traum, William Swartout, Jonathan Gratch, Stacy Marsella, Patrick Kenny, Eduard Hovy, Shri Narayanan, Ed Fast, Bilyana Martinovski, Rahul Baghat, Susan Robinson, Andrew Marshall, Dagen Wang, Sudeep Gandhe, and Anton Leuski. 2005. Dealing with doctors: A virtual human for non-team interaction. In *SIGdial*.

D. R. Traum, W. Swartout, J Gratch, and S Marsella. 2008. A virtual human dialogue model for non-team interaction. In Laila Dybkjaer and Wolfgang Minker, editors, *Recent Trends in Discourse and Dialogue*. Springer.

David Traum. 2003. Semantics and pragmatics of questions and answers for dialogue agents. In *proceedings of the International Workshop on Computational Semantics*, pages 380–394, January.

Michael White, Rajakrishnan Rajkumar, and Scott Martin. 2007. Towards broad coverage surface realization with CCG. In *Proc. of the Workshop on Using Corpora for NLG: Language Generation and Machine Translation (UCNLG+MT)*.

Huayan Zhong and Amanda Stent. 2005. Building surface realizers automatically from corpora using general-purpose tools. In *Proc. Corpus Linguistics '05 Workshop on Using Corpora for Natural Language Generation*.

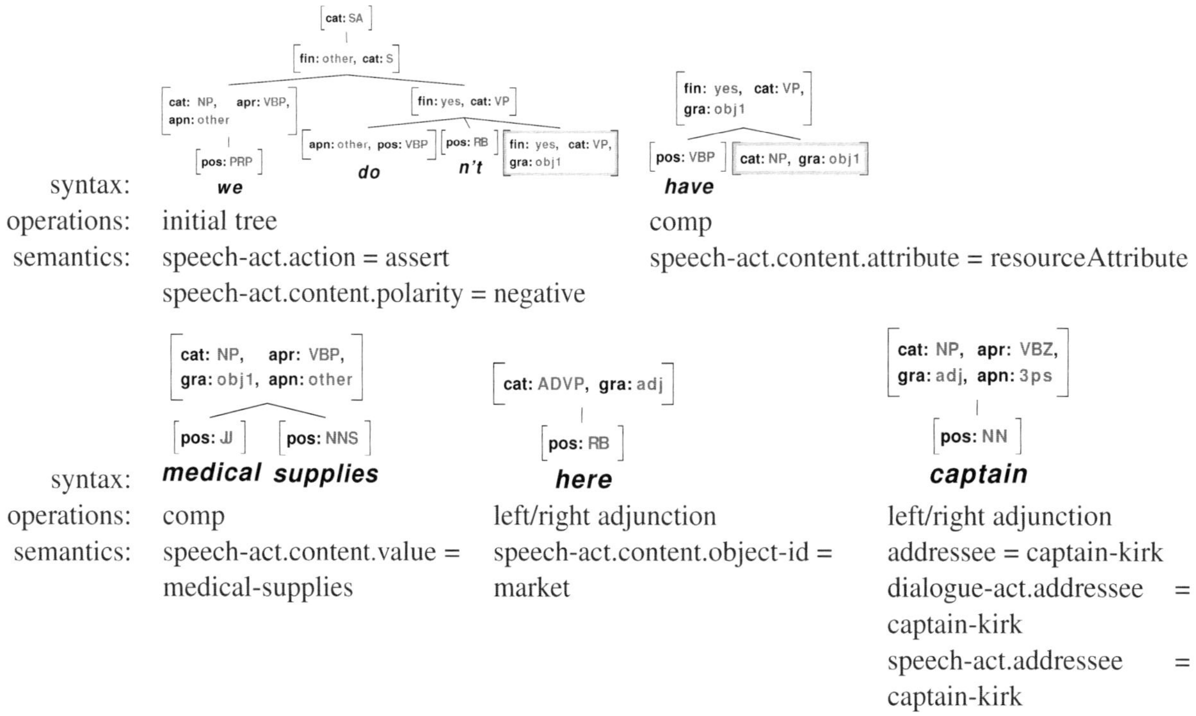

Figure 5: The linguistic resources automatically inferred from the training example in Figure 3.

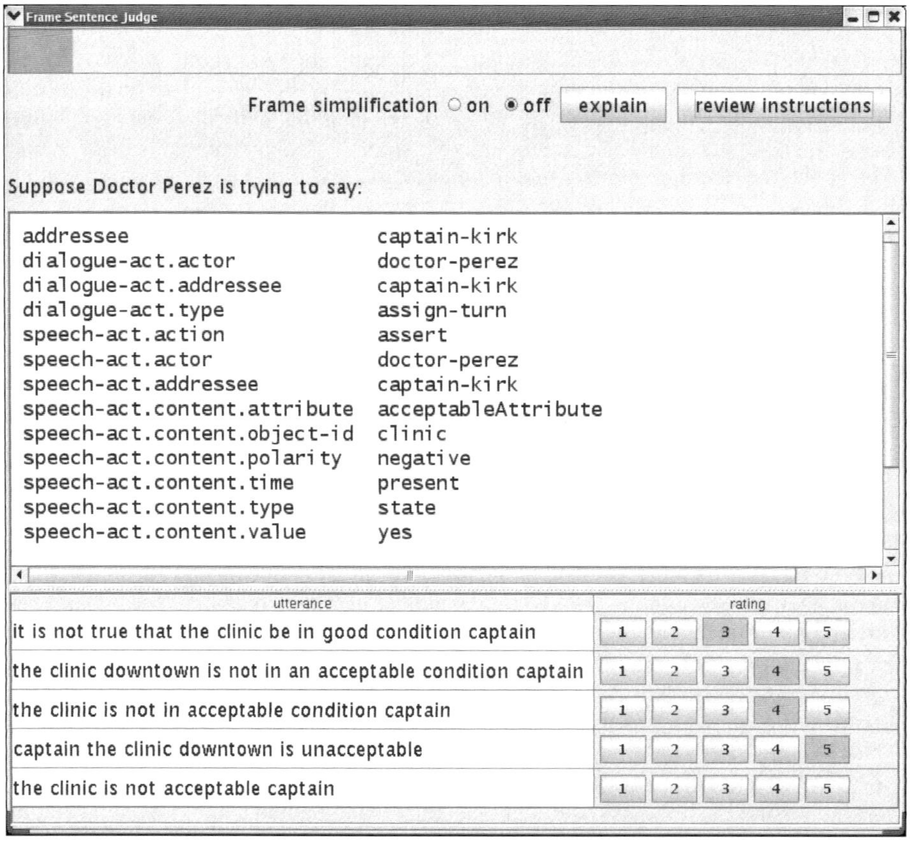

Figure 6: Human rating interface.

Input semantic form

addressee	captain-kirk
dialogue-act.actor	doctor-perez
dialogue-act.addressee	captain-kirk
dialogue-act.type	assign-turn
speech-act.action	assert
speech-act.actor	doctor-perez
speech-act.addressee	captain-kirk
speech-act.content.attribute	acceptableAttribute
speech-act.content.object-id	clinic
speech-act.content.time	present
speech-act.content.type	state
speech-act.content.value	yes

Outputs

Hand-authored

the clinic is acceptable captain

Generated (uncorrected syntax)

Rank	Time (ms)	
1	16	*the clinic is up to standard captain*
2	94	*the clinic is acceptable captain*
3	78	*the clinic should be in acceptable condition captain*
4	16	*the clinic downtown is currently acceptable captain*
5	78	*the clinic should agree in an acceptable condition captain*

Generated (corrected syntax)

Rank	Time (ms)	
1	47	*it is necessary that the clinic be in good condition captain*
2	31	*i think that the clinic be in good condition captain*
3	62	*captain this wont work unless the clinic be in good condition*

Sentence retriever

the clinic downtown is not in an acceptable condition captain

Figure 7: The utterances generated for a single test example by different evaluation conditions. Generated outputs whose rank (determined by derivation probability) was higher than 1 were not rated in the evaluation reported in this paper, but are included here to suggest the potential of our approach to provide a variety of alternative outputs for the same requested semantic form. Note how the output of sentence retriever has the opposite meaning to that of the input frame.

Author Index